# FACT FILE

# FACT FILE

Compiled by
## Theodore Rowland-Entwistle and Jean Cooke
Other Contributors
David Lambert and Jill Thomas

WHSMITH
EXCLUSIVE
· BOOKS ·

Editor    Rachel Pilcher

Designers    Michèle Arron
             Clare Finlaison

First published in 1989 by
Grisewood & Dempsey Ltd,
Elsley House
24–30 Great Titchfield Street
London W1P 7AD

Reprinted 1990

© Grisewood & Dempsey Ltd 1989

Printed in Yugoslavia

ISBN  0  906279  63  1

# Contents

**Colour Plates**

World Atlas

Flags of the World

---

**BILLIONS**

For many years there have been two meanings for the word 'billion'. In Britain and Continental Europe the word indicated one million million; in the United States one thousand million. Today international usage is following the US meaning, so all references to 'billion' in *Factfile* are to be taken as one thousand million.

# The Universe

**The universe is still a mystery to people. Was it really formed 15 billion years ago in one gigantic 'Big Bang'? Is the explosion still continuing as planets, asteroids, comets, moons and billions upon billions of stars hurtle further into deepest space?**

**Stars are vast spheres of gas that burn with different coloured light. Our Sun is a star and planet Earth spins around it, kept in orbit by gravity. Other stars give off no light: these are the 'black holes'. Their gravitational force is so strong that even light waves are sucked into them.**

All the stars, planets and other bodies we see in the heavens are known as the universe. Stars are huge spheres of gas which give off light and heat. Our Sun is a typical medium-sized star. It looks so much larger than other stars because it is close to the Earth.

The distances between stars are so vast that the easiest way to measure them is in terms of the time it takes their light to reach us. The Sun's light takes 8 minutes 20 seconds to travel to the Earth. The light from the next nearest star, called Proxima Centauri, takes 4 years 15½ weeks, or 4.3 light-years. The most distant stars are billions of light-years away.

### The countless stars?

Nobody knows for certain, but astronomers think there are at least 200 billion billion stars – that is 2 with twenty zeros after it. Some stars are much smaller than the Sun, and are known as dwarf stars. Others are between 100 and 1,000 times bigger, and are known as supergiants. Stars between 10 and 100 times the size of the Sun are called giants.

All stars have one thing in common: the force known as gravitation. Every object has this force, and pulls other objects towards it.

△ Quasars are the most distant objects we know. Each is about 100 times brighter than the brightest galaxies in our local star clusters. Quasar 3C 273, about 600 million light years away, is one of the closest and brightest quasars known.

The power of gravity depends on the mass of the object – that is, how much material it contains. On Earth, the effect of gravity is that if you let go of something, such as a ball, it falls to the ground, because the Earth's gravitational force is much stronger than that of the ball. A large star that is mostly gas may have less gravitational force than a small, more solid star.

△ How the Milky Way might appear from Earth if the solar system was a few hundred light years above the Galaxy's arms. In fact, the fierce energy waves from the blazing centre would have prevented life from developing on Earth.

### Black holes, quasars and pulsars

There are many different kinds of stars. They shine with different coloured light, ranging from white through blue and yellow to red. Some white stars are called white dwarfs. Their gravitational force has shrunk them, making them small and dense. Some stars that give off no light at all are believed to exist. They are called black holes. Their gravitational force is so strong that even light waves cannot escape from them.

There are numbers of star-like bodies in the heavens which are still a mystery. Quasars – short for quasi (almost) star-like objects – give off strong radio waves. Pulsars are similar, but send out their radio waves in regular pulses. There are also stars which give off X-rays, and others which emit heat rather than light.

▽ A pulsar, like this one in the Crab Nebula, is the spinning remains of a supernova, an exploding star. The beam of light and radio waves makes a pulse, like the circling beam of a light-house.

△ Astronomers use radio telescopes to collect signals from objects too far away to be seen through ordinary telescopes. This radio telescope at Parkes Observatory in Australia has a collecting dish 64 metres (210 feet) across.

▽ The diagram below shows the orbits of the main asteroids. These minor planets are small and, though much closer to the Earth than the stars, are difficult to detect in the night sky.

## Star clusters

Many stars are grouped in clusters called constellations. A major group of stars, containing many millions, is called a galaxy. We are part of a galaxy called the Milky Way. It has that name because some of its stars form a vast, milky-looking band of light across the night sky. It is a huge, spinning disc made of stars, about 100,000 light years across. Our Sun is about 30,000 light years from the centre of the disc. There are millions of galaxies – we just do not know how many.

## Planets, asteroids, comets

A planet is a heavenly body that revolves around a star. Our Sun has nine major planets revolving around it, forming the solar system. The Earth is one of the planets. A planet does not give off its own light, like a star, but shines with light reflected from the Sun.

There are also a group of small bodies, called the minor planets, or asteroids. They are found between the orbits of the major planets Mars and Jupiter. All but three of the major planets – Mercury, Venus and Pluto – have small, planet-like satellites revolving around them. They are called moons. The Earth has just one satellite, called the Moon, but other planets have several.

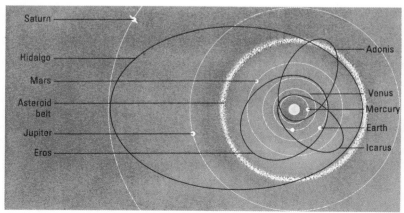

Finally, the solar system contains some wandering bodies called comets. They have very long, elliptical orbits, and shoot away into space after looping around the Sun. Some return after a few years, others not for thousands of years. Comets have been described as 'dirty snowballs', consisting of a mixture of dust, gas and particles of ice.

### How old is the universe?

The universe is thought to be at least 15 billion years old. Many scientists think that before that time all matter was collected together in one large ball, a sort of super black hole. Then there was an explosion, called the 'Big Bang.' Matter was scattered in all directions.

From that matter all the stars were formed. According to one theory, the effects of the Big Bang are still going on, and stars and galaxies are still spreading out from the centre of the explosion. Certainly, the galaxies are moving away from each other at high speed.

However, other astronomers believe there never was a Big Bang, and that the universe has always been roughly like it is today.

## The Constellations

A constellation is a group of conspicuous stars that can be seen in a particular portion of the night sky. Altogether there are 88 constellations. Of these, 48 can be seen from the northern half of the Earth or from the lands around the Equator.

Astronomers use the constellations as sky landmarks for fixing the position, not only of their own stars, but of any others that are detected with powerful telescopes.

The ancient Greeks gave the constellations the names of real and mythical beasts and their gods and heroes, because they fancied they saw patterns of stars that fitted these names. The patterns have changed since then.

△ People have always been excited, and often alarmed, by the sight of a visiting comet. Halley's comet was seen over Jerusalem in the year AD 66.

△ Halley's comet photographed from South Africa in 1910. It returns close to the Earth every 76 years.

When the constellations of the southern hemisphere were discovered within the past few hundred years, astronomers gave them similar names. The names are in Latin, because for centuries all scholarly books were written in that language.

## CONSTELLATIONS

| Latin name | English name | Latin name | English name |
|---|---|---|---|
| Andromeda | Andromeda | Indus | Indian |
| Antlia | Air Pump | Lacerta | Lizard |
| Apus | Bird of Paradise | Leo | Lion |
| Aquarius | Water Bearer | Leo Minor | Little Lion |
| Aquila | Eagle | Lepus | Hare |
| Ara | Altar | Libra | Scales |
| Argo Navis | Ship Argo | Lupus | Wolf |
| Aries | Ram | Lynx | Lynx |
| Auriga | Charioteer | Lyra | Lyre |
| Boötes | Herdsman | Mensa | Table |
| Caelum | Chisel | Microscopium | Microscope |
| Camelopardus | Giraffe | Monoceros | Unicorn |
| Cancer | Crab | Musca | Fly |
| Canes Venatici | Hunting Dogs | Norma | Rule (straight-edge) |
| Canis Major | Great Dog | Octans | Octant |
| Canis Minor | Little Dog | Orion | Orion (hunter) |
| Capricornus | Sea-Goat | Pavo | Peacock |
| Carina | Keel (of Argo) | Pegasus | Pegasus (winged horse) |
| Cassiopeia | Cassiopeia | Perseus | Perseus |
| Centaurus | Centaur | Phoenix | Phoenix |
| Cepheus | Cepheus | Pictor | Painter (or Easel) |
| Cetus | Whale | Pisces | Fishes |
| Chamaeleon | Chameleon | Piscis Austrinus | Southern Fish |
| Circinus | Pair of Compasses | Puppis | Poop (of Argo) |
| Columba | Dove | Pyxis | Mariner's Compass |
| Coma Berenices | Berenice's Hair | Reticulum | Net |
| Corona Australis | Southern Crown | Sagitta | Arrow |
| Corona Borealis | Northern Crown | Sagittarius | Archer |
| Corvus | Crow | Scorpius | Scorpion |
| Crater | Cup | Sculptor | Sculptor |
| Crux | Southern Cross | Scutum | Shield |
| Cygnus | Swan | Serpens | Serpent |
| Delphinus | Dolphin | Sextans | Sextant |
| Dorado | Swordfish | Taurus | Bull |
| Draco | Dragon | Telescopium | Telescope |
| Equuleus | Little Horse | Triangulum | Triangle |
| Eridanus | River Eridanus | Triangulum Australe | Southern Triangle |
| Fornax | Furnace | Tucana | Toucan |
| Gemini | Twins | Ursa Major | Great Bear (or Plough) |
| Grus | Crane | Ursa Minor | Little Bear |
| Hercules | Hercules | Vela | Sails (of Argo) |
| Horologium | Clock | Virgo | Virgin |
| Hydra | Sea-Serpent | Volans | Flying Fish |
| Hydrus | Watersnake | Vulpecula | Fox |

The positions of the constellations of the northern and southern hemispheres.

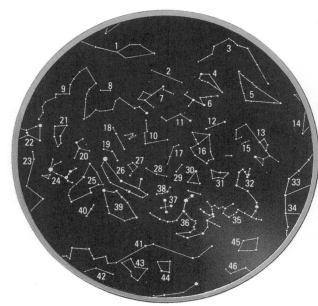

# Stars and Galaxies

You can tell stars from planets because their light seems to twinkle. Planets, which merely reflect the Sun's light, shine with a steady glow. The stars appear to move across the sky, but really this apparent motion is produced by the rotation of the Earth, just like the seeming movement of the Sun. Every star is a great glowing atomic furnace. It consists mainly of the two lightest gases, hydrogen and helium, which are burning all the time.

Galaxies are systems of stars. These are real systems, not apparent ones like the constellations. Galaxies have two main shapes, an ellipse or a spiral. Our own galaxy, the Milky Way, is a spiral galaxy. The galaxies are moving away from each other at ever-increasing speed. We know this because the lines of the spectrum of the light from each galaxy have moved towards the colour red, a phenomenon that astronomers term red shift.

| THE NEAREST STARS | |
|---|---|
| Name | Distance (light-years) |
| Proxima Centauri | 4.38 |
| Alpha-Centauri A | 4.37 |
| Alpha-Centauri B | 4.37 |
| Barnard's Star | 5.90 |
| Wolf 359 | 7.60 |
| Lalande 21185 | 8.13 |
| Sirius A | 8.80 |
| Sirius B § | 8.80 |
| Luyten 726–8 A | 8.88 |
| UV Ceti | 8.88 |
| Ross 154 | 9.44 |
| Ross 248 | 10.28 |
| Epsilon-Eridani | 10.76 |
| Luyten 789–6 | 10.76 |
| Ross 128 | 10.83 |
| 61 Cygni A | 11.09 |
| 61 Cygni B | 11.09 |
| Epsilon-Indi | 11.20 |
| Procyon A | 11.40 |
| Procyon B § | 11.40 |
| Struve 2398 A | 11.52 |
| Struve 2398 B | 11.52 |
| § White dwarf. | |

▽ Galaxies exist in groups. Our Milky Way Galaxy belongs to what scientists call the Local Group, of about 30 galaxies. This diagram shows the galaxies so far discovered at their correct distances apart, although their sizes are not to scale. The Milky Way Galaxy and the Andromeda Galaxy are by far the largest members of the group. There is another smaller spiral galaxy, but the other galaxies are all elliptical dwarfs.

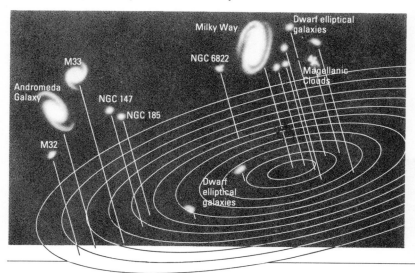

### THE BRIGHTEST STARS

| Name | Constellation | † Apparent magnitude | Distance (light-years) |
|---|---|---|---|
| Sun | — | −26.74 | — |
| Sirius | Canis Major | −1.45 | 8.8 |
| Canopus | Carina | −0.73 | 196 |
| Rigil Kent | Centaurus | −0.10 | 4.37 |
| Arcturus | Boötes | −0.06 | 37 |
| Vega | Lyra | 0.04 | 26 |
| Capella | Auriga | 0.08 | 46 |
| Rigel | Orion | 0.11 | 815 |
| Procyon | Canis Minor | 0.35 | 11.4 |
| Achernar | Eridanus | 0.48 | 127 |
| Hadar | Centaurus | 0.60 | 391 |
| Altair | Aquila | 0.77 | 16 |
| Betelgeuse | Orion | 0.80 | 652 |
| Aldebaran | Taurus | 0.85 | 68 |
| Acrux | Crux | 0.90 | 260 |
| Spica | Virgo | 0.96 | 261 |
| Antares | Scorpius | 1.00 | 424 |
| Pollux | Gemini | 1.15 | 36 |
| Fomalhaut | Piscis Austrinus | 1.16 | 23 |
| Deneb | Cygnus | 1.25 | 1630 |
| Mimosa | Crux | 1.26 | 490 |
| Regulus | Leo | 1.35 | 85 |

† A measure of brightness; the lower the number, the brighter the star.

△ There are millions of spiral galaxies, like our own Milky Way Galaxy. Each one turns very slowly, like a vast wheel of stars in space. This photograph of a nearby spiral galaxy gives us a good idea of what our own Galaxy must look like. The arms of this galaxy are more 'open' than the arms of our own star system, however, and the central nucleus is smaller.

# The Sun

The Sun provides us with light and heat, so it is extremely important to us. But it is really a very ordinary star, of the kind that astronomers call a 'yellow dwarf'. It has been shining for at least five billion years and it is certain to go on shining for at least five billion more.

Deep inside the Sun the temperature reaches millions of degrees. At such a temperature atoms of its main gas, hydrogen, join together to make the gas helium. This process is called fusion. Scientists are trying to make nuclear power plants here on Earth that will work in the same way.

The Sun's surface is seething as hot gases well up from underneath. On the surface we can see dark markings, known as sunspots. These spots come and go, and they appear to reach their maximum number every 11 years. The sunspots are about 2,000°C (3,600°F) cooler than the temperature of the rest of the Sun's surface. During sunspot activity the magnetic radiation from the Sun's surface changes. These changes cause interference with radio communications and compass needles on Earth.

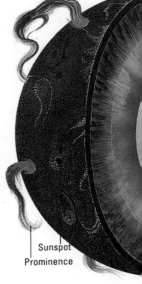

Sunspot
Prominence

△ The Sun looks bright because it is intensely hot. Yet the surface is dim and cool compared to the interior, which has a temperature of about 15 million degrees.

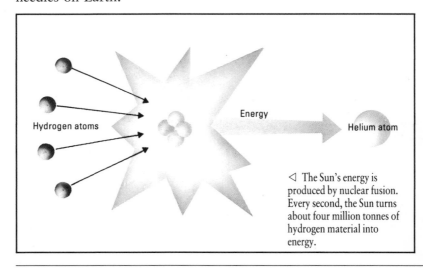

Hydrogen atoms

Energy

Helium atom

◁ The Sun's energy is produced by nuclear fusion. Every second, the Sun turns about four million tonnes of hydrogen material into energy.

Photosphere

Core

### SUN STATISTICS

**Diameter at equator:** 1,392,000 km (865,000 mi)
**Volume:** 1,303,600 times Earth's volume
**Mean density:** 1.41 (water = 1)
**Mass:** 333,000 times Earth's mass
**Gravity:** 28 times Earth's gravity
**Mean distance from Earth:** 149,000,000 km (92,960,000 mi)
**Escape velocity:** 618 km/sec (384 mi/sec)
**Surface temperature:** 6000°C
**Core temperature:** circa 15,000,000°C
**Spins on axis in:** 25.38 days
**Orbits galaxy in:** 225 million years
**Speed of travel through space:** 250 km/sec (155 mi/sec)
**Distance from centre of galaxy:** 30,000 light-years
**†Apparent magnitude:** −26.74

† *A measure of brightness: the lower the number, the brighter the star.*

▽ The Sun's daily path across the sky changes with the seasons of the year. The Sun is at its highest point in the sky at midsummer, and at its lowest point at midwinter.

△ During an eclipse of the Sun by the Moon, the glow of the Sun's corona can be seen.

Midsummer Sun

23½°

Spring and Autumn Sun

23½°

Midwinter Sun

South

SE

SW

E

W

NE

NW

# The Moon

The Moon is a satellite of the Earth – that is, it circles around the Earth. It takes 27⅓ days to do so, slightly less than a calendar month. Its bright surface reflects the light of the Sun. When the Moon is directly between the Earth and the Sun we cannot see it. This is the new Moon. As the Moon moves on, a thin crescent of light appears. The first quarter is when half the surface is lit.

Later, we see all the surface – the full Moon. Up to this point we say the Moon has been 'waxing'. After this it starts to 'wane'. When half is lit again the Moon is in its last quarter. The sunlit portion gets smaller until the Moon vanishes.

△ The Moon was first explored by humans between 1969 and 1972, when six teams of Apollo astronauts landed. This photograph shows the second man on the Moon, Edwin Aldrin, posing for the first man, Neil Armstrong, after the Apollo 11 landing of 21 July 1969.

The diameter of the Moon is 400 times smaller than that of the Sun, but the Moon is 400 times closer to the Earth. As a result, we see the Moon and Sun as about the same size. At certain times of the year, the Moon comes directly between us and the Sun and blots out the Sun from our sight for a few minutes. We say that an eclipse of the Sun has occurred. If the Earth's shadow comes between the Sun and the Moon, there is an eclipse of the Moon.

New Moon

Crescent phase

Gibbous phase

Full Moon

Last quarter

Crescent phase

△ We call the varying appearance of the Moon its 'phases'. First comes the new Moon. As the Moon waxes, a thin crescent appears and gets bigger until half the surface is lit. We call this the Moon's first quarter. Next comes the gibbous Moon; then the full Moon. As the Moon wanes, the sunlit portion gets smaller, until it disappears at the next new Moon.

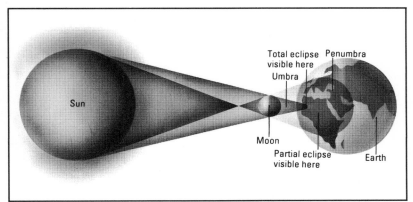

Total eclipse
visible here
Penumbra
Umbra
Sun
Moon
Partial eclipse
visible here
Earth

△ An eclipse of the Sun, or solar eclipse, happens when the Moon blocks the Sun's light from reaching the Earth. A total eclipse can be seen only from within the umbra – a region of shadow a few hundred kilometres across. Around it is a less shadowy area, the penumbra.

### MOON STATISTICS

**Diameter at equator**: 3476 km (2160 mi)
**Volume**: 1/49 Earth's volume
**Density**: 3.34 (water = 1)
**Mass**: 1/81 Earth's mass
**Gravity**: 1/6 Earth's gravity
**Closest distance from Earth**: 356,400 km (221,460 mi)
**Furthest distance from Earth**: 406,70 km (252,710 mi)
**Mean distance from Earth**: 384,400 km (238,860 mi)
**Spins on axis in**: 27⅓ days
**Orbits Earth in (sidereal month)**: 27⅓ days
**Synodic month (new Moon–new Moon)**: 29½ days

▷ We only ever see one face of the Moon. When the Moon was newly formed it was made of molten rock, spinning around once in a few hours. As it cooled, a hard skin or crust formed on the outside. The Earth's gravity, pulling at this crust, slowed the spin down and raised a 'bulge' a few kilometres high on one side. Now this bulge is always turned inwards, and the Moon keeps the same face towards the Earth.

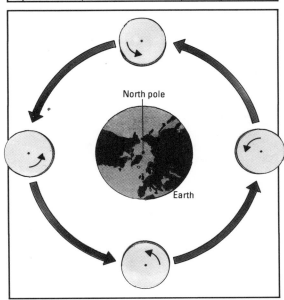

North pole

Earth

HOW THE PLANETS
FORMED

# The Solar System

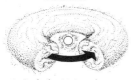

1. In the beginning, there was a spinning ring of gas and dust particles, circling the Sun.

2. The solid particles began to stick together, forming larger bodies, made mostly of carbon and ice.

3. The bodies became as big as planets, and began to 'pull' against each other. Some of the very small ice bodies became comets.

4. Eventually there were just nine large bodies going around the Sun in orbits: the major planets.

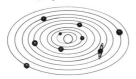

5. In time, the planets' orbits stabilized.

Nine planets orbit the Sun. We call the Sun's satellites the *solar system*, 'solar' meaning 'of the Sun'. The Earth is the third planet in distance from the Sun and – as far as scientists are aware to date – it is also the only planet on which there is life. The further a planet is from the Sun, the longer its year – the time it takes to go once around the Sun. The Earth takes 365¼ days. Mercury, the nearest to the Sun, takes only 88 days. Pluto, the most distant planet, has a year more than 247 Earth-years long.

In between the orbits of two of the planets, Mars and Jupiter, are thousands of smaller bodies called the asteroids or minor planets. The largest of these minor planets, Ceres, is only 687 km (427 miles) across. Most of the asteroids are less than 95 km (60 miles) in diameter. We do not know if these little planets are debris that resulted from the break-up of a larger planet, or whether they just failed to form one body when the solar system began.

## FAMOUS COMETS

Comets are small heavenly bodies made up of dust and ice. They have been described as 'dirty snowballs'. They orbit the Sun in very long ellipses, and some take thousands of years to complete one circuit of their orbit.

| Name | First observed | Orbital period (years) |
|---|---|---|
| Halley's Comet | 240 BC | 76 |
| Encke's Comet | 1786 | 3.3 |
| Great Comet of 1811 | 1811 | 3,000 |
| Pons-Winnecke Comet | 1819 | 6.0 |
| Biela's Comet | 1826 | 6.7 |
| Great Comet of 1843 | 1843 | 512.4 |
| Donati's Comet | 1858 | 2,040 |
| Schwassmann-Wachmann Comet | 1925 | 16.2 |
| Arend-Roland Comet | 1957 | 10,000 |
| Ikeya-Seki Comet | 1965 | 880 |
| Kouhoutek's Comet* | 1975 | – |
| Comet West | 1976 | – |

*observed from Skylab and Soyuz spacecraft

## THE PLANETS AND THEIR STATISTICS

| Name | Average distance from Sun, millions of km | (miles) | Diameter at equator km | (miles) | Circles Sun in: | Turns on axis in: |
|---|---|---|---|---|---|---|
| Sun | – | – | 1,392,000 | (865,000) | – | 25⅓ days |
| Mercury | 58 | (36) | 4850 | (3015) | 88 days | 59 days |
| Venus | 108 | (67) | 12,140 | (7545) | 224 days | 244 days |
| Earth | 150 | (93) | 12,756 | (7926) | 365¼ days | 23:56 hours |
| Mars | 228 | (142) | 6790 | (4220) | 687 days | 24:37 hours |
| Jupiter | 778 | (483) | 142,600 | (88,600) | 11.9 years | 9:50 hours |
| Saturn | 1427 | (887) | 120,200 | (74,700) | 29.5 years | 10:14 hours |
| Uranus | 2870 | (1783) | 49,000 | (30,500) | 84 years | 11 hours |
| Neptune | 4497 | (2794) | 50,000 | (31,200) | 164.8 years | 15:48 hours |
| Pluto | 5900 | (3660) | 3000 | (1800) | 247.7 years | 153 hours |

▷ This view of the Sun and planets shows how small the Earth is compared with the four 'giant planets'. But even the giants are tiny compared with the Sun.

▽ The nine planets of our system (in order from the Sun)
1. Mercury
2. Venus
3. Earth
4. Mars
5. Jupiter
6. Saturn
7. Uranus
8. Neptune
9. Pluto

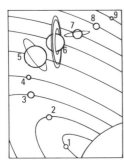

## ASTRONOMY TERMS

**asteroids** Thousands of small bodies that orbit the Sun between the orbits of Mars and Jupiter.

**astrobiology** Study of life on other worlds.

**astronomical unit** (AU) Mean distance between Earth and Sun. 93,000,000 miles or 150,000,000 km.

**astrophysics** Branch of astronomy concerned with physical nature of heavenly bodies.

**aurora** Phenomenon of the atmosphere seen around the polar regions, in form of colourful displays of light, attributed to sunspot activity. Northern Lights – Aurora Borealis; Southern Lights – Aurora Australis.

**big-bang theory** See *universe*.

**black holes** Supposed regions of space of intense gravitational force caused by collapse of star.

**celestial sphere** Imaginary sphere in which heavenly bodies seem to be projected from point of observation.

**chromosphere** Layer of crimson gas round the Sun.

**comet** Heavenly body consisting of the head, a relatively small, star-like nucleus surrounded by *coma*, a glowing cloud, with, usually, a *tail* millions of miles long made up of dust and gas. Comets, visible near the Sun, orbit it with periods of a few to thousands of years.

**constellation** Apparent grouping of stars together within definite region of the sky; 88 officially recognized and designated.

**corona** Sun's pearly-white outer layer of gas, extending more than a million miles, visible only during eclipse.

**eclipse** Obscuration of one heavenly body by another.

**equinox** Instant when the Sun is directly over our Equator, making equal day and night; occurs about 21 March and 23 September.

**evening star** Planet seen in western sky after sunset, especially Venus.

**galaxy** Vast system of stars (thousands of millions). Millions of galaxies exist, regular ones having spiral or elliptical forms.

**halo** (1) Luminous ring seen round Moon or Sun, caused by light refraction through high clouds. (2) Stars surrounding Milky Way in halo fashion.

**interstellar space** Beyond the Solar System, among the stars.

**light-year** Distance travelled by light in 1 year, 5.88 million million miles or 9.46 million million km.

**meridian** Imaginary line in sky passing through poles of celestial sphere and directly over observer.

**meteor** Phenomenon caused by small body entering Earth's atmosphere and emitting light; estimated 100 million per day.

**meteorite** Meteor reaching Earth before burning up; lumps of stone (*aerolites*) or iron (*siderites*) up to a 50-tonne specimen found near Grootfontein, Namibia.

**Milky Way** Our galaxy; contains estimated 200,000 million stars; spiral type.

**moon** Any natural satellite of planet. Earth's Moon is our only natural satellite.

▽ On June 21, the north pole is inclined towards the Sun, bringing mid-summer to the northern hemisphere while the south has midwinter. On December 21 the situation is reversed.

**The Seasons**

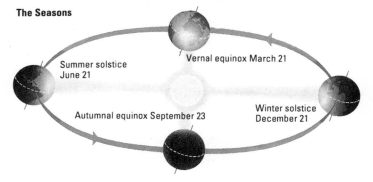

Summer solstice
June 21

Vernal equinox March 21

Autumnal equinox September 23

Winter solstice
December 21

**morning star** Planet seen in eastern sky before sunrise, especially Venus.

**nebula** (Lat. *mist*) Hazy mass of gases and particles in space.

**Northern Lights** See *aurora*.

**orbit** Path of one celestial body round another.

**parsec** Unit of distance equal to 3.258 light-years.

**photosphere** Visible surface of the Sun.

**planetarium** Projection instrument that demonstrates motions of heavenly bodies.

**planets** The nine major bodies moving in orbit around the Sun.

**quasar** Quasi-stellar radio sources – mysterious distant objects in the universe, powerful sources of radio waves and light.

**radio astronomy** Branch concerned with study of radio energy emitted by stars or regions in space.

**radio source** A single source of radio emission in space.

**radio telescope** Instrument that collects radio waves from space.

**red shift** Spectra of galaxies shift towards the red, indicating receding of galaxies.

**satellite** A body, natural or artificial, that orbits a celestial body.

**shooting star** Common type of meteor, caused by objects as small as 1 mm diameter.

**siderite** See *meteorite*.

**solar flare** Eruption of radiation on the Sun.

**Solar System** The Sun and its satellites.

**solar wind** Permanent particle radiation from the sun.

△ The Aurorae, or Northern and Southern Lights, are brilliant displays in the atmosphere.

**solstice** Instant when the Sun is farthest from Earth's Equator, making longest or shortest day; occurs about 21 June and 22 December.

**Southern Lights** See *aurora*.

**star** Heavenly body generating its own heat and light; nearest after Sun is Proxima Centauri (4.28 light-years); 5,000 stars are visible to the naked eye. Brightness is measured in terms of *star magnitude*.

**steady-state theory** See *universe*.

**Sun** Our star, basis of the Solar System, a glowing ball of gases, mainly hydrogen and helium. (See *chromosphere, corona, photosphere*).

**sunspots** Dark patches on the Sun, 2000°C cooler than normal; maximum activity in 11-year cycles; origin unknown (see *aurora*).

**transit** Passage of Mercury or Venus across the Sun's disc.

**universe** Everything that exists – matter, space, energy. Most astronomers set its age at 15 billion years; the universe seems to be expanding, like an inflating balloon. *Big-bang theory* suggests explosion of 'primeval atom' 100 million light-years in diameter – hence the expanding universe; *steady-state theory* suggests infinite universe, no beginning or end, matter continuously being created, changing, and 'aging'.

**zenith** Point in heavens directly overhead.

▽ A photograph of meteor tracks. Such brilliant displays as this are rare.

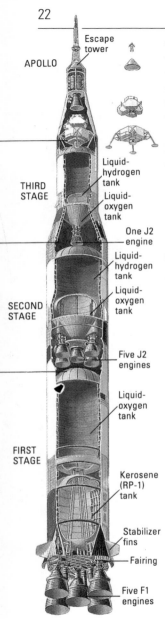

APOLLO

Escape tower

THIRD STAGE

Liquid-hydrogen tank

Liquid-oxygen tank

One J2 engine

Liquid-hydrogen tank

Liquid-oxygen tank

SECOND STAGE

Five J2 engines

Liquid-oxygen tank

FIRST STAGE

Kerosene (RP-1) tank

Stabilizer fins

Fairing

Five F1 engines

△ Cutaway view of the three-stage Saturn 5 rocket launcher used for the American-manned Apollo flights.

# Exploring Space

Only 60 years ago, the idea that people might one day fly in space and walk on the Moon seemed as far-fetched as any modern science fiction story. But it suddenly came close on October 4, 1957, when radio signals were picked up from space. They came from *Sputnik 1*, a tiny Soviet satellite, and the first man-made object to orbit the Earth.

Four years later came the first manned space flight, by the Russian cosmonaut Yuri Gagarin. American manned space flights followed. The first Moon landing was made on July 20, 1969, by the American astronauts Neil A. Armstrong and Edwin E. Aldrin, while their colleague Michael Collins orbited the Moon in a vehicle called the command module ready to pick them up for the return to Earth.

The first series of manned Moon landings was completed by the United States in the early 1970s. The next target is Mars, where the Soviets plan to land a mission in the 1990s.

However, the most important aspects of space exploration have been the practical uses of Earth satellites, and the scientific knowledge of our solar system we have gained. Satellites keep a regular watch on the world's weather. Weather men can actually see bad weather and potential disaster-makers such as hurricanes as they approach land, and can warn people to take the necessary precautions. Satellites have photographed every part of the Earth's surface, and confirmed the accuracy of our maps. They have also confirmed the growing hole in the ozone layer above Antarctica, first detected in 1985.

One of the biggest benefits has been in the field of communications. If a satellite orbits the Earth at a speed matching the Earth's rotation, it becomes 'fixed' in space above

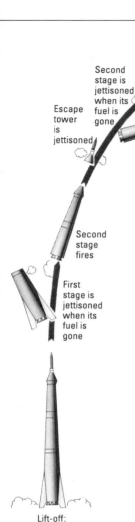

Second stage is jettisoned when its fuel is gone

Escape tower is jettisoned

Third stage fires and thrusts spacecraft into orbit

Third stage separates

Spacecraft continues in orbit

Second stage fires

First stage is jettisoned when its fuel is gone

Lift-off: first stage fires

△ How a three-stage rocket launches a spacecraft. The first stage fires at lift-off. When its fuel is used up, it separates and falls away. The second and third stages fire in turn to give the spacecraft sufficient speed to enter orbit.

one point on the ground. A group of three communications satellites placed around the world can receive radio and television signals from almost every part of the globe, and 'bounce' them back to receiving stations on Earth.

In this way we can now use satellites to relay telephone calls. Radio and TV can bring you events as they happen on the opposite side of the world.

Unmanned space probes have been sent to land on or fly past every one of the planets in our solar system. They have photographed the planets in close-up and relayed the pictures back to Earth. In this way we have discovered that water must once have existed on Mars and that Jupiter has 16 moons, three more than we can detect by telescope.

Only one kind of engine works in space – the rocket. When fuel is burned inside a rocket engine, it produces large volumes of gas. The gas exerts great pressure on the surface inside the engine. The pressure around the sides is the same. The upward pressure on the top is much greater than the pressure on the bottom. This is because the gas can escape through a nozzle at the bottom of the engine. Because the pressure at the top is much stronger than the pressure at the bottom, the result is an upward thrust which drives the rocket along.

Perhaps the most exciting developments are still going on: the creation of space laboratories where scientific work impossible within Earth's gravity can be carried out.

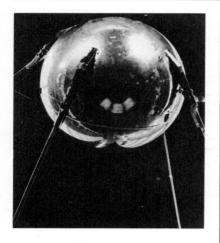

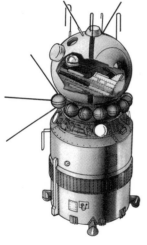

## STEPS INTO SPACE

**1957** First artificial Earth satellite: Russians launch *Sputnik 1* on October 4, heralding Space Age; November 3, Russians launch *Sputnik 2*, containing dog Laika, first mammal in space.

**1958** On January 31, Americans launch their first satellite, *Explorer 1*.

**1959** Russians launch *Lunik 1* (first probe to go near Moon), *Lunik 2* (first to crash-land on Moon), and *Lunik 3* (first photographs of hidden side of Moon).

**1960** US launch *Tiros 1*, first Earth weather satellite (clear photographs of cloud cover).

**1961** First man in space: Russian cosmonaut Yuri Gagarin makes one orbit in *Vostok 1* on April 12. First American astronaut Alan Shepard makes sub-orbital flight on May 5.

**1962** First American in orbit, John Glenn makes 3 orbits in *Friendship 7* (Mercury craft). *Ranger 4* becomes first US craft to reach Moon. First commercial communications satellite, *Telstar 1*, begins relaying TV programmes across Atlantic.

**1963** First woman in space is Russian cosmonaut Valentina Tereshkova.

**1964** Russians launch *Voskhod 1* with Vladimir Komarov, Boris Yegorov, and Konstantin Feoktistov aboad, first craft with more than one spaceman (made 16 orbits).

**1965** Alexei Leonov makes first space walk.

**1966** Russia's *Luna 9* makes soft landing on Moon and returns TV pictures. Neil Armstrong and Dave Scott make first space docking with unmanned craft. First American soft landing on Moon by *Surveyor 1*.

**1967** First space disasters: three US astronauts and one Soviet cosmonaut die.

**1968** First recovery of unmanned lunar probe, Russian *Zond 5*, from Indian Ocean on September 21. First manned lunar flight: *Apollo 8* (Frank Borman, James Lovell, William Anders) completes 10 orbits.

**1969** First docking of two manned spacecraft, with exchange of cosmonauts by space walk (*Soyuz 4* and *5*). In July *Apollo 11* lands lunar module on Moon: American astronaut Neil Armstrong becomes first man to walk on Moon. Second Moon landing (*Apollo 12*) in November.

◁ *Top*: Sputnik 1 was the first space satellite. *Centre*: The first Soviet cosmonauts flew in Vostok spacecraft. *Bottom*: Telstar was the first communications satellite.

**1970** *Apollo 13* has narrow escape from disaster. Russians soft-land unmanned *Luna 17* on Moon and use 8-wheeled Lunokhod 1, first propelled vehicle on Moon. Russian probe *Venera 7* lands on Venus (Dec 15) and transmits data back.

**1971** *Apollo 14* makes 3rd manned Moon landing. Three cosmonauts make longest space flight to date (23 days 17 hr 40 min), but die on return. *Apollo 15* makes 4th Moon landing. US probe *Mariner 9* becomes first artificial satellite of Mars.

**1972** Americans launch *Pioneer 10* on 21-month mission to Jupiter. *Apollo 16* and *Apollo 17* make final Moon landings, bringing back lunar samples.

**1973** Americans launch *Skylab 1*, unmanned portion of their first manned orbiting space station, including workshop and telescope mount. *Skylab 2, 3*, and *4* launched, each with three astronauts.

**1974** *Mariner 10* (launched by US 3.11.73) passes Venus and flies close to Mercury (March 29) for Man's first close-up look.

**1975** First joint Russian-American mission in space: *Soyuz 19* and *Apollo 18* dock while orbiting Earth. Astronauts and cosmonauts carry out exchange visits and experiments. Russian probes *Venera 9* and *Venera 10* soft-land on Venus.

**1976** *Helios B*, a research spacecraft carrying American and German instrumentation, comes within 27 million miles (43.4 million km) of the Sun. Soviet spacecraft *Luna 24* makes a soft landing on the Moon to take soil samples with automatic scoop.

**1977** The Soviet craft *Soyuz 24* docks successfully with orbiting *Salyut 5* space laboratory one day after launch. The US launch two *Voyager* spacecraft to fly to Jupiter and Saturn.

**1978** Two Soviet spacecraft dock with the orbiting *Salyut* space laboratory (Jan 11) thus achieving the first triple link-up in space.

**1980** Western Europe's *Ariane* rocket makes first test flight. *Voyager 1* flies past Saturn. Its instruments reveal that Saturn's rings are more numerous and complex than had been thought.

**1981** America's shuttle *Columbia* makes first test flight of 54½-hr, orbiting the Earth and gliding back to a perfect landing on a desert airstrip. *Voyager 2* flies near Saturn, before going on to visit Uranus and Neptune.

△ The American Mercury capsule was just big enough for one astronaut. The Mercury programme of manned spaceflights ended in 1963, after six flights, four of them orbital.

△ In 1983 the Pioneer spacecraft became the first object launched from Earth to leave the solar system.

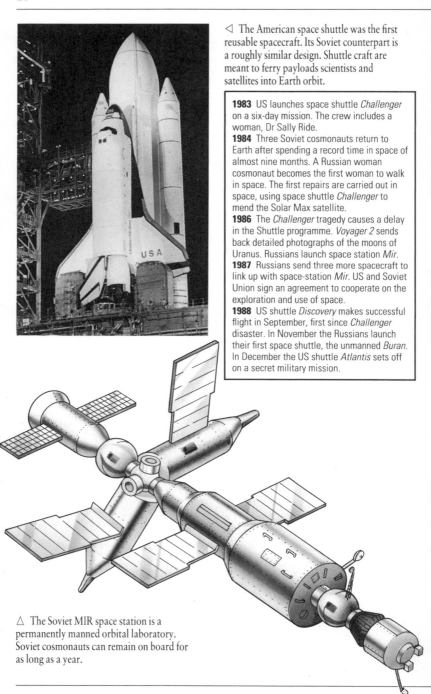

◁ The American space shuttle was the first reusable spacecraft. Its Soviet counterpart is a roughly similar design. Shuttle craft are meant to ferry payloads scientists and satellites into Earth orbit.

**1983** US launches space shuttle *Challenger* on a six-day mission. The crew includes a woman, Dr Sally Ride.

**1984** Three Soviet cosmonauts return to Earth after spending a record time in space of almost nine months. A Russian woman cosmonaut becomes the first woman to walk in space. The first repairs are carried out in space, using space shuttle *Challenger* to mend the Solar Max satellite.

**1986** The *Challenger* tragedy causes a delay in the Shuttle programme. *Voyager 2* sends back detailed photographs of the moons of Uranus. Russians launch space station *Mir*.

**1987** Russians send three more spacecraft to link up with space-station *Mir*. US and Soviet Union sign an agreement to cooperate on the exploration and use of space.

**1988** US shuttle *Discovery* makes successful flight in September, first since *Challenger* disaster. In November the Russians launch their first space shuttle, the unmanned *Buran*. In December the US shuttle *Atlantis* sets off on a secret military mission.

△ The Soviet MIR space station is a permanently manned orbital laboratory. Soviet cosmonauts can remain on board for as long as a year.

## SPACE ACCIDENTS

**1967, January** First space accident: three US astronauts (Ed White, Gus Grissom, Roger Chaffee) die in *Apollo 1* launch pad fire.

**1967, April** Cosmonaut Vladimir Komarov is killed when *Soyuz 1* crashes into ground.

**1970, April** Moon-bound *Apollo 13* is damaged by an explosion on the third day of its journey, but loops around the Moon and back to Earth.

**1971, June** After a record flight the three-man crew of Soviet spacecraft *Soyuz 11* are killed by a last-minute pressure failure.

**1986, January** US space shuttle *Challenger* explodes on take-off, killing all seven on board.

**1988, September** Three Soviet cosmonauts almost fail to return following a computer failure.

▽ The Voyager spacecraft showed the planet Saturn's rings in clearer detail than ever before. They are numerous and more complicated than had been previously suspected. This picture was taken from the dark side of the giant planet, at a distance of 700,000 kilometres (434,970 miles).

▽ Skylab was an American space station launched in 1973. Three astronauts could live in the crew quarters within the orbital workshop, a converted third stage Saturn rocket. Three crews visited Skylab, successfully repairing damage caused during its launch. Skylab was burnt up in the Earth's atmosphere in 1979.

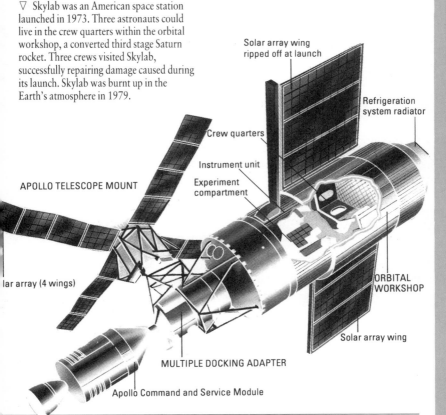

Solar array wing ripped off at launch

Refrigeration system radiator

Crew quarters

Instrument unit

APOLLO TELESCOPE MOUNT

Experiment compartment

lar array (4 wings)

ORBITAL WORKSHOP

Solar array wing

MULTIPLE DOCKING ADAPTER

Apollo Command and Service Module

# Planet Earth

**An atmosphere containing the element oxygen and an abundant supply of its compound, water, is found on planet Earth, and nowhere else in the solar system. These two ingredients are vital for life, which began here probably about 3½ billion years ago. During that unimaginable span of time, continents have formed and re-formed, ice ages have come and gone, and living things have evolved and some have become extinct.**

Our Earth is one of nine planets that orbit the Sun. It ranks fifth in size. It is the only one with abundant water and an atmosphere containing oxygen – the two things necessary for life. Space probes have not detected any definite signs of life on the other planets.

Some form of life on Earth may have begun as long ago as 3½ billion years. But the abundant life we see today has been in existence for only about 600 million years. That is less than one-eighth of the Earth's age. During that time many species (kinds) of plants and animals have come into existence and died out again. Geologists divide the past 600 million years of Earth's history into periods. There is a chart showing these periods and the kinds of living things that flourished during them on pages 30–31.

Although the continents appear to have always been where they are now, this is not so. Millions of years ago, all the continents were part of one supercontinent known as Pangaea. About 200 million years ago this huge supercontinent began to break up, and the separate continents gradually moved to where they are now. This process is called continental drift. The continents are still moving. The Atlantic Ocean, for example, is growing wider by at least 5 cm (2 inches) a year, as America drifts to the west.

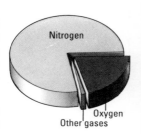

Nitrogen

Oxygen
Other gases

△ The two main gases in the atmosphere are nitrogen 78 per cent and oxygen 21 per cent. There is also an increasing amount of carbon dioxide and small quantities of other gases, water vapour, dust and salt particles.

The continents rest on plates. There are about 20 covering the surface of the Earth's crust. As the plates move, some of them bump into one another. Such collisions happen very slowly. Some of them thrust up mountains, such as the ranges of western North and South America and the Himalayas of Asia. At such places, one plate may be sliding under another. New material is welling up under the oceans to replace the lost part of the plate, and to push the plates along. The plates also slide sideways against one another. One place where this is happening is the San Andreas Fault in California. The plates do not move smoothly, but in jerks. When a jerk happens, we get an earthquake.

Many factors influence the world's climate and weather. From time to time, large parts of the Earth's surface are covered with thick sheets of ice. Scientist think these Ice Ages — also called glacials — occur every few million years. We are now in one of the warmer periods, called interglacials. During Ice Ages so much of the ocean water is locked up as ice that the sea level falls. That is how there was once a strip of land connecting Alaska to Siberia, and another linking Britain to the rest of Europe.

The most recent Ice Age lasted until about 10,000 years ago. During the Ice Age a large part of northern North America and Europe were covered with a sheet of ice up to 3,000 m (9,800 ft) thick.

During the Ice Age there were a great many glaciers, ice rivers. As glaciers creep slowly over the land they wear it away, smoothing out mountains and gouging out deep valleys. If you see very jagged mountains, such as the Alps, you can be sure that they are not very old — in Earth history terms, that is. But low, smooth mountains have been shaped by the ice. You can still see glaciers in cold mountain regions.

---

**EARTH'S VITAL STATISTICS**

**Age:** About 4,600 million years.

**Diameter:** From Pole to Pole through the Earth's centre, 12,700 km (7,930 miles); across the Equator through the Earth's centre 12,760 km (7,930 miles).

**Circumference:** Round the Poles 40,070 km (24,860 miles); round the Equator 40,070 km (24,900 miles).

**Area:** Land 148,800,000 sq km (57,400,000 sq miles) = 29 per cent; water 361,300,000 sq km (139,500,000 sq miles) = 71 per cent.

**Volume of the oceans:** 1,321 million cu km (317 million cubic miles).

**Average height of land:** 840 m (2,757 ft) above sea level.

**Average depth of oceans:** 3,795 m (12,450 ft) below sea level.

## EARTH'S LONG HISTORY

| Era | Period | Epoch | Millions of years ago |
|---|---|---|---|
| Cenozoic | Quaternary | Recent (Holocene) | |
| | | | 0.01 |
| | | Pleistocene | |
| | | | 2 |
| | Tertiary | Pliocene | |
| | | | 5 |
| | | Miocene | |
| | | | 25 |
| | | Oligocene | |
| | | | 35 |
| | | Eocene | |
| | | | 60 |
| | | Palaeocene | |
| | | | 65 |
| | | | 65 |
| Mesozoic | Cretaceous | | |
| | | | 145 |
| | Jurassic | | |
| | | | 210 |
| | Triassic | | |
| | | | 245 |
| | | | 245 |
| Palaeozoic | Permian | | |
| | | | 285 |
| | Carboniferous | | |
| | | | 360 |
| | Devonian | | |
| | | | 410 |
| | Silurian | | |
| | | | 440 |
| | Ordovician | | |
| | | | 505 |
| | Cambrian | | |
| | | | 570 |
| | | | 570 |

Pre-Cambrian time stretches back to the formation of the Earth, about 4,600 million years ago

*Highlights of plant and animal life*

Modern human beings emerged and civilization began.

Ice Age in northern hemisphere, woolly mammals survived the cold.

'Ape-men' appeared. Many large mammals died out as the weather got colder.

Many apes in Africa. Herds of mammals grazed on the spreading grasslands.

Early apes appeared. Many modern mammals began to evolve. Flowering plants increased.

Strange mammals, including early horses and elephants. Plants mostly modern types.

Mammals evolved rapidly after most reptiles had died out.

Dinosaurs and many other reptiles died out at the end of the period. Ammonites disappeared. First flowering plants.

Dinosaurs ruled the land. Flying reptiles. First birds. Ammonites common. Some small mammals.

First dinosaurs and large sea reptiles. First mammals. Ammonites common. Cycads and Bennettitaleans evolved. Conifers spread. Luxuriant forests.

Reptiles increased. Amphibians less important. Trilobites died out. Primitive conifers and ginkgoes.

Amphibians increased. First reptiles. Clubmosses, ferns and horsetails in coal-forming swamps.

The age of fishes (bony and cartilaginous). Amphibians evolved. Land plants more common.

Giant armoured fishes. First land/marsh plants. Large sea scorpions – terrors of the seas.

First vertebrates (jawless fishes). Graptolites and trilobites abundant. Echinoderms and brachiopods spread.

Fossils abundant. Graptolites, trilobites, primitive shellfish, corals, crustaceans, etc.

Life began about 3,500 million years ago. Oldest known fossils are organisms in Fig-Tree cherts (3,500 m yrs) and stromatolites (2,800 m yrs). But fossils rare – probably because creatures were soft-bodied (eg jellyfish, worms).

# Earthquakes and Volcanoes

Earthquakes and volcanoes often seem to go together. They are most likely to occur in areas where two plates meet (see page 38). Most of the world's active volcanoes occur in a band around the edge of the Pacific Ocean, called the 'Ring of Fire', that continues north of Australia through New Guinea and Indonesia.

Volcanoes are also likely to occur over 'hot spots', places in the Earth's crust where there are weaknesses. Many Pacific islands are the tops of old volcanoes which were once over such hot spots, before the plates moved on. Inside a volcano lava (hot liquid rock) spouts up from a central vent. As the lava cools it forms solid rock again.

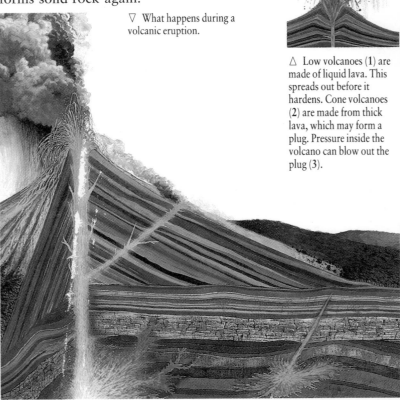

1

2

3

▽ What happens during a volcanic eruption.

△ Low volcanoes (1) are made of liquid lava. This spreads out before it hardens. Cone volcanoes (2) are made from thick lava, which may form a plug. Pressure inside the volcano can blow out the plug (3).

## NOTABLE EARTHQUAKES

**Shensi Province, China, 1556:** Over 800,000 people perished – more than in any other earthquake.

**Lisbon, Portugal, 1755:** About 60,000 people died and shocks were felt as far away as Norway.

**San Francisco, USA, 1906:** An earthquake and the fires it caused destroyed the city.

**Kwanto Plain, Japan, 1923:** Some 570,000 buildings collapsed. This was the costliest earthquake ever as measured by damage to property.

**Tangshan China, 1976:** About 242,000 people were reported killed in this industrial city.

**Lebu, Chile, 1977:** The strongest earthquake shock ever recorded.

**Armenia, USSR, 1988:** 45,000 people died; 20,000 people were injured; 400,000 people were made homeless and 3 cities were destroyed.

▽ Shock waves spread out from the epicentre of an earthquake.

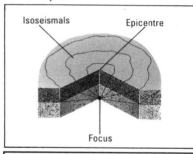

## MEASURING EARTHQUAKES

The intensity of an earthquake is measured on the Modified Mercalli Scale. The numbers of this scale refer to the effects produced:

1. Very slight. Felt only by instruments.
2. Felt by people resting.
3. Feels like passing traffic.
4. Furniture and windows rattle.
5. Can be felt outdoors. Clocks stop. Doors swing.
6. Furniture moves about. Cracks appear in walls.
7. People knocked over. Masonry cracks and falls.
8. Chimneys and monuments fall. Buildings move on foundations.
9. Heavy damage to buildings. Large cracks open in ground.
10. Most buildings destroyed. Landslides occur. Water thrown out of canals and lakes.
11. Railway lines badly bent.
12. No buildings left standing.

△ San Francisco after the 1906 earthquake.

## THE EARTHQUAKE ZONES OF THE WORLD

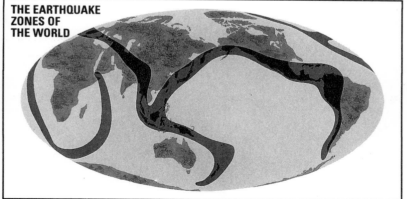

# The World's Water

Nearly three-quarters of the Earth's surface is covered by water. The oceans are mostly very deep. Near land the seas are shallower, because part of each continent slopes down under the sea at what is called the continental shelf. Several parts of the oceans are very deep indeed. They are called ocean trenches, and they occur where one plate of the Earth's crust is sliding under another. The deepest of these trenches is the Marianas Trench, in the Eastern Pacific. It is 11,033 m (36,198 ft) deep. The deepest trench in the Atlantic Ocean is the Puerto Rico Trench in the West Indies, which is 8,648 m (28,374 ft) deep.

The water of the oceans is salty. It is always being evaporated by the heat of the Sun, forming clouds which eventually fall as rain. Rain collects on land to form ponds and lakes, and flows back down rivers to the sea. Some water collects in huge natural reservoirs deep underground. There are stores of such water under the dry Sahara desert. Much of it fell as rain thousands of years ago.

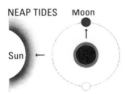

△ Most of the Earth's surface is watery, as this pie chart shows.

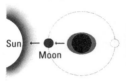

△ Spring tides are high because the Sun's gravitational pull is combined with the Moon's. Neap tides are low because the Moon and Sun are pulling at right angles to each other.

| SIZE OF THE OCEANS | | |
|---|---|---|
| | Sq km | Sq miles |
| Pacific Ocean | 181,000,000 | 70,000,000 |
| Atlantic Ocean | 106,000,000 | 41,000,000 |
| Indian Ocean | 73,500,000 | 28,400,000 |
| Arctic Ocean | 14,350,000 | 5,540,000 |

▽ This diagram shows the relative sizes of the four major oceans.

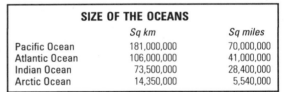

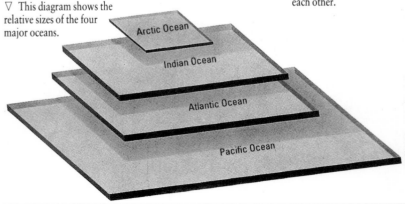

## LONGEST RIVERS

| | Km | Miles |
|---|---|---|
| Nile (Africa) | 6,695 | 4,160 |
| Amazon (South America) | 6,440 | 4,000 |
| Chang Jiang (China) | 6,380 | 3,964 |
| Mississippi-Missouri-<br>Red River (North America) | 5,970 | 3,710 |
| Ob-Irtysh (USSR) | 5,410 | 3,362 |
| Huang He (China) | 4,672 | 2,903 |
| Zaïre (Africa) | 4,667 | 2,900 |
| Amur (Asia) | 4,416 | 2,744 |
| Lena (USSR) | 4,400 | 2,734 |
| Mackenzie (Canada) | 4,240 | 2,635 |
| Mekong (Asia) | 4,180 | 2,600 |
| Niger (Africa) | 4,170 | 2,590 |

## LARGEST LAKES

| | Sq km | Sq miles |
|---|---|---|
| Caspian Sea (Asia/Europe) | 371,000 | 143,244 |
| Superior (North America) | 82,103 | 31,700 |
| Victoria (Africa) | 69,484 | 26,828 |
| Aral Sea (Asia) | 77,451 | 24,904 |
| Huron (North America) | 59,569 | 23,000 |
| Michigan (North America) | 57,757 | 22,300 |
| Tanganyika (Africa) | 32,893 | 12,700 |
| Baykal (Asia) | 31,499 | 12,162 |
| Great Bear (North America) | 31,328 | 12,096 |
| Malawi (Africa) | 28,878 | 11,150 |

△ This bar graph shows the world's longest rivers.

▽ Five lakes make up North America's Great Lakes. They are Erie, Superior, Huron, Michigan and Ontario. Shown here is Erie.

# World Record Breakers

The world contains many natural features, such as deserts and mountains, which are outstanding in size. Here is a selection. It has proved very difficult to measure some of them. For example, several measurements have been made of Mount Everest, which do not quite agree. Several different ways of measuring the depth of the Marianas Trench have been tried, again giving slightly different readings. The figures given here are the best available.

△ One of nature's most violent phenomena: an erupting volcano spews out lava in Iceland.

---

### DEEP, LONG AND HIGH

**Greatest ocean depth:** 11,033 m (36,198 ft), Marianas Trench, Pacific Ocean.

**Deepest underwater gorge:** 1,800 m (5,900 ft), near Esperance, Western Australia.

**Longest gorge:** 349 km (217 miles), Grand Canyon, Arizona.

**Highest navigated lake:** Titicaca, on the borders of Peru and Bolivia, 3,810 m (12,500 ft) above sea level.

**Deepest lake:** Baykal, central Asia, 1,940 m (6,365 ft).

---

### HIGHEST MOUNTAINS

|  | metres | feet |
|---|---|---|
| **Asia** | | |
| Everest (Himalaya-Nepal/Tibet) | 8848 | 29,028 |
| Godwin Austen (Pakistan/India) | 8611 | 28,250 |
| Kanchenjunga (Himalaya-Nepal/India) | 8597 | 28,208 |
| Makalu (Himalaya-Nepal/Tibet) | 8480 | 27,824 |
| Dhaulagiri (Himalaya-Nepal) | 8169 | 26,801 |
| Nanga Parbat (Himalaya-India) | 8126 | 26,660 |
| Annapurna (Himalaya-Nepal) | 8078 | 26,504 |
| **South America** | | |
| Aconcagua (Andes-Argentina) | 6960 | 22,834 |
| **North America** | | |
| McKinley (Alaska Range) | 6194 | 20,320 |
| **Africa** | | |
| Kilimanjaro (Tanzania) | 5895 | 19,340 |
| **Europe** | | |
| Elbruz (Caucasus-USSR) | 5633 | 18,481 |
| Mont Blanc (Alps-France) | 4807 | 15,771 |
| **Antarctica** | | |
| Vinson Massif | 5140 | 16,864 |
| **Australasia** | | |
| Jaja (New Guinea) | 5029 | 16,500 |

▷ The great waterfalls of the world are awesome spectacles.

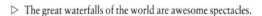

## FAMOUS WATERFALLS

| | Drop (m) | (ft) |
|---|---|---|
| **Africa** | | |
| Tugela (Africa) | 614 | 2,014 |
| **Asia** | | |
| Jog or Gersoppa (India) | 272 | 890 |
| **Australasia** | | |
| Sutherland (New Zealand) | 580 | 1,904 |
| Wallaman (Australia) | 347 | 1,137 |
| **Europe** | | |
| Mardalsfossen, Southern (Norway) | 655 | 2,149 |
| Gavarnie (France) | 422 | 1,385 |
| **North America** Yosemite (U.S.A., Cal.) | 739 | 2,425 |
| Della (Canada, B.C.) | 440 | 1,443 |
| **Southern America** | | |
| Angel (Venezuela)† | 979 | 3,212 |
| Glass (Brazil) | 404 | 1,325 |

*† World's highest waterfall*

## EROSION FACTS

**Weight of soil and rock** removed by rivers is about 140 tonnes a year from each square kilometre (363 from each square mile) of the Earth's crust.

**Thickness of land** worn away by rivers is about 30 cm (1 ft) a year as estimated for the United States.

**Deepest gorges** cut by rivers are those made by the rivers Indus, Brahmaputra and Ganges in India–Pakistan; they are more than 5 km (3 miles) deep.

## DESERTS

| | Sq km | Sq miles |
|---|---|---|
| Sahara (Africa) | 9,096,000 | 3,500,000 |
| **Australian Desert** | 1,550,000 | 600,000 |
| **Arabian Desert** | 1,300,000 | 500,000 |
| Gobi (Asia) | 1,300,000 | 500,000 |
| Kalahari (Africa) | 518,000 | 200,000 |
| Chihuahuan (USA) and Mexico) | 363,900 | 140,000 |
| **Mojave** (USA) | 39,000 | 15,000 |

## FACTS ABOUT VOLCANOES

**Active volcanoes:** There are about 535 of these, 80 below the sea.

**Largest known eruption:** Tamboro, Indonesia, in 1815. The volcano threw out about 150 cubic km (about 36 cubic miles) of matter and lost 1250 m (4100 ft) in height.

**Greatest disaster:** 35,000 people were drowned by a giant wave unleashed when Krakatau, Indonesia, exploded in 1883.

**Greatest volcanic explosion:** About 1470 BC, Santorini in the Aegean Sea exploded with maybe 130 times the force of the greatest H-bomb.

## FACTS ABOUT ICE

**More than one-tenth** of all the land on Earth is covered by ice at any given time.

**Largest ice sheet** is the Antarctic Ice Sheet, covering 13 million square km (5 million square miles).

**Longest glacier** is the Lambert-Fisher Ice Passage in Antarctica. It stretches over 500 km (300 miles).

**Largest iceberg** ever recorded was an Antarctic iceberg seen in 1956. It covered 31,000 square km (12,000 square miles), an area bigger than Belgium.

## LARGEST ISLANDS

| | Sq km | Sq miles |
|---|---|---|
| Greenland | 2,183,000 | 840,000 |
| New Guinea | 821,000 | 317,000 |
| Borneo | 727,900 | 280,100 |
| Madagascar | 589,081 | 226,658 |
| Baffin Island | 509,214 | 195,928 |
| Sumatra | 431,982 | 182,860 |
| Honshu | 228,204 | 87,805 |
| Great Britain | 218,800 | 84,200 |
| Victoria Island | 218,045 | 83,896 |
| Ellesmere Island | 196,917 | 75,767 |

▷ Sand dunes in Colorado, USA. The Earth's desert regions are the driest and most inhospitable environments for plants, animals and people.

▽ About 200 million years ago there was a single huge land mass. It later split into two super-continents, which eventually, after millions of years of drift, formed the continents we see today. Millions of years from now, the continents will have drifted still farther. For example, North and South America will probably have separated.

500 million years ago

325 million years ago

175 million years ago

50 million years ago

# Drifting Continents

Although its inhabitants are unaware of its daily changes the Earth is in a constant state of flux. Movements beneath the crust cause variations in the surface features which are revealed over a period of millions of years.

The Earth's crust is very thin compared with the diameter of the globe. It varies from 32 km (20 miles) thick under the continents to 8 km (5 miles) under the oceans. It lies over a layer of very hot rock called the mantle.

Scientists think that the mantle, which is so hot that its rock can melt, is constantly moving. It has convection currents, like those you see when a pan of thick soup is cooking on the stove. The theory is that it is these convection currents which move the plates along, causing continental drift. The movement is circular, welling up in the mid-ocean ridges, and going down at the ocean edges, as under the west coast of South America.

On a world map Africa and South America look as though they should fit together, and that is exactly what they did. The surprising thing is that India was separate from the rest of Asia. When it collided with Asia the force of the collision slowly pushed up a huge range of mountains, the Himalayas.

▽ Where two plates meet, rocks are either pushed up to form mountains or ridges, or sink down into the Earth's mantle to create trenches.

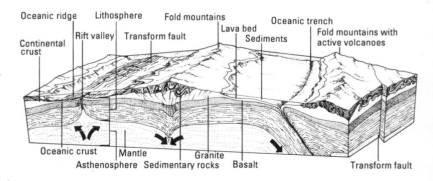

Oceanic ridge  Lithosphere  Fold mountains  Oceanic trench
Rift valley  Transform fault  Lava bed  Fold mountains with active volcanoes
Continental crust  Sediments
Oceanic crust  Mantle  Granite  Transform fault
Asthenosphere  Sedimentary rocks  Basalt

# The Weather

The atmosphere – the layer of air around the Earth – is constantly moving because it is unevenly heated by the Sun. Huge masses of warm air from the Equator and cold air from the Poles flow around the world, meeting each other. The warm air rises and the cold air sinks, and this movement causes the winds.

The air picks up water vapour evaporated from the oceans in the tropics, and rises, getting cooler. The vapour condenses into tiny droplets of water in the cool air and forms clouds. If it cools further, the droplets unite to form larger drops, which fall as rain. On very cold days the droplets form snowflakes. From storm clouds small pieces of ice may fall as hailstones.

△ The atmosphere of the Earth acts like an insulating wrapping, stopping the planet from getting too hot or too cold.

---

## WEATHER EXTREMES

**Hottest shade temperature recorded:** 57.7°C (136°F) at Al'Aziziyah, Libya, on September 13, 1922.

**Coldest temperature recorded:** −89.2°C (−128.6°F) at Vostock, Antarctica, on July 21, 1983.

**Highest average annual rainfall:** 11,770 mm (463 inches) at Tutunendo, Colombia.

**Driest place on earth:** Arica, Chile, averages 0.76 mm (0.030 inches) of rain per year.

**Greatest tides:** 16.3 m (53.4 ft) Bay of Fundy, Nova Scotia, Canada.

**Strongest surface wind recorded:** 372 km/h (231 mph) at Mt Washington, New Hampshire, USA, in 1934.

---

## BEAUFORT SCALE

In 1805 Admiral Sir Francis Beaufort worked out a scale for measuring wind speed. The scale is numbered from 1 to 12 and represents wind force out in the open, 10 metres (33 feet) above the ground.

| No. | Wind force | km/h | mph | Observable effects |
|---|---|---|---|---|
| 0 | calm | <1.6 | <1 | smoke rises vertically |
| 1 | light air | 1.6–4.8 | 1–3 | direction shown by smoke |
| 2 | slight breeze | 6.4–11.3 | 4–7 | felt on face; wind vanes move |
| 3 | gentle breeze | 12.9–19.3 | 8–12 | leaves, twigs move; flags extended |
| 4 | moderate breeze | 20.9–29.0 | 13–18 | dust, paper, small branches move |
| 5 | fresh breeze | 30.6–38.6 | 19–24 | small trees sway; flags ripple |
| 6 | strong breeze | 40.2–50.0 | 25–31 | large branches move; flags beat |
| 7 | moderate gale | 51.5–61.2 | 32–38 | whole trees sway; walking difficult |
| 8 | fresh gale | 62.8–74.0 | 39–46 | twigs break off; walking hindered |
| 9 | strong gale | 75.6–86.9 | 47–54 | slight damage – chimney-pots, slates |
| 10 | whole gale | 88.5–101.4 | 55–63 | severe damage; trees uprooted |
| 11 | storm | 103.0–115.9 | 64–72 | widespread damage |
| 12 | hurricane | >117.5 | >73 | devastation |

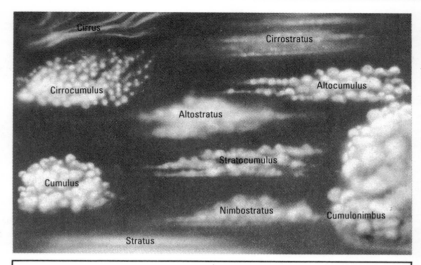

## TYPES OF CLOUDS

Clouds consist of masses of water drops or ice crystals in the atmosphere. They form when moisture in the air condenses.

**Altostratus:** A greyish sheet of cloud, with a hazy Sun above.

**Altocumulus:** Fleecy bands of cloud with blue sky between.

**Cirrus:** High, wispy clouds made of particles of ice.

**Cirrocumulus:** Thin, high lines of cloud with rippled edges.

**Cirrostratus:** Milky, thin, high cloud producing a halo around the Sun.

**Stratus:** Low, grey, sheet-like cloud covering the sky.

**Nimbostratus:** Low, grey, sheet-like cloud producing steady rain.

**Stratocumulus:** Like a low, dark, heavy kind of altocumulus.

**Cumulus:** A white heaped up cloud usually seen in fair weather.

**Cumulonimbus:** A towering cloud that may give heavy showers.

▷ Lightning is a huge electric spark.

## FACTS ABOUT STORMS

**Most thundery region on Earth:** The tropics and nearby regions. More than 3,000 thunderstorms occur there every night of the year.

**Fiercest storm winds:** Those whirling around in a tornado. They are thought to reach speeds of 800 km/h (500 mph).

**Speed of lightning:** The fastest flashes move at 140,000 km/sec (87,000 miles a second).

**Tornadoes:** A tornado is a storm that moves across the land at about 65 km/h (40 mph). It measures only about 200 m (650 ft) across, but its whirling winds can cause severe damage.

## SOME WEATHER TERMS

**climate** The average weather conditions of a place. Climate figures are averages of figures collected over a number of years, so extremes of heat and cold, drought and flood are hidden.

**hurricane** A severe tropical storm with spiralling winds and very low air pressure. The wind does a great deal of damage, the accompanying rain and high tides cause floods.

**Mediterranean climate** Summers are hot and dry; winters are warm and wet. Such a climate is found around the Mediterranean Sea and also in central California and Perth, Western Australia.

**monsoon** The word means season and usually refers to winds that bring an exceptionally wet season for part of the year. The most spectacular monsoon climates are in Asia.

**temperate lands** Those parts of the world between the tropics and the Polar areas which have a cold season and a hot season. Places such as the Mediterranean which have warm winters may be called warm temperate.

**precipitation** When used of the weather, refers to rain and snow.

▽ A depression or cyclone is an area of low air pressure. This satellite photograph shows a hurricane, a severe tropical cyclone. Hurricane winds spiral at up to 340 km/h (210 mph).

△ Weather forecasting has been aided by weather satellites like this one. Such satellites can spot and track weather systems as they develop.

▽ All maps are projections: from a globe (**A**), a cone (**B**) or a cylinder (**C**). The Mollweide projection (**D**) shows the entire surface of the Earth.

**A**

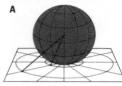

# Making Maps

It is impossible to make a completely accurate flat map of a curved surface such as the Earth, which is a sphere. So map-makers make 'projections' from a globe. Imagine a transparent globe touching a flat surface at one point. If a light could be placed in the centre of the globe, it would throw a shadow of the lines of latitude and longitude on to the paper. This projection (**A**) becomes more and more distorted away from the point of contact.

If you put a cone of paper on the globe, the light in the globe would give what is called a conical projection (**B**).

**B**

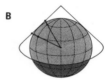

If you put a cylinder of paper around the globe, the resulting map would look like (**C**), the familiar projection invented by the Flemish cartographer Gerhardus Mercator in the 1500s. But the north and south of the map are badly distorted, and the lines of latitude appear to be parallel to each other, which they are not.

Flat maps of a small area of the world, like a country such as Britain, can be much more accurate, because the Earth's surface does not curve so much over such a comparatively short distance.

**C**

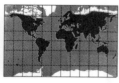

**D**

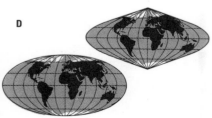

---

### MAP TERMS

**atlas** A book of maps.

**globe** A ball painted or printed to show the Earth in its true shape.

**legend** A small table that explains what the various symbols on a map mean.

**physical map** A map that shows the rivers, mountains and other physical features of the landscape.

**political map** A map in which the political boundaries of the various countries are shown, usually in different colours.

**road map** A map especially designed to help drivers find their way.

**thematic map** A maps that shows a certain aspect of geography, such as rainfall or population.

# Time Zones

The Earth rotates on its axis once every 24 hours. As a result the local time – by the Sun – changes by about 4 minutes for every 1° of longitude. Therefore we cannot use the same time all over the world. So the world has been divided into 24 time zones, each representing a difference of roughly 1 hour.

Within a zone, the time is the same. But if you cross into the next zone, you have to put your watch back (going west) or forward (going east) by 1 hour. The zone lines are not always straight, but follow country boundaries. In large countries such as the United States there are several time zones. For example, when it is noon in San Francisco, Cal., it is 1 pm in Denver, Col., 2 pm in Houston, Tex., and 3 pm in Washington D.C.

The line of longitude, or meridian, at 0° passes through Greenwich in London; this line is also called the Greenwich meridian. Exactly halfway round the world from 0° is the 180th meridian. Along most of it runs the International Date Line, where every new calendar day begins. People living just east of this line are almost a day behind those who live just west of it.

△ The Earth rotates on its axis once in 24 hours. This gives us day and night. At any one moment, part of the Earth is facing the Sun and people there have their clocks set at midday. On the opposite side of the Earth it is midnight.

▽ This map shows the world divided into time zones. The lines zigzag in some places to follow country borders where possible.

International Time Zones

## PLANET EARTH GLOSSARY

**atmosphere** The layer of moving air which surrounds the Earth. It consists of nitrogen, oxygen, water vapour and other gases. The atmosphere becomes thinner away from the Earth.

**axis** An imaginary straight line around which a spinning object rotates. The Earth's axis goes from the North Pole, through the centre of the Earth, to the South Pole.

**block mountains** Blocks of land raised up by vertical movements between faults in the Earth's crust.

**canyon** A deep, steep-sided valley, usually cut by a river in a *desert* area. The most famous is the Grand Canyon.

**coral** Coral is made by tiny creatures called polyps which live in warm sunny seas. They build skeletons outside their bodies. When they die new polyps build on the old skeletons to form coral reefs.

**core** The inner part of the Earth.

**crust** The outer layer of the Earth.

**delta** The Greek letter Δ (delta) is used to describe an area of sediments deposited at the mouth of some rivers, such as the Mississippi and the Nile.

**deserts** A dry area where few plants grow. The Sahara is the largest desert; the Atacama is the driest.

**dunes** Mounds or ridges of sand. They are found on some sandy coasts and in sandy *deserts*.

**earthquake** A sudden movement within the Earth's *crust* which causes shock waves which make the Earth's surface shake. Earthquake tremors are recorded on a seismograph.

**estuary** The mouth of a river where it enters the sea. Usually it is much wider than the rest of the river and it has tides.

**fault** A more or less vertical break in the Earth's crust, along which the rocks have moved. The rocks may move upward, downward or sideways.

**fiord (fjord)** A long, steep-sided inlet of the sea in a mountainous coastal area, as in Norway. Originally it was a valley eroded by a glacier. After the glacier melted, the valley was drowned as the sea level rose.

**fold mountains** Mountains formed by folding layers of rocks. When parts of the Earth's crust move together from each side, the rocks in between are folded.

**geyser** A hot spring which throws out a jet of hot water regularly or occasionally. The best-known geysers are in the USA, Iceland and New Zealand.

**glacier** A mass of ice which moves slowly downhill. It follows the easiest route – usually along a river valley which it deepens and straightens.

**iceberg** A lump of ice which has broken off from one of the two polar ice caps and floats in the sea. Only about one-tenth of an iceberg shows above water level.

**latitude** and **longitude** These are lines drawn on a globe. Lines which run through the poles north to south are called lines of longitude. The Equator and lines parallel to it are lines of latitude.

**meander** A bend in a river, usually in soft, relatively flat ground.

▽ The curved lines on a globe are lines of latitude (east-west) and lines of longitude (north-south).

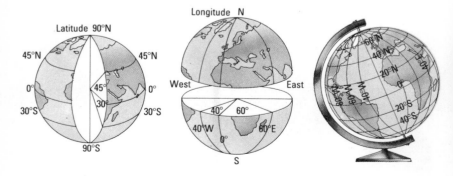

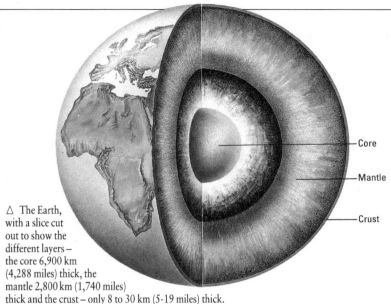

△ The Earth, with a slice cut out to show the different layers – the core 6,900 km (4,288 miles) thick, the mantle 2,800 km (1,740 miles) thick and the crust – only 8 to 30 km (5-19 miles) thick.

Core

Mantle

Crust

**oasis** An area in a desert with water at or near the surface. Crops can be grown, and people can live there.

**peninsula** An area of land almost surrounded by water, but not completely cut off from the mainland.

**plain** A lowland area with a fairly level surface, though there may be hills. The North European Plain and the Great Plains of North America are examples of very large plains.

**plateau** An upland area with a fairly level surface, though a plateau may have some hills and may be divided by deep valleys.

**sedimentary rocks** Rocks formed from sediments (small rock particles) which once accumulated on land or sea. Clay, sandstone and limestone are examples of sedimentary rocks.

**tropics** Lines of latitude marking where the sun is directly overhead on midsummer's day. On June 21 the sun is overhead at the Tropic of Cancer. On December 21 it is overhead at the Tropic of Capricorn.

▽ Fold mountains are formed when the Earth's crust squeezes rock layers upwards.

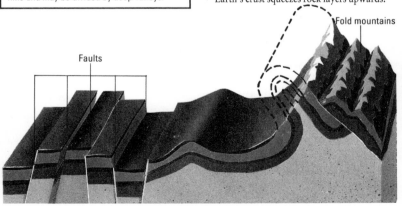

Fold mountains

Faults

# Countries of the world

There are over 5,000 million people in the world today living in more than 160 countries and speaking over 3,000 languages. Before World War II, Britain, France and other European countries ruled large empires; since that time most colonies have gained independence and, together with their former rulers, joined the United Nations in an attempt to keep world peace and form fruitful political and economic alliances.

There are more than 160 independent countries in the world. In addition, there are a number of countries that are not independent. They are either part of larger countries or are colonies, dependent territories or associated states. Many of them have internal self-government.

Examples of countries that are part of larger bodies include England, Scotland and Wales, which are part of the United Kingdom; and French Guiana, which is the overseas French *département* of Guyane Française, giving it the same status as the political divisions of mainland France.

There are few colonies left. They include Anguilla in the West Indies, Bermuda and Gibraltar, which are all British colonies. American Samoa, in the Pacific Ocean, is an example of a dependent territory. Others include the Australian territories of Christmas Island and the Cocos Islands, the Chilean territory of Easter Island an the Ecuadoran territory of the Galapagos Islands.

Associated states tend to have a greater measure of self-government than dependencies. Some are difficult to classify: for example, the West Indian island of Puerto Rico is completely self-governing, but its people are United States citizens, and it is almost one of the states.

△ An assembly of Indian princes. Until its independence in 1947, India was the jewel in Britain's imperial crown. The British Empire was the largest and most diverse in history.

## Former empires

Before World War II (1939–1945) many European countries had large empires, consisting of a mixture of dominions, colonies, protectorates and so-called 'spheres of influence', places that were virtually independent but relied for defence and other aid on a European country. Many lands of the Middle East were in this group. The Empire of India was administered by Britain, but many of its states were effectively self-governing.

The largest empires were the British and French empires. Smaller empires were controlled by Belgium, Italy, The Netherlands, Portugal and Spain. The Spanish empire originally included most of South America, but those colonies fought for, and won, independence in the early 1800s. Portugal's empire included Brazil.

After World War II most of the colonies began to press for independence. The European nations were glad to let them have it, partly because administering such large overseas lands was becoming too expensive, and partly because public opinion everywhere was in favour of self-government for all peoples. The process began with the break-up of the Indian Empire in 1947, but the largest number of new independent countries came into being in the 1960s, when most of the African states won their freedom.

## Peoples of the world

The total population of the world is over 5,000 million. The population is growing at the rate of 1.6 per cent a year. The number of people being born is greater than the number who are dying – there are about 29 births per thousand population, with deaths at 11 per thousand.

People live longer in the industrialized countries than in those that are developing. The place to be if you want to reach old age is Japan, where a newborn baby can expect to

▽ At the present time, as the graph shows, the population of the world is increasing rapidly. This is sometimes called a population explosion. Rates of increase vary in different parts of the world. For example, in Europe the increase is small (only 0.6 per cent per year) while in Africa and South America the population is increasing at 2.7 per cent.

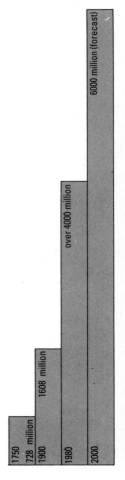

6000 million (forecast)

over 4000 million

1608 million

1750

728 million

1900

1980

2000

▽ The human race can be divided into three main groups. Caucasoids include north-western Europeans, most Indians and the Aborigines of Australia. Mongoloids mainly comprise the peoples of China and Japan and the Indians of North and South America. They are characterized by high cheek bones and small noses, straight black hair and yellowish skin. Negroids are African people and usually have black curly hair, broad noses and large lips.

Caucasoid

Mongoloid

Negroid

live to the age of 77. In Britain and the United States life expectancy is about 75 years. At the other end of the scale, in Afghanistan the life expectancy is about 37 years. In many African countries it is about 45 years. In all countries, women live longer than men.

All humans belong to the same species, but over thousands of years groups living in different parts of the world have evolved great varieties of size, skin colour, hair and eyes. For example, people living in countries where there is almost continuous hot sunshine have evolved darker skins, which help to protect against any harmful rays of the Sun.

The result is that there are many different kinds of people. These different kinds are called races, but scientists do not agree on what constitutes a race. The most common difference is in skin colour, and that has led to the unpleasant trait of racism: the misguided belief that people of one colour are inferior to those of another. Racism has led to much bloodshed and barbarity.

Improved communications has meant that the world has increasingly become a great melting pot of racial types. Britain and the United States are examples of multi-racial societies – that is, they have people of different races living side by side.

**Languages**
One thing that divides people is the language they speak. There about 160 main languages – that is, those spoken by 1,000,000 or more people. But altogether there are at least 3,000 separate languages, and countless dialects.

The languages with the most speakers are Mandarin Chinese (788,000,000), English (420,000,000), Hindi (300,000,000), Spanish (296,000,000) and Russian (285,000,000). Most languages are spoken in a limited area: for example, few people outside China speak Mandarin Chinese.

Many languages are spoken only in a single community of a few thousand people. For example, Papua New Guinea has a population of only 3,400,000 yet more than 700 languages are spoken there.

△ The world's peoples speak and read many languages. Newspapers reflect this rich variety of cultures.

By contrast, several languages are spoken by people of many lands, and are used as international languages. English, Spanish and French are among them. In many former French colonies of Africa people speak so many different local languages that French has been retained as the official language.

Other countries have two official languages: Kenya, a former British territory, uses the local Swahili, and also English. India, which has 14 major languages and more than 160 others with 700 dialects, has Hindi as its first official language, but many people use English as a common language.

Another barrier to communications has been the number of different alphabets in use. The Western alphabet – in which this book is written – is used in more countries than any other, even in those where it is not the main alphabet employed. It is one of the easiest to learn and to write, and it can be readily adapted to many languages.

Other important alphabets include Arabic, the Cyrillic script used in the Soviet Union, Greek and the scripts used for Hindi and its related language Urdu. Chinese has a different system of writing using about 50,000

△ Soldiers of a UN peace-keeping force. The UN has no army of its own but relies on contingents of troops from member-states, who also pay the cost of such operations. UN forces act as observers and 'police' in trouble spots, endeavouring to hold 'peace-lines' between warring factions.

▽ The emblem of the United Nations. The olive branches symbolize peace.

characters, each representing a word. Most Chinese use only about 10,000 characters, and a simplified version of the system was introduced in the 1950s. However, one advantage of the Chinese system is that the Chinese people, who speak many dialects and pronounce their words in many ways, can read written Chinese even when they cannot understand what other people are saying.

### International organizations

Over the centuries, countries have formed alliances of all kinds, for trade or political reasons. Some alliances were the result of conquest. Others, especially the British Empire, were created for purposes of trade. Many of the empire-builders of the 1800s sincerely believed that they were also bringing benefits to under-developed countries.

Many alliances have existed for mutual defence, such as the *Entente Cordiale* between Britain and France of 1904. Russia joined it in 1907 to make a *Triple Entente* which pledged the three countries to support each other in the event of war. The alliance came into action in 1914 when World War I broke out.

A different kind of alliance came into being in 1920 as a result of World War I. It was the League of Nations, formed with the express purpose of maintaining world peace. The League had some success in stopping small wars, but it was unable to prevent the outbreak of World War II in 1939, nor many of the conflicts leading up to it. However, out of World War II came a new body, the United Nations, which took over the role of the League of Nations.

### The United Nations

The United Nations was formed in 1945 by 50 countries, headed by Britain, the United States and the Soviet Union, who had been allies in World War II. Today nearly all the independent countries of the world are members. The member countries send representatives to the United Nations Assembly, which meets for one three-month session every year. Emergency special sessions may be called in between the regular meetings if a crisis develops.

More frequent meetings are held by the Security Council, which has representatives from 15 countries. Britain, the United States, France, China and the Soviet Union are permanent members, while 10 other countries are elected by the General Assembly to serve for two years at a time. The Security Council makes its decisions by a majority vote, with nine being the minimum number of votes for a majority. However, the five permanent members have the right of veto on any Security Council resolution.

## The Commonwealth

A smaller world body is the Commonwealth. It consists of 49 countries, mostly former British colonies, that were part of the old British Empire. It developed from the empire, and its member countries originally acknowledged the British sovereign as their head of state. Now that 25 Commonwealth countries are republics, with their own heads of state, Queen Elizabeth II is regarded as 'Head of the Commonwealth'.

Unlike the United Nations, the Commonwealth has no charter or treaty. It is described as 'a free association' of countries that are equal in status, and have their common background in the old empire. The Commonwealth exists for those countries' mutual assistance, cooperation and benefit. The Commonwealth Secretariat, based in London, acts as a coordinating body. Heads of government meet every two years at a Commonwealth Conference to discuss business. Each conference is held in a different member country, and is opened by the Queen.

▽ Members of the Commonwealth incorporate the likeness of Queen Elizabeth II in the design of their stamps.

## UNITED NATIONS: MEMBER COUNTRIES

| Country | Joined* | Country | Joined | Country | Joined |
|---|---|---|---|---|---|
| Afghanistan | 1946 | Central African | | Grenda | 1974 |
| Albania | 1955 | Republic | 1960 | Guatemala | 1945 |
| Algeria | 1962 | Chad | 1960 | Guinea | 1958 |
| Angola | 1976 | Chile | 1945 | Guinea-Bissau | 1974 |
| Antigua and | | China † | 1945 | Guyana | 1966 |
| Barbuda | 1981 | Colombia | 1945 | Haiti | 1945 |
| Argentina | 1945 | Comoros | 1975 | Honduras | 1945 |
| Australia | 1945 | Congo | 1960 | Hungary | 1955 |
| Austria | 1955 | Costa Rica | 1945 | Iceland | 1946 |
| Bahamas | 1973 | Cuba | 1945 | India | 1945 |
| Bahrain | 1971 | Cyprus | 1960 | Indonesia | 1950 |
| Bangladesh | 1974 | Czechoslovakia | 1945 | Iran | 1945 |
| Barbados | 1966 | Denmark | 1945 | Iraq | 1945 |
| Belgium | 1945 | Djibouti | 1977 | Ireland, Rep. of | 1955 |
| Belize | 1981 | Dominica | 1978 | Israel | 1949 |
| Benin | 1960 | Dominican Republic | 1945 | Italy | 1955 |
| Bhutan | 1971 | Ecuador | 1945 | Ivory coast | 1960 |
| Bolivia | 1945 | Egypt | 1945 | Jamaica | 1962 |
| Botswana | 1966 | El Salvador | 1945 | Japan | 1956 |
| Brazil | 1945 | Equatorial Guinea | 1968 | Jordan | 1955 |
| Brunei | 1984 | Ethiopia | 1945 | Kenya | 1963 |
| Bulgaria | 1955 | Fiji | 1970 | Kuwait | 1963 |
| Burkina Faso | 1960 | Finland | 1955 | Laos | 1955 |
| Burma | 1948 | France | 1945 | Lebanon | 1945 |
| Burundi | 1962 | Gabon | 1960 | Lesotho | 1966 |
| Byelorussian SSR | 1945 | Gambia | 1965 | Liberia | 1945 |
| Cambodia | 1955 | Germany, East | 1973 | Libya | 1955 |
| Cameroon | 1960 | Germany, West | 1973 | Luxembourg | 1945 |
| Canada | 1945 | Ghana | 1957 | Madagascar | 1960 |
| Cape Verde | 1975 | Greece | 1945 | Malawi | 1964 |

## UN: PRINCIPAL ORGANS

**General Assembly** consists of all members, each having one vote. Most of work done in committees: (1) Political Security, (2) Economic & Financial, (3) Social, Humanitarian & Cultural, (4) Decolonization (including Non-Self- Governing Territories), (5) Administrative & Budgetary, (6) Legal.

**Security Council** consists of 15 members, each with one vote. There are five permanent members – China, France, UK, USA and USSR – the others being elected for two-year terms. Main object: maintenance of peace and security.

**Economic and Social Council** is responsible under General Assembly for carrying out functions of the UN with regard to international economic, social, cultural, educational, health, and related matters.

**Trusteeship Council** administers Trust Territories.

**International Court of Justice** is composed of 15 judges (all different nationalities) elected by UN. Meets at The Hague.

**The Secretariat** is composed of the Secretary-General, who is chief administrative officer of the UN and is appointed by the General Assembly, and an international staff appointed by him. Secretary-Generals:

| | | |
|---|---|---|
| Trygve Lie (Norway) | 1.2.46 | to 10.4.53 |
| Dag Hammarskjöld (Sweden) | 10.4.53 | to 17.9.61 |
| U Thant (Burma) | 3.11.61 | to 31.12.71 |
| Kurt Waldheim (Austria) | 1.1.72 | to 31.12.81 |
| Javier Pérez de Cuéllar (Peru) | 1.1.82 | to |

| Country | Joined* | Country | Joined | Country | Joined |
|---------|---------|---------|--------|---------|--------|
| Malaysia | 1957 | St Lucia | 1979 | United States | 1945 |
| Maldives, Rep. of | 1965 | St Vincent & | | Uruguay | 1945 |
| Mali | 1960 | the Grenadines | 1980 | Vanuatu | 1981 |
| Malta | 1964 | São Tomé e Príncipe | 1975 | Venezuela | 1945 |
| Mauritania | 1961 | Saudi Arabia | 1945 | Vietnam | 1976 |
| Mauritius | 1968 | Senegal | 1960 | Western Samoa | 1976 |
| Mexico | 1945 | Seychelles | 1976 | Yemen Arab Republic | 1976 |
| Mongolian PR | 1961 | Sierra Leone | 1961 | Yemen PDR | 1967 |
| Morocco | 1956 | Singapore | 1965 | Yugoslavia | 1945 |
| Mozambique | 1975 | Solomon Islands | 1978 | Zaïre | 1960 |
| Nepal | 1955 | Somali Republic | 1960 | Zambia | 1964 |
| Netherlands | 1945 | South Africa | 1945 | Zimbabwe | 1980 |
| New Zealand | 1945 | Spain | 1955 | | |
| Nicaragua | 1945 | Sri Lanka | 1955 | | |
| Niger | 1960 | Sudan | 1956 | | |
| Nigeria | 1960 | Surinam | 1975 | | |
| Norway | 1945 | Swaziland | 1968 | | |
| Oman | 1971 | Sweden | 1946 | | |
| Pakistan | 1947 | Syria | 1945 | | |
| Panama | 1945 | Tanzania | 1961 | | |
| Papua New Guinea | 1975 | Thailand | 1946 | | |
| Paraguay | 1945 | Togo | 1960 | | |
| Peru | 1945 | Trinidad & Tobago | 1962 | | |
| Philippines | 1945 | Tunisia | 1956 | | |
| Poland | 1945 | Turkey | 1945 | *The UN came into existence | |
| Portugal | 1955 | Uganda | 1962 | in 1945. | |
| Qatar | 1971 | Ukrainian SSR | 1945 | †In 1971 the UN voted for the | |
| Romania | 1955 | USSR | 1945 | expulsion of Nationalist China | |
| Rwanda | 1962 | United Arab Emirates | 1971 | and the admittance of | |
| St Kitts-Nevis | 1983 | United Kingdom | 1945 | Communist China in its place. | |

## UNITED NATIONS AGENCIES

| | | | |
|---|---|---|---|
| FAO | Food and Agriculture Organization | ITU | International Telecommunications Union |
| GATT | General Agreement on Tariffs and Trade | UNCLOS | United Nations Conference on the Law of the Sea |
| IAEA | International Atomic Energy Agency | UNCTAD | United Nations Conference on Trade and Development |
| IBRD | International Bank for Reconstruction and Development (World Bank) | UNEF | United Nations Emergency Fund |
| ICAO | International Civil Aviation Organization | UNESCO | United Nations Educational, Scientific and Cultural Organization |
| IDA | International Development Association | UNICEF | United Nations Children's Emergency Fund |
| IFAD | International Fund for Agricultural Development | UNIDO | United Nations Industrial Development Organization |
| IFC | International Finance Corporation | UPU | Universal Postal Union |
| ILO | International Labour Organization | WHO | World Health Organization |
| IMCO | Inter-Governmental Maritime Consultative Organization | WIPO | World Intellectual Property Organization |
| IMF | International Monetary Fund | WMO | World Meteorological Organization |

## Other International Groups

There are a great many small international groups. Some exist to look after mutual defence interests, such as the North Atlantic Treaty Organization, the Warsaw Pact and the Arab League.

Others are concerned with trade, such as the European Community (the 'Common Market'), COMECON (Council for Mutual Economic Assistance) and the Latin American Integration Association.

### MEMBERS OF INTERNATIONAL ORGANIZATIONS

**COMECON:** Bulgaria, Cuba, Czechoslovakia, East Germany, Hungary, Mongolia, Poland, Romania, USSR, Vietnam.

**Commonwealth:** Antigua and Barbuda, Australia, Bahamas, Bangladesh, Barbados, Belize, Botswana, Brunei, Canada, Cyprus, Dominica, Fiji, Gambia, Ghana, Grenada, Guyana, India, Jamaica, Kenya, Kiribati, Lesotho, Malawi, Malaysia, Maldives, Malta, Mauritius, Nauru, New Zealand, Nigeria, Papua New Guinea, St Kitts-Nevis, St Lucia, St Vincent and the Grenadines, Seychelles, Sierra Leone, Singapore, Solomon Islands, Sri Lanka, Swaziland, Tanzania, Tonga, Trinidad & Tobago, Tuvalu, Uganda, United Kingdom, Vanuatu, Western Samoa, Zambia, Zimbabwe.

**European Community** (Common Market): Belgium, Denmark, France, Greece, Ireland, Italy, Luxembourg, Netherlands, Portugal, Spain, United Kingdom, West Germany.

**NATO** (North Atlantic Treaty Organization): Belgium, Canada, Denmark, France, West Germany, Greece, Iceland, Italy, Luxembourg, Netherlands, Norway, Portugal, Spain, Turkey, United Kingdom, United States.

**Organization of American States:** Antigua and Barbuda, Argentina, Bahamas, Barbados, Bolivia, Brazil, Chile, Colombia, Costa Rica, Cuba, Dominica, Dominican Republic, Ecuador, El Salvador, Grenada, Guatemala, Haiti, Honduras, Jamaica, Mexico, Nicaragua, Panama, Paraguay, Peru, St Kitts-Nevis, St Lucia, St Vincent and the Grenadines, Surinam, Trinidad and Tobago, United States, Uruguay, Venezuela.

**Warsaw Pact:** Bulgaria, Czechoslovakia, East Germany, Hungary, Poland, Romania, USSR.

### OTHER INTERNATIONAL ORGANIZATIONS

| | |
|---|---|
| **ASEAN** | Association of South-East Asian Nations |
| **EFTA** | European Free Trade Association |
| **OAS** | Organization of American States |
| **OAU** | Organization of African Unity |
| **OECD** | Organization for Economic Development and Co-operation |
| **OPEC** | Organization of Petroleum-Exporting Countries |

**Gazetteer of Independent Countries**
In the gazetteer which follows, all independent countries of the world are described in alphabetical order. One non-independent country, Namibia (South-West Africa), is included. The League of Nations assigned it to South Africa to administer in 1920.

Since 1971 the United Nations has regarded South Africa's continued rule of Namibia as illegal, and it pressed for the country to become independent. Moves towards independence began in 1989.

For many countries a small map appears next to the relevant article to show the area that the country covers and which are its neighbouring countries.

At the end is a ready-reference chart of all the independent countries. It includes each nation's area, population and capital.

# Independent Countries A–Z

**AFGHANISTAN,** a landlocked republic in south-eastern Asia. The land is mostly mountainous: major ranges include the Hindu Kush and the Pamirs. The north is arid. Rainfall generally averages 300 mm (12 in). Temperatures vary from 49°C (120°F) in the south in summer to −26°C (−15°F) in winter in the mountains. Nearly 80 per cent of the workers are farmers. Only 10 per cent of the land is cultivable, mostly in irrigated valleys. Many people are nomads: sheep are the most numerous animals. Natural gas is exported, but mining and manufacturing are small-scale. Islam was introduced in the 8th century. Modern Afghanistan was founded in 1747 by an Afghan chief, Ahmad Shah. A republic was declared in 1973.

**ALBANIA,** the smallest European communist nation, borders the Adriatic Sea. The climate on the dry coast is Mediterranean in type. The land is mostly mountainous. Farmland covers 17 per cent of Albania, with fertile basins in the wetter uplands where the rainfall averages 1800 mm (71 in). Scrub and oak and pine forest cover 44 per cent of the land and pasture another 25 per cent.

Farming is collectivized and 62 per cent of the workforce is employed on farms. But mining and manufacturing are the leading industries. Ottoman Turks introduced Islam in the 15th century. Albania became independent in 1912 and a kingdom in 1928. After World War II a communist republic was set up. Albania officially became an 'atheist state' in 1967.

**ALGERIA,** a large republic bordering the Mediterranean Sea in North Africa. The Sahara, which covers 85 per cent of the nation, yields oil and natural gas, and oil accounts for 90 per cent of the exports. People are moving from the countryside to the towns. Of the workers, agriculture now employs 30 per cent, industry 25 per cent and services 45 per cent. Most people live in the northern Atlas mountain region and the fertile coastal plains. Barley, fruit, grapes, olives, vegetables and wheat are grown. Livestock are raised in the uplands. Islam and the Arabic language were introduced in the 7th century, but Berber languages survived in some areas. France ruled Algeria from 1848, until it become independent in 1962.

**ANDORRA,** a tiny, mountainous co-principality in the Pyrenees between France and Spain. Sovereignty is technically exercised by the 'co-princes', the Spanish Bishop of Urgel and the French President, but an elected, 28-member General Council effectively rules the state. Tourism is the main industry. Tobacco is the chief cash crop.

**ANGOLA,** a republic in west-central Africa, including the small enclave of Cabinda. Behind the narrow coastal plain are plateaux. The climate is generally warmest and wettest in the north. Savanna covers much of the country, with forests in the south and north-east. Most people speak Bantu languages. The main groups are the Ovimbundu, the Mbundu and the Kongo. Tribalism has divided the nationalist movement in Angola. About 60 per cent of the people are farmers, mostly at subsistence level. The main food crops are cassava and maize. Mining is becoming increasingly important. Angola was a Portuguese colony until it become independent in 1975.

**ANTIGUA,** including the smaller and also low-lying islands of Barbuda and the uninhabited Redonda in the Leeward Islands, was a British colony but became an independent nation in the Commonwealth in 1981. The British monarch is its Head of State. Antigua exports cotton and rum, but tourism is the most important industry in this dry, sunny country. Discovered by Christopher Columbus in 1493. Antigua was named after a church in Seville, Spain. Most Antiguans are descendants of African slaves, but some are of European or Middle Eastern origin.

**ARGENTINA,** South America's second largest nation after Brazil, extends north-south through more than 32° of latitude. As a result the climate varies considerably. There are four main regions. The tropical, largely forested north is comparatively little developed. The west is arid, except around 'oases' where such towns as Mendoza and Tucumán have grown up, rising in the far west to the Andes Mountains. Here, on the border with Chile is Mt Aconcagua, the highest mountain in the western hemisphere. Southern Argentina, called Patagonia, consists of sparsely populated, wind-swept and semi-arid plateaux. In the far south is

half of the barren and cold archipelago, Tierra del Fuego. The fourth and most densely populated region is the central *pampas* (or plains) which cover nearly 25 per cent of the country. The soils of the pampas are fertile and the climate is mild. The *pampas* lie to the north-west and south of Buenos Aires, the elegant capital city. About 90 per cent of the people are of European descent, another 8 per cent being *mestizos* of mixed white and Indian origin, and 2 per cent pure Indians. Argentina is one of the world's leading food producers. Dairy products, hides, maize, meat, oats, vegetable oils, wheat and wool are major products. About 11 per cent of the country is cultivated and pastureland covers another 41 per cent. In recent years, mining (for coal and oil) and manufacturing have become important. The cities are growing quickly, and eight out of ten people live in them. The Spanish explorer Juan de Solás was the first European to see the Rio de la Plata estuary, into which the Paraguay and Uruguay rivers flow, in 1516. The first permanent Spanish settlers arrived in 1535. Spanish rule continued until independence in 1816. Argentina has been disturbed by political and economic turmoil. Between 1946 and 1987, the Republic of Argentina had 15 presidents, seven of whom were deposed.

**AUSTRALIA,** the world's sixth largest country, has very few people for its size, because large tracts are desert or semi-desert. About 90 per cent of the people live in towns, with more than 50 per cent concentrated in the four largest cities. The western part of Australia is a vast plateau, broken by occasional mountain ranges. The central plains extend from the Gulf of Carpentaria in the north to the Great Australian Bight in the south. These plains include the Great Artesian Basin, comprising western Queensland, the south-east of the Northern Territory, the north-east of south Australia and the northern part of New South Wales. Here artesian wells tap ground water that originally fell as rain on the Great Dividing Range in the east, and which has seeped through aquifers beneath the plains. The Lake Eyre basin in the south-west of the Great Artesian Basin is usually dry and covered by salt. The highest peak in the Great Dividing Range, an uplifted block of land, is Mt Kosciusko, in that part of the Range called the Australian Alps. The Range continues in the island state of Tasmania in the south-east, which is separated from the mainland by the shallow Bass Strait. In the north-east is the Great Barrier Reef, the world's longest reef, 2027 km (1260 mi) long. Australia's chief rivers are the Murray and its tributaries, including the Darling, in the south-east. The climate varies according to the latitude. The north is tropical with summer monsoon rains. In the south, winters are cooler and rains are brought by the prevailing westerlies. However, about two-thirds of Australia is too dry for farming. The tropical region in the north contains tropical forest and savanna, and crops, such as sugar-cane, flourish in Queensland. Deserts cover most of Western Australia, the southern part of Northern Territory, much of South Australia and the eastern parts of New South Wales. The mid-latitude grasslands are west of the Great Dividing Range in south-central Queensland and central New South Wales. The coastlands of New South Wales and south-eastern Victoria form a warm temperate zone, where eucalypt forests grow. The south-western part of Western Australia and parts of South Australia and western Victoria have a Mediterranean climate, with much scrub woodland vegetation. The cool temperate climate of Tasmania supports forests of beech and eucalypts. Australia has a wide range of animals, including kangaroos, koalas, platypuses and wallabies. Birds include the flightless emu and cassowary and the lyre bird. The first people in Australia were probably the Tasmanian Aborigines who were driven into Tasmania by the Australian Aborigines who arrived from Asia about 16,000 years ago. The Tasmanian Aborigines became extinct in 1876 and contact with Europeans caused the Australian Aborigines to decline in numbers. Today there are about 100,000 Australian Aborigines, but many are of mixed ancestry. About 80 out of 100 Australians are of British origin. Many recent settlers have come from other parts of Europe. Australia has vast mineral reserves and is a major world producer of bauxite, iron ore and lead. Other metal ores, coal and oil are also mined, together with thorium and uranium. The main product of the country is wool. Beef and dairy products are of great importance. Only about 2 per cent of the land is cultivated, but yields are high and crops are varied because of the wide climatic range. Manufacturing industries are mostly in the towns and cities. The main steel centres are Newcastle, Wollongong and Whyalla. Dutch navigators landed in northern and eastern Australia in the early 17th century and, in 1788, a British convict settlement was established on the present site of Sydney. In 1793 the first free settlers arrived. Gold rushes in the 1850s and 1890s accelerated immigration. Australia is a member of the Commonwealth and the British monarch, represented by a Governor-General, is Head of State.

**AUSTRIA,** a federal republic in central Europe. The Alps cover about 75 per cent of the land and tourism is a major industry, especially winter sports. The Danube river valley in the north is the chief farming region. Livestock are also important: the uplands contain much summer pasture. Forests occupy about 40 per cent of the land. Iron ore and lignite are mined, forming the basis of the iron and steel industry. Vienna is the main manufacturing and cultural centre and more than half the people live in towns. Austria, part of the Holy Roman Empire, became a possession of the Habsburg family in 1282. From 1438 this family supplied all but one of the Holy Roman Emperors. After the Empire ended (1806), the Habsburg ruler became Emperor of Austria. In 1938 Germany annexed Austria. It became a federal republic in 1955.

**BAHAMAS,** a group of 14 large and about 700 small islands with a mild climate, to the south-east of Florida. Tourism is the main industry. Christopher Columbus discovered the islands in 1492: the island of San Salvador was possibly his first landing place. The Bahamas became a British colony in 1717. Full independence within the Commonwealth was achieved in 1973. About 85 per cent of the people are descendants of African Blacks (former slaves).

---

### STATISTICS

To see the statistics of each country's area and population, plus its capital, turn to pages 102–106.

**BAHRAIN,** a densely populated island nation in the Persian Gulf. The capital Manama is on the largest island, also called Bahrain. This hot, arid country is an important oil producer, and revenue from oil sales has been used to provide free education, health care and other services. The Arabs occupied Bahrain in the 7th century. In 1861, it became a British protectorate. It became a fully independent sheikhdom in 1971.

**BANGLADESH,** a densely populated country in Asia, is one of the world's poorest. It has a tropical monsoon climate, with hot, dry winters and hot, wet summers. It is mostly flat, largely occupying the fertile deltas of the Ganges, Brahmaputra and other rivers. The rivers are the main transport arteries but they often flood causing disease and starvation. Coastal floods are also caused when cyclones in the Bay of Bengal drive the sea inland. About 71 per cent of the mainly Muslim Bengali population is engaged in agriculture. In 1980 only 11 per cent of the population was urban. Formerly part of British India, Bangladesh became the province of East Pakistan in 1947. A bitter civil war between East and West Pakistan in 1971 ended with the secession of East Pakistan, which became the People's Republic of Bangladesh.

**BARBADOS,** the most easterly island in the West Indies, is mostly flat with a mild climate. More than 90 per cent of the people are descendants of African slaves, the rest being white or of mixed origin. Sugar and sugar products (molasses and rum) are the main products but tourism is now the chief industry. Barbados was a British colony from 1628 to 1966, when it became an independent member of the Commonwealth.

**BELGIUM,** a densely populated, prosperous industrial nation in western Europe. Two-thirds of the land is flat, but the largely forested Ardennes rise in the south-east. The navigable Meuse and Scheldt rivers drain the fertile central plains. Antwerp, near the mouth of the Scheldt, is the main port. The climate is mild. Three languages are spoken: Flemish (a Dutch dialect) in the north; French by the Walloons in the south; and German by a small group in the south-east. Conflict between Flemish- and French-speakers has led to rioting and complaints about discrimination. More than 70 per cent of the people are town-dwellers. The lowlands are intensely cultivated. Most farms are small and many farmers also have jobs in industry. The main crops are cereals, notably wheat, flax, potatoes and sugar beet. Coal is mined in the north-eastern Campine (Kempen) region, which has become a major industrial area. The older industrial areas are in the south, in the Sambre-Meuse valley. This zone is based on coalfields which extend from Mons to Liège, but extraction of the coal has become expensive and the region has declined in consequence. Antwerp is a major industrial centre, some industries being based on imported oil, as is Brussels whose varied industries produce luxury goods such as lace. Textiles are important, particularly in Flanders; the main centre is Ghent. Belgium came under the Austrian Habsburgs in 1477 and the Spanish Habsburgs in 1506. After a spell of independence (1598–1621), it came successively under Spain, Austria, France and the Netherlands. It declared its independence in 1830. The Kingdom of Belgium is a constitutional, representative and hereditary monarchy, with an elected Senate and Chamber of Deputies. Belgium is a founder member of the European Community.

**BELIZE,** which faces the Caribbean Sea in Central America, is flat in the north, with uplands in the south. Forests flourish and sugar-cane is the chief cash crop in this hot, wet nation. More than half the people are Creoles; most of the others are of Mayan Indian, Black, Carib or European descent. Belize was declared a British colony in 1862, although neighbouring Guatemala has claimed it since 1821. Belize became an independent country within the Commonwealth in 1981.

GULF OF MEXICO

CARIBBEAN SEA

MEXICO

BELIZE

GUATEMALA

HONDURAS

**BENIN,** a People's Republic on the Gulf of Guinea in West Africa. Behind the sandy coast are low plateaux, with the highest land in the north-west. The formerly forested south has an equatorial climate but winters are dry in the tropical northern savanna. The Black African population is divided into 50 groups, the largest being the Fon, Adja, Bariba and Yoruba. Nearly half the people work in agriculture. The chief food crops are maize and millet and the chief cash crop is palm kernels and oil. Oil was discovered offshore in the late 1970s. Benin (known as Dahomey until 1975) was ruled by France from the 1890s to 1960, when it became independent.

**BHUTAN,** a mountainous landlocked kingdom between China and India. Most people, who are of Tibetan or Hindu Nepalese origin, live in fertile valleys where the climate is warm and wet. Nine out of every 10 workers are in agriculture. Some rice, fruit and timber are exported. Most manufactures and fuels must be imported. Contact with the West began in 1774. An elected National Assembly can dismiss the king. India has responsibility for Bhutan's foreign affairs.

**BOLIVIA,** a landlocked republic in South America. The Andes mountains in the south-west contain a central plateau, the Altiplano, where most Bolivians live. It has a cool climate, contrasting with the hot Amazon rain forests in the north-east. Lake Titicaca, the world's highest navigable lake, is on the border with Peru. More than half of the people are American Indians, a third are *mestizos* and the rest of European origin. Agriculture employs 51 per cent of the people, but mining is the most valuable

industry. Bolivia is the world's 2nd largest tin producer and antimony, copper, lead, oil and natural gas, silver and wolfram are also mined. Spain ruled Bolivia from 1532 to 1825, when it won independence.

**BOTSWANA,** a thinly populated, landlocked republic in southern Africa. Most of the country is a plateau, and the climate is warm. The rainfall is three times as heavy in the north as in the south-west. The Kalahari, a semi-desert, covers 84 per cent of the country and only a few nomadic Bushmen live there. Most people belong to the Bantu-speaking Tswana group, including the Bamangwato and Bangwaketse. Minerals now dominate the economy: diamonds, copper and nickel are the main exports. Most people work in agriculture. Arable land covers only 2 per cent of the country, but cattle farming is important. Botswana became the British protectorate of Bechuanaland in 1885. It became fully independent within the Commonwealth in 1966 before which time it was called Bechuanaland.

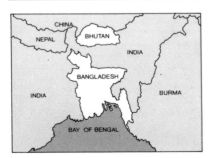

### STATISTICS

To see the statistics of each country's area and population, plus its capital, turn to pages 102–106.

**BRAZIL,** the world's 5th largest nation, occupies nearly half of South America. In the north, the equatorial Amazon basin contains the world's largest rain forest, which is now being reduced as economic development proceeds. The Amazon river is the world's second longest, with a greater volume than any other. It is navigable into Peru. South of the forest is a huge tropical grassland. This region is still little developed despite the inauguration in its heart of the new capital of Brasília in 1960. The north-east around Recife and Salvador has a forested coastal plain, but the inland plateaux are dry: long droughts cause much hardship to an already impoverished population. The central coastal region is the most densely populated and includes the great industrial cities of São Paulo and Rio de Janeiro. Inland are fertile plateaux and pleasant, mineral-rich highlands. The plateaux near São Paulo are Brazil's main coffee-producing region. The southern region around Porto Alegre has a temperate climate: pastoral farming is important. About 75 per cent of Brazil's population is of Portuguese or other European origin. There are many people of mixed European/Indian/Black African descent; colour prejudice is almost absent. Agriculture provides work for two-fifths of the people. Brazil leads the world in producing bananas and coffee, and it is among the top world producers of beef, veal, cocoa, cotton, maize, sugar-cane, soya beans and tobacco. It is Latin America's leading producer of vehicles, steel and cement. Brazil was a Portuguese colony from 1500 to 1822, when it became an empire. It became a republic in 1889.

**BRUNEI,** a small Sultanate in north-western Borneo. Behind the narrow coastal plain, the interior is rugged and forested. The climate is tropical. Some 68 per cent of the people are of Malay origin and 25 per cent are Chinese. Oil is the main product. Natural gas, rubber and timber are also exported. Brunei was a British protectorate between 1888 and 1971. It became independent in 1984.

**BULGARIA,** a Communist People's Republic facing the Black Sea in south-eastern Europe. The climate is transitional between Mediterranean and continental, the latter prevailing in the north and in the mountains. The mountains include the Balkans in the north and the higher Rhodope Mts in the south. The capital Sofia is in a fertile mountain basin. The River Danube plain is in the north, but the central plains are the main farming region, producing fruit, mulberry leaves, attar of roses, sugar beet, tobacco and wine. Lignite, copper, iron ore and oil are mined and manufactures include cement, iron and steel goods and textiles. COMECON countries account for 80 per cent of Bulgaria's trade. Tourism is increasing. The Turks ruled Bulgaria from 1396. Bulgaria became independent in 1878.

**BURKINA FASO,** formerly Upper Volta, a West African republic. Low plateaux cover most of the country. The east is in the River Niger basin; the centre and west are drained by the Black, Red and White Volta rivers. Burkina Faso has a hot, tropical climate. The main rainy season is July–October, but droughts are common. Most people are Blacks; the Mossi (48 per cent) are the largest single group. Four-fifths of the people farm the land, raising cattle, sheep and goats. Cotton and other cash crops are grown in the south and south-west. The country was ruled by France from 1896 to 1960, when it became independent.

**BURMA (renamed the Union of Myanmar in June 1989),** a Socialist Republic in south-eastern Asia. The north, east and west are mountainous. but the southern valleys of the Irrawaddy and Sittang rivers are fertile. The Irrawaddy delta is one of the world's great rice-growing areas. The climate is tropical, with heavy rainfall in the delta. Two-thirds of the people are Tibeto-Burmese and there are many small groups of isolated hill peoples. Half the people are farmers. Forests cover half the country and teak is a major product. Many minerals, including oil and natural gas, are mined. Britain took Burma between 1823 and 1855. It became independent in 1948.

**BURUNDI,** a small, densely populated, landlocked republic in east-central Africa. Part of Lake Tanganyika is in the Rift Valley in the west, with highlands and high plateaux in the east. There are a few pygmies, but the main ethnic groups are the Bantu-speaking Hutu (85 per cent) and the Hamitic Tutsi (13 per cent). Agriculture employs 85 per cent of the people. The Tutsi entered the area from the north in the 17th century. They founded a feudal society under their *mwami* (king), making the Hutu serfs. Burundi was ruled by Germany from 1890 to 1916, and was under Belgian administration until independence in 1962. Hutu attempts to overthrow the Tutsi government have all failed, leading to the deaths of thousands of Hutu.

**CAMBODIA** is a South-East Asian nation. It was originally called Cambodia then, briefly, the Khmer Republic and then Kampuchea. Much of the land is low-lying, in the drainage basin of the lower Mekong River; hills surround the plain. Cambodia has a tropical monsoon climate and dense forests cover nearly half the land. Khmers make up 90 per cent of the population. There are Chinese and Vietnamese minorities. The economy is based on agriculture, mainly on growing rice. The country was a French colony from 1863 to independence in 1953.

**CAMEROON,** a republic in west-central Africa, bordering the Gulf of Guinea. Behind narrow coastal plains are plateaux that slope down in the north to the Lake Chad basin. The main uplands are on the western border: the highest peak is the volcanic Mt Cameroon on the coast. The equatorial south is forested; the tropical centre contains wooded savanna; the drier north has open grassland. Most people are Blacks, speaking one of about 200 Bantu or Sudanic languages. Agriculture employs eight out of 10 people. Mining (for bauxite and oil) is becoming important. After being ruled by Germany, Britain and France, Cameroon became completely independent in 1961.

**CANADA,** the world's 2nd largest nation after the USSR. There are seven main regions. The *Appalachian region* in the north-east is an extension of the Appalachian region in the USA. The *St Lawrence and Lower Great Lakes* region is Canada's most densely populated. The *Canadian Shield* is a vast region of ancient rocks, mineral deposits, and innumerable lakes and rivers. The *Hudson Bay* lowland is a plain between the Canadian Shield and Hudson Bay. The *Western Interior Plains* are between the Canadian Shield and the *Western Mountains*, which include the Canadian Rockies and the Coast Range. In the far north are the bleak *Arctic Islands*. Canada has extremely cold winters, especially north of the Arctic Circle. Southern Canada has warm, moist summers. Forests cover 35 per cent of Canada. There are also vast grasslands and tundra regions. The origins of the people are as follows: British (45 per cent), French (29 per cent), German (6 per cent), Italian (3 per cent) and Ukrainian (3 per cent). Most of the rest come from other parts of Europe. American Indians and Inuit number 289,000 and 17,500

CANADA

### STATISTICS

To see the statistics of each country's area and population, plus its capital, turn to pages 102–106.

respectively. Canada has two official languages, English and French. Quebec is the main French-speaking province. Only 7.2 per cent of the land is cultivated, but Canada is one of the world's leading producers of barley, fruit, oats, wheat, rye and timber. Livestock ranching and dairy farming are also important. Canada is among the top six world producers of asbestos, copper, gold, iron ore, lead, molybdenum, natural gas, nickel, potash, silver, uranium and zinc. But more important than mining is manufacturing. The chief industrial area is the St Lawrence and Lower Great Lakes region. Much traffic is carried along the St Lawrence Seaway, the world's longest artificial seaway. The Dominion of Canada, comprising Quebec, Ontario, Nova Scotia and New Brunswick, was established in 1867. Canada is now a federation of 10 self-governing provinces and two territories.

**CAPE VERDE,** an island republic west of Senegal in West Africa. The 10 large islands and five islets are of volcanic origin. The climate is tropical, but the rainfall is very unreliable. Most people are of mixed Portuguese and African origin; 28 per cent are classed as 'pure' Africans. Most people are subsistence farmers, but severe droughts in the 1970s forced many people to emigrate and the government has had to provide work for destitute farmers. Portugal claimed the islands in 1460. Independence was achieved in 1975.

**CENTRAL AFRICAN REPUBLIC,** a landlocked nation, consists largely of plateaux high above sea-level. The climate is warm, and there is heavy rainfall in the south of the country. The south is forested, but wooded savanna covers most of the land. Wildlife is abundant. Most people speak Sudanese languages. Nearly nine out of every 10 people work on the land. Diamonds are mined and large uranium deposits have been found, but manufacturing is on a small scale. The country became part of French Equatorial Africa in the 1880s. It became independent in 1960.

**CHAD,** a landlocked nation in north-central Africa. Lake Chad, the remains of an inland sea, is in the west. Southern Chad is savanna-covered, but sandy deserts and bare rocky uplands, notably the high Tibesti massif, are in the north. About 100 languages are spoken in Chad. In the south, where most of the population lives, most people are Blacks. Muslim Arabs and Berbers live in the north. Cultural divisions have caused much civil conflict and periodic war since the mid-1960s. Agriculture employs 86 per cent of the workers in this poor nation. Cotton is the chief crop. Chad became a French colony in 1897 and an independent republic in 1960.

**CHILE,** a long, narrow country stretching through 38° of latitude in South America. From west to east there are generally three regions: coastal uplands, central lowland basins and valleys, and the high Andes. In the glaciated south, the coastal uplands are islands, the central lowlands becoming arms of the sea. Chile's climate changes north-south. The north is hot and arid, including the rainless Atacama Desert with its large mineral reserves. Central Chile, where most Chileans live, has hot summers and mild, moist winters. The forested south with its beautiful fiords is cool: heavy rain falls in all seasons. Cape Horn, South America's stormy tip, is in the far south. People of mixed European and Indian origin make up 68 per cent of the population, Europeans 30 per cent, and Araucanian Indians 2 per cent. Agriculture provides work for about 15 per cent of the people. The main farm products are barley, fruit, maize, wheat, oats, rice and wine. Minerals include copper, which makes up 48 per cent of the exports, molybdenum, iron ore, nitrates and oil. Chile has one of the largest fishing industries in the world. Manufacturing industries are powered mainly by hydro-electricity. Chile was a Spanish colony for about 300 years before becoming independent in 1818.

**CHINA,** the world's 3rd largest country, contains about 20 per cent of the world's population. The land is extremely varied. In the north-east is the basin of the Huang He, one of the world's longest rivers. It cuts through a clay-rich plateau which has coloured its waters yellow. To the north lie the central plain and eastern highlands of Manchuria. To the south, beyond the Qin Ling Mountains, lies the Chang Jiang basin of Central China. The Chang Jiang is Asia's longest river. China's third important river basin is that of the Xi Jiang in the south-east, south of the South China Highlands. Outer or Western China contains the high and vast Tibetan plateau which rises in the south to the Himalayan range, crowned by Mt Everest. In the far west are other ranges including the lofty Pamirs and Tien Shan. North-eastern China contains some large deserts, including the vast Tarim and Dzungaria basins. The Gobi desert straddles the frontier between Nei Monggol (in China) and Mongolia. The climate varies from north to south. North-eastern China has bitterly cold winters and warm summers, with moderate rainfall. Central China has milder winters and more rainfall, while south-eastern China has a sub-tropical monsoon climate and many places get heavy rain. About 94 per cent of the population are Han, or true, Chinese. But there are also large national minorities, including Manchus, Mongols, Tibetans and Uighurs, who maintain their own cultures. The population is densest in the fertile river basins and along the coasts of eastern China. Some 25 per cent of the population lives in urban areas. The rural population has been encouraged to live in communes, which are groups of villages where up to 20,000 people work together, share the produce and receive wages that are geared to production. More than half the people work on the land. China leads the world in millet, rice and tobacco production. It is among the top three producers of barley, cotton, groundnuts (peanuts), maize, potatoes, silk, sorghum, tea and wheat. It has more pigs than any other country, plus cattle, sheep and goats. There is also an important fishing industry. China has huge mineral resources – many untapped. It is among the world's top producers of antimony, asbestos, coal, iron ore, mercury, tin and tungsten. The oil industry is expanding. The main industrial centres are in Manchuria, Sichuan and the large cities. Coal is the main source of energy for manufacturing. China's written history goes back 3,500 years and it is one of the world's oldest living civilizations. Its inventions have included gunpowder, paper and printing, porcelain and silk. It was ruled by emperors until it became a republic in 1912. War with Japan (1937–45) was followed by civil war between the Nationalists and Communists. The Communists under Mao Zedong were victorious in 1949 and the People's Republic of China was established.

**COLOMBIA,** a republic in north-western South America, includes three ranges of the Andes whose high, fertile valleys contain most of the people. In eastern Colombia, grasslands merge into the forests of the upper Amazon and Orinoco basins. The coastal lowlands are hot and wet. The highlands are cooler and less rainy. The grasslands have dry winters but wet summers. More than two-thirds of the people are of mixed American Indian and European origin; most others are of pure American Indian, European or Black descent. The chief export, coffee, is grown in the highlands. Seventy per cent of the people live in urban areas. Spaniards opened up the region in the early 16th century. Spanish rule was overthrown in 1819.

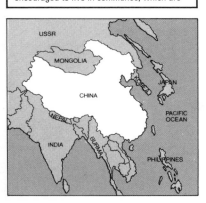

### STATISTICS

To see the statistics of each country's area and population, plus its capital, turn to pages 102–106.

**COMOROS,** an island Federal and Islamic Republic, lies at the northern end of the Mozambique Channel, Geographically, there are 4 islands: Njazidja, Nzwani, Mahoré (or Mayotte) and Mwali. The republic contains three of them, but Mayotte is a French territory. The islands are mountainous: Mt Kartala is an active volcano. The population is mixed, including elements from Africa, Asia and Europe. These tropical islands have few resources and most people are subsistence farmers. They came under French protection in 1886–1909 and became a colony in 1912. In 1946 they became a French overseas department. Comoros, apart from Mayotte, became independent in 1976.

**CONGO,** a People's Republic in equatorial Africa. Behind a narrow coastal plain is an upland region; the north is a swampy plain drained by the Congo (Zaïre) and Oubangui rivers. High temperatures and heavy rainfall, except on the coast, have encourged the growth of rain forests and wooded savanna. Most people speak Bantu languages (including Kongo, Téké and Mbochi); 12,000 pygmies live in central Congo. About one-third of the people work on the land, and a third in industry: oil extraction and processing industries are especially important. Discovered by Europeans in 1482, Congo later became a slave trade centre. French rule was established in the 1880s. Full independence was achieved in 1960.

**COSTA RICA,** a Central American republic, has coastlines on the Caribbean Sea and the Pacific Ocean. Inland it is mountainous with volcanic peaks. Fertile plateaux lie between the mountains. About 70 per cent of the people live in the largest of these, the Central Plateau. More than 80 per cent of the population is of European origin. Most non-whites are of mixed European and American Indian origin. The main cash crop is coffee. Costa Rica is one of the more prosperous nations of Central America. Spain ruled the country from around 1530 to 1821. Dictatorships and revolutions marred its early years of independence but it has enjoyed democracy since 1919.

**CUBA,** the largest nation in the West Indies. Small islands, reefs and mangrove swamps skirt much of the coast. More than half of the land is flat and fertile. Forested mountain ranges occupy about 25 per cent of the land, the rest being gently undulating country. The climate is tropical, with heavy rainfall. About 75 per cent of the people are descendants of Spaniards, the rest being Blacks or mulattos. About two-thirds of the people are town-dwellers, and a quarter work on the land. About 34 per cent of Cuba is cultivated, most farms being government-owned. Sugar and its by-products, molasses and rum, are the main products. Minerals, tobacco, bananas and fish are also exported. Columbus discovered Cuba in 1492 and Spain ruled it between 1511 and 1898. US influence was strong in the 20th century until Communist guerrillas seized power in 1959.

**CYPRUS,** an island republic in the north-eastern Mediterranean Sea. There are fertile coastal plains and a broad central plain (the Mesaoria). The Kyrenia and Karpass mountains are in the north and the Troödos mountains in the south. The climate is typically Mediterranean. Greek Cypriots form 80 per cent of the population, Turkish Cypriots 18 per cent, and Armenian, Maronite and other minorities also live there. Most people feel themselves to be Greeks or Turks rather than Cypriots. About 60 per cent of the land is cultivated; one-third of the work-force is employed in farming. Agriculture supplies about half of the exports and minerals (notably copper) about 30 per cent. Cyprus was a British colony from 1927 to 1960, when it gained independence. In 1974 Turkish forces occupied the north. The island was partitioned, the northern 40 per cent being proclaimed the 'Turkish Cypriot Federated State'.

**CZECHOSLOVAKIA,** a landlocked Communist republic in eastern Europe. The saucer-shaped Bohemian plateau, bounded by mountains, is in the east. It is drained by

# WORLD ATLAS

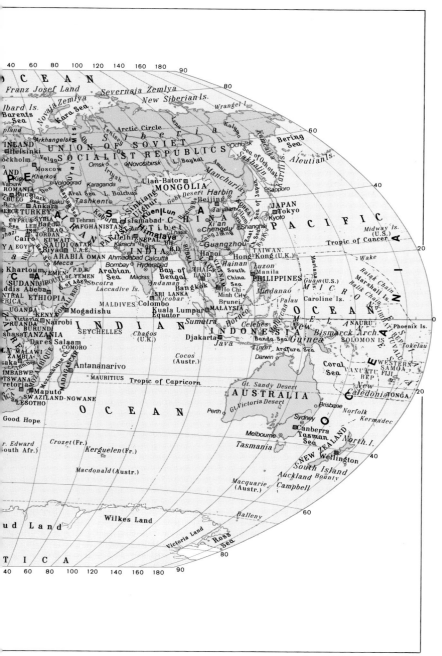

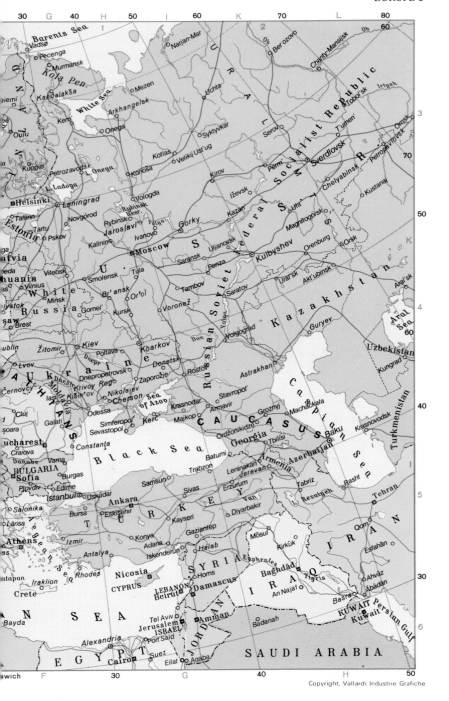

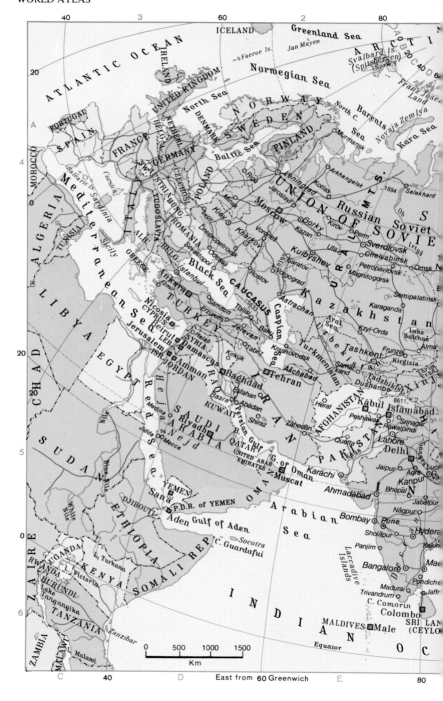

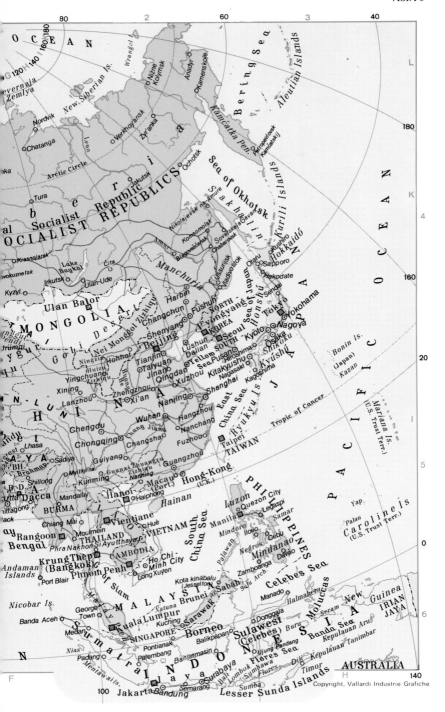

80     2     60     3     40

O C E A N

G 120 140 160 180 180

evernaja Zemlya

Nordvik   New Siberian Is.

Wrangel I.

L

Nizne Kolymsk

Chatanga

180

Arctic Circle

b   e   r   i   a

Anadyr

Kamenskoje

B e r i n g   S e a

Aleutian Islands

Tura

Jakutsk

Ochotsk

Kamtchatka Pen.

Petropawlowsk (Kamtchatkij)

Krasnojarsk

al   Socialist Republic

O C I A L I S T   R E P U B L I C S

Nikolajevsk na-Amure

Sea of Okhotsk

K

vokuznetsk

Verkhoyansk

Zyr'anka

Nizne

Kyzyl

Lena

Irkutsk   Ulan-Ude

Lake Baykal

Cita

Manchuria

Komsomolsk

Blagoveščensk

Chabarovsk

Ussurijsk

Vladivostok

Amur

S a h a l i n

Južno Sachalinsk

Sovetskaja-Gavan

Otaru   Sapporo

Kuşhiro

H o k k a i d ó

Hakodate

Sendai

N

160

Ulan Bator

M O N G O L I A

Gobi Desert

Nei Monggol Zizhiqu

Harbin

Changchun

Shenyang

Fushun

N O R T H

P'yongyang

K O R E A

Seoul

SOUTH

Sea of Japan

Honshū

Niigata

Tokyo

Yokohama

Nagoya

P A C I F I C

20

Beijing

Tianjin

Taiyuan

Jinano

Qingdao

Lushun

Dalian

Yellow Sea

Pusan

Kitakyushu

Nagasaki

Kyoto

Osaka

Hiroshima

Shikoku

Kyushu

Kagoshima

Bonin Is. (Japan) Kazan

Ningxia

Huizu

Yinchuang

Hohhot

Zhengzhou

Xuzhou

Shanghai

East China Sea

Xining   Lanzhou   Zhengzhou   Xi'an

Nanjing

Hangzhou

Ryukyus

Tropic of Cancer

160

Chengdu

Wuhan

Chang Jiang

Nanchang

Chongqing

Changsha

Fuzhou

Taipei

TAIWAN

I

Guiyang

Guangzhou

5

Guanxi Zhuangzu

Nanning

Macau (Port)

Hong Kong (U.K.)

Kunming

Mandalay

Hanoi

Haiphong

Hainan

Luzon

Quezon City

P H I L I P P I N E S

Yap

Palau Caroline Is (U.S. Trust Terr.)

Dacca

Shillong

Chiang Mai

Vientiane

Hué

Manila

Mindoro

Iloilo

Samar

Cebu

BURMA

Moulmein

THAILAND

V I E T N A M

South China Sea

Negros

Mindanao

Davao

0

Rangoon

Bengal

Phra Nakhon Si Ayutthaya

Ho Chi Minh City

Long Xuyen

Zamboanga

Sulu Arch.

Celebes Sea

Krung Thep (Bangkok)

CAMBODIA

Phnom Penh

Gulf of Siam

Kota kinabalu (Jesselton)

Brunei Sabah

Manado

Halmaheras

Moluccas

New Guinea

IRIAN JAYA

Port Blair

Andaman Islands

George Town

M A L A Y S I A

Sarawak

Kuching

Borneo

Sulawesi (Celebes)

Donggala

Seram

Buru

Banda Sea

Nicobar Is.

Banda Aceh

Medan

Natuna

Kuala Lumpur

SINGAPORE

Pontianak

Balikpapan

Ujung Pandang

Flores Sea

Kepulauan Aru

Nias

Padang

Palembang

Banjarmasin

I N D O N E S I A

Sumatra

Java

Surabaya

Lombok

Flores

Dili

Kepulauan Tanimbar

Timor

AUSTRALIA

Mentawai Is.

100

Jakarta   Bandung

Semarang

Sumba

Bali   Sumbawa

Lesser Sunda Islands

140

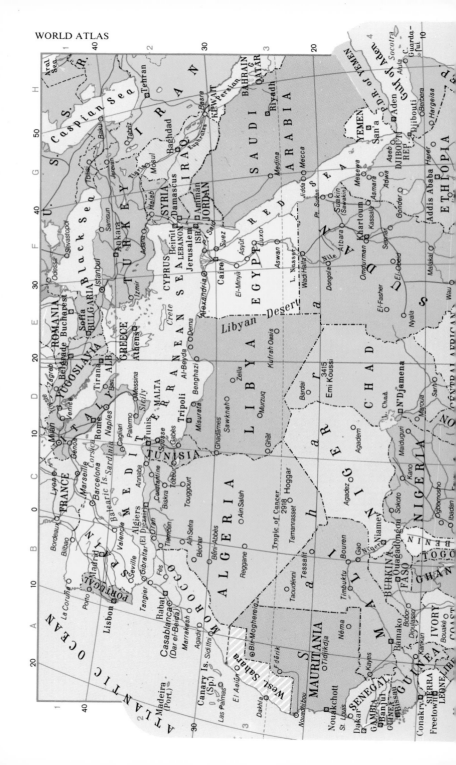

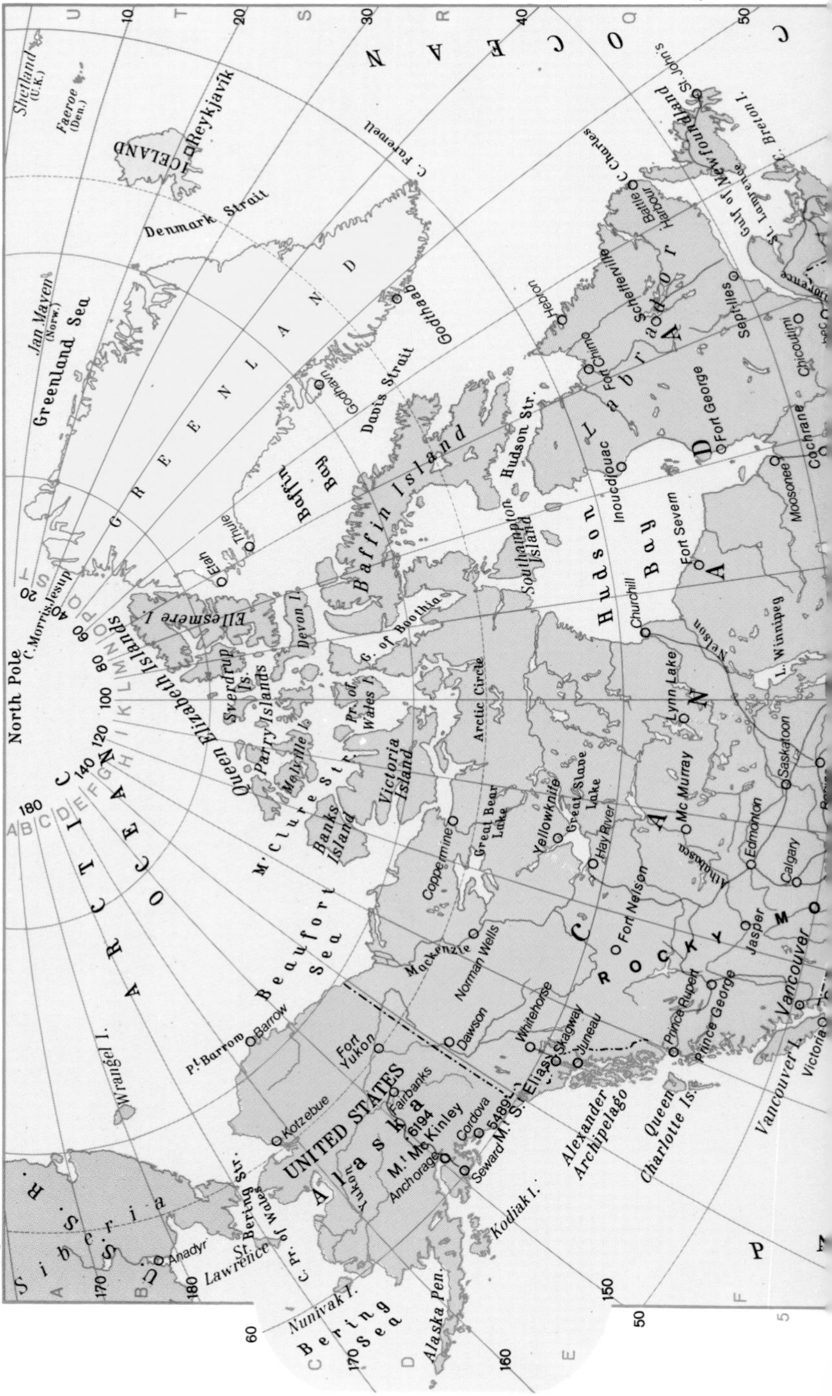
A R C T I C O C E A N
North Pole
Greenland Sea
Jan Mayen (Norw.)
Faeroe (Den.)
Shetland (U.K.)
ICELAND
Reykjavík
Denmark Strait
G R E E N L A N D
C. Farewell
Godthaab
Godhavn
Thule
Etah
C. Morris Jesup
Baffin Bay
Davis Strait
Baffin Island
Ellesmere I.
Queen Elizabeth Islands
Sverdrup Is.
Parry Islands
Devon I.
Melville I.
Pr. of Wales I.
G. of Boothia
Southampton Island
Hudson Str.
Hudson Bay
Victoria Island
Banks Island
M'Clure Str.
Beaufort Sea
Arctic Circle
Great Bear Lake
Great Slave Lake
Yellowknife
Coppermine
Norman Wells
Mackenzie
Dawson
Whitehorse
Fort Yukon
Pt. Barrow
Barrow
Wrangel I.
Siberia
U.S.S.R.
Anadyr
Bering Str.
St. Lawrence I.
C. Pr. of Wales
Kotzebue
UNITED STATES
Alaska
Yukon
Fairbanks
Mt. McKinley
6194
Anchorage
Cordova
Seward
Mt. St. Elias
5489
Skagway
Juneau
Alexander Archipelago
Queen Charlotte Is.
Kodiak I.
Alaska Pen.
Nunivak I.
Bering Sea
C A N A D A
L a b r a d o r
Hebron
Fort Chimo
Schefferville
Battle Harbour
C. Charles
Newfoundland
St. John's
C. Breton I.
Gulf of St. Lawrence
Sept-Îles
Chicoutimi
Fort George
Inoucdjouac
Churchill
Fort Severn
Moosonee
Cochrane
Nelson
L. Winnipeg
Lynn Lake
Mc Murray
Athabasca
Edmonton
Calgary
Saskatoon
Hay River
Fort Nelson
Jasper
Prince Rupert
Prince George
Vancouver
Vancouver I.
Victoria
R O C K Y M

UNITED STATES
MEXICO
BAHAMAS
CUBA
DOMINICAN REP.
JAMAICA
HONDURAS
NICARAGUA
GUATEMALA
BELIZE
EL SALVADOR
COSTA RICA
PANAMA
VENEZUELA
COLOMBIA

ANTILLES
Bermuda Is. (U.K.)

ATLANTIC OCEAN
PACIFIC OCEAN

Gulf of Mexico
Caribbean Sea
Greater Antilles
Lesser Antilles

New Haven
New York
Philadelphia
Baltimore
Washington D.C.
Pittsburgh
Cleveland
Buffalo
Toronto
Erie
L. Erie
L. Ontario
Toledo
Chicago
Milwaukee
L. Michigan
St. Paul
Minneapolis
Des Moines
Omaha
Pierre
Casper
Cheyenne
Denver
M.t Elbert 4399
Pocatello
Boise City
Snake
Great Salt Lake
Salt Lake City
Carson City
Reno
Sacramento
Oakland
San Francisco
C. Mendocino
Fresno
Las Vegas
S. Bernardino
Los Angeles
San Diego
Tijuana
Mexicali
Tucson
Phoenix
M.t Whitney 4418
Santa Fe
Albuquerque
El Paso
Ciudad Juárez
Chihuahua
Oklahoma City
Wichita
Topeka
Kansas City
St. Louis
Indianapolis
Cincinnati
Columbus
Richmond
Norfolk
Raleigh
Columbia
Charleston
Savannah
Jacksonville
Knoxville
Nashville
Memphis
Atlanta
Montgomery
Birmingham
Jackson
Arkansas
Missouri
Mississippi
Ohio
Tulsa
New Orleans
Houston
Galveston
Corpus Christi
San Antonio
Austin
Fort Worth
Dallas
Matamoros
Nuevo Laredo
R. Grande
Bravo
Monterrey
Torreón
Durango
Ciudad Obregón
Guaymas
Hermosillo
Mazatlán
Culiacán
La Paz
C. Falso
Pta. Eugenia
Lower California
Gulf of California
Revilla Gigedo Is.
Tropic of Cancer
Clipperton (Fr.)
Manzanillo
Guadalajara
León
S. Luis Potosí
Tampico
Veracruz
Puebla
Mexico City
Oaxaca
Acapulco de Juárez
Tehuantepec
Mérida
C. Catoche
Yucatán Str.
Tampa
Miami
Havana
Nassau
Santiago de Cuba
Kingston
San Juan
Port-au-Prince
Santo Domingo
Puerto Rico (U.S.)
Belmopan
Guatemala
S. Salvador
Tegucigalpa
Managua
San José
Panama
Canal Zone
Medellín
Bogotá
Barranquilla
Cartagena
Maracaibo
Caracas
Florida

Km
0    500    1000

ATLANTIC

Tropic of Cancer

Equator

D West from 60 Greenwich

S. Paulo (Braz.)

Fernando de Noronha (Braz.)

Rio Gr. do Norte
C. São Roque
Natal
João Pessoa
Paraíba
Recife
Pernambuco
Maceió
Alagôas
Sergipe

Fortaleza (Ceará)
Ceará
Teresina
Piauí
Parnaíba

Maranhão
São Luís
Belém
Pará
Tocantins
Carolina

BRAZIL

Cayenne
French Guiana
Paramaribo
SURINAM
Amapá
Macapá
New Amsterdam
Georgetown
GUYANA
Obidos
Santarém
Roraima
2810
Boa Vista
Roraima
Amazonas
Moura
R. Manicoré
Manaus
R. Negro
Pará

Barbuda (U.K.)
ANTIGUA
Guadeloupe (Fr.)
DOMINICA
Martinique (Fr.)
ST. LUCIA
ST. VINCENT
BARBADOS
Bridgetown
GRENADA
Port-of-Spain
TRINIDAD AND TOBAGO

Lesser Antilles

Puerto Rico (U.S.)
San Juan
St. Thomas (U.S.)
Virgin Is. (U.S., U.K.)

Curaçao (Neth.)

Caribbean Sea

Greater Antilles

JAMAICA
Kingston

HAITI
Port-au-Prince

DOMINICAN REP.
Santo Domingo

CUBA
Havana
Santa Clara
Santiago de Cuba
Guantánamo

BAHAMAS
Nassau
Miami

UNITED STATES
Florida
Tampa
Florida Str.

Gulf of Mexico

Yucatan Channel

MEXICO
Mérida

Caracas
Cumaná
VENEZUELA
Ciudad Bolívar
Orinoco
Valencia
San Cristóbal
S. Fernando de Atabapo
Maracaibo
L. de Maracaibo

COLOMBIA
Barranquilla
Cartagena
Magdalena
Medellín
Manizales
Bogotá
Cali
Buenaventura
Pasto

ECUADOR
Quito
Guayaquil
Chimborazo
Cuenca
Iquitos
Cerro de Pasco

Cayman (U.K.)

Belize
Belmopan
BELIZE
GUATEMALA
HONDURAS
Tegucigalpa
San Salvador
EL SALVADOR
NICARAGUA
Managua
L. Nicaragua
COSTA RICA
San José
PANAMA
Panamá
Canal (U.S.)

Cocos I. (Costa Rica)

Malpelo I. (Col.)

Galápagos Islands (Ecuad.)

Cerro de Pasco
Chiclayo
Trujillo
Chimbote
Piura
Pta. Parinas
Cajamarca
PERU
Ucayali
Callao

Pôrto Velho
Rondônia
Riberalta
Rio Branco
Acre
Cuzeiro do Sul
Humaitá
R. Madeira

PACIFIC

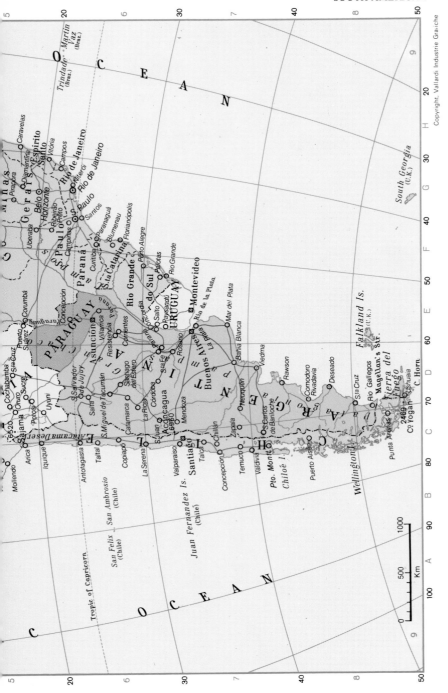

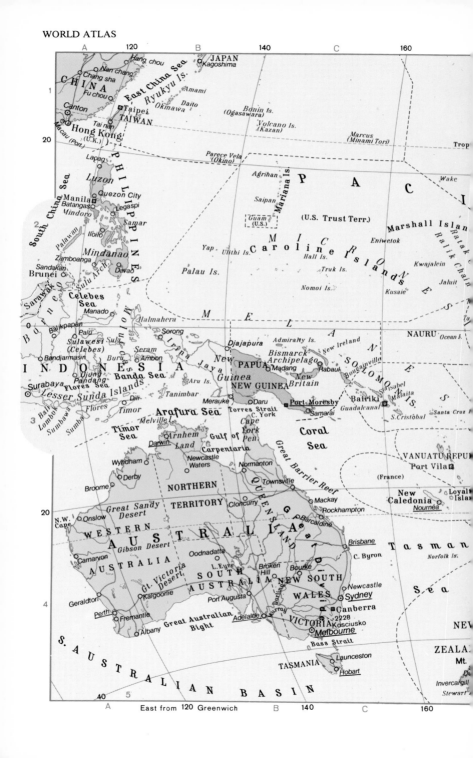

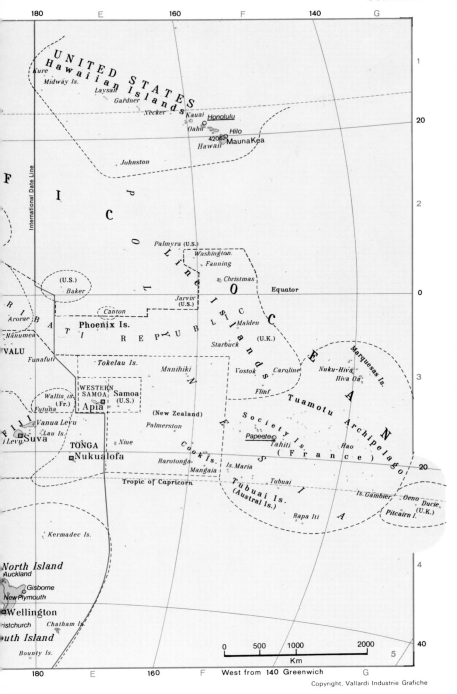

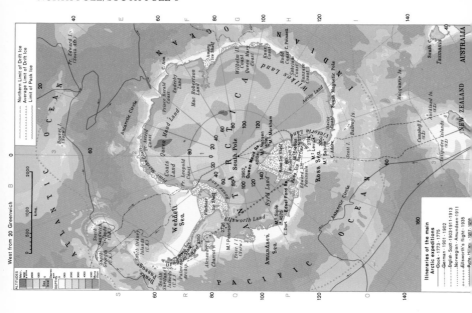

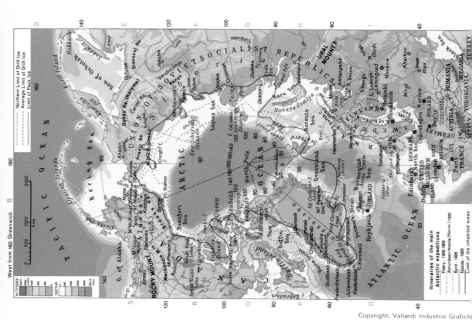

# FLAGS
# OF THE
# WORLD

# Flags of the World

Afghanistan

Albania

Algeria

Andorra

Angola

Antigua
and Barbuda

Argentina

Australia

Austria

Bahamas

Bahrain

Bangladesh

Barbados

Belgium

Belize

Benin

Bhutan

Bolivia

Botswana

Brazil

Brunei

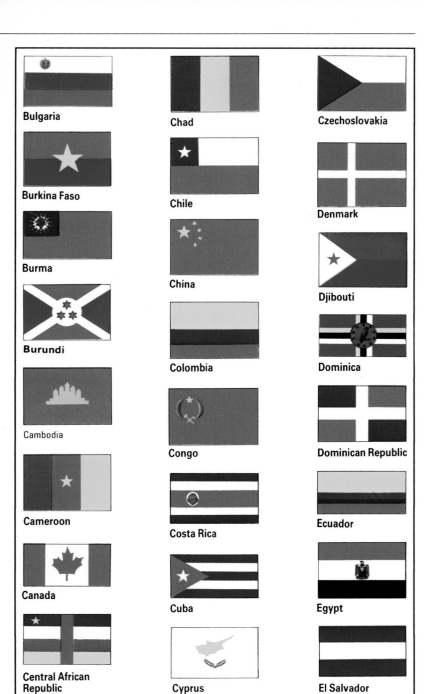

Bulgaria

Chad

Czechoslovakia

Burkina Faso

Chile

Denmark

Burma

China

Djibouti

Burundi

Cambodia

Colombia

Dominica

Cameroon

Congo

Dominican Republic

Canada

Costa Rica

Ecuador

Central African
Republic

Cuba

Egypt

Cyprus

El Salvador

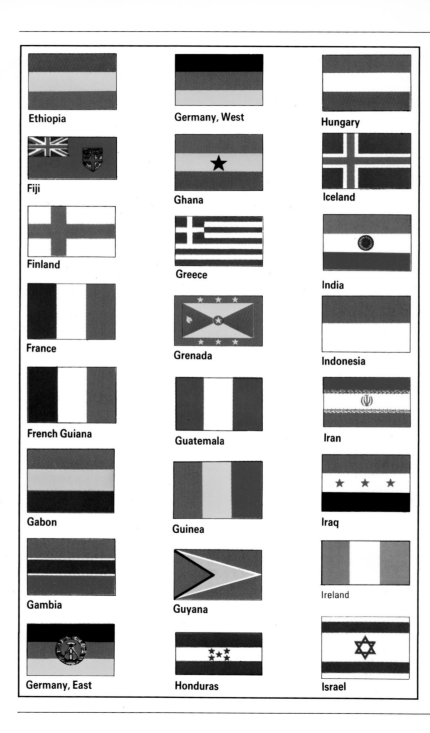

**Ethiopia**

**Germany, West**

**Hungary**

**Fiji**

**Ghana**

**Iceland**

**Finland**

**Greece**

**India**

**France**

**Grenada**

**Indonesia**

**French Guiana**

**Guatemala**

**Iran**

**Gabon**

**Guinea**

**Iraq**

**Gambia**

**Guyana**

Ireland

**Germany, East**

**Honduras**

**Israel**

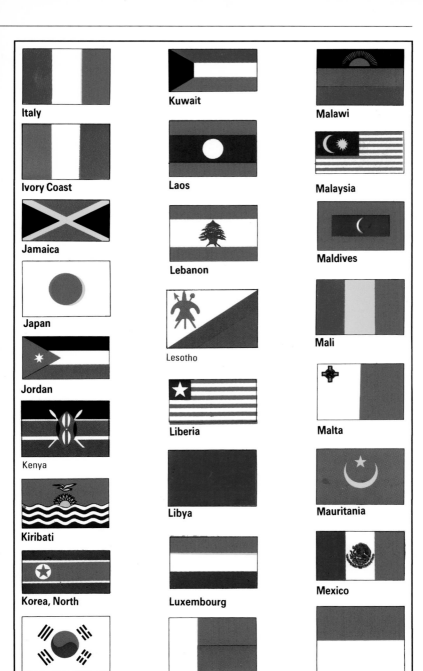

Italy

Ivory Coast

Jamaica

Japan

Jordan

Kenya

Kiribati

Korea, North

Korea, South

Kuwait

Laos

Lebanon

Lesotho

Liberia

Libya

Luxembourg

Madagascar

Malawi

Malaysia

Maldives

Mali

Malta

Mauritania

Mexico

Monaco

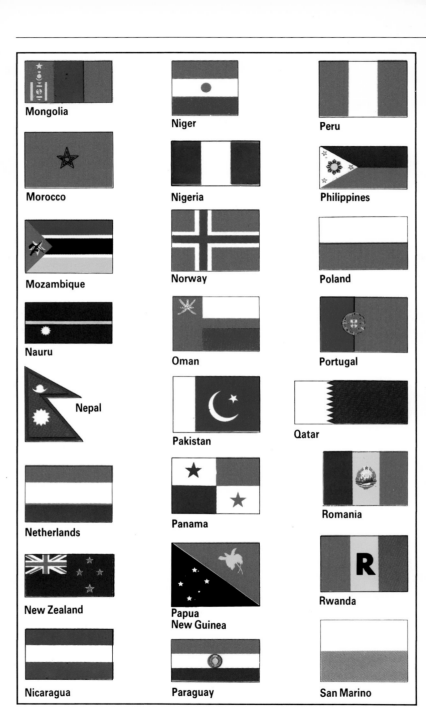

Mongolia

Niger

Peru

Morocco

Nigeria

Philippines

Mozambique

Norway

Poland

Nauru

Oman

Portugal

Nepal

Pakistan

Qatar

Netherlands

Panama

Romania

New Zealand

Papua
New Guinea

Rwanda

Nicaragua

Paraguay

San Marino

**Saudi Arabia**

**St Christopher Nevis**

**Syria**

**Senegal**

**St Lucia**

**Tanzania**

**Sierra Leone**

**St Vincent and Grenadines**

**Thailand**

**Singapore**

**Sudan**

**Togo**

**Solomon Islands**

**Surinam**

**Tonga**

**South Africa**

**Swaziland**

**Trinidad and Tobago**

**Spain**

**Sweden**

**Tunisia**

**Sri Lanka**

**Switzerland**

**Turkey**

**Tuvalu**

**UAE
(United Arab Emirates)**

**Uganda**

**United Kingdom**

**Uruguay**

**USA**

**USSR**

**Vanuatu**

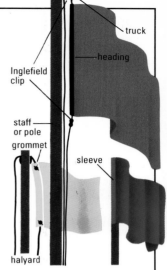

**Vatican City**

**Venezuela**

**Vietnam**

**Western Samoa**

**Yemen AR**

**Yemen PDR**

**Yugoslavia**

**Zaire**

**Zambia**

**Zimbabwe**

truck

heading

Inglefield
clip

staff
or pole

grommet

sleeve

halyard

Red Cross

Red Crescent

Magen David

the upper Elbe (the Vltava) on which Prague stands. Moravia, in the centre, is largely lowland, with rivers draining to the Danube. Slovakia, in the east, is mainly upland, with some plains in the south. The climate is continental. The people include the Czechs (65 per cent of the population), in Bohemia and Moravia, the Slovaks (30 per cent) and various minorities. Industry, which is nationalized, is the main occupation. The country is rich in coal and lignite and has many metal ores, although metals are imported. Farmland covers 55 per cent of the country. Crops include barley, hops, rye, sugar beet and wheat. The republic was created in 1918, and became a communist state in 1948.

**DENMARK,** the smallest but most densely populated nation in northern Europe. It consists of the low-lying Jutland peninsula and about 500 islands, the largest of which, Sjaelland, contains the capital, Copenhagen. Two thirds of the land is fertile farmland or pasture. Animal products (bacon, butter, cheese and eggs) are particularly important, as is sea fishing. The leading sector of the economy is manufacturing. Products include superb silverware, furniture, processed food, chemicals, engineering goods, machinery and ships. The Faeröe Islands and Greenland are semi-independent parts of Denmark.

**DJIBOUTI,** a small republic on the Red Sea in north-eastern Africa. The land is mostly hot desert. The people include the Somali-speaking Issas, the nomadic Afars (or Danakils), both of whom are Muslims, and some Europeans, Arabs and other foreigners. Stock raising is the main occupation. The country became a French colony in 1881, called French Somaliland. In 1967 it was

renamed the Territory of the Afars and Issas. It became independent in 1977, calling itself Djibouti.

**DOMINICA,** volcanic island republic in the Windward Islands in the eastern Caribbean Sea. Its wet tropical climate supports dense forests. Most people are Blacks or of mixed origin. There is a small Carib American Indian community, mostly of mixed origin. Agriculture and tourism are the main industries. Dominica was under British rule from 1805 until independence in 1978.

**DOMINICAN REPUBLIC,** a nation occupying the eastern half of Hispaniola, an island in the West Indies. The land is mountainous and the climate tropical. Rain forests are widespread, and the valleys are fertile. More than 70 per cent of the population is of mixed Black and European descent, 15 per cent is White and 10 per cent is Black. More than half the workers are in agriculture. Sugar is the chief export. Bauxite, nickel, gold and silver are mined and there is some light industry. Tourism is increasingly important. Columbus discovered Hispaniola in 1492. Spain lost the area to France in 1795 but ruled it again in 1809–21. From 1822 to 1844 Haitians occupied the area. The Dominican Republic was founded in 1844, but its history has been marred by violence and civil war.

**ECUADOR,** a republic on the Equator in north-western South America, includes the 15 Galápagos Islands to the west. The Pacific coastlands have a high average annual temperature. The Andes ranges are much cooler. The hot Amazon basin occupies eastern Ecuador. More than half the people are American Indians. There are also people of European, African and mixed descent. Fewer than half the people work on the land. Oil is the leading industrial product. The Incas ruled the area from about 1470 until Spaniards conquered it in 1533. Independence was achieved in 1822 and Ecuador became a separate republic in 1830.

### STATISTICS
To see the statistics of each country's area and population, plus its capital, turn to pages 102–106.

**EGYPT,** an Arab Republic in north-eastern Africa. The fertile, irrigated Nile valley contains 99 per cent of the population, although it covers less than 4 per cent of the country. The Nile flows through Egypt. Near the Mediterranean Sea it divides into two branches, the Dumyat (Damietta) and Rashid (Rosetta), which enclose the triangular delta. The rest of Egypt is desert. The western (Libyan) desert contains several large oases and depressions, notably the Qattara depression, which is below sea level. The eastern, or Arabian, desert rises to highlands that border the Red Sea. But the highest peak, Jabal Katrinah, is in the Sinai peninsula, east of the Suez Canal. This international waterway, opened in 1869, links the Mediterranean and Red seas. Average temperatures in Egypt are high, and rainfall is low. Most Egyptians are Arabs, but there are Berber, Nubian and Sudanese minorities. Egypt is a poor country, although it is the 2nd most industrialized in Africa. Nearly half the people live in urban areas. Energy comes mainly from hydro-electric stations, especially at the Aswan High Dam. Manufactures include cement, chemicals, plastics, steel, sugar and textiles. Some phosphates, iron ore and oil are mined. Just over half the people work on the land. The chief export is cotton, but most farmers are peasants (*fellahin*) who practise subsistence farming. Tourism is important. Ancient Egypt's pyramids and other monuments are special attractions. Ancient Egypt's history is divided into 30 dynasties. The first began in 3100 BC, when Upper and Lower Egypt were united. It reached its peak under King Thutmose III (1490–36 BC). From 525 BC Egypt was mostly under foreign rule. In 30 BC it became part of the Roman empire and, in AD 395, it was the centre of the Coptic Christian Church. Arabs occupied Egypt in 639–642, introducing Islam and Arabic. In 1517 Egypt became part of the Ottoman empire. It was under British control 1881–1922, when it became an independent kingdom. Egypt was declared a republic in 1953 and, in 1956, nationalized the Suez Canal.

**EL SALVADOR,** a densely populated republic in Central America, has a coastline on the Pacific Ocean. The country is mountainous. The climate is warm and wet.

About 90 per cent of the population is of mixed European and American Indian descent. Agriculture employs 52 per cent of the workforce, the main crops being coffee and cotton. Spain conquered the area in 1526. Independence from Spain was achieved in 1821 and El Salvador became an independent republic in 1841. The country has suffered from political instability.

**EQUATORIAL GUINEA,** a republic in west-central Africa, comprises Río Muni on the mainland and the islands of Bioko (formerly Fernando Póo) and Pagalu. The islands are volcanic; Río Muni contains hills and plateaux. The climate is equatorial. The Bantu Fang form the majority in Río Muni. Fang, Bubi (the original inhabitants) and Fernandinos (descendants of liberated slaves) live on the islands. Most people are farmers: coffee is the main crop. Spain took the territory in the 1840s. Independence was achieved in 1968.

**ETHIOPIA,** a republic in north-eastern Africa. The highlands are divided into two blocks by the deep Rift Valley. Lowlands occur in the east near the Red Sea coast. The main river, the Blue Nile, flows from Lake Tana in the north. The lowlands are hot and arid, contrasting with the cooler, moister uplands. About 100 languages are spoken: most belong to the Cushitic, Semitic or Nilotic families. Cushites include the nomadic Galla, the largest single ethnic group. The Amhara, who form the ruling class, speak a Semitic language, while Nilotic languages are spoken by Negroid people in the east. Four out of five people work on the land. Coffee makes up about 75 per cent of the exports. Ethiopia is the home of an ancient monarchy which embraced Christianity in the 4th century AD. The monarchy was abolished in 1974.

**FIJI,** a nation in the south-central Pacific. Two mountainous, volcanic islands, Viti Levu and Vanua Levu, make up 87 per cent of the total area, although there are 320 other small islands. About 48 per cent of the people are Indians (mainly Hindus); 44 per cent are Melanesians; there are also Europeans, Chinese and other Pacific islanders. Agriculture is the main activity and tourism is important. Discovered in 1643, the islands became a British colony in 1874 and an independent nation within the Commonwealth in 1970.

**FINLAND,** a republic in north-eastern Europe, it contains 55,000 lakes, and water covers 9 per cent of the country. Much of Lapland in the north is within the Arctic Circle. Winters are long and severe, but the short summers are warm. Forests cover more than four-fifths of the country and timber has been the mainstay of the economy. Farming is mostly confined to the far south. Russia occupied Finland in 1809 but Finland declared itself independent in 1917, becoming a republic in 1919.

**FRANCE,** the 2nd largest nation in Europe after the USSR. Mountain ranges (the French Alps which contain France's highest peak, Mont Blanc, and the lower Jura Mts) form the south-eastern border. The Vosges Mts are in the north-east, overlooking the Rhine rift valley, and the scenic Massif Central is in south-central France. The north-west peninsula, including Brittany, is lower but also scenic, with a superb indented coastline. The Paris basin is a saucer-shaped depression enclosed by rings of hills with outward facing scarps. The Aquitaine basin in the south-west is a low plain, partly fringed by coastal sand dunes. It extends to the high Pyrenees along the border with Spain. The Rhône-Saône valley, in the south-east between the Massif Central and the south-eastern mountains, ends in the marshy Camargue. The climate varies from the moist, temperate north to the Mediterranean coastlands, with their hot, dry summers and mild, moist winters. The climate also changes from west to east. Rain falls all the year round except for the Mediterranean region. Several minority languages are spoken: Breton, a Celtic tongue, in Brittany; Basque in the Western Pyrenees; Catalan in the eastern Pyrenees; Provençal in the south-east; and German in the north-east. Foreign-born people, including Portuguese, Algerians, Spaniards and Italians, make up 6.5 per cent of the population. Some 78 per cent of the people live in towns. The chief mineral resource is iron ore, notably in Lorraine. Some coal, oil and natural gas are mined. Energy also comes from hydro-electric stations and the River Rance tidal power station in Brittany. There is a wide range of manufacturing industries. Paris is known especially for its luxury and fashion products; Lyon is known for textiles; Marseille and Bordeaux are major industrial ports; and Lille, on the north-western coalfield, is the centre of a large industrial region. Farming is also important, and nine out of every 100 people work on the land. A high proportion of the farms are small and unmechanized, but France is a leading producer of wheat, barley, oats, flax and sugar beet and has a lot of livestock, including dairy cattle. France is famous for its quality wines and cheeses. The tourist industry is a major source of foreign earnings. France is a founder member of the European Community. The Romans conquered the country (then called Gaul) in the 50s BC. In AD 486 the country became an independent kingdom. The monarchy was overthrown by the French Revolution of 1789. After years of turmoil during which France was successively a republic, an empire, a monarchy, a republic again and then once more a monarchy, it finally settled down as a republic in 1875.

## STATISTICS

To see the statistics of each country's area and population, plus its capital, turn to pages 102–106.

**GABON,** a republic on the equator in west-central Africa. Behind the coastal plain are plateaux and mountains. Most of Gabon is in the River Ogooué drainage basin. Average annual temperatures and rainfall are high. Rain forests cover 75 per cent of the land. About 40 languages are spoken: the Bantu-speaking Fang form the largest ethnic group; a few pygmies form the smallest. About 70 per cent of the population is engaged in agriculture, the chief cash crops being cocoa, coffee, palm oil and bananas. But the main wealth of Gabon comes from oil and natural gas, manganese and uranium. France established a settlement on the coast in 1843 and founded Libreville for free slaves in 1849. Gabon became a French colony in the 1880s and an independent republic in 1980.

**GAMBIA,** in West Africa, is the smallest nation in mainland Africa. It is a narrow strip of land bordering the Gambia River, being entirely enclosed by Senegal except along its short Atlantic coast. The climate is tropical. Wooded savanna covers much of the land. The largest of the five main ethnic groups are the Mandingo and the Fulbe (or Fulani). Eighty-five out of every hundred people work on the land. The only major cash crop is groundnuts. Tourism is expanding rapidly. Gambia became a British colony in 1888. Full independence was achieved in 1965 and Gambia became a republic in 1970.

**GERMANY, EAST,** officially the German Democratic Republic, a communist country in Eastern Europe. The Baltic sea coast is fringed by sand bars and lagoons. The north is part of the North European Plain, with many lakes and marshes, and vast areas of heathlands. Soil fertility is generally low. The south, which is more fertile, contains low plateaux and mountains, including the Harz Mountains and the Thüringer Wald in the south-west and the Erzgebirge in the south-east. The main rivers are the Elbe which flows into West Germany, and the Oder-Neisse rivers which form the frontier with Poland. The climate is continental, and rainfall is moderate. About 77 per cent of the population lives in urban areas, working in industry and services. East Germany is now one of the world's top 10 industrial powers. Most factories are government-owned. About one-third of the output comes from

engineering industries. Consumer goods, precision and optical goods, chemicals, textiles and plastics are all important. The main industrial centres are the Dresden, Erfurt, Gera, Halle, Karl-Marx-Stadt and Leipzig districts in the south and the area around Berlin. Mines produce lignite, potash, copper, iron ore, nickel, tin and uranium. Agriculture employs 10 per cent of the workforce. Barley, oats, potatoes, rye, sugar beet and wheat are leading crops. Germany was partitioned after World War II, and East Germany, including East Berlin, corresponds to the former Soviet Occupation Zone. It has been independent since 1949.

**GERMANY, WEST,** officially the Federal Republic of Germany. The coasts on the Baltic and North seas are fringed by sandy islands and dunes. The northern plains are drained by the Elbe, Weser and Ems rivers. The natural vegetation is moorland and heath, but large areas have been cleared for farming. Central Germany contains hills, plateaux and low horsts (block mountains). The leading region is the industrial Ruhr · valley, with its rich coalfield. South-western Germany, the chief farm region, includes horsts that border the Rhine rift valley. The horsts include the Black Forest and the Odenwald. The south-east is an upland zone which includes the scenic Bavarian Alps in the far south. The Danube, which rises in the Black Forest, is Europe's 2nd longest river after the Volga in the USSR. It drains much of the south-east. The centre and south have slightly warmer summers and colder winters than the north. Rainfall is moderate. After World War II millions of refugees from East Germany and eastern Europe flooded in; nearly 25 per cent of West Germans today are former refugees. Also in recent years,

many immigrants, or 'guest workers', from Turkey, Yugoslavia, Italy and other places have found jobs in the country: there were 1.6 million such workers in West Germany in 1987. West Germany is a highly industrialized nation, having achieved an 'economic miracle' since 1945. The largest city, West Berlin, is an enclave in East Germany. Hamburg and Bremen are the chief seaports, but the river port of Duisburg, at the confluence of the Ruhr and Rhine, has a greater annual tonnage of shipping than Hamburg. The ships ply to Rotterdam in the Netherlands which handles a substantial part of German trade. West Germany is the world's 8th largest coal-producer (the main coalfields being the Ruhr, Aachen and Saar), the 3rd largest producer of lignite and it also produces some potash, salt, metal ores and oil. Chemical and iron and steel industries underpin the economy. Other major industries include electrical engineering, machinery, textiles and vehicles. Agriculture employs only 4 per cent of the workforce, but farming remains important. The main crops in the north are potatoes and rye. In the central uplands and south-west, crops include fruit, grapes (for wine), hops, tobacco, sugar beet and wheat. The south-east is mainly pastoral. West Germany is a member of the European Community. For hundreds of years, Germany was a loose federation of small states. It was united in 1871 under the leadership of Prussia, whose king became emperor, After World War II it was split into two, West Germany becoming a federal republic in 1949.

**GHANA,** a republic in West Africa. It is mostly low-lying and contains the man-made Lake Volta. The most fertile region is in the hilly south-west. The only highlands are in the south-east. The climate is hot and wet, with more rain in the south-west than elsewhere. The people are Blacks, and they speak about 100 languages and dialects. Agriculture employs 54 per cent of the workforce. The main crop and export is cocoa. Bauxite, diamonds, gold and manganese are mined, but manufacturing is small-scale. Portuguese mariners reached Ghana in 1471. The area was the British colony of Gold Coast from 1875 until independence in 1957. Ghana became a republic in 1960.

**GREECE,** a republic in south-eastern Europe. It contains the southern part of the mountainous and deeply indented Balkan peninsula and many islands. The southern Peloponnesus is linked to the north by the narrow Isthmus of Corinth. The northern part of the peninsula contains the Pindus Mts and Greece's highest peak, Mt Olympus. It also includes the Plain of Thessaly, the largest lowland apart from the coastal plains of Macedonia and Thrace in the north-east. Islands make up 20 per cent of the area of Greece. The Cyclades are 220 islands east of the Peloponnesus in the Aegean Sea. The South Sporades (or Dodecanese), including Rhodes, are Aegean islands nearer to Turkey than Greece. The North Sporades are north-east of Euboea. The Ionian Islands, including Corfu, lie off the west coast. In the south, the largest island, Crete, covers 8331 sq km (3217 sq mi). The climate is Mediterranean, with hot, arid summers and mild, moist winters, but winters are severe in the mountains. Greece has many processing industries and manufactures are now the leading exports. Only one-third of the land is cultivable. Citrus fruits, grapes, olives, tobacco and wheat are major crops. Sheep, goats and cattle are raised. Tourism brings in foreign exchange. The merchant navy, one of the world's largest, is another money-earner. Thousands of Greeks emigrate every year, finding work especially in Australia, West Germany and the US. Greece came under Roman rule in 146 BC, and formed part of the Ottoman (Turkish) empire from AD 365 to 1830, when it became independent. Greece is a member of the European Community.

---

**STATISTICS**

To see the statistics of each country's area and population, plus its capital, turn to pages 102–106.

**GRENADA,** a West Indian nation, the southernmost in the Windward Islands. The land is mountainous and largely forested. Temperatures remain very warm throughout the year. Descendants of African slaves form the largest ethnic group. Most of the rest are of mixed Black and European descent. The main exports are cocoa, nutmegs and bananas. Tourism is becoming important. Columbus discovered the island in 1498. In 1674–1763 it was a French colony. Thereafter, except for a period of French rule in 1779–83, it was ruled by Britain until it became a fully independent monarchy in the Commonwealth in 1974.

**GUATEMALA,** a Central American republic. Coastal lowlands face the Pacific Ocean in the south-west; a central highland region with 27 volcanoes, some active, is in the earthquake-prone centre; a low forested plain covers the north; and there is a short Caribbean coastline. The altitude modifies the climate. The capital, Guatemala City, is in the hills and is pleasantly warm with heavy rainfall. The lowlands are hotter and generally wetter. More than 50 per cent of the people are American Indians; most of the rest are of mixed European and American Indian origin. About half the people are farmers, mainly in the highlands. Coffee is the main crop. Mining is becoming important, especially for nickel. Spain conquered the area in the 1520s. Guatemala became independent in 1821.

**GUINEA,** a West African republic. Behind the Atlantic coastal plain is the Fouta Djallon plateau, where the Gambia, Niger and Senegal rivers rise. The north-east contains the Upper Niger plains, while the south-east is mountainous, rising to Mt Nimba on the border with Ivory Coast and Liberia. Guinea has a tropical monsoon climate and savanna covers most areas. Most people are Blacks and a large number of tribal languages are spoken. Eight out of 10 people work on the land. The leading industry is bauxite mining: Guinea is the world's 2nd largest producer. It is a very important export for the country, together with a processed form called alumina. France annexed part of Guinea in 1849 and gradually extended its rule. In 1958 the people of Guinea voted to become independent.

**GUINEA-BISSAU,** a West African republic. The land is mostly low-lying, with a broad coastal plain and flat offshore islands. It has a tropical monsoon climate. Most people are Black belonging to various tribal groups. There is a small mulatto community of Guinean and Cape Verdean descent. It has played an important part in the government. Most people are subsistence farmers. The main food crop is rice; the main cash crop is groundnuts. There is no mining and little manufacturing. Portuguese explorers first sighted the coast in 1446. In 1836–79 Portugal ruled the country jointly with the Cape Verde Islands, establishing close ties that were to continue. A long guerrilla war began in 1963, led by Guineans and Cape Verdeans. Guinea-Bissau become independent in 1974, followed by Cape Verde in 1975.

**GUYANA,** a republic in north-eastern South America. Behind the flat, cultivated coastal zone, the land rises to a hilly upland and then to the Guiana Highlands in the east and south. Forest covers 83 per cent of the land with grassland in the highest mountain areas. The main river is the Essequibo. The climate is tropical. Most people live in the coastal zone: 51 per cent are of Asian origin; 33 per cent are descendants of Black African slaves; about 10 per cent are of mixed origin; and 5 per cent are American Indians who live mostly in the forested interior. Bauxite is the main resource and diamonds and gold are also mined. The chief cash crop is sugar and the main food crop is rice. Guyana was the British colony of British Guiana until independence in 1966.

**HAITI,** a republic in the western part of the West Indian island of Hispaniola. The interior consists of wooded mountains: the Massif du Nord, the Massif de la Selle (in the south-east), and the Massif de la Hotte (in the south-west). Most people live on the fertile plains which make up about one-fifth of the country. About 95 per cent of the people are of Black African descent. The mulattoes who form 5 per cent make up a social elite. Voodoo is the chief religion. Most people are subsistence farmers. The chief cash crops are coffee and sugar. Haiti was a French colony from 1697 to 1804, when a revolution brought independence.

**HONDURAS,** a wedge-shaped Central American republic. It has a coastline on the Caribbean Sea and an outlet to the Pacific Ocean through the Gulf of Fonseca. Behind the hot and humid Caribbean coastal plain, there are mountains and high plateaux with a healthy climate. Most Hondurans are of mixed European and American Indian origin. Honduras is Central America's poorest nation. Nearly two-thirds of the people are farmers. Bananas and coffee are the main cash crops. Forests cover 45 per cent of the country and timber is exported. Some lead, zinc and silver are also exported and there are many, mostly small, manufacturing and processing industries. Spain ruled Honduras between 1525 and 1821. It was part of a Central American Federation but became fully independent in 1838.

**HUNGARY,** a landlocked People's Republic in eastern Europe. It is mostly low-lying and drained by the Danube and the Tisza, its tributary. The fertile, hilly Little Alföld is in the north-west. It is separated from the Great Alföld, or Hungarian Plain (56 per cent of the country), by a limestone ridge, the Bakony Forest. Low mountains north-east of Budapest are renowned for their wine. Winters are cold and summers hot. Hungarians, or Magyars, are of Finno-Ugric and Turkic descent, mixed with local peoples. Industry is developing rapidly. Bauxite, coal and some other minerals are produced, but many raw materials must be imported. More than 50 per cent of the factories, all of which are nationalized, are in or around Budapest. Farming employs 18 per cent of the workforce. Arable land, orchards and vineyards cover 53 per cent of the land, pasture 14 per cent and forests 17 per cent. Maize and wheat are the main crops. Hungary and Austria jointly controlled the Austro-Hungarian Empire from 1867 until it broke up in 1918. Hungary became a communist state in 1948.

**ICELAND,** an island republic in the North Atlantic Ocean. Large snowfields, glaciers, volcanoes, hot springs (which are used to heat homes in Reykjavík, the capital) and a deeply indented coastline are features of this rugged island. The warm North Atlantic Drift keeps the southern coasts ice-free in winter. Summers are cool. Less than 1 per cent of the land is cultivated; the main crops are hay, potatoes and turnips. Fishing is the main industry. Norwegian Vikings colonized Iceland in AD 874. In 1262 it was united with Norway and, in 1380, it came under Denmark. Independence was achieved in 1918. In 1963 it acquired a new volcanic island, Surtsey, which appeared from the sea.

**INDIA,** the world's 7th largest country in area, but the 2nd largest in terms of population. The Himalayan mountains in the north include India's highest peak, Nanda Devi. In the north-west Kashmir contains parts of the Karakoram and Hindu Kush ranges. The Indus, Ganges and Brahmaputra rivers rise in the Himalayas. The fertile northern plains of India are densely populated. To the south, the Vindhya range borders the Deccan, a huge, triangular-shaped plateau. It is bounded by two other ranges: the Western Ghats and the lower Eastern Ghats. The main rivers, the Cauvery, Krishna and Godavari, flow from west to east into the Bay of Bengal. The climate and vegetation vary greatly. The highest mountains have an Arctic climate; the Thar desert borders Pakistan; Cherrapunji in the north-east holds the world rainfall record for one year – 1041.8 inches (26,461 mm) were recorded in 1860–61; and the Deccan lies in the tropics. Most of India has three seasons: winter in October–February when it is cool and dry; the hot season in March–June; and the rainy season, June–September, when monsoon winds are drawn into eastern India from the south-west. Hundreds of languages are spoken in India, but the government recognizes only the two official languages, Hindi and English, and 14 other national languages: Assamese, Bengali, Gujerati, Kannada, Kashmiri, Malayalam, Marathi, Oriya, Punjabi, Sanskrit, Sindhi, Tamil, Telegu and Urdu. India is a mainly poor agricultural nation; 74 per cent of the workers farm the land. India is the world's top producer of groundnuts, hemp, sugar-cane and tea; the 2nd leading producer of millet, rice and

**STATISTICS**

To see the statistics of each country's area and population, plus its capital, turn to pages 102–106.

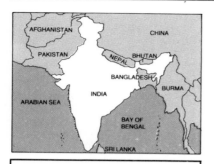

sorghum; the 3rd largest producer of coconuts, copra and tobacco; and the 4th producer of cotton and wheat. It has more cattle than any other nation, but Hinduism forbids their slaughter. India has various minerals, including bauxite, coal, iron ore and manganese. Manufacturing has expanded greatly since 1947; the chief products are textiles, but there is also much heavy industry. Various kings ruled India until 1858, when Britain took over. Independence was achieved in 1947 when British India was partitioned into the mainly Hindu India and the Muslim Pakistan.

**INDONESIA,** a republic in South-East Asia made up of more than 13,000 islands. The largest regions are Kalimantan (part of Borneo), Sumatra, West Irian (part of New Guinea), Sulawesi (Celebes) and Java, the most densely populated island. There are many mountain ranges and more active volcanoes than in any other country: 77 have erupted in recent times. The climate is equatorial, hot and wet all the year round. Rain forests cover large areas. Most people are of Malay origin, mixed with Melanesians and Australasians, and at least 70 languages are spoken. Agriculture employs 60 per cent of the workforce. Rice is the main food. Coffee, copra, palm oil and kernels, rubber, tea and tobacco are major cash crops. Forestry is important. Indonesia is the leading oil producer in the Far East. Manufacturing is important, including shipbuilding, textiles, cement and chemicals. Indonesian princes adopted Islam in the 16th century as a political weapon against Portuguese traders. It gradually replaced Hinduism. Dutch influence began in the late 16th century and the territory became Dutch in 1799. The Republic of Indonesia was formed in 1949.

**IRAN,** a republic in south-western Asia. Around a barren plateau, which contains the Dasht e Kavir (Great Salt Desert) and the Dasht e Lut (Great Sand Desert), are mountains: the highest are the northern Elburz Mts; the Zagros Mts in the west and south; and several ranges in the east. The only fertile areas are near the Caspian Sea and in mountain foothills. The central plateau is arid and hot, but the Zagros Mts can be bitterly cold. About 90 per cent of the people are Shia Muslims. Two-thirds of the people are Persian in type and one-fourth are Turki. There are some Arabs, and Sunni Muslim Kurds live in the north. Forty per cent of the people are farmers. Cereals, fruit, cotton and tobacco are grown. Income from oil has been used to develop heavy industries and improve social services. Ancient Persia was a powerful empire between 550 and 330 BC. The country was Islamized in AD 641. Iran was ruled by a shah (king) until 1979, when it became an Islamic Republic.

**IRAQ,** a republic in south-western Asia. It contains Mesopotamia, the valleys of the Tigris and Euphrates rivers where the ancient civilizations of Babylonia and Assyria arose. There are swamps in the south where the two rivers join, deserts in the west and mountains in the north-east. Summers are hot and winters cool. More than half of the people are Shia Muslims. Sunni Muslim Kurds live in the north, forming about 15 per cent of the population. Oil production dominates the economy. The main crops are dates, cereals, pulses and cotton. Manufacturing is expanding. Iraq was Islamized in AD 637 and, in 1638, it became part of the Ottoman Empire. British forces occupied Iraq in World War I and stayed until it became an independent monarchy in 1932. In 1958, however, the monarchy was overthrown and a republic was proclaimed.

**IRELAND, REPUBLIC OF,** occupies 80 per cent of the island of Ireland. It contains 26 counties, divided into four provinces: Connacht, Leinster, Munster and Ulster. The six north-eastern counties of Ulster constitute Northern Ireland, which is part of the United Kingdom. Central Ireland is a lowland, containing areas of peat bog and some rich farmland. A broken rim of uplands surrounds the plain. The highest peak, Carrantuohill, is in County Kerry in the south-west. The River Shannon is the longest river in the British Isles. Along its course are several lakes, including Lough Ree and Lough Derg. Ireland has mild, wet winters and cool, wet summers. Most people are of Celtic or mixed Celtic and English descent. About 30 per cent speak Irish, but English is used in daily life. Farming forms the basis of the economy. Arable land and pasture cover two-thirds of the land. Major crops are barley, hay, oats, potatoes, sugar beet and wheat, and cattle, sheep and pigs are raised. There are many processing industries. The only large-scale manufacturing industries are in Dublin and Cork: most of the minerals and raw materials needed are imported. Fishing employs about 9,000 men. Tourism is important. The main exports are chemicals, computers, meat, dairy products and textiles. The Normans invaded Ireland in the 12th century and the island came under English rule. Much of Ireland's subsequent history was concerned with a struggle against English rule. In 1801 the Act of Union created the United Kingdom of Great Britain and Ireland. In 1919–21 the Irish fought for independence, finally achieving dominion status as the Irish Free State. Northern Ireland remained part of the UK. Ireland became a republic in 1949. It is a member of the European Community.

**ISRAEL,** a Middle Eastern republic created in 1948. The Galilee highlands containing Mt Meron are in the north. To the east is an extension of the East Africa Rift Valley, enclosing the Sea of Galilee (Lake Tiberias), the River Jordan and, in the south, the Dead Sea. South of the Galilee Highlands are fertile plains and hilly regions. The Negev in the far south is desert. The coast has a Mediterranean climate; the rainfall decreases inland and to the south. More than 80 per cent of the people are Jews: the rest are Arabs. Israel makes most industrial products and diamond finishing is the most valuable industry. Farming is efficient because of extensive irrigation and co-operative and collective farming methods. Cereals, citrus fruits, cotton, olives, tobacco and vegetables are important. About 1 million tourists visit Israel yearly. Israel is part of the ancient land of Palestine. It was the cradle of Judaism and Christianity. Britain ruled Palestine from 1917 to 1948.

**ITALY,** a republic in southern Europe. It consists largely of a long peninsula projecting like a boot between the Adriatic Sea to the east and the Ligurian and Tyrrhenian seas to the west. The scenic Alps, Italy's highest region, form a broad arc in the north. They overlook the North Italian plain which consists mainly of the Po river drainage basin. This is Italy's most densely populated region. The Po is Italy's longest river. The Apennine Mts occupy much of peninsular Italy. Within the Apennines are many fertile valleys and basins, and there are some rich coastal plains. Most rivers are short. The most important are the Arno on which Florence stands and the Tiber which flows through Rome. In the south-west are a series of volcanoes: Vesuvius is near the port of Naples; Stromboli and Vulcano in the Lipari Islands; and Etna, Europe's highest volcano, in Sicily. Sicily is the largest of Italy's 70 or so islands. Italy's second largest island is Sardinia to the west. Southern Italy is subject to earthquakes: it lies near a subduction zone in the Earth's crust.

### STATISTICS

To see the statistics of each country's area and population, plus its capital, turn to pages 102–106.

Southern Italy has hot, dry summers and mild winters. Winter rainfall is highest in the mountains and it increases northwards. Winters are colder in the more continental North Italian plain. The Alps are cold and snowy. Oil and natural gas are extracted in the North Italian plain and in Sicily, but oil and coal have to be imported. Hydro-electric projects are numerous and supply 30 per cent of Italy's electricity. Generally, Italy lacks minerals, and metal ores are major imports. Leading industrial products include textiles, especially silk, engineering goods, including transport equipment and motor vehicles, office and household equipment, chemicals and iron and steel. The chief industrial region is the triangular area formed by Turin, Milan and Genoa. Farmland covers about two-thirds of the land, but agriculture employs only 13 per cent of the workforce. Major crops include barley, citrus and other fruits, grapes (for wine-making), maize, olives, sugar beet, tobacco, vegetables and wheat. Italy is a major milk producer and its cheeses, such as Gorgonzola, are famous. There is a huge tourist industry. The Romans ruled Italy for about a thousand years until AD 476. It then became a series of small city-states, but was unified as a kingdom in 1861. It became a republic in 1946, and is a founder member of the European Community (EC).

**IVORY COAST (Côte d'Ivoire),** a republic in West Africa with a coastline on the Gulf of Guinea. Behind the broad coastal lowlands are high plains. The main highlands are in the north-west: the highest peak, Mt Nimba, is on the Ivory Coast-Liberia-Guinea border. The south has an equatorial climate. The north is often scorched by the north-easterly Harmattan, a wind from the Sahara. There is some forest in the south but savanna is the

main type of vegetation. About 60 languages and dialects are spoken by the Black peoples but French is the official language. Ivory Coast is prosperous by African standards, but prosperity is confined mostly to the south-east. Four-fifths of the people farm the land. Ivory Coast leads the world in cocoa production and is the 4th largest coffee producer. There is some mining, but the processing and consumer goods industries make a larger contribution to the economy. Ivory Coast became a French colony in 1893. and achieved independence in 1960.

**JAMAICA,** a West Indian island nation. The land is mainly mountainous, with spectacular scenery. The coast has a tropical climate, although the Blue Mountains have a very high average annual rainfall. The coasts are drier. More than 75 per cent of the people are Blacks, 14 per cent are of mixed black and white origin, and there are minorities of Asians, Afro-Asians and whites. Jamaica is the world's 3rd largest producer of bauxite, the main export. Bananas and sugar are the main farm products. About three people out of ten work on the land. Tourism is a major industry. Discovered by Columbus in 1494, Jamaica was ruled by Spain until 1655 when the English captured it. Full independence within the Commonwealth was achieved in 1962.

**JAPAN,** an island nation in the Far East that is separated from the Asian mainland by the Sea of Japan. There are 4 large islands (Honshu, Hokkaido, Kyushu and Shikoku) and about 3,000 small ones, including the Ryukyu island chain that stretches towards Taiwan. The islands are largely mountainous, the most rugged region being the Japanese Alps on Honshu, including the highest peak

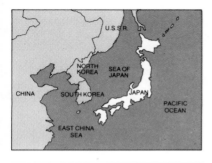

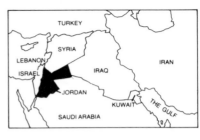

Fujiyama, a dormant volcano south-west of Tokyo which last erupted in 1707. Japan contains more than 160 volcanoes; 54 are active. Earthquakes are common; about 1,500 occur every year, but most cause little damage. Japan has a monsoon climate, with plentiful rain. The heaviest rains fall in June–July and September–October and typhoons are common. Most people are descendants of people who came from mainland Asia and Pacific islands. Japan is Asia's most prosperous and industalized nation. About eight people out of ten live in towns. Some minerals, including coal and copper, are mined, but the amounts are generally too small for the needs of manufacturers. Hence, many materials, including iron ore and oil, must be imported. Japan has a wide range of light and heavy industry. It is the world's 2nd largest manufacturer of cars and is a leading producer of many different types of electronic equipment. It is the world's 3rd largest producer of electrical energy, after the US and the USSR. Japan leads the world in producing motor cycles, merchant ships and television sets. Most of Japan is too mountainous for farming; forests cover nearly 70 per cent of the land. Farming produces rice, barley, fruit, soya beans and wheat. Japan has a large fishing fleet, but has to import some types of food. According to tradition, Japan's monarchy dates from 660 BC. Emperors have ruled Japan, at least in name, ever since. After World War II, Japan adopted a constitutional monarchy, and became one of the world's leading industrial powers.

**JORDAN,** a kingdom in south-western Asia. Its official name is the Hashemite Kingdom of Jordan. The fertile western uplands (the West Bank, occupied by Israel) overlook the Rift Valley which contains the River Jordan and the Dead Sea. The valley continues south to the Gulf of Aqabah, Jordan's only outlet to the sea. The east consists mainly of barren uplands. About 87 per cent of Jordan is desert. Some highland regions are cooler and have adequate rainfall. Most people are Arabs. Farmers grow fruit and vegetables and raise sheep and goats. The main export is phosphates. British forces occupied what is now Israel and Jordan in World War I. Transjordan became a separate country in 1923 and full independence was achieved in 1946.

**KENYA,** an East African republic. Behind the narrow coastal plain is a large grassy or savanna-covered plateau broken by volcanic mountains, including the highest peak, Mt Kenya. The East African Rift Valley in Kenya contains lakes Nakuru, Naivasha and Turkana. Part of Lake Victoria is in the south-east. The climate on the coast is equatorial, but it is much cooler on the plateau. Only 15 per cent of Kenya has a reliable rainfall. There are about 40 language groups: the largest are the Kikuyu and Luo. Farming is the main occupation, employing about eight people out of every ten. The chief cash crops are coffee and tea, and cattle, sheep and goats are raised. Manufacturing is growing rapidly. The wildlife, scenery and beaches attract many thousands of tourists each year. Kenya became a British protectorate in 1895, a colony in 1920, and independent in 1963. It remains a member of the Commonwealth.

### STATISTICS

To see the statistics of each country's area and population, plus its capital, turn to pages 102–106.

**KIRIBATI,** an island republic in the Central Pacific. It includes Ocean (Banaba) Island, the 16 Gilbert Islands, eight of 11 Line Islands (the rest are uninhabited US dependencies), and the eight Phoenix Islands. The climate is hot and generally wet. Most people are Micronesians. Copra is the only export. The Gilbert and Ellice Islands became a British protectorate in 1892. The Ellice Islands became a separate country, Tuvalu, in 1975. Kiribati (pronounced *Kiribas*) became fully independent in 1979.

**KOREA, NORTH,** officially the Democratic People's Republic of Korea. The northern part of a peninsula, North Korea is mostly mountainous, the population being concentrated in coastal plains in the east. Only 16 per cent of the land is cultivable, but nearly half the people are farmers. Rice is the main crop in irrigated areas: maize, millet and wheat grow in drier places. There are many minerals – coal, copper, iron ore, lead, manganese, nickel, tungsten and zinc. There are many light and heavy industries. Korea was partitioned in 1945, and North Korea became a communist state. War raged between the two Koreas from 1950 to 1953.

**KOREA, SOUTH,** a republic in the Far East. The land is mostly mountainous with many islands in the west. Winters are dry, but rainfall is plentiful over the year. Forests cover 70 per cent of the land. Since partition, industry has overtaken agriculture. Tungsten is the chief mineral; small deposits of many other minerals occur. The chief manufactures are light consumer goods, but chemical and heavy industries are growing. The chief crops are rice and other grains and tobacco. Livestock raising and fishing are also important. Korea became a united kingdom in the 7th century AD. It was occupied by Mongols between the 13th and 14th

centuries and it was conquered by China in 1627. Korea became a Japanese colony in 1910. It became the two countries of North and South Korea in 1945.

**KUWAIT,** a small Emirate at the head of the Persian Gulf. This low-lying, desert nation has low and erratic rainfall. The average summer temperature is hot, sometimes extremely hot. Winters are cooler. Most people are Arabs. Kuwait is one of the world's 10 top oil producers, and revenue from oil sales finances one of the world's most elaborate welfare states. In 1899 Kuwait accepted British protection for certain rights. Kuwait became independent in 1914, but Britain remained responsible for Kuwait's foreign policy until 1961, when Kuwait became fully independent.

**LAOS,** a poor, landlocked People's Democratic Republic in South-East Asia. Forested mountains and plateaux cover much of the country: most people live in the Mekong River plains. Laos has a tropical monsoon climate, with most rain in May–September. The Lao-Lum (or Valley Lao, a Thai people) make up 56 per cent of the population; the Lao-Theung, consisting of many groups of animist tribes in the uplands, make up 34 per cent; and the Lao-Soung, including the Meo and Yao who are shifting agriculturalists, make up 9 per cent. Among the minorities, the Chinese and Vietnamese are important in business. Four out of five people work on the land. Rice is the main food crop; timber and coffee are the main exports. Tin is the only important mineral. A united kingdom was established in what is now Laos and northern Thailand in the 14th century. Laos became a French protectorate in 1893, and became independent in 1954.

**LEBANON,** a Middle Eastern republic. Behind the narrow coastal plain are the western Lebanon Mts, an interior plateau containing the fertile Bekaa valley, and the Anti-Lebanon Mts in the east. The climate is Mediterranean in type. Most people are Arabs, but only 60 per cent of them are Muslims; the rest are Christians. Lebanon has long been a financial and commercial base and, in normal times, it has a major tourist industry. Hence, services are the leading sector of the economy, followed by

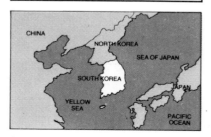

**LIBYA,** a nation in north Africa, officially the Socialist People's Libyan Arab Jamahiriyah. (*Jamahiriyah* means 'state of the masses'). About 95 per cent of Libya is desert or semi-desert. The land rises towards the south. Most people live in the north-eastern and north-western coastal plains, where temperatures are high and rainfall is moderate. Most are of Arab or Berber origin. Libya is a wealthy country because of its oil. The main food crops are cereals, dates, olives and vegetables. The Turks controlled Libya from 1551 to 1911, when Italy occupied Tripoli. Italy lost Libya in World War II, after which Libya became independent, first as a monarchy (1951) and later as a republic (1969).

**LIECHTENSTEIN,** a small principality, lies between Austria and Switzerland, with which it has close links. It uses Swiss currency and is united with Switzerland in a customs union. The Rhine and Ill river plains are in the north, with mountains in the south. Farming includes the cultivation of cereals, fruit and vines and cattle rearing. Light industry, the sale of postage stamps and tourism are leading sources of revenue. Liechtenstein was founded in 1719. It was part of the German Confederation from 1815, but it has been independent since 1866. It is a constitutional monarchy.

**LUXEMBOURG,** a Grand Duchy between Belgium, France and West Germany. The north is part of the Ardennes plateau, with fertile lowlands in the south. The climate is mild and moist. Iron ore is the chief resource and there are large iron and steel works. About 52 per cent of the land is farmed: barley, oats, potatoes, sugar beet and wheat are major crops. Luxembourg became a Grand Duchy in 1354. It has been under the control of Spain, Austria, France, and the Netherlands, but has been independent since 1890 when it broke away from the Netherlands. It is a constitutional monarchy, and became a founder member of the European Community in 1957.

industry and agriculture. Consumer goods are manufactured and cereals and fruit are the main farm products; 38 per cent of the land is cultivated. Lebanon was the heart of the ancient Phoenician empire. It came under the Romans in 64 BC and under Ottoman rule from 1517. France ruled Lebanon from 1918 to 1946, when it became a fully independent republic. Since 1975 it has suffered civil war.

**LESOTHO,** a landlocked kingdom enclosed by South Africa. It was formerly called Basutoland. Mostly mountainous, it includes the high Drakensberg range, but most people live in the western lowlands and the southern Orange River valley. The climate is continental, with warm, moist summers and cold, dry winters. The people, called Basotho, speak Sesotho and English. Agriculture employs one-third of the workforce. The chief food crops are cereals and vegetables. The main exports are wool, mohair and alluvial diamonds. The nation became a British protectorate in 1884 and an independent kingdom in 1966.

**LIBERIA,** a republic in West Africa. Behind the coastal plain, with its mangrove swamps and savanna country, are forested plateaux and grassy highlands. The climate is very warm, with heavy rainfall. There are 16 main language groups. The 50,000 or so Americo-Liberians, descendants of freed slaves, have been important in ruling Liberia. About 70 per cent of the people work the land, growing rubber, cassava and rice. Iron ore is the country's main product. Liberia has a large merchant navy: many foreign ships register in Liberia because of the low fees. In 1822 the American Colonization Society founded Monrovia, now the capital, for freed slaves. In 1847 Liberia became an independent republic.

---

### STATISTICS

To see the statistics of each country's area and population, plus its capital, turn to pages 102–106.

**MADAGASCAR,** an island republic separated from the African mainland by the Mozambique Channel. A high plateau covers about 66 per cent of the country; volcanic peaks, such as the Massif du Tsaratanana, rise above it. The coastal plain in the east is narrow, with broader lowlands in the west. The forested east coast is hot and humid. The grassy and savanna-covered plateau is cool, with abundant rainfall. The north-west is wet but the south-western lowlands are semi-desert. The people are of Indonesian and African origin: the largest of the main 18 groups is the Merina. The people speak Malagasy, which is based on the Merina language. Farmers form 86 per cent of the workforce. Rice is the main food and coffee, cloves and vanilla are the main cash crops. There is little mining but there are many small processing industries, and oil refining is important. Portuguese mariners discovered the island in 1500. France made it a protectorate in 1885. Independence was achieved in 1960.

**MALAWI,** a landlocked republic in southern Africa. It includes part of Lake Malawi (Nyasa) in the East Africa Rift Valley. The River Shire flows from the lake into the Zambezi in Mozambique. There are scenic highlands west of Lake Malawi, but the highest peak, Mt Mlanje, is east of the River Shire. The highlands are wetter and cool. The people speak a number of Bantu languages. Two out of every five workers are engaged in agriculture. Maize is the chief food crop. Tobacco accounts for 49 per cent of the exports and tea for 24 per cent. The territory became the British Central African Protectorate in 1891: it was renamed Nyasaland in 1907. It became independent as Malawi in 1964 and declared itself a republic in 1966.

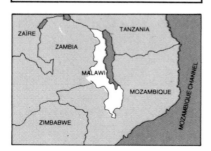

**MALAYSIA,** a South-East Asian monarchy. It contains the southern Malay peninsula, and Sabah and Sarawak in northern Borneo. Forested mountains cover large areas. The most important lowlands are in the Malay peninsula. The climate is tropical. The Malay peninsula contains 84 per cent of the population. In the country as a whole, 47 per cent are Malays, 34 per cent are Chinese, 9 per cent are Indians and Pakistanis, 5 per cent are Dayaks and 5 per cent belong to other groups. Tin is the main mineral, and Malaysia is the world's leading tin producer. Some oil is also produced and manufacturing is increasing. Half the people are farmers, growing rubber, palm (for oil) and rice. Timber is also important. Portuguese traders reached Malacca in 1509 but the Dutch took over in 1641. Malaya, Sabah and Sarawak were all under British protection from the 1800s until 1963, when the independent country of Malaysia was formed. At first Singapore was part of it, but broke away in 1965. Malaysia's Constitution provides that the 9 Rulers of the Malay states elect one of their number every 5 years to be *Yang di-Pertuan Agong* (Supreme Head of the Federation).

**MALDIVES,** an island republic 650 km (400 mi) south-west of Sri Lanka. It includes about 2,000 coral islands. Fishing is the main industry. Coconuts, millet and fruit are grown. The Maldives came under British protection in 1887. Full independence was achieved in 1965.

**MALI,** a landlocked republic in north-western Africa. Plains cover most of Mali, with uplands in the north-east and south. The River Niger flows in a broad arc through southern Mali. The climate is warm. The south has adequate rainfall; the north is desert. There are people of Arab and Berber origin, such as Tuaregs, and some of mixed origin, such as the Fulbe (Fulani). But more than 80 per cent of the population is Black. Almost 90 per cent of the people work on the land. The chief cash crop is cotton. In 1880 France made the area a protectorate. Full independence was achieved in 1960.

**MALTA,** a Mediterranean island republic, south of Sicily, includes Malta, Gozo, Comino, and two islets. It has warm summers

and mild winters. Most people are of Arab, Italian and English descent. More people work in manufacturing than in agriculture or fishing. Tourism is important. Malta was a British colony from 1814 until it gained independence in 1964.

**MAURITANIA,** an Islamic Republic in north-western Africa. Low plateaux cover most of the country which lies largely in the Sahara. But the fertile River Senegal plains are in the south-west. Average annual temperatures are between 25°C and 32°C (77–90°F) and there are large daily variations in the Sahara. The average rainfall is 660 mm (26 inches) per year in the savanna-covered south. The north has little rainfall. About 80 per cent of the population is of Arab and Berber origin. The others are Blacks. Agriculture, particularly livestock rearing, employs eight out of ten workers. Sea fishing is important but the chief resource is iron ore: Mauritania is Africa's 3rd largest producer. Copper is also mined. France ruled Mauritania from 1903 to 1960, when it won independence.

**MAURITIUS,** an island nation east of Madagascar in the Indian Ocean. It includes the mountainous, volcanic island of Mauritius and Rodrigues, which is about 560 km (350 mi) to the east. The climate is warm and humid. The people are of Asian Hindu descent (53 per cent), Asian Muslim descent (17 per cent), and European, mixed and African descent (28 per cent). Sugar and its by-products form the basis of the economy. Tourism is increasing. Britain captured Mauritius from France in 1810. It achieved independence in the Commonwealth in 1968.

**MEXICO,** a republic in North America. It is largely mountainous, with high plateaux and volcanic peaks. The lowlands are in the Yucatan peninsula and along the Pacific and Gulf of Mexico coasts. The chief mountain ranges are the Sierra Madre Occidental and the Sierra Madre Oriental which enclose the central plateaux. These are dotted with lakes and volcanoes: one, Citlaltépetl, is Mexico's highest peak. The long peninsula, Lower or Baja California, is mostly separated from the rest of Mexico by the Gulf of California. It is a rugged, arid region. Mexico straddles the Tropic of Cancer, but there are three main climatic regions determined by the altitude: the tropical *tierra caliente*, the mild *tierra templada*, in which Mexico City is situated; and the high *tierra fría* with its cold winters. Rainfall in central Mexico is adequate, but the north-west is arid. People of mixed European and American Indian origin form 55 per cent of the population; American Indians 29 per cent and Europeans 15 per cent. Crops vary according to the altitude. They include coffee, cotton, maize, sisal and sugar. Cattle, sheep, goats and pigs are reared. Mexico is a major oil producer. Coal, copper, gold, iron ore, lead, manganese, mercury, silver, zinc and other minerals are mined. Manufacturing includes light and heavy industry: textiles and steel are leading manufactures. Spain ruled Mexico from 1521 to 1821. The country became a republic in 1824.

**MONACO,** a tiny principality on the Mediterranean Sea in south-eastern France. There are four districts: Monaco-Ville, the capital; la Condamine, a resort area; Monte-Carlo, a luxury resort with a famous casino; and Fontvieille. French currency is used. Monaco became fully independent in 1861. It is a constitutional monarchy.

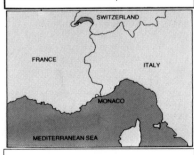

**STATISTICS**

To see the statistics of each country's area and population, plus its capital, turn to pages 102–106.

**MONGOLIA,** a landlocked People's Republic in northern Asia. A featureless plateau covers much of Mongolia, with mountains in the west and the Gobi desert, which covers one-third of the country, in the south. The main rivers are the Selenga, which flows into Lake Baykal, and the Kerulen, a tributary of the Amur River. The climate is severe. Most people were formerly nomadic herdsmen, but all farmland is now organized in large state or collective farms: these farms own 80 per cent of the animals – sheep, goats, cattle and horses – that are reared. Some oil, coal and other minerals are produced, but manufacturing is small-scale. The Mongol Empire became powerful in the 13th century under Genghis Khan. Mongolia became a Chinese province in 1691 and an independent Buddhist kingdom in 1912. In 1924 the communist Mongolian People's Republic was set up.

**MOROCCO,** a monarchy in north-eastern Africa. The folded Atlas ranges cover much of the country: the highest point is Djebel Toubkal in the High Atlas range. The Anti-Atlas in the south is an uplifted rim of the African plateau. The fertile Rharb-Sebou lowlands and the Moulouya valley are in the north. Low plateaux border the narrow coastal plain in central Morocco. The north has a Mediterranean climate, but the south is cooler. The south and east merge into the Sahara. Most people are Arabs. About 30 per cent are Berbers and there is a small European minority. Over half the people work on the land. Barley, citrus fruit, grapes and wheat are important crops, and sheep, cattle and goats are reared. Forestry and fishing are also important, but the main resource is phosphates. Iron ore, lead, manganese, oil, zinc and other minerals are mined. France ruled most of Morocco from 1912, although Spain held the north. Morocco became an independent kingdom in 1956.

**MOZAMBIQUE,** a People's Republic in south-eastern Africa. Coastal plains cover 44 per cent of the land, plateaux and hills 43 per cent and uplands 13 per cent. Lake Nyasa (Malawi) is shared with Malawi and Tanzania. There is a man-made lake behind the Cabora Bassa Dam on the Zambezi river. The centre and north have a tropical climate. The far south is subtropical. The rainfall is generally low. There are 12 major Bantu-speaking tribes and more than 30 minor ones. Agriculture employs 67 per cent of the people in this poor nation. Leading crops are cashew nuts, copra, cotton, groundnuts, maize, rice, sisal, sugar-cane and tobacco. Some coal is mined and the towns contain some industries. Portugal became established in Mozambique in the early 16th century. A guerrilla war (1964–74) preceded independence in 1975. The Constitution of 1978 vests power in the sole political party, FRELIMO, and declares socialism to be the national objective.

**NAMIBIA,** a South African-ruled country moving towards independence. Behind the coastal plain (the Namib desert) is the central plateau. The Kalahari, a semi-desert, is in the east. The north is tropical and the south sub-tropical. The Namib is almost rainless: the northern interior is the wettest place. The people include Europeans (12 per cent), people of mixed origin (6 per cent), Khoisan and related peoples, including Nama (Hottentots) and Bushmen (16 per cent) and Bantu-speaking people who make up the rest of the population. Diamonds, lead, tin, zinc and uranium are mined. In 1920 the League of Nations mandated South Africa to rule the country. United Nations' attempts to achieve independence for Namibia intensified in 1989.

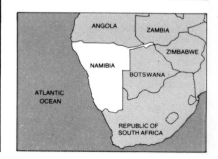

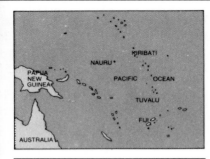

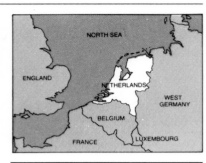

**NAURU,** an island republic close to the equator in the western Pacific Ocean. A raised atoll, it contains rich phosphate deposits on which the economy is based. Half the people are Polynesians, while the rest are other Pacific islanders, Chinese or Europeans. The League of Nations mandated Britain to rule Nauru in 1920. Full independence was achieved in 1968.

**NEPAL,** a landlocked monarchy between China and India. It includes some of the world's highest peaks in the Himalayas, including Mt Everest on the Chinese border. Two-thirds of Nepal is mountainous. There are temperate valleys and warm plains near the Indian border. The people are of Tibetan or Indian descent, including the warlike Gurkhas. Most people are farmers, but manufacturing is developing. The country is a constitutional monarchy.

**NETHERLANDS,** a prosperous monarchy, is one of the Low Countries. It is at the western edge of the North European Plain. About 40 per cent of the country is below sea-level at high tide: the sea is held back by dykes which enclose polders (reclaimed areas), making up more than 25 per cent of the land.

The centre of the country consists of the flood plains of the Rhine and Maas (Meuse) rivers, and their branches (the IJssel, Lek and Waal). The Schelde river enters the sea in the south-west. The coastal region contains many islands, deep estuaries, marshes, sand dunes and polders. The highest land is in the south-east (Limburg). The Netherlands is one of the world's most densely populated nations. Nearly 70 per cent of the land is farmed, but only six out of every 100 people work on it. Most farms are small but the yields are among the world's highest. Butter, cheese and eggs are major products. Leading crops include flowers and bulbs, potatoes, sugar beet and wheat. There is little mining apart from the extraction of natural gas and oil. The chief manufacturing region is the Randstadt, a ring of cities around the polders of the west-centre: Rotterdam with its port Europoort, The Hague, Haarlem, Amsterdam and Utrecht. Eindhoven is another industrial centre. Petroleum products, ships, radio and television sets, textiles, and china and earthenware goods are major products. The country has been largely independent since the late 16th century.

**NEW ZEALAND,** a member nation of the Commonwealth, in the south-western Pacific Ocean. It contains two large islands, North Island and South Island, with Stewart Island, the Chatham Islands, and some smaller islands. North Island, where most people live, contains fertile plains, a volcanic central plateau, and fold mountain ranges in the

---

### STATISTICS

To see the statistics of each country's area and population, plus its capital, turn to pages 102–106.

east. Active volcanoes include Ngauruhoe and Tongariro. Lake Taupo in the centre is in a crater of an extinct volcano. North of the lake, hot springs are utilized to produce electricity. The eastern fold mountains continue in South Island as the Southern Alps, which reach their highest point in Mt Cook. Glaciers flow down high valleys and the south-western coast is glaciated with scenic fiords. The major lowlands include the Canterbury Plains in the east and the Otago plateau in the south-east. New Zealand has a cool, temperate climate. Nine out of 10 New Zealanders are of European, mostly British, origin; 8 per cent are Maoris and 1 per cent other Pacific peoples. Farming is efficient and yields are high. Wool, beef, lamb, mutton and dairy products are the leading exports. Arable farming is less important than livestock, but cereals, fruit, tobacco and vegetables are all important. New Zealand has a few minerals, including some coal and ironsands. Nearly 70 per cent of the electricity, however, is generated by hydro-electric stations. Maoris probably settled in New Zealand in the 14th century. The Dutch navigator Abel Tasman reached New Zealand in 1642. British settlers went to New Zealand in the early 1800s, and it became a British colony in 1841. It became an independent dominion in 1907. The British monarch, represented by a Governor-General, is Head of State.

**NICARAGUA,** a Central American republic. Forested plains border the Caribbean Sea. In the centre is a highland region with some active volcanoes. It is broadest and highest in the north. The Pacific coastlands contain two huge lakes, Managua and Nicaragua. The country has a hot and humid climate. About 80 per cent of the people are of mixed white and American Indian origin, 10 per cent are blacks and 4 per cent are pure American Indians. Coffee, cotton and meat are major products. Gold, silver and copper are mined

and manufacturing is expanding. Spain conquered Nicaragua in the early 16th century. The country became independent in 1821, but in 1823–38 it was part of the Central American Federation. It was torn by rebellion in the 1980s.

**NIGER,** a poor landlocked republic in north-central Africa. The highest peaks are in the Aïr massif in the north; plateaux and plains cover most of Niger. The only river is the Niger in the south-west. The north is mostly in the hot Sahara, although there is some pasture in the Aïr massif. Nomadic Tuaregs live in the Sahara, but most of the people are Black Africans who live in the south. Most of them are engaged in agriculture. Live animals, animal products, groundnuts and vegetables are important products. Niger has large uranium deposits. The country was a French colony from 1900 to 1960, when it became independent.

**NIGERIA,** a Federal Republic in West Africa, and Africa's most populous nation. Most of the country is drained by the Niger and Benue rivers. North of these rivers are the high plains of Hausaland and higher plateaux. The land descends to the Sokoto plains in the north-west and the Lake Chad internal drainage basin in the north-east. South and west of the Niger River are hilly uplands bordered by a broad coastal plain which extends to the huge, swampy Niger delta. In the south-east the land rises to mountains on the Cameroon border. The climate is equatorial. Forest is the typical vegetation in the south with savanna in the north and semi-desert in the Chad basin. About 250 languages and dialects are spoken in Nigeria, but English is the official language. The largest groups are the Muslim Hausa and

Fulani in the north, the Ibo in the south-east and the Yoruba in the south-west. More than half the people work on the land. Oil is Nigeria's main source of wealth. Revenue from oil sales is being used to diversify the economy and to improve Nigeria's towns, including the building of a new federal capital at Abuja in central Nigeria. Southern Nigeria was a centre of the slave trade from the 15th century. Britain abolished the slave trade in 1807 and extended its control over the country. Nigeria became independent in 1960 and a republic in 1963.

**NORWAY,** a monarchy in the western part of the mountainous Scandinavian peninsula. The Kjölen mountains form much of the border with Sweden. In the south there is an extensive region of high plateaux and mountains, including the highest peak, Galdhöppigen. The only large lowlands are in the south-east. The climate is mild, especially in winter, when the western coasts are warmed by the North Atlantic Drift. Even at North Cape, Norway's and Europe's most northerly point, the sea never freezes. Norway is thinly populated. Only 2 per cent of the land is cultivated and food must be imported. Coniferous forests cover 26 per cent of the land and the pulp and paper industry is important. Fishing is the main activity for people who live in the fiords or on the 50,000 or so islands. Norway has rich oil reserves in the North Sea: it is Western Europe's 2nd largest oil producer. Iron ore, copper, lead and zinc are also mined and a high proportion of Norway's exports come from the electro-metallurgical, electro-chemical and paper industries. Hydro-electric power stations provide electricity for most purposes. Norway's large merchant shipping fleet is another major source of income.

Between 1380 and 1814 Norway was united with Denmark under Danish rule. After a brief period of independence, Norway entered into a union with Sweden. In 1905 Norway broke away and became independent again as a constitutional monarchy.

**OMAN,** a Sultanate in the south-eastern corner of the Arabian peninsula. Behind the fertile northern coast (the Batinah north-west of Muscat) is a barren upland that merges into an arid interior plateau. The only other fertile region is in the far south (Dhufar). The climate is hot, with hardly any rain. Arabs make up 90 per cent of the population. There are also some Indians, Iranians, Blacks and Pakistanis. Most people are farmers or fishermen, but the oil industry dominates the economy. Oil is the main source of wealth. Dates, dried fish, limes and other fruit, tobacco and vegetables are also produced. Britain established a special relationship with the area in 1891. Oman is now an independent, absolute monarchy, but retains ties with Britain.

### STATISTICS

To see the statistics of each country's area and population, plus its capital, turn to pages 102–106.

PAKISTAN, an Islamic Republic in southern Asia. The land is mountainous in the north where the Hindu Kush and Himalayas rise. Central and southern Pakistan contain fertile plains drained and irrigated by the Indus River and its tributaries. The south-west includes the arid Baluchistan plateau and the Thar desert is in the south-east. Winters are cold in the mountainous north and cold north-easterly winds chill the northern plains in November–February. In the hot season, March–May, temperatures are high. Rainfall is higher in the north than in the south. Pakistanis are descendants of the many peoples who have invaded the area. Several languages are spoken, including Urdu, Punjabi, Sindhi, Pashto and Baluchi. More than two thirds of the people of this extremely poor country live in rural areas. Agriculture is the main activity. Leading crops are rice, winter wheat, cotton, maize and sugar-cane. Hydro-electricity is important and Pakistan has large reserves of natural gas. Textiles, cement, sugar and fertilizers are leading manufactures. The Indus valley was the home of early civilizations dating from 2500 BC. Islam was introduced in the 8th century AD. Pakistan was part of the Indian Empire, and under British rule from the late 1700s until 1947, when Pakistan became a separate Muslim state. In 1971 East Pakistan broke away to become Bangladesh.

PANAMA, a narrow Central American republic linking North and South America. Behind the Pacific and Caribbean coastal plains the interior is mountainous, the highest peak being Mt Chiriqui in the west. Panama is at its narrowest at the point where the Panama Canal cuts through to link the Atlantic and Pacific Oceans. The United States governed the Panama Canal Zone, a strip of land along the Canal, until 1979 when it reverted to Panama, although the US retains control over the Canal itself until 1999. Panama has a tropical climate. More than 75 per cent of the people are of mixed white and American Indian descent. Bananas, rice and sugar-cane are major crops and there are copper reserves. But Panama's chief resource is the Canal. Panama became independent from Spain in 1819 as part of Colombia, and a separate nation in 1914.

PAPUA NEW GUINEA, a nation in the south-western Pacific Ocean. It consists of the eastern part of New Guinea, the Bismarck Archipelago, including Manus Is, New Britain and New Ireland; Bougainville and Buka in the northern Solomon Is; the D'Entrecasteaux Is; the Louisiade Archipelago and the Trobriand Is; and about 600 smaller islands. New Guinea contains forested mountain ranges and broad, swampy river valleys. There are 40 active volcanoes in the north: this volcanic zone extends eastwards through the islands. The climate is hot and humid, but the uplands are cooler. About 700 languages are spoken by the various tribal groups, a few of which have never come into contact with Western civilization. Most of them farm the land. The main resource, copper, is mined on Bougainville. Coffee, cocoa, copra, timber and fish are other major products. The territory was under Australian rule from 1906 until 1975, when it achieved full independence as a monarchy in the Commonwealth.

PARAGUAY, a landlocked republic in South America. Its main river, the Paraguay, divides it into the Chaco, a thinly populated, flat region of marsh and scrubland in the west, and a fertile plain and hills, rising to the Paraná plateau, in the east. The climate is subtropical. About 75 per cent of the people are of mixed American Indian and white descent, 21 per cent are of European origin, and 3 per cent are pure American Indians. Half the people work in agriculture. Cotton and soya beans are major crops. Forestry is also important: the bark of the quebracho tree is used to make tannin. Yerba maté, the plant from which a green tea is made, grows wild. Mining is unimportant and most manufacturing is involved in processing farm products. Paraguay broke away from the former Spanish Empire in 1811.

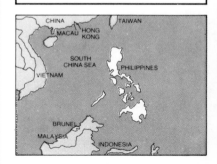

**PERU,** a republic in western South America. Behind the narrow, arid coastal plain are high Andean ranges. These mountains, which reach their highest peak at Mt Huascarán, contain the headwaters of the Amazon River, notably the Maranon and Ucayali. Lake Titicaca, the world's highest navigable lake, straddles the border with Bolivia. Eastern Peru is in the low Amazon basin. The climate is tropical, but the highlands are cooler. People of mixed American Indian and white origin and a roughly equal number of pure American Indians make up the bulk of the population. Sugar, cotton, coffee and wool are leading crops. Fishing is a major industry. Peru produces oil and a variety of minerals, which provide its main wealth. These include copper, lead, zinc, silver and iron ore. Spain ruled Peru from the 1500s until independence in 1821.

**PHILIPPINES,** a South-East Asian republic consisting of more than 7,000 islands. The largest, Luzon and Mindanao, together make up two-thirds of the land area. The large islands are volcanic and mountainous, but many islands are small coral outcrops. The country has a tropical monsoon climate. The plains are hot and humid: the uplands are cooler. Most Filipinos are of Malay-Polynesian origin. There are also some people of Pygmy, European and mixed descent. The Philippines is Asia's only predominantly Christian country. Rice and maize are the main food crops. Coconut products and sugar-cane are major cash crops. Copper is the leading mineral. Textiles, footwear, chemicals, beverages and food are leading manufactures. Spain ruled the Philippines from 1565 to 1898, when the archipelago was ceded to the United States. It became independent in 1946.

**POLAND,** a People's Republic in eastern Europe. Behind the lagoon-fringed Baltic coast is a broad plain, the northern part of which is mostly covered by infertile glacial deposits and forest. The central lowlands, in which Warsaw, Poznań and Lódź are situated, are more fertile. A low plateau in the south rises to the Sudeten Mts in the south-west and the Carpathians in the south-east. The plateau contains much fertile land and the major industrial region built around the Upper Silesian coalfield. The south is drained by the Oder and Vistula river systems. Summers become warmer from north to south. Farmland covers 60 per cent of Poland: unusually for a Communist country, 75 per cent is privately owned. Cereals, potatoes and sugar beet are major crops, and farmers raise cattle, pigs, poultry and sheep. Poland is the world's 4th largest coal producer and it has large reserves of copper, lignite, lead, nickel, salt, sulphur and zinc. But much iron ore for the large steel industry is imported. It is now one of the world's 15 top industrial nations. Poland's frontiers have changed several times in the last 200 years. In 1795 it disappeared from the map when it was partitioned among Austria, Prussia and Russia. Poland was proclaimed an independent republic in 1918 but, in 1939, it was divided between Germany and the USSR. It again became independent in 1945, and a Communist government was set up. All attempts by the government to nationalize farmland and discourage religious worship have failed.

## STATISTICS

To see the statistics of each country's area and population, plus its capital, turn to pages 102–106.

**PORTUGAL,** a republic in the Iberian peninsula of south-west Europe. Much of the land is an extension of the Spanish meseta: there are plateaux and continuations of the central Sierras of Spain. Lowlands border the coast. Portugal has hot, dry summers and mild, moist winters, but the rainfall decreases and temperatures increase from north to south. Cereals are the main crops. About 12 per cent of the land is devoted to vineyards and olive groves. Forests cover one-third of Portugal, which leads the world in cork production. In fishing, sardines and cod form the bulk of the catch. Portugal produces coal, copper and some iron ore. Manufacturing, including iron and steel, chemicals and textiles, is increasing, as is tourism. Portugal's modern frontiers were established in the 13th century and Spain recognized Portugal as an independent kingdom in 1385. In the 15th century Portugal initiated the Age of Exploration and built up a large overseas empire, now gone, in the 1400s and 1500s. In 1910 the monarchy was abolished and a republic proclaimed. Between the 1930s and early 1970s Portugal had a very limited form of democracy but in 1974 full democracy was restored.

**QATAR,** an Arab Emirate occupying a peninsula in the Persian Gulf. This hot, arid and mostly desert nation has little agriculture, although fruit and vegetables are grown. Oil dominates the economy, and its revenues have been used to finance an elaborate welfare state. After being under Turkish rule Qatar became a British protectorate in 1916, and fully independent in 1971 when Britain withdrew from the Gulf.

**ROMANIA,** a Socialist Republic on the Black Sea. Transylvania forms the heart of Romania. It includes a central plateau surrounded by the Bihor Mts to the west, the Carpathians to the east and the Transylvanian Alps to the south, where the country's highest peak is situated. In the far west are fertile plains. Other plains lie in the east and south. They are drained by the River Danube and its tributaries. A limestone plateau (Dobrogea) borders the Black Sea coast. The climate is continental. The people are descendants of several peoples, including the Romanized Dacian tribes of the Danube valley and Slavs. The Romanian language is

based on Latin and contains many Slav words. Farmland covers 63 per cent of the country; most is government-owned. Cereals, potatoes, oilseeds and sugar beet are major crops and cattle, pigs and sheep are raised. There are rich mineral resources, including oil and natural gas, coal, lignite, copper, chromite, gold, iron ore, manganese and zinc. Manufacturing is increasing. Romania was formed in 1861 by the union of Moldavia and Walachia, two provinces. It became a communist state in 1947 after the king abdicated.

**RWANDA,** a small, poor, landlocked republic in east-central Africa. The East Africa Rift Valley in the west contains part of Lake Kivu. It is bordered by highlands that descend in a series of plateaux to the River Kagera in the east. It has an equatorial climate. Bantu-speaking Hutu form 90 per cent of the population. There are also Nilo-Hamitic Tutsi and Pygmy, European and Asian minorities. Most people farm the land. The main cash crop is coffee. Cassiterite, the chief ore of tin, is mined and there are various small-scale manufacturing industries. Rwanda was ruled successively by Germany and Belgium before independence in 1962.

### SAINT CHRISTOPHER AND NEVIS,

popularly St Kitts-Nevis, an island country in the Leeward Islands of the West Indies. It consists of the two small islands of St Christopher, where most of the people live, and Nevis. The country has a warm climate with good rainfall. Most of the people are descendants of Black Africans. The country earns its living from tourism and growing cane sugar. Britain ruled the two islands from 1713 until independence in 1983.

### SAINT LUCIA,

a picturesque island nation in the Windward Is in the West Indies. Volcanic in origin, it has a tropical climate; bananas, cocoa, coconut oil and copra, and textiles are exported. Tourism is developing. The island was ruled by Britain from 1814 until it achieved full independence within the Commonwealth in 1979.

### SAINT VINCENT AND THE GRENADINES,

a West Indian nation in the Windward Is, consists of the volcanic island of St Vincent and the small islands that make up the Northern Grenadines. The climate is tropical. Most people are Blacks or of mixed origin. Farming is the main activity, but tourism is expanding. It was a British colony from 1805, and became a full independent member of the Commonwealth in 1979.

### SAMOA, WESTERN,

a Pacific island nation north-east of Fiji. The largest islands are Savai'i and Upolu. There are also two small islands, Manono and Apolima, and several uninhabited islets. The islands are volcanic in origin and have a tropical climate. The people are Polynesians and Christianity is the main religion. The chief products are bananas, cocoa and coconuts. The country was ruled successively by Germany and New Zealand until it became a fully independent monarchy in 1962. It became a member of the Commonwealth in 1970.

### SAN MARINO,

Europe's smallest independent republic. It is landlocked and situated in central Italy, south of Rimini. Its capital is on the slopes of Mt Titano, a spur of the Apennines. Most people are farmers, but tourism is the main industry. Building stone, textiles and wine are exported. San Marino was founded in the AD 300s.

### SÃO TOMÉ AND PRÍNCIPE,

an African island republic in the Gulf of Guinea. It includes the volcanic island of São Tomé, Príncipe to the north, and some smaller islands. The people are descendants of slaves from the mainland and Europeans. Agriculture is the main activity. From 1522 the islands were governed as a province of Portugal until independence in 1975.

### SAUDI ARABIA,

a kingdom occupying much of the Arabian peninsula. Behind the narrow, Red Sea coastal plain is a highland zone, including the Hejaz in the north and the Asir highlands in the south. To the east of these there are plateaux that slope gently towards the Persian Gulf coastal plain. The plateaux, which cover 90 per cent of the country, include the Nafud Desert in the north and the Rub'al-Khali (the 'Empty Quarter') in the south. The lowlands are hot, but the higher land is cooler. Rainfall is low, and hardly any

### STATISTICS

To see the statistics of each country's area and population, plus its capital, turn to pages 102–106.

falls in the Rub'al-Khali. Most Saudis are Muslim Arabs. Mecca, the birthplace of the Prophet Muhammad, and Medina are the two holiest places of Islam. The economy is dominated by oil; only the USSR and US produce more. There is a small amount of manufacturing and agriculture but the country cannot yet produce all the food it requires and has to import most of its food. The country was under the nominal rule of the Ottoman Turks from 1517 to 1916, when they were driven out. In 1927 the Sultan of Nejd, Abd Al-Aziz Ibn Saud, founded modern Saudi Arabia and became its king.

**SENEGAL,** a West African republic. It is mostly low-lying and covered by savanna. There is a low plateau in the south-east. Senegal is drained by the Senegal, Saloum, Gambia and Casamance rivers. The climate on the coast is pleasant but the interior is hot. The rainfall increases from the arid north to the south. Most of the people are Black Africans. Three-quarters of them work in agriculture, growing groundnuts (peanuts) and raising cattle, sheep and goats. The capital, Dakar, is West Africa's most industrialized city. Tourism is growing. France ruled Senegal as a colony from 1887. It became an independent republic in 1960.

**SEYCHELLES,** an Indian Ocean island republic north-east of Madagascar. There are about 90 islands. The rugged Mahé, or Granitic, islands make up 80 per cent of the area: the rest are flat coral islands. The largest island, Mahé, contains the capital, Victoria. The climate is tropical. Most people are Creoles, of mixed French and African origin. There are also some Chinese, Europeans and Indians. Tourism and agriculture are the main activities. Britain ruled the islands from 1810 until independence in the Commonwealth in 1976.

**SIERRA LEONE,** a West African republic. Behind the broad coastal plain are interior plateaux and mountains. The climate is tropical, and rainfall is heavy. Most people are Black Africans: there are 18 main groups. A minority is composed of descendants of freed slaves. Rice is the main food crop and coffee, cacao and palm kernels are the chief cash crops. Diamonds and bauxite are the chief exports. Forestry and fishing are expanding, as is manufacturing, and tourism is being developed. In 1787 Britain founded Freetown, the capital, as a settlement for freed slaves. Sierra Leone was a colony from 1808 until full independence in 1961. The country became a republic in 1971.

**SINGAPORE,** a prosperous island republic off the southern tip of the Malay peninsula. A causeway links Singapore Island to the mainland. There are many islets that make up 8 per cent of the country. The climate is hot and humid. The main groups of people are Chinese (76 per cent), Malays (15 per cent) and Indians (7 per cent). The country has four official languages – Chinese, English, Malay and Tamil. There is little agriculture. Manufacturing is extremely important. The many products include ships, chemicals, electronic equipment, machinery, steel and textiles. Other important industries are oil refining, and food and timber processing. The port of Singapore is one of the world's largest and Singapore is a major financial centre. Britain took over the island in 1824. It was part of Malaysia from 1963 but it became a separate republic in 1965.

**SOLOMON ISLANDS,** an island nation in the Commonwealth in the south-western Pacific. It lies to the east of New Guinea. The

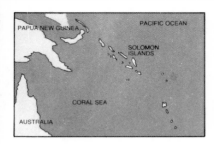

largest of the Solomon Islands is Guadalcanal which, like the other large islands in the group, is volcanic and mountainous. The climate is equatorial. Most people are Melanesians. Agriculture, forestry and fishing are the main activities: copra, timber and palm-oil are major exports. The Solomons became a British protectorate in 1893–99. Full independence was achieved in 1978.

**SOMALI REPUBLIC,** in the Horn of Africa, faces the Gulf of Aden in the north and the Indian Ocean to the east. Behind the narrow northern coastal plain are highlands containing Somalia's highest peaks. The south consists of plateaux and plains. It contains the only permanent rivers: the Wabi Shebele and the Juba. Rainfall increases from the north to the south. Temperatures are high throughout the year. The main types of vegetation are semi-desert and savanna. Nearly all the people are Muslims. About 75 per cent are nomads, herding goats, sheep, camels and cattle. The main arable areas are in the southern river valleys. The north became a British protectorate in 1884, while Italy took the south in 1905. The two territories merged and became an independent republic in 1960.

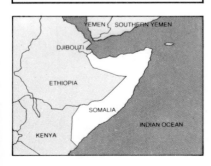

**SOUTH AFRICA,** a republic since 1961. The interior is a vast, saucer-shaped plateau, with an uptilted rim. The Orange and Limpopo rivers drain much of the plateau. Around the plateau, the land descends in steps to the sea. Most of South Africa has a subtropical climate, and a low rainfall; about 50 per cent is arid. The population includes Black Africans (70.2 per cent), people of European origin (17.5 per cent), people of mixed descent (9.4 per cent) and Asians (2.9 per cent). The whites control the country. Since 1948 a policy of apartheid has been pursued, whereby each ethnic group is supposed to develop separately. Hence, 10 African tribal Homelands have been set up for the main black groups, including the Zulu, Xhosa, Tswana, Sepedi and Seshoeshoe. South Africa produces most of the non-communist world's gold and many other minerals, including asbestos, coal, diamonds, copper, iron ore, manganese, tin, uranium and zinc. Industry produces nearly all the goods the country needs, and farms grow most of its food. The chief food crop is maize, but a wide variety of cash crops is produced. Forestry, fishing and tourism are also important. During the 1800s Boers (Dutch settlers) and British settlers clashed over South Africa and fought two wars. In 1910 the country was united as the Union of South Africa, an independent member of the Commonwealth. Since 1948 the white minority government of South Africa has been increasingly criticized for its racial separatism. In 1961 South Africa declared itself a republic and left the Commonwealth.

## STATISTICS

To see the statistics of each country's area and population, plus its capital, turn to pages 102–106.

**SPAIN,** a kingdom in the Iberian peninsula. Most of Spain is a *meseta*, or plateau, which is broken by several mountain ranges, including the Sierra de Gredos and the Sierra de Guadarrama near the capital, Madrid. The fold ranges of the Pyrenees and the Cantabrian Mts are in the north, while the Sierra Nevada in the south contains Mulhacén, Spain's highest peak. The coastal plains vary in width. Some, like those around Alicante and Valencia, are fertile. Four major rivers, the Duero, Tagus, Guadiana and Guadalquivir, rise in the Meseta and discharge into the Atlantic. The Ebro River rises in the Cantabrian Mts and flows into the Mediterranean. The Balearic Islands (notably Majorca, Minorca and Ibiza) form a province in the Mediterranean. The volcanic Canary Islands, off southern Morocco, consist of two provinces: Las Palmas de Gran Canaria and Santa Cruz de Tenerife. The northern Atlantic coast region has mild wet winters and cool summers; the south has warmer summers. The national language of Spain is Castilian. Basque, which is not clearly related to any other language in the world, is spoken in the north in the provinces bordering the Bay of Biscay. Catalan is spoken in the north-east and Galician in the north-west. In 1980, regional governments were established for the Basques and Catalans, and in 1981 a similar government was set up in Galicia. In 1980 74 per cent of Spain's people lived in urban areas, as compared with 57 per cent in 1960. This change reflected a fall in the relative importance of agriculture in the economy. Industry employs 43 per cent of the population, services 39 per cent and agriculture 18 per cent. Important minerals include coal, iron ore, copper, lead and zinc. Hydro-electric and nuclear power stations supply half Spain's electrical energy. The leading manufacturing centres are Madrid and the Mediterranean port of Barcelona. Textiles are the leading manufactures, but Spain has a wide range of light and heavy industry. Tourism is a major source of foreign exchange. Crops vary according to the climate; irrigation is practised in many arid areas. Barley, citrus fruit, grapes (for wine), olives, potatoes, wheat and vegetables are leading crops. Spain is Europe's 3rd largest wine producer. There is a large fishing fleet. Moors from Morocco invaded Spain in 711, and occupied a large part of it. They were driven out by 1492. The modern kingdom of Spain came into being in 1479, when the two small kingdoms of Castile and Aragon were united. Spain built up a huge overseas empire, but lost most of it in the early 1800s. The country is a member of the European Community.

**SRI LANKA,** called Ceylon until 1972, is a South Asian island republic and member of the Commonwealth. It is mostly low-lying; the central highlands which cover less than 20 per cent of the land reach their highest peak in Pidurutalagala. The climate is tropical, with moderate to heavy rainfall and high temperatures. Most people are Sinhalese, but 18 per cent are Tamils and 7 per cent are Moors. About 36 per cent of Sri Lanka is cultivated. Rice is the main food. Tea, rubber and coconuts are the main cash crops. Gemstones and graphite are mined and there is a variety of manufacturing industries. The Sinhalese, from northern India, conquered the island in the 6th century BC, Tamils arrived in the 11th century AD and Arabs (Moors) in the 12th and 13th centuries. The country was the British colony of Ceylon from 1796 until independence in 1948. It became the republic of Sri Lanka in 1972.

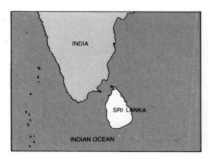

**SUDAN,** Africa's largest nation. The land is mostly flat. It includes much of the Upper Nile basin. Highlands border the Red Sea plains in the north-east, the Darfur highlands are in the west, but the highest peak, Kinyeti, is in the far south. The average annual temperature is high. Rainfall varies from extremely low in the north to plentiful. Much of Sudan is desert but large areas of *sudd* (masses of floating plants) occur in the Nile region. In the north most people are Muslim Arabs, Hamites and Blacks; Blacks predominate in the south. Agriculture is the main occupation, producing cotton for export. Farmers raise cattle, sheep and goats. Many people grow barely enough food to eat; droughts, floods and famine have been a severe problem. Britain and Egypt ruled Sudan jointly as a condominium from 1899. The country became fully independent as a republic in 1956.

**SURINAM,** a republic in north-eastern South America, formerly called Dutch Guiana. Behind the wide marshy coastal plain are savanna-covered hills that rise to forested highlands. The climate is tropical and the rainfall plentiful. About 35 per cent of the people are Creoles of mixed African and European origin, 35 per cent are East Indians, 15 per cent are Javanese, 9 per cent are descendants of runaway slaves, 2 per cent are Chinese and 2 per cent are pure American Indians. Farming is confined to the coastal plain. Fruit, rice and sugar cane are major crops. Forestry is also important, but the most valuable resource is bauxite. Surinam was a Dutch colony from 1667 until independence in 1975.

**SWAZILAND,** a landlocked kingdom in southern Africa between South Africa and Mozambique. There are 4 regions aligned north-south, forming rolling grasslands and open plains dotted with bushes. Rainfall is higher in the west than in the east. The Swazis are Black Africans speaking the Bantu language siSwati. Most of them live in rural areas. The main crops are citrus fruits, cotton, maize, pineapples, rice, sorghum, sugar cane and tobacco, and people raise cattle, goats and sheep. Asbestos and coal are mined and there are various factories in the towns. Tourism and remittances from Swazis working abroad are sources of foreign exchange. Britain ruled Swaziland from 1902 until independence in the Commonwealth was achieved in 1968.

**SWEDEN,** a Scandinavian European monarchy. Norrland, north of latitude 61° North, contains vast coniferous forests and many streams and lakes in the valleys. Mountains run along the border with Norway; the highest peak, Kebnekaise, is in the north-west. In the far north of this thinly-populated region is part of Lapland, where some Lapps still follow their traditional nomadic way of life. South of Norrland, between Göteborg and Stockholm, is the Central Lake region, where lakes Vänern and Vättern are situated. This region has a milder climate than Norrland. South of the Lake region are the infertile southern uplands. Scania in the far south is the most fertile region. Most of Sweden has long, cold winters and short, warm summers. Sweden is one of the world's most prosperous nations. It has little coal but hydro-electric and nuclear power stations produce most of

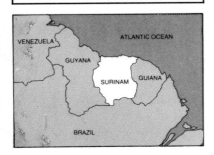

---

### STATISTICS

To see the statistics of each country's area and population, plus its capital, turn to pages 102–106.

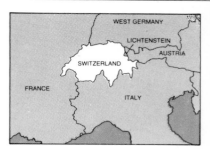

its electric energy. There are major reserves of metal ores, notably iron ore. Steel and steel products are the chief manufactures. Forests cover 57 per cent of Sweden and timber and wood pulp are major exports. Only 8 per cent of the land is cultivated: cereals, potatoes, sugar beet and cattle fodder are grown. Sweden was united with Denmark and Norway in 1397. It broke away in 1523. From 1814 to 1905 it was again united with Norway.

**SWITZERLAND,** a landlocked federal republic in Europe. The Jura Mts run from north-east to south-west along the border with France. These mountains are separated by a central plateau, the *Mittelland*, from the spectacularly scenic Alps, which make up 60 per cent of Switzerland. The plateau contains 75 per cent of the population. It has many lakes between Lake Geneva in the south-west and Lake Constance in the north-east. Switzerland contains the head-waters of the Inn, Rhine, Rhône and Ticino rivers. The average annual temperature range on the plateau is low to moderate, with moderate rainfall. The mountains are colder and wetter, although much of the precipitation falls as snow. Switzerland is a multilingual nation: 69 per cent of the population speak German, 18 per cent French, 12 per cent Italian and 1 per cent Romansch (which is related to Latin). Dairy farming is the main agricultural activity. Cereals, potatoes, sugar beet and fruits are grown and wine is produced. Switzerland is highly industrialized. Its superb precision instruments made it famous, but chemicals, processed foods, glassware, machinery, metal products and textiles are all important today. Tourism is a major source of foreign exchange. Switzerland was formed by a league of cantons (provinces) and won independence in

1648. The country has remained neutral in all wars since 1815. There are 23 self-governing cantons and a federal parliament, which is in Bern, the capital.

**SYRIA,** an Arab republic in south-western Asia. Behind the coastal plain, with its Mediterranean climate, is a low mountain range that overlooks the fertile River Orontes valley. The River Euphrates drains the inland plains in the north. The highest peaks are in the Anti-Lebanon range in the south-west. To the east, the land slopes down to the hot Syrian desert. The rainfall decreases from west to east: about 60 per cent of Syria has very low rainfall. About 90 per cent of the people are Arabs, 6 per cent are Kurds and there is a Palestinian minority. Cotton is the leading crop. Oil is produced and manufacturing is increasing. Tourism is important in peaceful times. Syria was under foreign rule for most of its history, finally winning independence in 1946.

**TAIWAN,** an island republic (formerly called Formosa) off the coast of China. It is largely mountainous, with fertile plains in the west. The climate is tropical. Nearly all the people are Chinese. Rice, sugar-cane, sweet potatoes and tea are major crops. Taiwan

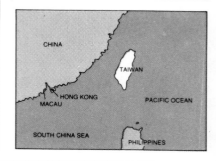

produces coal, some oil and natural gas, and various metals. But manufactures, including textile and electrical goods, dominate the exports. Taiwan became Chinese in the 1680s. Japan ruled it between 1895 and 1945. When the Communists took over China in 1949, their Nationalist opponents set up a government on Taiwan. The economy expanded rapidly with US aid. Taiwan represented China in the UN until 1971, when the People's Republic of China was admitted instead.

**TANZANIA,** a united republic in East Africa, consisting of mainland Tanganyika and the coral islands of Zanzibar and Pemba. Most of Tanganyika is a high plateau broken by arms of the East African Rift Valley: the western arm encloses lakes Nyasa (Malawi) and Tanganyika; the eastern arm contains smaller salt lakes. Lake Victoria lies in the north-west. There are mountains in the north and south. Mt Kilimanjaro is Africa's highest peak. The climate is equatorial, but is cooler on the plateau. Savanna vegetation is the most common. The wildlife is rich and national parks cover 3 per cent of the land: tourism is expanding. The people are divided into 120 tribal groups. About 94 per cent of the people speak Bantu languages. Others speak Cushitic and Khoisan tongues. The majority of Tanzanians work on the land. Major crops are coffee, cotton, cashew nuts and sisal. Zanzibar is a leading producer of cloves. Diamonds are mined, but manufacturing is small-scale. Britain ruled Tanganyika under mandate from 1919 until independence in 1961. Zanzibar, a British protectorate from 1890, became independent in 1963 but joined with Tanganyika in 1964, adopting the official title of the United Republic of Tanzania. The country concentrates on rural development.

**THAILAND,** a South-East Asian kingdom, called Siam until 1939. The fertile Chao Phraya river basin, the main farming region, is bordered by mountains in the east, west and north, where the highest peak, Inthanon, is situated. North-eastern Thailand, a plateau drained by the Mekong River, is infertile. The climate is tropical and most areas have plentiful rainfall. About 85 per cent of the people are Thais. There is a sizeable Chinese community, tribesmen in remote areas (Karen, Khmu, Mao and Yao), Malays and Indians. Three-quarters of the people work on the land. The main products are rice, rubber and tin. Manufacturing is increasing. The Thai state was founded in the 14th century. Its area was reduced in the 19th century but it remained independent. It was an absolute monarchy until 1932 when it became a constitutional monarchy.

**TOGO,** a West African republic. The Togo-Atacora Mts in the centre separate a low plateau in the north from the fertile southern plains. The climate is tropical. The rainfall increases from the coast inland. There are about 30 tribal groups among the Black African population. Farming is the main activity: cocoa and coffee are the leading crops. Phosphates make up 39 per cent of the exports, but manufacturing is small-scale. Togo was a German protectorate from 1884. France and Britain divided it between them during World War I. In 1957 the western (British) section joined Ghana. French Togo was made a fully independent republic in 1960.

## STATISTICS

To see the statistics of each country's area and population, plus its capital, turn to pages 102–106.

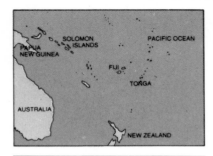

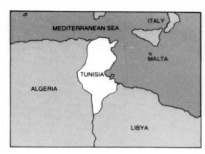

**TONGA,** or the Friendly Islands, an island kingdom in the South Pacific. The 169 islands and islets are divided into 3 groups: Vava'u in the north; Ha'apai in the centre; and Tongatapu in the south, where the capital is situated. There are both coral and volcanic islands. The climate is pleasant. Most people are Polynesians. The country is basically agricultural. Coconuts and bananas are leading products and some are exported. The islands were a British protectorate from 1900 until independence within the Commonwealth was achieved in 1970.

**TRINIDAD AND TOBAGO,** a West Indian republic of two islands close to South America. Trinidad covers 94 per cent of the country. Both islands are hilly and have a tropical climate. The people include Blacks, (45 per cent), East Indians (35 per cent), people of mixed origin (17 per cent), Europeans (2 per cent) and Chinese (1 per cent). Oil is the main product. Citrus fruits, cocoa, coffee and sugar-cane are grown. Sugar is used in the production of rum and molasses. Columbus discovered the islands in 1498. They were ruled by Britain from 1802 until independence within the Commonwealth in 1962. Trinidad and Tobago became a republic in 1976.

**TUNISIA,** a North African republic. An extension of the Atlas Mts is in the north, surrounded by plains. A depression containing salt lakes, the Chott el-Djerid, is in the centre. Saharan plateaux, are in the south. The country becomes drier from north to south. Most people are Arabs or Berbers. Nearly half the people work in agriculture. Major crops are cereals, olives, grapes (for wine), fruit and vegetables. Fishing is important. Mining for oil, phosphates and metal ores is increasing; manufacturing is also growing. Tourism is important. The Arabs conquered Tunisia in AD 647. France made Tunisia a protectorate in 1883. Full independence as a monarchy was achieved in 1956 and a republic was proclaimed in 1957.

**TURKEY,** a republic partly in Europe but mostly in Asia. European Turkey lies west of the Dardanelles, the Sea of Marmara and the Bosporus. These waterways link the Mediterranean and Black seas. European Turkey is a fertile, low-lying region. Asian Turkey (Anatolia) has fertile coastal plains with a Mediterranean climate. Central Anatolia, a mainly flat plateau, has a very low rainfall. About 90 per cent of the people speak Turkish; Kurds make up 7 per cent of the population. Nearly 31 per cent of Turkey is cultivated. Major crops include barley, cotton, grapes (for wine), fruit, nuts, raisins, sugar beet and wheat, and large numbers of cattle, sheep and goats are raised. Turkey produces coal and lignite, chromium and some iron ore, copper and oil. Manufactures include iron and steel, petroleum products, paper, cement, chemicals, textiles and machinery. Tourism is growing. Ottoman Turks captured the former Byzantine capital, Istanbul (then called Constantinople), in

1493, and built up a huge empire stretching north into Europe and south and west into south-western Asia and northern Africa. It was ruled by sultans. The Ottoman Empire declined in size during the 1700s and 1800s, and finally disappeared in 1918, during World War I. In 1923 Turkey became a republic.

**TUVALU,** an independent member of the Commonwealth (formerly the Ellice Islands) north of Fiji in the South Pacific. The islands are coral atolls. The people are Polynesians. Coconuts and copra are major products. The Gilbert and Ellice Islands became a British protectorate in 1892. The Ellice Islands broke away from the Micronesian Gilbert Islands (now Kiribati) in 1975 to become Tuvalu. Full independence was achieved in 1978.

**UGANDA,** a landlocked republic in equatorial Africa. Part of Africa's largest lake, Victoria, is in the south-east; the marshy Lake Kyoga is in the centre; and lakes Edward and Mobutu Sese Seko are in the Rift Valley in the west. The Ruwenzori Range borders the Rift Valley. Most of Uganda is a high plateau, warm with plentiful rainfall. Uganda has about 40 tribal groups. Two-thirds of the people, including the largest single group, the Baganda, speak

Bantu languages. Some Nilotic languages are also spoken. Most people are farmers. Coffee, cotton, tea, hides and skins are produced, and copper is mined. Manufacturing is developing. Uganda was under British rule for about 70 years until independence in 1962.

**UNION OF SOVIET SOCIALIST REPUBLICS,** the USSR, is the world's largest nation. It spreads from eastern Europe right across Asia to the Pacific Ocean. The European part, west of the Ural Mts, covers 25 per cent of the country, but it contains 75 per cent of the population. Much of the land is flat, including the fertile Ukraine, but there are many hilly areas. Major rivers are the Dnepr and Don which flow into the Black Sea, and the Volga which empties into the Caspian Sea. The Caspian Sea is the world's largest lake, while the Volga, is Europe's longest river. The Caucasus in the south contain Mt Elbruz, which is Europe's highest point. East of the Urals is the West Siberian Plain, drained by the River Ob. Between the Yenisey and Lena rivers is the central Siberian plateau. In the far east is a series of mountain ranges. The south-east, which is drained by the Amur River, contains Lake Baykal, the world's deepest lake. South of the West Siberian plain are the Kazakh plateau, several mountain ranges, including the Pamir, Altai and Tien Shan, and in the west the plains around the Aral Sea. The climate varies from the Arctic north to the warm Mediterranean climate along the Black and Caspian sea coasts. Inland areas have a continental climate, with freezing winters. The north-west and the Caucasus region are the wettest places. There are deserts east of the Caspian Sea (the Kara Kum and the Kyzyl Kum). About 60 languages are spoken in the USSR. The largest groups are Russians (52.2 per cent), Ukrainians (16 per cent), Uzbeks (4.8 per cent), Belorussians (3.6 per cent), Kazakhs (2.5 per cent), Tatars (2.4 per cent), Azerbaijanis (2.1 per cent), Armenians (1.6 per cent), Georgians (1.4 per cent),

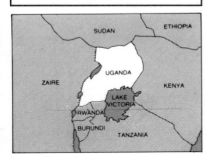

### STATISTICS
To see the statistics of each country's area and population, plus its capital, turn to pages 102–106.

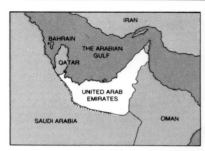

Moldavians (1.1 per cent), Tadzhiks (1.1 per cent), Lithuanians (1.1 per cent) and Turkmenians (0.8 per cent). The USSR is divided into 15 republics. The largest, the Russian Soviet Federal Socialist Republic (RSFSR) covers 76 per cent of the country. Arable land covers 10 per cent and pasture 17 per cent of the land. Crops vary with the climate. The USSR is a world leader in producing apples, barley, coniferous wood, milk, mutton, lamb and goat's meat, oats, potatoes, rye, sugar beet and wheat. Forests cover about one-third of the USSR. Most of the land and all industry are government-owned, but most farm workers have a private plot. The USSR has vast mineral resources. It leads the world in asbestos, coal, oil, iron ore, lead, manganese, mercury, nickel, potash and silver production. But manufacturing is the chief economic sector. The main industrial areas are: the Moscow region, the Ukraine; the Urals; Transcaucasia; and the area around Leningrad. Only the US produces more electrical energy than the USSR, and the USSR is the world's top steel producer. Russia was invaded by Mongol hordes in the 1200s. By 1480 the principality of Moscow had driven out the Mongols and begun to unify Russia. The grand princes of Moscow took the title of *tsar* (emperor). Tsars ruled Russia until 1917, when a revolution during World War I brought the Bolsheviks (communists) to power under Lenin. In 1922 the country took the name Union of Soviet Socialist Republics. After World War II the USSR became a super-power.

**UNITED ARAB EMIRATES,** an oil-rich federation of seven Emirates (formerly the Trucial States), with coastlines on the Persian Gulf and the Gulf of Oman. The Emirates are Abu Dhabi, Ajman, Dubai, Fujairah, Ras al Khaimah, Sharjah and Umm al Qaiwain. The main resource of this flat, hot, desert nation is oil. About 70 per cent of the people are Arabs. The rest are Iranians or other Asians. Britain was responsible for the states' armed forces and foreign relations from 1820 to 1971.

**UNITED KINGDOM OF GREAT BRITAIN AND NORTHERN IRELAND,** an island monarchy off the west coast of Europe. It is known as Britain or the UK. Great Britain consists of England, Scotland and Wales. The Channel Islands (Jersey, Guernsey and Guernsey's dependencies: Alderney, Brechou, Great Sark, Herm, Jethou, Lihou and Little Sark) and the Isle of Man in the Irish Sea are dependencies of the British Crown, but they are largely self-governing. Scotland has three main land regions. The highlands are divided by Glen More into the rugged north-western highlands and the Grampians, which include the UK's highest mountain, Ben Nevis. The main island groups are Orkney and Shetland to the north and the Hebrides to the west. The central lowlands are the most densely populated region, with coalfields, the leading cities and much farmland. Scotland's southern uplands are a mainly farming region. Northern England contains the Cumbrian Mts (or the Lake

District), with England's highest peak, Scafell Pike, and the Pennines which run north–south. Coalfields near the edge of the Pennines have stimulated the growth of major industrial regions. England's other highland region includes Exmoor and Dartmoor in the south-west. Lowland England contains many fertile plains, crossed by ranges of low hills. Wales is a mainly highland country, rising to Snowdon. South Wales contains a large coalfield on which a major industrial region has been built. Northern Ireland contains uplands and plains. In the east Lough Neagh is the UK's largest lake. The UK's longest rivers are the Severn and the Thames, on which the capital, London, stands. The UK has a moist, temperate climate, moderated by the warm North Atlantic Drift (Gulf Stream). Nine out of ten people live in towns. Farming is highly efficient but much food is imported. Major crops are cereals, potatoes, sugar beet and green vegetables. Cattle, sheep and pigs are raised. Fishing is an important source of food. The UK's industrial economy was originally based on its abundant coal and iron ore resources. Coal-mining has declined, but the economy has been boosted by the exploitation of oil and natural gas in the North Sea. Manufactures are extremely varied. Invisible earnings from banking, insurance, tourism and other services make a vital contribution to the economy. The UK's early history is one of successive invasions by Iberians, Celts, Romans, Angles, Saxons, Jutes, Norseman and finally in 1066 Normans, who conquered England. In 1282 England overran Wales and annexed it. In 1603 the Scottish king, James VI, also became king of England, though the two countries were not finally united until 1707. England began the conquest of Ireland in the 1100s, but it was not until 1801, after much bloodshed, that Ireland became part of the United Kingdom of Great Britain and Ireland. The southern part of Ireland broke away in 1922 and is now independent. In the 1700s and 1800s the UK became the first country to change the basis of its economy from agriculture to industry. From the 1960s onward many Blacks and Asians from the Commonwealth settled in the UK, transforming it into a multi-racial society. In 1973 the UK joined the European Economic Community (EEC).

**UNITED STATES OF AMERICA,** a federal republic and the world's 4th largest nation. The bulk of the US lies between Canada and Mexico. The 49th state, Alaska, is in north-western North America, while the 50th state, Hawaii, is in the North Pacific Ocean, about 3870 km (2400 mi) south-west of San Francisco. Alaska and Hawaii became states in 1959. The main part of the US contains five land regions. The southern coastal plains are broadest around the Gulf of Mexico. The Atlantic coastal plains are broadest in the south and narrowest in New England. The Atlantic coast is deeply indented and contains several natural harbours. West of the Atlantic seaboard are the Appalachian Mts, running roughly from Newfoundland (Canada) in the north-east to Alabama in the south. The central (interior) lowlands stretch westwards from the Appalachians. In the north are the five Great Lakes. To the south, the central plains are drained by the Mississippi River and its tributaries, notably the Missouri and Ohio. To the west are the higher Great Plains. Beyond these plains the land rises to the western highlands, made up of the folded Rocky mountains, the Sierra Nevada range and the Cascade range, where the volcano Mt St Helens erupted in 1980. The Colorado River in the south-west has carved the Grand Canyon. The Pacific slope contains fertile valleys and coastal ranges. One feature is the 960 km (597 mi) long San Andreas Fault in California. Movements along the fault cause earthquakes. Alaska also has much earthquake and volcanic activity and the Alaska range contains North

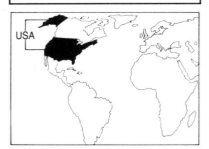

### STATISTICS

To see the statistics of each country's area and population, plus its capital, turn to pages 102–106.

America's highest peak, Mt McKinley. Hawaii consists of a string of volcanic and coral islands. The climate varies greatly from Arctic conditions in Alaska to deserts in the south-west, including Death Valley, the US's lowest point at 86 m (282 ft) below sea level, and a humid, sub-tropical climate in the south-east. California has a pleasant Mediterranean climate, but much of the interior has a continental climate, with hot summers, cold winters and a relatively low annual rainfall. About 83 per cent of the people are of European descent, and 12 per cent are Black, the descendants of slaves. A few are American Indians, the earliest inhabitants. There are also Asians. Farming is highly efficient and the US is among the world's top producers of cotton, fruit, maize, oats, soya beans, sugar beet, tobacco, timber, wheat and livestock. The US is one of the world's top producers of copper, iron ore, oil and natural gas, lead, phosphates, sulphur and uranium. The US is the world's most industrialized nation, accounting for about half of the world's industrial goods. The first inhabitants, American Indians, entered North America at least 30,000 years ago, crossing the Bering Strait from Asia. They travelled over a huge sheet of ice covering the Strait at that time. Europeans discovered the continent in the 1490s, and quickly began settling. The United States was founded in 1776 by 13 British colonies which rebelled and declared themselves independent. The new country grew quickly to include all the territory between the Mexican and Canadian borders. After World War II the US was established as one of the world's super-powers.

**URUGUAY,** a South American republic facing the Atlantic Ocean. It is mostly low-lying, with hills in the north. The River Negro,

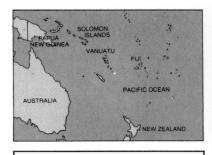

a tributary of the Uruguay on the western border, drains the central region. Temperature and rainfall are both moderate. More than 90 per cent of the people are of European descent. Most others are of mixed European and American Indian descent. About 89 per cent of the land is farmed; 90 per cent of this is pasture, grazing cattle and sheep; livestock products are the chief exports. Crops include fruit, maize, rice, sugar and wheat. There are processing, oil refining, light engineering, transport, chemical and textile industries. From 1726 Uruguay was part of the Spanish empire. It became an independent nation in 1828.

**VANUATU,** an island republic in the south-western Pacific Ocean, formerly called the New Hebrides. There are about 80 islands which are mountainous and volcanic. The climate is tropical and the rainfall is generally abundant. Most people are Melanesians. Copra and fish are exported. Tourism is growing. Britain and France jointly ruled the islands from 1906 until independence in 1980.

**VATICAN CITY STATE,** the world's smallest independent state, is in north-western Rome, on a hill on the right bank of the River Tiber. It contains the government of

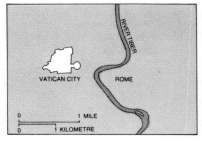

the Roman Catholic Church, headed by the Pope, and the magnificent St Peter's Basilica. It has been the residence of the Pope since the 5th century and was formerly the hub of the Papal States in central Italy. Its independence was officially recognized in 1929 when the Lateran Treaty was signed.

**VENEZUELA,** an oil-rich republic in northern South America. The hot Maracaibo lowlands surround Lake Maracaibo, a freshwater lake open to the sea, beneath which are the largest known oil deposits in the continent. Overlooking the lowlands are the Venezuelan highlands, extensions of the Andes. The central plain is drained by the Orinoco, one of the world's longest rivers. This plain is covered by llanos (savanna). The south-eastern Guiana Highlands are thinly populated. They contain the world's highest waterfall, Angel Falls, with a drop of 979 m (3,212 ft). A lot of the southern part of this region is covered with tropical forests. The climate is equatorial. About 70 per cent of the people are mestizos (of mixed White and American Indian origin), 18 per cent are Blacks or mulattos, 10 per cent are Whites and 2 per cent are American Indians. About four people out of five live in the towns. The chief resource is oil: Venezuela is a leading producer and most is exported to the United States. Other minerals, including diamonds, gold and iron ore, are being exploited and manufacturing has been expanding quickly. Particularly important are textiles, lumber and products and chemicals derived from oil and natural gas. Coffee, cotton, maize, rice and sugar-cane are major crops; beef and dairy cattle are reared in the central plains. Spain ruled the area from the 16th century. It was liberated from Spain in 1821, but became part of a republic called Gran Colombia until 1830.

**VIETNAM,** a Socialist Republic in South-East Asia. The northern Red River delta is ringed by hills and mountains, including Fan Si Pan, the nation's highest peak. In central Vietnam, a narrow coastal plain is backed by the Annamite range. In the far south is the huge delta of the Mekong River. Temperatures are high throughout the year in the south, but are cooler in the north. The rainfall is generally abundant. About 84 per cent of the people are Vietnamese (Kinh). There are also Khmers, Thais and various tribal groups. Rice, maize, sugar-cane, sweet potatoes and cotton are major crops. Farmers raise cattle and pigs. Fishing is also important. The north is rich in minerals, including coal, lignite, bauxite, chromite, iron ore, manganese and titanium. Manufacturing has been steadily increasing. From the 1880s Vietnam was part of the colony of French Indo-China. In 1954 it was given independence as two countries, North Vietnam and South Vietnam. War between the two started in 1959. It ended with the defeat of South Vietnam and the reunification of the country as a Socialist Republic with close relations with the USSR in 1976.

**YEMEN ARAB REPUBLIC** (North Yemen) is in the south-western Arabian peninsula. The Red Sea coastal plain, called the Tihama, is backed by mountains. The coastal plain is hot with very low rainfall and has little population. The highlands have more rain and contain Arabia's best farmland. Most people are Arabs; 90 per cent live in rural areas. Agriculture is the main occupation. Cereals,

## STATISTICS

To see the statistics of each country's area and population, plus its capital, turn to pages 102–106.

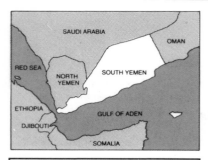

coffee, cotton, fruit and vegetables are grown and hides and skins are important products. Oil deposits were discovered in the early 1980s and oil production is an important industry. Some salt is mined and manufacturing is expanding. From AD 897 Yemen was ruled by an *imam*, a religious and political leader. Yemen was part of the Ottoman Empire in 1849–1918. In 1962 the *imam* was overthrown and a republic proclaimed.

**YEMEN PEOPLE'S DEMOCRATIC REPUBLIC,** in the southern Arabian peninsula, was formerly the Federation of South Arabia, including Aden. Behind the narrow coastal plain are mountains, a fertile valley (the Hadhramawt) and large deserts in the east. Temperatures are high and the rainfall low in Aden, but parts of the Hadhramawt have moderate rain. Most people are Arabs. The chief crops are cereals; cotton is the main cash crop. Farmers keep goats and sheep. Fishing is also important. Aden has an oil refinery and oil products, made from imported oil, are exported. Transit trade is generally important. Britain annexed Aden in 1839, which became a major strategic and trading centre after the opening of the Suez Canal in 1869. The country became independent in 1967.

**YUGOSLAVIA,** a Socialist Federal Republic on the Adriatic Sea. Large areas are mountainous; the mountains are extensions of the Alpine system. The mountains on the coast have been submerged, so former ridges now form long, narrow islands parallel to the coast and former valleys are inlets. There are more than 600 islands along the coast. To the north and east is hill country descending to the interior plains drained by the Danube river system. The coastal climate is typically Mediterranean, but the interior plains, the main farming region, have a continental climate. Most people are South Slavs: The Serbs and Croats are the two largest groups; the Slovenes live in the north; and the Montenegrins and Macedonians live in the south. Various non-Slav minorities live mainly in the east and south. The division of Yugoslavia into six republics reflects its cultural diversity. About half the people live in towns but more and more people are leaving country areas to seek better-paid jobs in the cities. Farmers grow cereals, cotton, fruit, olives, sugar beet, sunflower seeds and tobacco, and raise sheep, pigs and cattle. Forestry is important. Yugoslavia has many mineral resources and manufacturing has steadily expanded since 1945. Yugoslavia was founded in 1918 as a union of the independent countries of Serbia and Montenegro with lands formerly ruled by Austria and Turkey. It became a communist country after World War II.

**ZAÏRE,** a republic in west-central Africa, is the continent's 2nd largest nation. Most of the country lies in the drainage basin of the River Zaïre (formerly Congo), which is one of

the world's longest at 4828 km (3000 mi). There are highlands and plateaux in the south and east along the Rift Valley where Zaïre's border passes through lakes Tanganyika, Kivu, Edward and Mobutu Sese Seko (formerly Albert). The climate is equatorial. There is rain forest in the centre and savanna in the north and south. About 200 language and ethnic groups live in Zaïre. About two-thirds of the people speak Bantu languages: Hamitic, Nilotic, Sudanic and pygmy languages are also spoken. Agriculture is the chief occupation. The chief cash crops are coffee, cotton, palm products and rubber. Fishing is important but livestock can be reared only in areas free from the disease-carrying tsetse fly. The main mining region is Shaba, where copper (the most valuable export), cobalt, manganese, silver, uranium and zinc are mined. Some oil is produced and diamonds are mined in the Kasai provinces. Hydro-electricity is being developed and manufacturing is growing. The country became the personal property of King Leopold of Belgium in 1884, and later became the colony of Belgian Congo. Independence came in 1960.

**ZAMBIA,** a landlocked republic in south-central Africa, called Northern Rhodesia until 1964. It consists mostly of a high plateau. In the south and east are the Zambezi and Luangwa rivers. The Zambezi has been dammed to form Lake Kariba, which Zambia shares with Zimbabwe. Kariba's hydro-electric plants have given Zambia an abundance of electrical energy. Parts of lakes Mweru and Tanganyika are in Zambia, as is the entire Lake Bangweulu. The main mountains are in the north-east. The climate is tropical. Wildlife is abundant in the savanna, which covers most of Zambia. Six major Bantu languages and 66 dialects are spoken. The chief resource is copper, which accounts for 90 per cent of the exports. Cobalt, lead and zinc are also exported as are maize and tobacco, the main cash crop. There are processing and metal industries. After more than 50 years under British protection the country became independent in 1964.

**ZIMBABWE,** a landlocked republic in southern Africa, formerly called Rhodesia. The north is in a deep trough through which the River Zambezi flows. Lake Kariba, a man-made lake on the Zambezi, is shared with Zambia, as is the electricity produced at Kariba dam. Central Zimbabwe (the high veld) has a pleasant climate. The lowlands in the south, drained by the Limpopo river, are much hotter and arid. About 96 per cent of the people are Black Africans who speak Bantu languages. The largest groups are the Ndebele in the south and the Shona in the north. Most other people are of European descent. European farming is efficient but African farming is mostly at subsistence level. Tobacco, sugar-cane, tea and fruit are the leading cash crops. Asbestos, chrome, coal and gold are mined. Manufacturing is important in the towns. Between 1898 and 1923. Southern Rhodesia (as Zimbabwe was then called) was ruled by a British High Commissioner based in South Africa. In 1923 it became a self-governing British colony. In 1965 the white government declared independence, but Britain refused to agree because the Black majority had little power. Finally independence with a majority Black government was achieved in 1980.

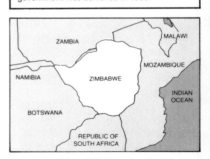

### STATISTICS

To see the statistics of each country's area and population, plus its capital, turn to pages 102–106.

# Country Data by Continents

**EUROPE**

| Country | Area sq km | sq miles | Population | Capital |
|---|---|---|---|---|
| Albania | 28,750 | 11,100 | 3,000,000 | Tirana |
| Andorra | 486 | 188 | 49,000 | Andorra la Vella |
| Austria | 83,850 | 32,374 | 7,500,000 | Vienna |
| Belgium | 30,507 | 11,780 | 9,900,000 | Brussels |
| Bulgaria | 110,910 | 42,823 | 8,900,000 | Sofia |
| Czechoslovakia | 127,855 | 49,365 | 15,500,000 | Prague |
| Denmark | 43,080 | 16,633 | 5,100,000 | Copenhagen |
| Finland | 337,006 | 130,120 | 4,900,000 | Helsinki |
| France | 572,923 | 221,207 | 55,000,000 | Paris |
| Germany, East (German Democratic Republic – D.D.R.) | 108,178 | 41,768 | 16,700,000 | East Berlin |
| Germany, West (Federal Republic of Germany) | 248,574 | 95,975 | 61,000,000 | Bonn |
| Greece | 132,467 | 51,146 | 10,100,000 | Athens |
| Hungary | 93,030 | 35,919 | 10,800,000 | Budapest |
| Iceland | 103,053 | 39,790 | 244,000 | Reykjavík |
| Ireland, Republic of | 70,284 | 27,137 | 3,600,000 | Dublin |
| Italy | 301,223 | 116,303 | 57,400,000 | Rome |
| Liechtenstein | 160 | 62 | 28,000 | Vaduz |
| Luxembourg | 2,585 | 998 | 400,000 | Luxembourg City |
| Malta | 316 | 122 | 400,000 | Valletta |
| Monaco | 1.6 | 0.6 | 28,000 | Monaco |
| Netherlands | 40,844 | 15,770 | 14,500,000 | Amsterdam; The Hague is the seat of government |
| Norway | 324,217 | 125,180 | 4,200,000 | Oslo |
| Poland | 312,680 | 120,727 | 37,500,000 | Warsaw |
| Portugal (including Azores and Madeira) | 92,082 | 35,553 | 10,400,000 | Lisbon |
| Romania | 237,500 | 91,700 | 22,800,000 | Bucharest |
| San Marino | 62 | 24 | 23,000 | San Marino |
| Spain | 504,728 | 194,896 | 39,000,000 | Madrid |
| Sweden | 449,960 | 173,730 | 8,300,000 | Stockholm |
| Switzerland | 41,287 | 15,940 | 6,500,000 | Bern |
| United Kingdom | 244,044 | 94,226 | 56,400,00 | London |
| U.S.S.R. | 22,402,090 | 8,649,496 | 280,000,000 | Moscow |
| Vatican City State | 0.44 | 108.7 acres | 1,000 | Vatican City |
| Yugoslavia | 255,803 | 98,766 | 23,300,000 | Belgrade |

## NORTH & CENTRAL AMERICA

| Country | Area sq km | sq miles | Population | Capital |
|---|---|---|---|---|
| Antigua and Barbuda | 443 | 170 | 82,000 | St. John's |
| Bahamas | 13,934 | 5,380 | 240,000 | Nassau |
| Barbados | 430 | 166 | 250,000 | Bridgetown |
| Belize | 22,965 | 8,867 | 170,000 | Belmopan |
| Canada | 9,976,090 | 3,851,790 | 25,600,000 | Ottawa |
| Costa Rica | 50,700 | 19,575 | 2,700,000 | San José |
| Cuba | 114,524 | 44,218 | 10,200,000 | Havana |
| Dominica | 750 | 290 | 74,000 | Roseau |
| Dominican Republic | 48,733 | 18,816 | 6,800,000 | Santo Domingo |
| El Salvador | 21,393 | 8,260 | 5,100,00 | San Salvador |
| Grenada | 344 | 133 | 86,000 | St. George's |
| Guatemala | 108,888 | 42,042 | 8,600,000 | Guatemala City |
| Haiti | 27,750 | 10,714 | 5,800,000 | Port-au-Prince |
| Honduras | 112,087 | 43,277 | 4,600,000 | Tegucigalpa |
| Jamaica | 10,960 | 4,232 | 2,300,000 | Kingston |
| Mexico | 1,972,545 | 761,604 | 81,700,000 | Mexico City |
| Nicaragua | 130,000 | 50,193 | 3,300,000 | Managua |
| Panama | 75,648 | 29,208 | 2,200,000 | Panama |
| Saint Christopher (St Kitts) and Nevis | 262 | 100 | 40,000 | Basseterre |
| Saint Lucia | 616 | 238 | 120,000 | Castries |
| Saint Vincent and the Grenadines | 388 | 150 | 100,000 | Kingstown |
| Trinidad and Tobago | 5,128 | 1,980 | 1,200,000 | Port-of-Spain |
| United States | 9,372,570 | 3,618,770 | 240,800,000 | Washington D.C. |

## SOUTH AMERICA

| Country | Area sq km | sq miles | Population | Capital |
|---|---|---|---|---|
| Argentina | 2,758,826 | 1,065,189 | 31,100,000 | Buenos Aires |
| Bolivia | 1,098,582 | 424,165 | 6,200,000 | La Paz (seat of government); Sucre (legal capital) |
| Brazil | 8,511,917 | 3,286,470 | 143,300,000 | Brasília |
| Chile | 756,942 | 292,257 | 12,300,000 | Santiago |
| Colombia | 1,138,908 | 439,735 | 30,000,000 | Bogotá |
| Ecuador | 283,560 | 109,483 | 9,700,000 | Quito |
| Guyana | 214,970 | 83,000 | 770,000 | Georgetown |
| Paraguay | 406,750 | 157,047 | 4,100,000 | Asunción |
| Peru | 1,277,440 | 496,222 | 20,200,000 | Lima |
| Surinam | 163,265 | 63,037 | 380,000 | Paramaribo |
| Uruguay | 176,215 | 68,037 | 3,000,000 | Montevideo |
| Venezuela | 912,046 | 352,143 | 17,800,000 | Caracas |

## ASIA

| Country | Area sq km | sq miles | Population | Capital |
|---|---|---|---|---|
| Afghanistan | 652,090 | 251,773 | 15,000,000 | Kabul |
| Bahrain | 668 | 258 | 440,000 | Manama |
| Bangladesh | 143,998 | 55,598 | 104,200,000 | Dhaka |
| Bhutan | 47,000 | 18,147 | 1,400,000 | Thimphu |
| Brunei | 5,765 | 2,226 | 240,000 | Bandar Seri Begawan |
| Burma (renamed the Union of Myanamar in 1989) | 678,030 | 261,789 | 37,600,000 | Rangoon (renamed Yangon) |
| Cambodia | 181,035 | 69,898 | 6,400,000 | Phnom Penh |
| China | 9,596,915 | 3,705,390 | 1,045,500,000 | Beijing |
| Cyprus | 9,250 | 3,572 | 700,000 | Nicosia |
| India | 3,280,466 | 1,266,595 | 783,900,000 | Delhi |
| Indonesia | 1,904,335 | 735,268 | 176,800,000 | Jakarta |
| Iran | 1,647,990 | 636,293 | 46,600,000 | Teheran |
| Iraq | 434,920 | 167,924 | 16,000,000 | Baghdad |
| Israel | 29,324 | 7,847 | 4,200,000 | Jerusalem |
| Japan | 377,765 | 145,856 | 121,400,000 | Tokyo |
| Jordan | 97,738 | 37,737 | 2,800,000 | Amman |
| Korea, North | 120,538 | 46,540 | 20,500,000 | Pyongyang |
| Korea, South | 98,484 | 38,025 | 43,300,000 | Seoul |
| Kuwait | 17,820 | 6,880 | 1,800,000 | Al Kuwait |
| Laos | 236,797 | 91,428 | 3,700,000 | Vientiane |
| Lebanon | 10,400 | 4,015 | 2,600,000 | Beirut |
| Malaysia | 330,868 | 127,316 | 15,800,000 | Kuala Lumpur |
| Maldives | 298 | 115 | 180,000 | Malé |
| Mongolia | 1,564,992 | 604,247 | 1,900,000 | Ulan Bator |
| Nepal | 145,392 | 56,136 | 17,400,000 | Katmandu |
| Oman | 212,457 | 82,030 | 1,300,000 | Muscat |
| Pakistan | 803,940 | 310,403 | 101,800,000 | Islamabad |
| Philippines | 300,000 | 115,830 | 58,100,000 | Manila |
| Qatar | 11,000 | 4,247 | 305,000 | Doha |
| Saudi Arabia | 2,175,580 | 839,996 | 11,500,000 | Riyadh |
| Singapore | 580 | 224 | 2,600,000 | Singapore |
| Sri Lanka | 65,610 | 25,332 | 16,600,000 | Colombo |
| Syria | 185,180 | 71,498 | 10,900,000 | Damascus |
| Taiwan | 35,962 | 13,885 | 19,600,000 | Taipei |
| Thailand | 514,000 | 198,456 | 52,400,000 | Bangkok |
| Turkey | 780,573 | 301,380 | 51,800,000 | Ankara |
| United Arab Emirates | 82,900 | 32,000 | 1,300,000 | Abu Dhabi |
| Vietnam | 332,557 | 128,400 | 62,000,000 | Hanoi |
| Yemen Arab Republic | 195,000 | 75,290 | 6,300,000 | San'a |
| Yemen People's Democratic Republic | 332,966 | 128,560 | 2,300,000 | Aden |

## AFRICA

| Country | Area sq km | sq miles | Population | Capital |
|---|---|---|---|---|
| Algeria | 2,378,896 | 918,497 | 22,800,000 | Algiers |
| Angola | 1,246,700 | 481,353 | 8,200,000 | Luanda |
| Benin | 112,620 | 43,483 | 4,100,000 | Porto Novo |
| Botswana | 600,370 | 231,804 | 1,100,000 | Gaborone |
| Burkina Faso | 274,200 | 105,870 | 7,100,000 | Ouagadougou |
| Burundi | 27,836 | 10,760 | 4,800,000 | Bujumbura |
| Cameroon | 480,620 | 185,568 | 10,000,000 | Yaoundé |
| Cape Verde | 4,532 | 1,750 | 318,000 | Praia |
| Central African Republic | 622,980 | 240,534 | 2,700,000 | Bangui |
| Chad | 1,284,000 | 495,756 | 5,200,000 | N'Djamena |
| Comoros | 2,170 | 838 | 420,000 | Moroni |
| Congo | 342,000 | 132,046 | 1,900,000 | Brazzaville |
| Djibouti | 22,000 | 8,494 | 300,000 | Djibouti |
| Egypt | 1,001,420 | 386,650 | 50,500,000 | Cairo |
| Equatorial Guinea | 28,055 | 10,832 | 360,000 | Malabo |
| Ethiopia | 1,221,894 | 471,776 | 43,900,000 | Addis Ababa |
| Gabon | 267,665 | 103,346 | 1,000,000 | Libreville |
| Gambia | 11,295 | 4,360 | 800,000 | Banjul |
| Ghana | 238,537 | 92,098 | 13,500,000 | Accra |
| Guinea | 245,976 | 94,964 | 5,700,000 | Conakry |
| Guinea-Bissau | 36,125 | 13,948 | 900,000 | Bissau |
| Ivory Coast | 322,460 | 124,503 | 10,500,000 | Abidjan |
| Kenya | 582,644 | 224,960 | 21,000,000 | Nairobi |
| Lesotho | 30,344 | 11,716 | 1,500,000 | Maseru |
| Liberia | 99,067 | 38,250 | 2,300,00 | Monrovia |
| Libya | 1,759,532 | 679,359 | 4,000,000 | Tripoli |
| Madagascar | 587,040 | 226,657 | 10,200,000 | Antananarivo |
| Malawi | 118,484 | 45,747 | 7,300,000 | Lilongwe |
| Mali | 1,240,000 | 478,764 | 7,900,000 | Bamako |
| Mauritania | 1,030,700 | 397,954 | 1,700,000 | Nouakchott |
| Mauritius | 2,046 | 790 | 1,000,000 | Port Louis |
| Morocco | 446,547 | 172,413 | 23,700,000 | Rabat |
| Mozambique | 801,560 | 309,484 | 14,000,000 | Maputo |
| Namibia | 824,292 | 318,260 | 1,100,000 | Windhoek |
| Niger | 1,267,000 | 489,189 | 6,700,000 | Niamey |
| Nigeria | 923,763 | 356,667 | 105,400,000 | Lagos |
| Rwanda | 26,338 | 10,169 | 6,500,000 | Kigali |
| São Tomé and Príncipe | 963 | 372 | 108,000 | São Tomé |
| Senegal | 196,192 | 75,750 | 70,000 | Dakar |
| Seychelles | 443 | 170 | 167,000 | Victoria |
| Sierra Leone | 71,740 | 27,700 | 4,000,000 | Freetown |
| Somali Republic | 637,914 | 246,300 | 7,800,000 | Mogadishu |

| AFRICA *continued*<br>Country | Area<br>sq km | sq miles | Population | Capital |
|---|---|---|---|---|
| South Africa | 1,223,404 | 472,360 | 33,200,000 | Pretoria (seat of government); Cape Town (legal capital) |
| Sudan | 2,503,900 | 966,757 | 22,900,000 | Khartoum |
| Swaziland | 17,363 | 6,704 | 690,000 | Mbabane |
| Tanzania | 945,050 | 364,886 | 22,400,000 | Dodoma |
| Togo | 56,000 | 21,622 | 3,100,000 | Lomé |
| Tunisia | 163,610 | 63,170 | 7,400,000 | Tunis |
| Uganda | 241,785 | 93,354 | 15,200,000 | Kampala |
| Zaïre | 2,345,400 | 905,563 | 31,300,000 | Kinshasa |
| Zambia | 752,614 | 290,586 | 7,000,000 | Lusaka |
| Zimbabwe | 390,580 | 150,803 | 9,000,000 | Harare |

## OCEANIA

| Country | Area<br>sq km | sq miles | Population | Capital |
|---|---|---|---|---|
| Australia | 7,682,422 | 2,966,200 | 15,800,000 | Canberra |
| Fiji | 18,275 | 7,056 | 700,000 | Suva |
| Kiribati | 689 | 266 | 63,000 | Tarawa |
| Nauru | 21 | 8 | 8,000 | Nauru |
| New Zealand | 268,675 | 103,736 | 3,300,000 | Wellington |
| Papua New Guinea | 461,687 | 178,260 | 3,400,000 | Port Moresby |
| Solomon Islands | 27,557 | 10,640 | 300,000 | Honiara |
| Tonga | 700 | 270 | 100,000 | Nuku'alofa |
| Tuvalu | 26 | 10 | 8,500 | Fongafale |
| Vanuatu | 14,763 | 5,700 | 136,000 | Port Vila |
| Western Samoa | 2,934 | 1,133 | 200,000 | Apia |

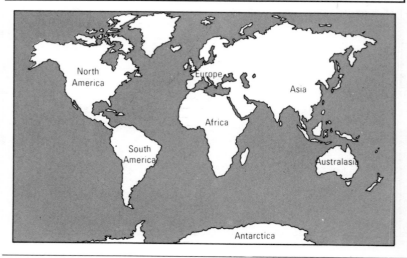

## PROVINCES AND TERRITORIES OF CANADA

| Province or territory | Area sq km | Area sq miles | Population 1980 | Capital |
|---|---|---|---|---|
| Alberta | 661,187 | 255,300 | 2,009,000 | Edmonton |
| British Columbia | 948,599 | 366,276 | 2,567,000 | Victoria |
| Manitoba | 650,089 | 251,014 | 1,030,000 | Winnipeg |
| New Brunswick | 73,437 | 28,356 | 701,000 | Fredericton |
| Newfoundland | 404,518 | 156,194 | 574,000 | St John's |
| Northwest Territory | 3,379,693 | 1,304,978 | 43,000 | Yellowknife |
| Nova Scotia | 55,491 | 21,426 | 847,000 | Halifax |
| Ontario | 1,068,586 | 412,606 | 8,500,000 | Toronto |
| Prince Edward Is. | 5,657 | 2,184 | 123,000 | Charlottetown |
| Quebec | 1,540,685 | 594,894 | 6,299,000 | Quebec |
| Saskatchewan | 570,113 | 220,121 | 957,100 | Regina |
| Yukon Territory | 536,326 | 207,088 | 22,0000 | Whitehorse |

## STATES AND TERRITORIES OF AUSTRALIA

| State or territory | Area sq km | Area sq miles | Population 1979 | Capital |
|---|---|---|---|---|
| Australian Capital Territory | 2,432 | 939 | 227,200 | Canberra |
| New South Wales | 801,428 | 309,450 | 5,111,600 | Sydney |
| Northern Territory | 1,347,519 | 520,308 | 117,700 | Darwin |
| Queensland | 1,727,522 | 667,036 | 2,213,900 | Brisbane |
| South Australia | 984,377 | 380,091 | 1,297,200 | Adelaide |
| Tasmania | 68,322 | 26,379 | 420,100 | Hobart |
| Victoria | 227,618 | 87,889 | 3,874,500 | Melbourne |
| Western Australia | 2,527,621 | 975,973 | 1,257,000 | Perth |

## REPUBLICS OF THE USSR

| | Population 1980 | Capital | | Population 1980 | Capital |
|---|---|---|---|---|---|
| Armenia | 3,000,000 | Yerevan | Lithuania | 3,400,000 | Vilnius |
| Azerbaijan | 6,100,000 | Baku | Moldavia | 4,000,000 | Kishinev |
| Belorussia | 9,600,000 | Minsk | Russian SFRS | 138,400,000 | Moscow |
| Estonia | 1,500,000 | Tallinn | Tadzikistan | 3,900,000 | Dushanbe |
| Georgia | 5,000,000 | Tbilisi | Turkmenistan | 2,800,000 | Ashkhabad |
| Kazakhstan | 14,900,000 | Alma-Ata | Ukraine | 50,000,000 | Kiev |
| Kirgizia | 3,600,000 | Frunze | Uzbekistan | 15,800,000 | Tashkent |
| Latvia | 2,500,000 | Riga | | | |

## PROVINCES OF SOUTH AFRICA

| Province | Area sq km | Area sq miles | Population | Seat of government |
|---|---|---|---|---|
| Cape of Good Hope | 721,001 | 278,395 | 6,732,000 | Cape Town |
| Natal | 86,967 | 33,580 | 4,237,000 | Pietermaritzburg |
| Transvaal | 283,917 | 109,627 | 8,718,000 | Pretoria |
| Orange Free State | 129,152 | 49,869 | 1,716,000 | Bloemfontein |

# Administrative Areas of the United Kingdom

## ENGLISH COUNTIES

| | Population 1981 census | County Town |
|---|---|---|
| Avon | 909,408 | Bristol |
| Bedfordshire | 504,986 | Bedford |
| Berkshire | 675,153 | Reading |
| Buckinghamshire | 565,992 | Aylesbury |
| Cambridgeshire | 575,177 | Cambridge |
| Cheshire | 926,293 | Chester |
| Cleveland | 565,775 | Middlesbrough |
| Cornwall and the Isles of Scilly | 430,506 | Truro |
| Cumbria | 483,427 | Carlisle |
| Derbyshire | 906,929 | Matlock |
| Devon | 952,000 | Exeter |
| Dorset | 591,990 | Dorchester |
| Durham | 604,728 | Durham |
| East Sussex | 652,568 | Lewes |
| Essex | 1,469,065 | Chelmsford |
| Gloucestershire | 499,351 | Gloucester |
| Hampshire | 1,456,367 | Winchester |
| Hereford & Worcester | 630,218 | Worcester |
| Hertfordshire | 954,535 | Hertford |
| Humberside | 847,666 | Kingston upon Hull |
| Isle of Wight | 118,192 | Newport |
| Kent | 1,463,055 | Maidstone |
| Lancashire | 1,373,118 | Preston |
| Leicestershire | 842,577 | Leicester |
| Lincolnshire | 547,560 | Lincoln |
| Norfolk | 693,490 | Norwich |
| Northamptonshire | 527,532 | Northampton |
| Northumberland | 299,905 | Newcastle upon Tyne |
| North Yorkshire | 666,610 | Northallerton |
| Nottinghamshire | 982,631 | Nottingham |
| Oxfordshire | 515,079 | Oxford |
| Shropshire | 375,610 | Shrewsbury |
| Somerset | 424,988 | Taunton |
| Staffordshire | 1,012,320 | Stafford |
| Suffolk | 596,354 | Ipswich |
| Surrey | 999,393 | Kingston upon Thames |
| Warwickshire | 473,620 | Warwick |
| West Sussex | 658,562 | Chichester |
| Wiltshire | 518,167 | Trowbridge |

## FORMER METROPOLITAN COUNTIES

These counties were created in 1974 when local government was reorganized. Their councils were abolished in 1986.

| | Population |
|---|---|
| Greater London | 6,696,008 |
| Greater Manchester | 2,594,778 |
| Merseyside | 1,513,070 |
| South Yorkshire | 1,301,813 |
| Tyne and Wear | 1,143,245 |
| West Midlands | 2,644,634 |
| West Yorkshire | 2,037,510 |

## SCOTTISH REGIONS

| | Population 1981 census | Administrative HQ |
|---|---|---|
| Borders | 99,248 | Newton St Boswells |
| Central | 273,078 | Stirling |
| Dumfries & Galloway | 145,078 | Dumfries |
| Fife | 326,480 | Glenrothes |
| Grampian | 470,596 | Aberdeen |
| Highland | 200,030 | Inverness |
| Lothian | 735,892 | Edinburgh |
| Strathclyde | 2,397,827 | Glasgow |
| Tayside | 391,529 | Dundee |
| *Island Authorities* | | |
| Orkney | 18,906 | Kirkwall |
| Shetland | 27,716 | Lerwick |
| Western Isles | 31,766 | Stornaway |

## COUNTIES OF NORTHERN IRELAND

| | Population 1981 census | County Town |
|---|---|---|
| Antrim | 356,000 | Belfast |
| Armagh | 134,000 | Armagh |
| Down | 312,000 | Downpatrick |
| Fermanagh | 50,000 | Enniskillen |
| Londonderry | 131,000 | Londonderry |
| Tyrone | 139,000 | Omagh |

## WELSH COUNTIES

| | Population 1981 census | County Town | | Population 1981 census | County Town |
|---|---|---|---|---|---|
| Clwyd | 390,173 | Mold | Mid-Glamorgan | 537,866 | Cardiff |
| Dyfed | 329,977 | Carmarthen | Powys | 110,467 | Llandrindod |
| Gwent | 439,684 | Cwmbran | South Glamorgan | 384,633 | Cardiff |
| Gwynedd | 230,468 | Caernarfon | West Glamorgan | 367,194 | Swansea |

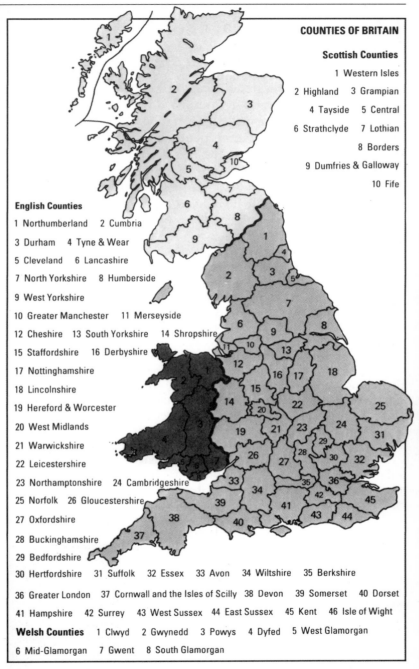

### COUNTIES OF BRITAIN

#### Scottish Counties

1 Western Isles
2 Highland   3 Grampian
4 Tayside   5 Central
6 Strathclyde   7 Lothian
8 Borders
9 Dumfries & Galloway
10 Fife

### English Counties

1 Northumberland   2 Cumbria

3 Durham   4 Tyne & Wear

5 Cleveland   6 Lancashire

7 North Yorkshire   8 Humberside

9 West Yorkshire

10 Greater Manchester   11 Merseyside

12 Cheshire   13 South Yorkshire   14 Shropshire

15 Staffordshire   16 Derbyshire

17 Nottinghamshire

18 Lincolnshire

19 Hereford & Worcester

20 West Midlands

21 Warwickshire

22 Leicestershire

23 Northamptonshire   24 Cambridgeshire

25 Norfolk   26 Gloucestershire

27 Oxfordshire

28 Buckinghamshire

29 Bedfordshire

30 Hertfordshire   31 Suffolk   32 Essex   33 Avon   34 Wiltshire   35 Berkshire

36 Greater London   37 Cornwall and the Isles of Scilly   38 Devon   39 Somerset   40 Dorset

41 Hampshire   42 Surrey   43 West Sussex   44 East Sussex   45 Kent   46 Isle of Wight

**Welsh Counties**   1 Clwyd   2 Gwynedd   3 Powys   4 Dyfed   5 West Glamorgan

6 Mid-Glamorgan   7 Gwent   8 South Glamorgan

# History

The colourful pageant of history tells of the conflicts and achievements of the human race, of bloody wars and milestones of civilization. It is studded with the names of statesmen and conquerors, explorers, inventors and artists; it also records the way ordinary people lived in times past. Records of daily life and world events have been kept since writing was invented 5,500 years ago; archaeologists search among ruins for clues to what happened before that in the two million years people have lived on Earth.

History is the story of people and what they did in the past. For most people, the life they led was very ordinary. Like the newspapers you read today, writers who chronicled the events of their time tended to write down only the outstanding events. For some periods of history, we have only the sketchiest idea of everyday life.

However, it is the important events that distinguish one period of history from another. Rulers exerted an enormous influence on their people. They could declare wars, negotiate peace settlements, exact taxes, control finances and make laws.

Some rulers have had much more influence than others. The most notorious have been the conquerors. Alexander the Great set out to conquer the whole world, as it was known in his day. From Macedonia, in Greece, he extended his empire over the Middle East, including Egypt, Persia (modern Iran), and Afghanistan as far as the Indus River valley, now in Pakistan.

Another conqueror was the French general Napoleon Bonaparte, who, at the height of his power, ruled most of Europe. Neither his career nor that of Alexander lasted long: Alexander died of fever at the age of 33; Napoleon was sent into exile at 46. By

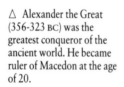

△ Alexander the Great (356-323 BC) was the greatest conqueror of the ancient world. He became ruler of Macedon at the age of 20.

▽ Lord Protector of England and brilliant military strategist, Oliver Cromwell. He died in 1658.

contrast, a third great general, George Washington, lived to be 67. He fought not to conquer but to liberate his country from colonial rule, and went on to become the first president of the United States.

The history of the whole world shows that people developed at very different times, and that great events in one part of the world were completely unknown to people living in other places. For example, while Roman soldiers were defending Hadrian's Wall in northern Britain against attacks from the Picts and Scots, across the Atlantic the Maya were beginning to build huge temple pyramids in Central America.

At the time Leif Ericsson discovered the land he called Vinland, in North America, the ancient Empire of Ghana was flourishing in West Africa, Polynesians were colonizing New Zealand, and in England the Saxon king Ethelred the Unready was paying Danish invaders large sums in gold to go away.

Human beings have lived on Earth for about two million years. The first humans appear to have lived in eastern Africa. By 100,000 years ago they had spread over most of Africa and Europe, and large parts of Asia. People migrated from Asia into North America less than 40,000 years ago, when they travelled across a huge ice sheet where the Bering Strait now is.

△ The Bayeux tapestry tells the story of the Norman conquest of England. At the battle of Hastings in 1066 William of Normandy defeated Harold Godwinsson, his rival for the English crown, and established Norman rule over England.

▽ At the battle of Austerlitz in 1805, the French emperor Napoleon won his greatest victory, defeating a combined army of Austrian and Russian troops.

△ Greek hoplites were the 'shock troops' of their day.

People were unable to record the events of their times until the invention of writing, a mere 5,500 years ago. So we have to piece together the events before that from what ancient peoples have left behind, such as their cave dwellings, or the ruins of buildings such as Stonehenge in England or the temples of Malta.

In the Chronology of World History on pages 128–148 we deal only with events within the time of written history.

Over the centuries there have been hundreds of wars and thousands of battles. Indeed, even in times of apparent peace people have been fighting somewhere in the world. These are a few of the most important conflicts.

## MAJOR WARS

| Name | Date | Won by | Against |
|------|------|--------|---------|
| Peloponnesian War | 431–404 BC | Peloponnesian League, led by Sparta, Corinth | Delian League, led by Athens |
| Punic Wars | 264–146 BC | Rome | Carthage |
| Hundred Years War | 1337–1453 | France | England |
| Wars of the Roses | 1455–1485 | House of Lancaster | House of York |
| Thirty Years War | 1618–1648 | France, Sweden, the German Protestant states | The Holy Roman Empire, Spain |
| Civil Wars, English | 1642–1651 | Parliament | Royalists |
| Spanish Succession, War of the | 1701–1713 | England, Austria, Prussia, the Netherlands | France, Bavaria, Cologne, Mantua, Savoy |
| Austrian Succession, War of the | 1740–1748 | Austria, Hungary, Britain | Bavaria, France, Poland, Prussia, Sardinia, Saxony, Spain |
| Seven Years War | 1756–1763 | Britain, Prussia, Hanover | Austria, France, Russia, Sweden |
| American War of Independence | 1775–1783 | Thirteen Colonies | Britain |
| Napoleonic Wars | 1792–1815 | Austria, Britain, Prussia, Russia, Spain, Sweden | France |
| War of 1812 | 1812–1814 | United States | Britain |
| Mexican-American War | 1846–1848 | United States | Mexico |
| Crimean War | 1853–1856 | Britain, France, Sardinia, Turkey | Russia |
| Civil War, American | 1861–1865 | 23 Northern States (The Union) | 11 Southern States (The Confederacy) |
| Franco-Prussian War | 1870–1871 | Prussia and other German states | France |
| Chinese-Japanese War | 1894–1895 | Japan | China |

| Name | Date | Won by | Against |
|---|---|---|---|
| Spanish-American War | 1898 | United States | Spain |
| Boer (South African) War | 1899–1902 | Britain | Boer Republics |
| Russo-Japanese War | 1904–1905 | Japan | Russia |
| World War I | 1914–1918 | Belgium, Britain and Empire, France, Italy, Japan, Russia, Serbia, United States | Austria-Hungary, Bulgaria, Germany, Ottoman Empire |
| Chinese-Japanese War | 1931–1933 | Japan | China |
| Abyssinian War | 1935–1936 | Italy | Abyssinia (Ethiopia) |
| Civil War, Spanish | 1936–1939 | Junta de Defensa Nacional (Fascists) | Republican government |
| Chinese-Japanese War | 1937–1945 | China | Japan |
| World War II | 1939–1945 | Australia, Belgium, Britain, Canada, China, Denmark, France, Greece, Netherlands, New Zealand, Norway, Poland, South Africa, Soviet Union, United States, Yugoslavia | Bulgaria, Finland, Germany, Hungary, Italy, Japan, Romania |
| Korean War | 1950–1953 | South Korea and United Nations forces | North Korea and Chinese forces |
| Vietnam War | 1957–1975 | North Vietnam | South Vietnam, United States |
| Six-Day War | 1967 | Israel | Egypt, Syria, Jordan, Iraq |
| Civil War, Nigerian | 1967–1970 | Federal government | Biafra |
| Civil War, Pakistani | 1971 | East Pakistan (Bangladesh) and India | West Pakistan |
| October War | 1973 | Ceasefire arranged by UN: fought by Israel against Egypt, Syria, Jordan, Iraq, Sudan, Saudi Arabia, Lebanon | |
| Gulf War | 1980–1988 | Ceasefire arranged with UN help; fought by Iraq against Iran | |

◁ Enola Gay, the USAAF B29 bomber that dropped the atomic bomb on Hiroshima on 6 August 1945. The use of atomic bombs against the cities of Hiroshima and Nagasaki forced Japan's surrender and ended World War II.

## MAJOR BATTLES

**490 BC Marathon** Force of 10,000 Athenians and allies defeated 50,000 Persian troops, crushing a Persian invasion attempt.

**AD 732 Tours** The Franks under Charles Martel defeated the Muslims, halting their advance in western Europe.

**1066 Hastings** About 8,000 troops under Duke William of Normandy defeated an equal force under Saxon king Harold II. England came under Norman rule.

**1415 Agincourt** Henry V of England with 10,000 troops defeated 30,000 Frenchmen, and recaptured Normandy.

**1453 Siege of Constantinople** Ottoman Turkish army captured the city and destroyed the Byzantine Empire. The Turks gained a foothold in Europe.

**1571 Lepanto** Allied Christian fleet of 208 galleys under Don John of Austria defeated Ali Pasha's Turkish fleet of 230 galleys; last great battle with galleys (pictured below).

**1588 Armada** Spanish invasion fleet of 130 ships was defeated by 197 English ships.

**1757 Plassey** Robert Clive with an Anglo-Indian army of 3,000 defeated the Nawab of Bengal's army of 60,000, setting Britain on the road to domination in India.

**1777 Saratoga** British troops under John Burgoyne surrendered to American colonial forces under Horatio Gates. Defeat led France to join war against Britain.

**1781 Yorktown** Charles Cornwallis with 8,000 British troops surrendered to a larger force under George Washington, ending the American War of Independence.

**1798 Nile** Horatio Nelson commanding a British fleet of 15 ships destroyed a 17-ship French fleet under Francis Paul Brueys in Aboukïr Bay, cutting off Napoleon Bonaparte's French army in Egypt.

**1805 Trafalgar** British fleet of 27 ships under Horatio Nelson shattered Franco-Spanish fleet of 33 ships, ending Napoleon's hopes of invading England.

**1805 Austerlitz** Emperor Napoleon I with 65,000 French troops defeated an 83,000-strong Austro-Russian army under the Austrian and Russian emperors.

**1813 Leipzig** Napoleon I with 190,000 French troops was surrounded and crushed by an allied force of 300,000 Austrian, Prussian, Russian and Swedish troops.

**1815 Waterloo** A British, Dutch, and Belgian force of 67,000 fought off 74,000 French troops under Napoleon I until the arrival of the Prussian army.

**1863 Gettysburg** Federal forces under George Meade defeated Robert E. Lee's Confederate army, a turning point in the American Civil War.

**1914 Marne** French and British armies halted German forces invading France.

**1916 Verdun** In a six-month struggle, French forces held off a major attack by German armies. French losses were 348,000 men, the German losses 328,000.

**1917 Passchendaele** British forces launched eight attacks over 102 days in heavy rain and through thick mud, gaining five miles and losing 400,000 men.

**1940 Britain** German air force launched an attack lasting 114 days. The smaller Royal Air Force defeated the attack.

**1942 Midway** A 100-ship Japanese fleet led by Isoruku Yamamoto aiming to capture Midway Island was defeated by American fleet half the size, under Raymond Spruance.

**1942 El Alamein** British Eighth Army under Bernard Montgomery drove German Afrika Korps under Erwin Rommel out of Egypt and deep into Libya.

**1942–3 Stalingrad** Twenty-one German divisions tried to capture Stalingrad (now Volgograd), but siege was broken and Friedrich von Paulus had to surrender with more than 100,000 German troops.

**1944 Normandy** Allied forces under Dwight D. Eisenhower invaded German-held northern France in biggest-ever sea-borne attack.

**1944–5 Ardennes Bulge** Last German counter-attack in west through Ardennes Forest failed; Germans lost 100,000 casualties and 110,000 prisoners.

△ World War II: German and Soviet troops fighting on the Eastern Front in 1941. The Germans failed to capture Moscow, and the severe Russian winter froze both men and machines.

▽ Chateau Wood devastated by gunfire during World War I. The war dragged on for four years, centred in Europe around the Western and Eastern fronts. Soldiers lived and fought in appalling conditions.

We owe our present knowledge of the world to a number of brave men – and a few women – who had the urge to explore distant lands that were unknown to them. Because people knew so little about the shape and size of the Earth, the earliest explorers needed real courage. For example, many of the Portuguese navigators trying to find a sea route to India thought the Earth was flat, and were afraid that if they ventured too far they might fall off the edge of the world.

△ Henry the Navigator (1394–1460) encouraged Portugal's seafarers.

## EXPLORATION AND DISCOVERY

| Place | Achievement | Explorer or discoverer | Date |
|---|---|---|---|
| Pacific Ocean | discovered | Vasco Núñez de Balboa (Sp.) | 1513 |
| World | circumnavigated | Ferdinand Magellan and Juan Sebastian del Cano (Port. for Sp.) | 1519–1521 |
| **Africa** | | | |
| Congo (river) | discovered | Diogo Cão (Port.) | c. 1483 |
| Cape of Good Hope | sailed round | Bartolomeu Dias (Port.) | 1488 |
| Niger (river) | explored | Mungo Park (Scot.) | 1795 |
| Zambezi (river) | discovered | David Livingstone (Scot.) | 1851 |
| Sudan | explored | Heinrich Barth (Germ. for GB) | 1852–1855 |
| Victoria Falls | discovered | Livingstone | 1855 |
| Lake Tanganyika | discovered | Richard Burton & John Speke (GB) | 1858 |
| Congo (river) | traced | Sir Henry Stanley (GB) | 1877 |
| **Asia** | | | |
| China | visited | Marco Polo (Ital.) | c. 1272 |
| India (Cape route) | visited | Vasco da Gama (Port.) | 1498 |
| Japan | visited | St Francis Xavier (Sp.) | 1549 |
| China | explored | Ferdinand Richthofen (Germ.) | 1868 |

△ Marco Polo (1254–1324) journeyed to the court of the Chinese emperor Kublai Khan at Peking (shown here on a map of 1459).

△ Robert Peary (1856–1920)

△ Hernando Cortes (1485–1547)

△ Captain James Cook (1728–1779)

**North America**

| North America | discovered | Leif Ericsson (Norse) | c.1000 |
|---|---|---|---|
| West Indies | discovered | Christopher Columbus (Ital. for Sp.) | 1492 |
| Newfoundland | discovered | John Cabot (Ital. for Eng.) | 1497 |
| Mexico | conquered | Hernando Cortés (Sp.) | 1519–1521 |
| St Lawrence (river) | explored | Jacques Cartier (Fr.) | 1534–1536 |
| Mississippi (river) | discovered | Hernando de Soto (Sp.) | 1541 |
| Canadian interior | explored | Samuel de Champlain (Fr.) | 1603–1609 |
| Hudson Bay | discovered | Henry Hudson (Eng.) | 1610 |
| Alaska | discovered | Vitus Bering (Dan. for Russ.) | 1728 |
| Mackenzie (river) | discovered | Sir Alexander Mackenzie (Scot.) | 1789 |

**South America**

| South America | visited | Columbus | 1498 |
|---|---|---|---|
| Venezuela | explored | Alonso de Ojeda (Sp.) | 1499 |
| Brazil | discovered | Pedro Alvares Cabral (Port.) | 1500 |
| Río de la Plata | discovered | Juan de Solis (Sp.) | 1516 |
| Tierra del Fuego | discovered | Magellan | 1520 |
| Peru | conquered | Francisco Pizarro (Sp.) | 1532–1538 |
| Amazon (river) | explored | Francisco de Orellana (Sp.) | 1541 |
| Cape Horn | discovered | Willem Schouten (Dut.) | 1616 |

**Australasia, Polar regions, etc.**

| Greenland | visited | Eric the Red (Norse) | c.986 |
|---|---|---|---|
| Australia | discovered | unknown | 1500s |
| Spitsbergen | discovered | Willem Barents (Dut.) | 1596 |
| Australia | visited | Abel Tasman (Dut.) | 1642 |
| New Zealand | sighted | Tasman | 1642 |
| New Zealand | visited | James Cook (Eng.) | 1769 |
| Antarctic Circle | crossed | Cook | 1773 |
| Antarctica | sighted | Nathaniel Palmer (US) | 1820 |
| Antarctica | circumnavigated | Fabian von Bellingshausen (Russ.) | 1819–1821 |
| Australian interior | explored | Charles Sturt (GB) | 1828 |
| Antarctica | explored | Charles Wilkes (US) | 1838–1842 |
| Australia | crossed (S–N) | Robert Burke (Ir.) & William Wills (Eng.) | 1860–1861 |
| Greenland | explored | Fridtjof Nansen (Nor.) | 1888 |
| Arctic | explored | Abruzzi, Duke of the (Ital.) | 1900 |
| North Pole | reached | Robert Peary (US) | 1909 |
| South Pole | reached | Roald Amundsen (Nor.) | 1911 |
| Antarctica | crossed | Sir Vivian Fuchs (Eng.) | 1957–1958 |

The president of the United States is one of the most powerful people in the world. Not only is he the country's head of state, but he is also the chief executive, whose duty is to make sure the law of the land is carried out, and the commander-in-chief of the armed forces. Forty-one men have held this office since the first, George Washington, took the oath in 1789.

△ George Washington (1732–99)

## AMERICAN PRESIDENTS

| President (party) | Term |
|---|---|
| 1 George Washington (F) | 1789–1797 |
| 2 John Adams (F) | 1797–1801 |
| 3 Thomas Jefferson (DR) | 1801–1809 |
| 4 James Madison (DR) | 1809–1817 |
| 5 James Monroe (DR) | 1817–1825 |
| 6 John Quincy Adams (DR) | 1825–1829 |
| 7 Andrew Jackson (D) | 1829–1837 |
| 8 Martin Van Buren (D) | 1837–1841 |
| 9 William H. Harrison* (W) | 1841 |
| 10 John Tyler (W) | 1841–1845 |
| 11 James K. Polk (D) | 1845–1849 |
| 12 Zachary Taylor* (W) | 1849–1850 |
| 13 Millard Fillmore (W) | 1850–1853 |
| 14 Franklin Pierce (D) | 1853–1857 |
| 15 James Buchanan (D) | 1857–1861 |
| 16 Abraham Lincoln† (R) | 1861–1865 |
| 17 Andrew Johnson (U) | 1865–1869 |
| 18 Ulysses S. Grant (R) | 1869–1877 |
| 19 Rutherford B. Hayes (R) | 1877–1881 |
| 20 James A. Garfield† (R) | 1881 |
| 21 Chester A. Arthur (R) | 1881–1885 |
| 22 Grover Cleveland (D) | 1885–1889 |
| 23 Benjamin Harrison (R) | 1889–1893 |
| 24 Grover Cleveland (D) | 1893–1897 |
| 25 William McKinley† (R) | 1897–1901 |
| 26 Theodore Roosevelt (R) | 1901–1909 |
| 27 William H. Taft (R) | 1909–1913 |
| 28 Woodrow Wilson (D) | 1913–1921 |
| 29 Warren G. Harding* (R) | 1921–1923 |
| 30 Calvin Coolidge (R) | 1923–1929 |
| 31 Herbert C. Hoover (R) | 1929–1933 |
| 32 Franklin D. Roosevelt* (D) | 1933–1945 |
| 33 Harry S. Truman (D) | 1945–1953 |
| 34 Dwight D. Eisenhower (R) | 1953–1961 |
| 35 John F. Kennedy† (D) | 1961–1963 |
| 36 Lyndon B. Johnson (D) | 1963–1969 |
| 37 Richard M. Nixon (R) | 1969–1974 |
| 38 Gerald R. Ford (R) | 1974–1977 |
| 39 James E. Carter (D) | 1977–1981 |
| 40 Ronald Reagan (R) | 1981–1989 |
| 41 George H. W. Bush (R) | 1989– |

◁ Thomas Jefferson (1743–1826)

▽ US President F.D. Roosevelt with Winston Churchill and Joseph Stalin.

△ Ronald Reagan was succeeded as US President by his two-term Vice-President, George Bush.

*Died in office.  †Assassinated in office.
F = Federalist. DR = Democratic-Republican.
D = Democratic. W = Whig. R = Republican. U = Union.

Past rulers of Britain held immense power, and were effectively dictators. After the Civil Wars of 1642–1651 they lost much of their power, and the rest was removed during the next hundred years.

However, although the present Queen's duties are largely ceremonial, as head of state, the government of the country is carried on in her name. The monarch provides continuity, no matter which political party is in power.

△ Henry VIII, by Holbein.

## BRITISH RULERS
### Rulers of England

**Saxons**

| | |
|---|---|
| Egbert | 827–839 |
| Ethelwulf | 839–858 |
| Ethelbald | 858–860 |
| Ethelbert | 860–866 |
| Ethelred I | 866–871 |
| Alfred the Great | 871–899 |
| Edward the Elder | 899–924 |
| Athelstan | 924–939 |
| Edmund | 939–946 |
| Edred | 946–955 |
| Edwy | 955–959 |
| Edgar | 959–975 |
| Edward the Martyr | 975–978 |
| Ethelred II the Unready | 978–1016 |
| Edmund Ironside | 1016 |

**Danes**

| | |
|---|---|
| Canute | 1016–1035 |
| Harold I Harefoot | 1035–1040 |
| Hardicanute | 1040–1042 |

**Saxons**

| | |
|---|---|
| Edward the Confessor | 1042–1066 |
| Harold II | 1066 |

**House of Normandy**

| | |
|---|---|
| William I the Conqueror | 1066–1087 |
| William II | 1087–1100 |
| Henry I | 1100–1135 |
| Stephen | 1135–1154 |

**House of Plantagenet**

| | |
|---|---|
| Henry II | 1154–1189 |
| Richard I | 1189–1199 |
| John | 1199–1216 |
| Henry III | 1216–1272 |
| Edward I | 1272–1307 |
| Edward II | 1307–1327 |
| Edward III | 1327–1377 |
| Richard II | 1377–1399 |

**House of Lancaster**

| | |
|---|---|
| Henry IV | 1399–1413 |
| Henry V | 1413–1422 |
| Henry VI | 1422–1461 |

**House of York**

| | |
|---|---|
| Edward IV | 1461–1483 |
| Edward V | 1483 |
| Richard III | 1483–1485 |

**House of Tudor**

| | |
|---|---|
| Henry VII | 1485–1509 |
| Henry VIII | 1509–1547 |
| Edward VI | 1547–1553 |
| Jane | 1553 |
| Mary I | 1553–1558 |
| Elizabeth I | 1558–1603 |

### Rulers of Scotland

| | |
|---|---|
| Malcolm II | 1005–1034 |
| Duncan I | 1034–1040 |
| Macbeth (usurper) | 1040–1057 |
| Malcolm III Canmore | 1057–1093 |
| Donald Bane | 1093–1094 |
| Duncan II | 1094 |
| Donald Bane (restored) | 1094–1097 |
| Edgar | 1097–1107 |
| Alexander I | 1107–1124 |
| David I | 1124–1153 |
| Malcolm IV | 1153–1165 |
| William the Lion | 1165–1214 |
| Alexander II | 1214–1249 |
| Alexander III | 1249–1286 |
| Margaret of Norway | 1286–1290 |
| (*Interregnum* 1290–1292) | |
| John Balliol | 1292–1296 |
| (*Interregnum* 1296–1306) | |
| Robert I (Bruce) | 1306–1329 |
| David II | 1329–1371 |

| House of Stuart | |
|---|---|
| Robert II | 1371–1390 |
| Robert III | 1390–1406 |
| James I | 1406–1437 |
| James II | 1437–1460 |
| James III | 1460–1488 |
| James IV | 1488–1513 |
| James V | 1513–1542 |
| Mary | 1542–1567 |
| James VI* | 1567–1625 |

*Became James I of Great Britain in 1603.

### Rulers of Great Britain

| House of Stuart | |
|---|---|
| James I | 1603–1625 |
| Charles I | 1625–1649 |
| (*Commonwealth* 1649–1659) | |

| House of Stuart (restored) | |
|---|---|
| Charles II | 1660–1685 |
| James II | 1685–1688 |
| William III } jointly | 1689–1702 |
| Mary II } | 1689–1694 |
| Anne | 1702–1714 |

| House of Hanover | |
|---|---|
| George I | 1714–1727 |
| George II | 1727–1760 |
| George III | 1760–1820 |
| George IV | 1820–1830 |
| William IV | 1830–1837 |
| Victoria | 1837–1901 |

| House of Saxe-Coburg | |
|---|---|
| Edward VII | 1901–1910 |

| House of Windsor | |
|---|---|
| George V | 1910–1936 |
| Edward VIII | 1936 |
| George VI | 1936–1952 |
| Elizabeth II | 1952– |

## BRITISH PRIME MINISTERS

| Prime Minister (party) | Term |
|---|---|
| Sir Robert Walpole (W) | 1721–42 |
| Earl of Wilmington (W) | 1742–43 |
| Henry Pelham (W) | 1743–54 |
| Duke of Newcastle (W) | 1754–56 |
| Duke of Devonshire (W) | 1756–67 |
| Duke of Newcastle (W) | 1757–62 |
| Earl of Bute (T) | 1762–63 |
| George Grenville (W) | 1763–65 |
| Marquess of Rockingham (W) | 1765–66 |
| Earl of Chatham (W) | 1766–67 |
| Duke of Grafton (W) | 1767–70 |
| Lord North (T) | 1770–82 |
| Marquess of Rockingham (W) | 1782 |
| Earl of Shelburne (W) | 1782–83 |
| Duke of Portland (Cln) | 1783 |
| William Pitt (T) | 1783–1801 |
| Henry Addington (T) | 1801–04 |
| William Pitt (T) | 1804–06 |
| Lord Grenville (W) | 1806–07 |
| Duke of Portland (T) | 1807–09 |
| Spencer Perceval (T)* | 1809–12 |
| Earl of Liverpool (T) | 1812–27 |
| George Canning (T) | 1827 |
| Viscount Goderich (T) | 1827–28 |
| Duke of Wellington (T) | 1828–30 |

▽ William Ewart Gladstone (1809–98), four times British prime minister.

◁ The head of Queen Victoria was shown on Britain's first postage stamp, the 'penny black' of 1840. The young queen was to become Britain's longest-reigning monarch.

| Prime Minister (party) | Term | Prime Minister (party) | Term |
|---|---|---|---|
| Earl Grey (W) | 1830–34 | Herbert Asquith (L) | 1908–15 |
| Viscount Melbourne (W) | 1834 | Herbert Asquith (Cln) | 1915–16 |
| Sir Robert Peel (T) | 1834–35 | David Lloyd-George (Cln) | 1916–22 |
| Viscount Melbourne (W) | 1835–41 | Andrew Bonar Law (C) | 1922–23 |
| Sir Robert Peel (T) | 1841–46 | Stanley Baldwin (C) | 1923–24 |
| Lord John Russell (W) | 1846–52 | James Ramsay MacDonald (Lab) | 1924 |
| Earl of Derby (T) | 1852 | Stanley Baldwin (C) | 1924–29 |
| Earl of Aberdeen (P) | 1852–55 | James Ramsay MacDonald (Lab) | 1929–31 |
| Viscount Palmerston (L) | 1855–58 | James Ramsay MacDonald (Cln) | 1931–35 |
| Earl of Derby (C) | 1858–59 | Stanley Baldwin (Cln) | 1935–37 |
| Viscount Palmerston (L) | 1859–65 | Neville Chamberlain (Cln) | 1937–40 |
| Earl Russell (L) | 1865–66 | Winston Churchill (Cln) | 1940–45 |
| Earl of Derby (C) | 1866–68 | Winston Churchill (C) | 1945 |
| Benjamin Disraeli (C) | 1868 | Clement Atlee (Lab) | 1945–51 |
| William Gladstone (L) | 1868–74 | Sir Winston Churchill (C) | 1951–55 |
| Benjamin Disraeli (C) | 1874–80 | Sir Anthony Eden (C) | 1955–57 |
| William Gladstone (L) | 1880–85 | Harold Macmillan (C) | 1957–63 |
| Marquess of Salisbury (C) | 1885–86 | Sir Alec Douglas-Home (C) | 1963–64 |
| William Gladstone (L) | 1886 | Harold Wilson (Lab) | 1964–70 |
| Marquess of Salisbury (C) | 1886–92 | Edward Heath (C) | 1970–74 |
| William Gladstone (L) | 1892–94 | Harold Wilson (Lab) | 1974–76 |
| Earl of Rosebery (L) | 1894–95 | James Callaghan (Lab) | 1976–79 |
| Marquess of Salisbury (C) | 1895–1902 | Margaret Thatcher (C) | 1979– |
| Arthur Balfour (C) | 1902–05 | | |
| Sir Henry | | *Assassinated | |
| Campbell-Bannerman (L) | 1905–08 | W = Whig. T = Tory. Cln = Coalition. P = Peelite. | |
| | | L = Liberal. C = Conservative. Lab. = Labour | |

△ Benjamin Disraeli, later Earl of Beaconsfield (1804–81). As prime minister, Disraeli enjoyed the favour of Queen Victoria (who intensely disliked his rival, Gladstone). The flamboyant Disraeli gave the Queen a new interest in Britain's growing Empire.

▽ Margaret Thatcher, Britain's first woman prime minister and the longest-serving premier the country has had this century.

The pope is the head of the Roman Catholic Church, and is purely the religious leader of just one religious group. But in the past the pope was the leader of the only Christian Church. The Eastern Orthodox Church broke away in 1054, and the Reformation, beginning in the 1500s, limited the power of the pope still more. But the pope remained an important political figure in Europe until the late 1800s, and even ruled parts of Italy directly.

△ Pope John Paul II.

### POPES

List of popes and their dates of accession. Antipopes and doubtful popes are not included.

| | | | | | | |
|---|---|---|---|---|---|---|
| St Peter | 42 | St Anastasius I | 399 | St Vitalian | 657 |
| St Linus | 67 | St Innocent I | 401 | Adeodatus II | 672 |
| St. Anacletus (Cletus) | 76 | St Zosimus | 417 | Donus | 676 |
| St Clement I | 88 | St Boniface I | 418 | St Agatho | 678 |
| St Evaristus | 97 | St Celestine I | 422 | St Leo II | 682 |
| St Alexander I | 105 | St Sixtus III | 432 | St Benedict II | 684 |
| St Sixtus I | 115 | St Leo I (the Great) | 440 | John V | 685 |
| St Telesphorus | 125 | St Hilary | 461 | Conon | 686 |
| St Hyginus | 136 | St Simplicius | 468 | St Sergius I | 687 |
| St Pius I | 140 | St Felix III | 483 | John VI | 701 |
| St Anicetus | 155 | St Gelasius I | 492 | John VII | 705 |
| St Soterus | 166 | Anastasius II | 496 | Sisinnius | 708 |
| St Eleutherius | 175 | St Symmachus | 498 | Constantine | 708 |
| St Victor I | 189 | St Hormisdas | 514 | St Gregory II | 715 |
| St Zephyrinus | 199 | St John I | 523 | St Gregory III | 731 |
| St Callistus I | 217 | St Felix IV | 526 | St Zachary | 741 |
| St Urban I | 222 | Boniface II | 530 | Stephen II (III)* | 752 |
| St Pontian | 230 | John II | 533 | St Paul I | 757 |
| St Anterus | 235 | St Agapetus I | 535 | Stephen III (IV) | 768 |
| St Fabian | 236 | St Silverius | 536 | Adrian I | 772 |
| St Cornelius | 251 | Vigilius | 537 | St Leo III | 795 |
| St Lucius I | 253 | Pelagius I | 556 | Stephen IV (V) | 816 |
| St Stephen I | 254 | John III | 561 | St Paschal I | 817 |
| St Sixtus II | 257 | Benedict I | 575 | Eugene II | 824 |
| St Dionysius | 259 | Pelagius II | 579 | Valentine | 827 |
| St Felix I | 269 | St Gregory I (the Great) | 590 | Gregory IV | 827 |
| St Eutychian | 275 | Sabinianus | 604 | Sergius II | 844 |
| St Caius | 283 | Boniface III | 607 | St Leo IV | 847 |
| St Marcellinus | 296 | St Boniface IV | 608 | Benedict III | 855 |
| St Marcellus I | 308 | St Deusdedit | 615 | St Nicholas I | 858 |
| St Eusebius | 309 | (Adeodatus I) | | Adrian II | 867 |
| St Melchiades | 311 | Boniface V | 619 | John VIII | 872 |
| St Sylvester I | 314 | Honorius I | 625 | Marinus I | 882 |
| St Marcus | 336 | Severinus | 640 | St Adrian III | 884 |
| St Julius I | 337 | John IV | 640 | Stephen V (VI) | 885 |
| Liberius | 352 | Theodore I | 642 | Formosus | 891 |
| St Damasus I | 366 | St Martin I | 649 | Boniface VI | 896 |
| St Siricius | 384 | St Eugene I | 654 | Stephen VI (VII) | 896 |

| | | | | | |
|---|---|---|---|---|---|
| Romanus | 897 | Lucius III | 1181 | Gregory XIII | 1572 |
| Theodore II | 897 | Urban III | 1185 | Sixtus V | 1585 |
| John IX | 898 | Gregory VIII | 1187 | Urban VII | 1590 |
| Benedict IV | 900 | Clement III | 1187 | Gregory XIV | 1590 |
| Leo V | 903 | Celestine III | 1191 | Innocent IX | 1591 |
| Sergius III | 904 | Innocent III | 1198 | Clement VIII | 1592 |
| Anastasius III | 911 | Honorius III | 1216 | Leo XI | 1605 |
| Landus | 913 | Gregory IX | 1227 | Paul V | 1605 |
| John X | 914 | Celestine IV | 1241 | Gregory XV | 1621 |
| Leo VI | 928 | Innocent IV | 1243 | Urban VIII | 1623 |
| Stephen VII (VIII) | 928 | Alexander IV | 1254 | Innocent X | 1644 |
| John XI | 931 | Urban IV | 1261 | Alexander VII | 1655 |
| Leo VII | 936 | Clement IV | 1265 | Clement IX | 1667 |
| Stephen VIII (IX) | 939 | Gregory X | 1271 | Clement X | 1670 |
| Marinus II | 942 | Innocent V | 1276 | Innocent XI | 1676 |
| Agapetus II | 946 | Adrian V | 1276 | Alexander VIII | 1689 |
| John XII | 955 | John XXI | 1276 | Innocent XII | 1691 |
| Leo VIII | 963 | Nicholas III | 1277 | Clement XI | 1700 |
| Benedict V | 964 | Martin IV | 1281 | Innocent XIII | 1721 |
| John XIII | 965 | Honorius IV | 1285 | Benedict XIII | 1724 |
| Benedict VI | 973 | Nicholas IV | 1288 | Clement XII | 1730 |
| Benedict VII | 974 | St Celestine V | 1294 | Benedict XIV | 1740 |
| John XIV | 983 | Boniface VIII | 1294 | Clement XIII | 1758 |
| John XV | 985 | Benedict XI | 1303 | Clement XIV | 1769 |
| Gregory V | 996 | Clement V | 1305 | Pius VI | 1775 |
| Sylvester II | 999 | John XXII | 1316 | Pius VII | 1800 |
| John XVII | 1003 | Benedict XII | 1334 | Leo XII | 1823 |
| John XVIII | 1004 | Clement VI | 1342 | Pius VIII | 1829 |
| Sergius IV | 1009 | Innocent VI | 1352 | Gregory XVI | 1831 |
| Benedict VIII | 1012 | Urban V | 1362 | Pius IX | 1846 |
| John XIX | 1024 | Gregory XI | 1370 | Leo XIII | 1878 |
| Benedict IX | 1032 | Urban VI | 1378 | St Pius X | 1903 |
| Gregory VI | 1045 | Boniface IX | 1389 | Benedict XV | 1914 |
| Clement II | 1046 | Innocent VII | 1404 | Pius XI | 1922 |
| Benedict IX† | 1047 | Gregory XII | 1406 | Pius XII | 1939 |
| Damasus II | 1048 | Martin V | 1417 | John XXIII | 1958 |
| St Leo IX | 1049 | Eugene IV | 1431 | Paul VI | 1963 |
| Victor II | 1055 | Nicholas V | 1447 | John Paul I** | 1978 |
| Stephen IX (X) | 1057 | Callistus III | 1455 | John Paul II | 1978 |
| Nicholas II | 1059 | Pius II | 1458 | | |
| Alexander II | 1061 | Paul II | 1464 | | |
| St Gregory VII | 1073 | Sixtus IV | 1471 | | |
| Victor III | 1086 | Innocent VIII | 1484 | | |
| Urban II | 1088 | Alexander VI | 1492 | *The original Stephen II died | |
| Paschal II | 1099 | Pius III | 1503 | before consecration, and was | |
| Gelasius II | 1118 | Julius II | 1503 | dropped from the list of popes in | |
| Callistus II | 1119 | Leo X | 1513 | 1961; Stephen III became Stephen | |
| Honorius II | 1124 | Adrian VI | 1522 | II and the numbers of the other | |
| Innocent II | 1130 | Clement VII | 1523 | popes named Stephen were also | |
| Celestine II | 1143 | Paul III | 1534 | moved up. | |
| Lucius II | 1144 | Julius III | 1550 | †Benedict IX was driven from office | |
| Eugene III | 1145 | Marcellus II | 1555 | for scandalous conduct; but | |
| Anastasius IV | 1153 | Paul IV | 1555 | returned briefly in 1047. | |
| Adrian IV | 1154 | Pius IV | 1559 | **John Paul I died after only 33 | |
| Alexander III | 1159 | St Pius V | 1566 | days as Pontiff. | |

124

The British Queen is head of state of a number of Commonwealth countries besides the United Kingdom. She is represented in them by governors-general, who act as heads of state except when the Queen visits those countries.

▽ Jawaharlal Nehru (1889–1964) led India to independence from Britain in 1947, and became the country's first prime minister.

## CANADIAN PRIME MINISTERS

| | |
|---|---|
| Sir John MacDonald | 1867–1873 |
| Alexander Mackenzie | 1873–1878 |
| Sir John MacDonald | 1878–1891 |
| Sir John Abbott | 1891–1892 |
| Sir John Thompson | 1892–1894 |
| Sir Mackenzie Bowell | 1894–1896 |
| Sir Charles Tupper | 1896 |
| Sir Wilfred Laurier | 1896–1911 |
| Sir Robert L. Borden | 1911–1920 |
| Arthur Meighen | 1920–1921 |
| W. L. Mackenzie King | 1921–1930 |
| R. B. Bennett | 1930–1935 |
| W. L. Mackenzie King | 1935–1948 |
| Louis St Laurent | 1948–1957 |
| John G. Diefenbaker | 1957–1963 |
| Lester B. Pearson | 1963–1968 |
| Pierre Elliott Trudeau (below) | 1968–1979 |
| Joe Clark | 1979–1980 |
| Pierre Elliott Trudeau | 1980–1984 |
| John Turner | 1984 |
| Brian Mulroney | 1984– |

▽ Pierre Trudeau, twice prime minister of Canada.

## INDIAN PRIME MINISTERS

| | |
|---|---|
| Jawaharlal Nehru | 1950–1964 |
| Lal Bahadur Shastri | 1964–1966 |
| Indira Gandhi | 1966–1977 |
| Morarji Desai | 1977–1979 |
| Indira Gandhi | 1979–1984 |
| Rajiv Gandhi | 1984– |

## AUSTRALIAN PRIME MINISTERS

| | |
|---|---|
| Edmund Barton | 1901–1903 |
| Alfred Deakin | 1903–1904 |
| John C. Watson | 1904 |
| George Houston Reid | 1904–1905 |
| Alfred Deakin | 1905–1908 |
| Andrew Fisher | 1908–1909 |
| Alfred Deakin | 1909–1910 |
| Andrew Fisher | 1910–1913 |
| Joseph Cook | 1913–1914 |
| Andrew Fisher | 1914–1915 |
| William M. Hughes | 1915–1923 |
| Stanley M. Bruce | 1923–1929 |
| James H. Scullin | 1929–1931 |
| Joseph A. Lyons | 1932–1939 |
| Robert Gordon Menzies | 1939–1941 |
| Arthur William Fadden | 1941 |
| John Curtin | 1941–1945 |
| Joseph Benedict Chifley | 1945–1949 |
| Robert Gordon Menzies | 1949–1966 |
| Harold Edward Holt | 1966–1967 |
| John Grey Gorton | 1968–1971 |
| William McMahon | 1971–1972 |
| Edward Gough Whitlam | 1972–1975 |
| John Malcolm Fraser | 1975–1983 |
| Robert James Hawke | 1983– |

## PRIME MINISTERS OF NEW ZEALAND

| | | | |
|---|---|---|---|
| Henry Sewell | 1856 | Harry Albert Atkinson | 1887–1891 |
| William Fox | 1856 | John Ballance | 1891–1893 |
| Edward William Stafford | 1856–1861 | Richard John Seddon | 1893–1906 |
| William Fox | 1861–1862 | William Hall-Jones | 1906 |
| Alfred Domett | 1862–1863 | Joseph George Ward | 1906–1912 |
| Frederick Whittaker | 1863–1864 | Thomas Mackenzie | 1912 |
| Frederick Aloysius Weld | 1864–1865 | William Ferguson Massey | 1912–1925 |
| Edward William Stafford | 1865–1869 | Francis Henry Dillon Bell | 1925 |
| William Fox | 1869–1872 | Joseph Gordon Coates | 1925–1928 |
| Edward William Stafford | 1872 | Joseph George Ward | 1928–1930 |
| George Marsden Waterhouse | 1872–1873 | George William Forbes | 1930–1935 |
| William Fox | 1873 | Michael J. Savage | 1935–1940 |
| Julius Vogel | 1873–1875 | Peter Fraser | 1940–1949 |
| Daniel Pollen | 1875–1876 | Sidney J. Holland | 1949–1957 |
| Julius Vogel | 1876 | Keith J. Holyoake | 1957 |
| Harry Albert Atkinson | 1876–1877 | Walter Nash | 1957–1960 |
| George Grey | 1877–1879 | Keith J. Holyoake | 1960–1972 |
| John Hall | 1879–1882 | Sir John Marshall | 1972 |
| Frederick Whitaker | 1882–1883 | Norman Kirk | 1972–1974 |
| Harry Albert Atkinson | 1883–1884 | Wallace Rowling | 1974–1975 |
| Robert Stout | 1884 | Robert Muldoon | 1975–1984 |
| Harry Albert Atkinson | 1884 | David Lange | 1984– |
| Robert Stout | 1884–1887 | | |

Assassination is the murder of a political leader or any other public figure. These killings are carried out for revenge, to remove a tyrant or a political opponent, or sometimes for financial gain. The word 'assassin' orginally meant an eater of hashish (a drug). A group of such drug-takers carried out many murders in Persia in the 1100s.

Assassinations have been a tragic feature all through history. One, the murder of Archduke Franz Ferdinand of Austria in 1914, sparked off World War I. Four US presidents – Lincoln, Garfield, McKinley and Kennedy – have been assassinated, and so has one British prime minister, Spencer Perceval.

Perhaps the three most famous people to have been assassinated since the end of World War II are President Kennedy of the USA, because his attacker bore a political grudge against him; Rev. Martin Luther King Jr., Black civil rights leader, by a white escaped convict; and songwriter and former Beatle, John Lennon, by a young man who was mentally ill.

△ President Anwar El Sadat of Egypt worked for a peace treaty with Israel. He was assassinated in 1981.

# HISTORIC ASSASSINATIONS

| Victim | Details of assassination | Date |
|--------|--------------------------|------|
| Philip II, king of Macedonia | Pausanias, young noble with a grudge | 336 BC |
| Julius Caesar, Roman dictator | Stabbed by Brutus, Cassius and others | 44 BC |
| St Thomas à Becket, English archbishop | Slain by four knights in cathedral | 1170 |
| James I of Scotland | Plot: Sir Robert Graham | 1437 |
| David Beaton, Scottish chancellor/ cardinal | Band of Protestant nobles in St Andrews Castle | 1546 |
| Lord Darnley, husband of Mary Queen of Scots | Blown up; plot | 1567 |
| William the Silent, Prince of Orange | Shot by Balthasar Gérard | 1584 |
| Henry III of France | Stabbed by fanatic monk (Jacques Clément) | 1589 |
| Henry IV of France (de Navarre) | Stabbed by fanatic (François Ravaillac) | 1610 |
| Gustavus III of Sweden | Plot: shot by Johan Ankarström | 1792 |
| Jean Marat, French revolutionary | Stabbed in bath by Charlotte Corday | 1793 |
| Spencer Perceval, British prime minister | Shot by bankrupt broker John Bellingham | 1812 |
| Abraham Lincoln, US president | Shot by actor, J. Wilkes Booth, in theatre | 1865 |
| Alexander II, emperor of Russia | Nihilist bomb | 1881 |
| James Garfield, US president | Shot at station by Charles Guiteau (grudge) | 1881 |
| Sadi Carnot, French president | Stabbed by anarchist | 1894 |
| Elizabeth, empress of Austria | By Italian anarchist at Geneva | 1898 |
| Humbert I, king of Italy | By anarchist at Monza | 1900 |
| William McKinley, US president | Shot by anarchist, Leon Czolgosz, at Buffalo | 1901 |
| Francis Ferdinand, archduke of Austria | Alleged Serbian plot: shot in car by Gavrilo Princip at Sarajevo (sparked World War I) | 1914 |
| Rasputin, powerful Russian monk | By Russian noblemen | 1916 |
| Michael Collins, Irish Sinn Fein leader | Ambushed and shot | 1922 |
| 'Pancho' Villa, former Mexican bandit/ rebel | Ambushed in car | 1923 |
| Paul Doumer, French president | Shot by mad Russian émigré, Paul Gorgoulov | 1932 |
| Engelbert Dollfuss, Austrian chancellor | Shot by Nazis in chancellery | 1934 |
| Alexander I of Yugoslavia Jean Louis Barthou, French foreign minister | By Macedonian terrorist at Marseille | 1934 |
| Leon Trotsky, exiled Russian communist leader | Axed in Mexico by Ramón Mercader | 1940 |
| Mahatma Gandhi, Indian nationalist leader | Shot by Hindu fanatic, Nathuran Godse | 1948 |
| Abdullah ibn Hussein, king of Jordan | In Jerusalem mosque | 1951 |
| Liaquat Ali Khan, Pakistani premier | By fanatics at Rawalpindi | 1951 |
| Anastasio Somoza, Nicaraguan president | Shot by Rigoberto López Pérez, in León | 1956 |
| Carlos Castillo Armas, Guatemalan president | By one of own guards | 1957 |
| Faisal II of Iraq | Military coup in Baghdad | 1958 |
| S.W.R.D. Bandaranaike, Ceylonese premier | By Buddhist monk in Colombo | 1959 |
| Rafael Trujillo Molina, Dominican Republic dictator | Car machine-gunned | 1961 |
| Ngo Dinh Diem, S. Vietnamese president | By generals in coup | 1963 |
| John F. Kennedy, US president | Shot in car, in Dallas, Texas* | 1963 |
| Malcolm X (Little), US Black Muslim leader | Shot at rally | 1965 |
| Hendrik Verwoerd, South African premier | Stabbed by parliamentary messenger, Dimitri Tsafendas (later ruled mentally disordered) | 1966 |
| Rev. Martin Luther King Jr., US Black civil rights leader | Shot on hotel balcony by James Earl Ray, in Memphis, Tennessee | 1968 |

△ Thomas à Becket is murdered by Henry II's knights.

△ Robert Kennedy, brother of murdered President J.F. Kennedy, was himself assassinated in a Los Angeles hotel in 1968.

◁ Mahatma Gandhi led a non-violent campaign to free India from British rule. He was assassinated by a Hindu fanatic shortly after India's independence.

| | | |
|---|---|---|
| Robert F. Kennedy, US senator | Shot by Arab immigrant, Sirhan Sirhan | 1968 |
| Luis Carrero Blanco, Spanish premier | Explosion under car; Basque terrorists (ETA) | 1973 |
| King Faisal of Saudi Arabia | Shot by nephew Prince Faisal ibn Musad | 1975 |
| Christopher Ewart-Biggs, British ambassador to Republic of Ireland | Car blown up by landmine planted by IRA | 1976 |
| Aldo Moro, five times prime minister of Italy | Kidnapped by 'Red Brigade' terrorists and later found dead | 1978 |
| Sir Richard Sykes, British ambassador in The Hague | Shot by IRA | 1979 |
| Airey Neave, British Conservative MP | Car bomb at House of Commons; IRA | 1979 |
| Earl Mountbatten of Burma, uncle of Queen Elizabeth II | Explosion in sailing boat off coast of Ireland; IRA | 1979 |
| Anastasio Somoza Debayle, president of Nicaragua | Shot by revolutionaries during Sandinista coup | 1980 |
| John Lennon, musician/songwriter and ex-Beatle | Shot in street in New York by Mark David Chapman | 1980 |
| William R. Tolbert, president of Liberia | Executed by army during coup | 1980 |
| Ziaur Rahman, president of Bangladesh | Shot by army officers during abortive military take over | 1981 |
| Anwar El Sadat, president of Egypt | Shot by rebel soldiers | 1981 |
| Benigno Aquino, Philippine opposition leader | Shot at airport on return from voluntary exile | 1983 |
| Mrs Indira Gandhi, prime minister of India | Shot by her Sikh bodyguards | 1984 |
| Olaf Palme, Swedish prime minister | Shot in street while walking home | 1986 |

*Accused, Lee Harvey Oswald, himself shot by Jack Ruby while awaiting trial.

# CHRONOLOGY OF WORLD HISTORY

BC

**c.3500** Sumerians develop flourishing civilization along Euphrates river.

**c.3400** Upper and Lower Egypt united to form one nation.

**c.2100** Abraham migrates from Ur.

**c.2000** Bronze Age begins in northern Europe.

**c.1750** Hammurabi of Bablyon draws up first known legal code.

**1500s** Shang Dynasty of China founded.

**1570** Hyksos invaders of Egypt defeated.

**1450** Minoan civilization flourishes in Crete: begins to decline soon after.

**1410** Reign of Amenhotep III of Egypt: golden age of nation at height.

**1400** Beginning of Iron Age in India and Asia Minor (Turkey).

**1358** Tutankhamen becomes pharaoh of Egypt: restores old religion destroyed by his predecessor Akhenaton.

**1292–1225** Rameses II pharaoh of Egypt; Abu Simbel temple built.

**1230–1200** Israelites leave Egypt and make their way to Canaan (Palestine).

**c.1100** Assyrian empire founded in Mesopotamia.

**c.1020** Saul becomes first king of Israel.

**c.1000** Chou dynasty founded in China.

**1000–961** David king of Israel.

**922** Death of David's son Solomon: kingdom divided into Judah and Israel.

**800s** Homer composes the *Iliad* and the *Odyssey* in ancient Greece.

**814** Phoenicians found Carthage.

**776** Earliest known Olympic Games

**753** Traditional date of founding of Rome

**722** Assyrians conquer Israel.

**689** Assyrians capture and destroy Babylon.

**670** Assyrians ravage Egypt; destruction of Thebes and Memphis.

**626** Nabopolassar liberates Babylon from Assyrian rule and becomes king.

**612** Babylonians, Medes, and Scythians overthrow Assyrian empire, destroying capital, Nineveh.

**586** Nebuchadnezzar of Babylon seizes Jerusalem and takes people of Judah into captivity.

**563** Siddhartha Gautama, later the Buddha, born at Lumbini, Nepal.

**550–530** Reign of Cyrus the Great, founder of Persian empire.

**551** Birth of K'ung Fu-tzu – Confucius, Chinese philosopher.

**539** Jews allowed to return to Jerusalem; rebuilding of city begins.

**535–404** Persians rule Egypt.

**510** Last king of Rome, Tarquin, deposed; city becomes republic.

**499–494** Ionian war: Greek revolt against Persian rule.

**494** Thirty cities of Latium form Latin League against Etruscans.

**492** First Persian expedition against Athens ends when storm destroys Persian fleet.

**490** Athenians crush second Persian expedition at Battle of Marathon.

**485** Xerxes king of Persia.

**480** Persian fleet defeated by Greeks at Battle of Salamis.

**479** Greek soldiers rout Persians at Battle of Plataea; end of Persian attempt to subdue Greece.

**460** Pericles becomes leader of Athenians.

◁ According to legend, the founders of Rome were Romulus and Remus who as babies were suckled by a she-wolf.

**431–421** Great Peloponnesian War between Athens and Sparta.

**415–404** Second Peloponnesian War, ending with Spartan capture of Athens.

**403** Thirty Tyrants seize power in Athens.

**399** Philosopher Socrates put to death for teaching heresies to the young.

**395–387** Corinthian War: coalition of Argos, Athens, Corinth, Thebes against Sparta; Sparta victorious.

**391** Romans conquer Etruscans.

**390** Gauls under Brennus sack Rome.

**352–336** Philip II king of Macedon; rise of Macedon to power in Greece.

**350** Persians suppress revolt of Jews.

**338** Philip of Macedon conquers Greece.

**336–323** Reign of Alexander III, the Great.

**335** Alexander destroys Thebes.

**332** Alexander conquers Egypt and Jerusalem, destroys Tyre.

**331** Alexander overthrows Persian empire, defeating Darius III and capturing Babylon.

**326** Greeks under Alexander extend empire to Indus river in what is now Pakistan.

**323** Death of Alexander; birth of Euclid.

**320** Egyptians under Pharaoh Ptolemy Soter capture Jerusalem.

**305** Seleucus I Nicator founds Seleucid dynasty in Syria, Persia and Asia Minor.

**305** Romans extend their rule over southern Italy.

**301** Egyptians conquer Palestine.

**295–294** Demetrius captures Athens and makes himself master of Greece.

**290** Romans finally defeat Samnite attempt to usurp Roman power in Italy.

**280** Achaean League of 12 Greek city-states formed.

**274** Pyrrhus of Epirus conquers Macedonia; killed two years later.

**264–241** First Punic War between Rome and Carthage; Carthage defeated and surrenders Sicily.

**221** Ch'in dynasty (to 207); founded by Shih Huang-te, who builds the Great Wall.

**218–201** Second Punic War.

**218** Carthaginians under Hannibal cross Alps to invade Italy; defeat Romans at Trebbia.

△ The Carthaginian general Hannibal crossing the Alps in 218 BC.

**216** Hannibal defeats Romans at Cannae.

**206** Romans under Scipio drive Carthaginians out of Spain.

**202** Carthaginians defeated at Zama.

**202** Han dynasty founded in China.

**200–197** Romans drawn into war against Macedonia; Philip V of Macedon defeated.

**192** Rome defeats Sparta.

**182** Suicide of Hannibal to avoid capture by Romans.

**171–167** Perseus of Macedonia attacks Rome; crushingly defeated; Roman rule in Macedonia.

**168** Antiochus IV Epiphanes of Syria persecutes Jews and desecrates Temple in Jerusalem.

**167** Revolt of Jews under Judas Maccabeus against Antiochus.

**153** Jews win independence from Syrian rule.

**149–146** Third Punic War ends in destruction of Carthage.

**88–82** Civil war in Rome; Lucius Cornelius Sulla emerges victor.

**87** Sulla defeats attack by Mithradates, King of Pontus, and captures Athens.

**86** Civil war in China.

**82** Sulla dictator of Rome.

**73–71** Revolt of gladiators and slaves under Spartacus; defeated by consuls Gnaeus Pompeius (Pompey) and Licinius Crassus.

**65** Roman armies under Pompey invade Syria and Palestine.

**64** Romans occupy Jerusalem.

**61** Gaius Julius Caesar becomes Roman governor of Spain.

| | |
|---|---|
| **60** | Pompey, Crassus and Caesar form First Triumvirate to rule Rome. |
| **58–51** | Caesar conquers Gaul and invades Britain; British pay tribute to Rome. |
| **53** | Death of Crassus in battle. |
| **52** | Pompey appointed sole consul in Rome. |
| **49** | Caesar crosses Rubicon river in Italy to challenge Pompey for power. |
| **48** | Pompey, defeated at Pharsalus, flees to Egypt and is assassinated. |
| **47** | Caesar appoints Cleopatra and her brother Ptolemy XII joint rulers of Egypt; Cleopatra disposes of Ptolemy. |
| **45** | Caesar holds supreme power in Rome. |
| **44** | Brutus, Cassius and others murder Caesar. |
| **43** | Mark Antony, Marcus Lepidus and Caesar's nephew Octavian form Second Triumvirate. |
| **43** | Cleopatra queen of Egypt. |
| **36** | Mark Antony marries Cleopatra; prepares to attack Octavian. |
| **31** | Battle of Actium: Octavian's fleet defeats Antony and Cleopatra, who commit suicide. Rome conquers Egypt. |
| **27** | Octavian emperor of Rome, with title of Augustus. |
| **6** | Romans seize Judaea. |
| **4** | Birth of Jesus Christ at Bethlehem (probable date). |

**AD**

| | |
|---|---|
| **9** | Battle of Teutoburg Forest: German leader Arminius wipes out three Roman legions. |
| **14** | Augustus dies; succeeded by stepson Tiberius. |
| **26** | Pontius Pilate appointed Procurator of Judaea. |
| **27** | Baptism of Jesus by John the Baptist. |
| **30** | Jesus crucified on Pilate's orders on charge of sedition. |
| **32** | Saul of Tarsus converted; baptized as Paul. |
| **37–41** | Caligula emperor of Rome; orders Romans to worship him as god. |
| **41–54** | Claudius emperor of Rome. |
| **43–51** | Roman conquest of Britain under Aulus Plautius. |

◁ The most famous Roman – Julius Caesar (100–44 BC).

| | |
|---|---|
| **54–68** | Reign of Emperor Nero. |
| **64** | Fire destroys Rome; Christians persecuted; St Paul and St Peter put to death. |
| **65** | Gospel of St Mark probably written. |
| **66–70** | Revolt of Jews; subdued by Vespasian and his son Titus. |
| **68** | Suicide of Nero; Galba becomes Emperor of Rome. |
| **69–79** | Reign of Vespasian. |
| **77–84** | Roman conquest of northern Britain. |
| **79** | Vesuvius erupts, destroying Pompeii, Herculaneum and Stabiae. |
| **98–117** | Reign of Trajan; Roman empire at greatest extent. |
| **122** | Emperor Hadrian (ruled 117–138) visits Britain; orders building of wall to keep out Picts and Scots. |
| **132–135** | Jewish revolt led by Simon Bar-Cochba suppressed; Romans disperse Jews from Palestine (*Diaspora*). |
| **161–180** | Marcus Aurelius emperor: Roman empire at its most united. |
| **177** | Increased persecution of Christians in Rome. |
| ***c.*200–800** | Maya empire flourishes in Central America. |
| **205–211** | Revolts and invasions in Britain suppressed by Emperor Septimus Severus. |

| | |
|---|---|
| **212** | Emperor Caracalla (211–217) gives Roman citizenship to all free men in the empire. |
| **220** | Han dynasty in China ends. |
| **226** | Artaxerxes founds new Persian empire. |
| **249** | Emperor Decius (249–251) inaugurates first general persecution of Christians. |
| **253–259** | Franks, Goths and Alamanni cross empire's frontiers and invade Italy. |
| **268** | Goths sack Sparta, Corinth, Athens. |
| **284–305** | Reign of Diocletian. |
| **285** | Empire divided into West (based on Rome) and East (based on Nicomedia in Bythnia). |
| ***c*.300** | Buddhism spreading throughout China. |
| **303–313** | New persecution of Christians. |
| **306–337** | Constantine the Great emperor of Rome. |
| **313** | Edict of Milan proclaims toleration for Christians throughout the Roman empire. |
| **314** | Council of Arles: meeting of Christian leaders at which Constantine presides. |
| **320** | Gupta empire founded in India. |
| **324** | Eastern and Western empires reunited under Constantine's rule. |
| **325** | First world council of Christian Church at Nicaea in Asia Minor. |
| **330** | Foundation of Constantinople on site of village of Byzantium, as capital of Roman Empire. |
| **360** | Huns invade Europe; Picts and Scots cross Hadrian's Wall to attack north Britain. |
| **369** | Picts and Scots driven out of Roman province of Britain. |
| **378** | Battle of Adrianople: Visigoths defeat and kill Emperor Valens, and ravage Balkans. |
| **379–395** | Reign of Theodosius the Great; on his death, Roman Empire is again split up. |
| **407** | Roman troops leave Britain to fight Barbarians in Gaul. |
| **410** | Goths under command of Alaric sack Rome. |
| **425–450** | Jutes, Angles and Saxons invade Britain. |
| **451** | Battle of Châlons: Franks and allies defeat Attila the Hun. |
| **476** | Goths depose Emperor Romulus Augustus, ending western Roman empire; date generally regarded as beginning of Middle Ages. |
| **481** | Clovis king of Franks. |
| **493** | Theodoric the Ostrogoth conquers Italy. |
| **496** | Clovis converted to Christianity; increases Frankish power. |
| **527–565** | Justinian the Great, Byzantine (eastern Roman) emperor. |
| **529–565** | Justinian has Roman laws codified. |
| **534** | Franks conquer Burgundy. |
| **534** | Eastern Empire reconquers northern Africa from Vandals. |
| **535** | Byzantine troops occupy southern Italy. |
| **550** | St David introduces Christianity into Wales. |
| **552** | Buddhism introduced into Japan. |
| **554** | Byzantine armies complete conquest of Italy. |
| **563** | St Columba preaches Christianity to the Picts in Scotland. |
| **568** | Lombards conquer north and central Italy. |
| **570** | Prophet Muhammad born at Mecca. |
| **581** | Sui dynasty founded in China. |
| **590** | Gregory the Great becomes pope. |
| **597** | St Augustine converts south-eastern England to Christianity for Rome. |
| **611–622** | Persians conquer Palestine and Egypt; Jerusalem sacked. |
| **616** | Visigoths drive Romans from Spain. |
| **618** | T'ang dynasty founded in China. |
| **622** | The Hegira: Muhammad flees from Mecca to Yathrib, afterwards called Medina. |
| **624** | Japan adopts Buddhism. |
| **625** | Muhammad begins dictating material later gathered into the *Koran*. |
| **622–630** | Byzantine emperor Heraclius drives Persians from Egypt and Palestine. |
| **628** | Muhammad enunciates principles of Islamic faith. |
| **632** | Death of Muhammad. |
| **634–641** | Muslim Arabs conquer Syria, Jerusalem, Mesopotamia, Egypt, and overthrow Persian empire. |
| **634–642** | Oswald, king of Northumbria, introduces Celtic Christian Church to northern England. |

**646** Taikwa, Japanese edict of reform; Japanese begin to copy Chinese culture.

**664** Synod of Whitby: Oswy, king of Northumbria, joins England to Church of Rome.

**711–715** Spain conquered by Moors.

**712** Islamic state set up in Sind, now part of Pakistan.

**717–718** Arab siege of Constantinople fails.

**720** Moors invade France.

**732** Charles Martel of Franks defeats Moorish invaders at Poitiers.

**752** Pepin the Short elected king of Franks.

**756** Donation of Pepin: Franks agree to popes' controlling central Italy.

**771–814** Reign of Charlemagne, king of Franks.

**773–774** Charlemagne conquers Lombardy.

**778** Moors defeat Franks at Roncesvalles.

**781** Christian missionaries reach China.

**786–809** Rule of Harun Al-Raschid as Caliph of Baghdad.

**787** First attacks by the Northmen (Vikings) on England.

**800** Pope Leo III crowns Charlemagne as Roman Emperor of the West.

**814** Division of Charlemagne's empire following his death.

▽ Charlemagne (c.742–814), Frankish ruler and first Holy Roman Emperor.

**827–839** Egbert, first Saxon king claiming to rule all England.

**832** Muslims capture Sicily.

**c.850** Jainism and Hinduism established as main religions of northern India.

**871–899** Reign of Alfred the Great in southern England.

**874** Northmen begin settling in Iceland.

**878** Treaty of Wedmore divides England between Saxons and Danes.

**885** Paris besieged by Vikings.

**896** Magyar tribes conquer Hungary.

**906** Magyars begin invasion of Germany.

**907** End of T'ang dynasty in China; civil war breaks out.

**919–936** Reign of Henry I (the Fowler) of Germany.

**926** Athelstan, king of England, conquers Wales and southern Scotland.

**935** Wenceslaus of Bohemia – 'good King Wenceslaus' – murdered by brother.

**936–973** Reign of Otto I, the Great, of Germany.

**955** Battle of the Lechfeld: Otto the Great repulses Magyars.

**960** Sung dynasty founded in China.

**962** Revival of Roman empire in West: Pope John XII crowns Otto of Germany as Holy Roman Emperor.

**978** Ethelred II, the Redeless, becomes king of England.

**986** Eric the Red founds colonies in Greenland.

**987** Hugh Capet elected king of Franks; Capetian dynasty founded.

**988** Foundation of Al-Azhar University in Cairo.

**994** London besieged by Olaf Trygvason of Norway and Sweyn of Denmark.

**c.1000** Polynesian settlers reach New Zealand.

**c.1000** Ancient Empire of Ghana flourished in west Africa.

**c.1000** Leif Ericsson of Norway discovers Vinland in North America.

**1004–1013** Danish attacks on England, bought off by Ethelred II.

**1014** Canute (Cnut) becomes king of Denmark and Norway.

**1016** Canute also becomes king of England, deposing Ethelred.

**1040** Macbeth murders Duncan, king of Scots, and becomes king.

**1042–1066** Edward the Confessor, son of Ethelred, king of England.

| | |
|---|---|
| **1058** | Malcolm III Canmore becomes king of Scots, having killed Macbeth in 1057 in battle near Aberdeen. |
| **1066** | Harold II chosen king of England; invasion of England by William of Normandy, who seizes throne. |
| **1075–1122** | Struggle between popes and German emperors over right to appoint bishops. |
| **1076** | Pope Gregory VII excommunicates German Emperor Henry IV. |
| **1077** | Penance at Canossa: Henry submits to the Pope. |
| **1084** | Normans under Robert Guiscard sack Rome. |
| **1096–1099** | First Crusade to free Holy Land (Palestine) from Muslim rule; capture of Jerusalem. |
| **1100** | William II (Rufus) of England shot while hunting; brother Henry I becomes king. |
| **1106** | Henry I wrests Normandy from elder brother Robert. |
| **1113** | Order of the Knights of St John founded. |
| **1119** | Order of Knights Templars founded. |
| **1122** | Concordat of Worms ends disputes between emperors and popes. |
| **1147–1149** | Second Crusade: Christian armies disagree and crusade fails. |
| **1152–1190** | Frederick I (Barbarossa) king of Germany and Holy Roman Emperor. |

| | |
|---|---|
| **1154–1189** | Reign of Henry II of England; much of France under English rule. |
| **1174–1193** | Rule of Saladin as Sultan of Egypt and Syria. |
| **1182** | Expulsion of Jews from France. |
| **1187** | Saladin captures Jerusalem. |
| **1189–1192** | Third Crusade, led by Frederick Barbarossa, Philip II of France, and Richard I of England; Acre and Jaffa captured. |
| **1192–1194** | Richard of England prisoner of Leopold of Austria and Emperor Henry VI. |
| **1197–1212** | Civil war in Germany following death of Emperor Henry VI; ends with election of Frederick II (*Stupor Mundi*). |
| ***c.*1200** | Settlement of Mexico by Aztecs; Incas found their first kingdom in Peru. |
| **1200–1450** | German cities form Hanseatic League to promote their trade. |
| **1202–1204** | Fourth Crusade: Crusaders, in debt to Venice, capture Constantinople for Venetians. |
| **1206** | Mongol leader Temujin proclaimed *Genghis Khan* (Emperor within the seas). |
| **1210** | Francis of Assisi founds Franciscan order of monks. |
| **1211–1222** | Mongol invasion of China. |
| **1212** | Children's Crusade: 30,000 children from France and Germany set off to free Holy Land; many die. |

▽ Routes taken by Crusaders to the Holy Land.

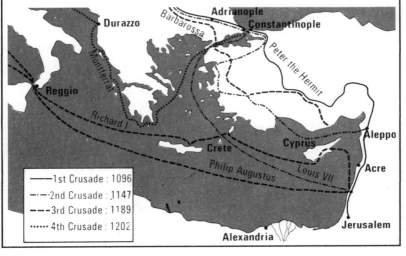

△ The seal of King John, as set upon Magna Carta in 1215.

**1215** King John of England agrees to Magna Carta, statement of the rights of his subjects.

**1215** St Dominic founds Dominican order of friars.

**1217–1221** Fifth Crusade fails to liberate Holy Land.

**1223** Mongol invasion of Russia.

**1224** Carmelite order of friars founded.

**1228–1229** Sixth Crusade led by Emperor Frederick II regains Jerusalem.

**1238** Mongol warriors capture Moscow.

**1240** Russian hero Alexander Nevsky defeats Swedish force at River Neva.

**1241** 'Golden Horde' Mongol kingdom established on banks of River Volga.

**1244** Muslims recapture Jerusalem.

**1248** St Louis (Louis IX of France) leads Seventh Crusade; captured by Muslims and ransomed in 1254.

**1256** Foundation of Augustinian order.

**1260–1294** Kublai Khan becomes ruler of Mongol Empire and founds Yüan dynasty in China.

**1268** Egyptians capture Antioch, held by Christians.

**1270** Eighth and last Crusade, led by St Louis, who dies during it.

**1271–1295** Marco Polo visits court of Kublai Khan, travels in Asia, and returns to Venice.

**1273** Rudolf I of Habsburg becomes Holy Roman Emperor, founding Habsburg dynasty.

**1282** Edward I of England conquers Wales.

**1290** Expulsion of Jews from England.

**1295** First truly representative parliament summoned in England.

**1301** Edward I of England creates his son Edward as the first Prince of Wales.

**1302** Papal Bull *Unam sanctam* proclaims papal superiority over national rulers.

**1305–1378** Avignonese Papacy: seven popes based at Avignon in France because of unrest in Italy.

**1306** Robert Bruce leads Scottish revolt against English rule.

**1314** Scotland becomes independent after Bruce defeats English at Battle of Bannockburn.

**1325** Aztecs found Tenochtitlán, now Mexico City.

**1334–1351** The Black Death (bubonic plague) ravages Europe, killing one in four.

**1337** Hundred Years War between England and France starts when Edward III of England takes title of King of France.

**1339** English invasion of France begins.

**1346** Edward III defeats French army at Battle of Crécy: long-bow proved to be the most formidable weapon.

**1356** English under Edward the Black Prince capture John II of France at Battle of Poitiers.

**1360** First part of Hundred Years War ended by Treaty of Bretigny.

**1368** Ming Dynasty begins in China.

**1369** War breaks out again between England and France.

**1369–1405** Reign of Tamerlane, Mongol ruler of Samarkand, and conqueror of much of southern Asia.

**1371** Robert I becomes first Stuart king of Scotland.

**1374** Peace between England and France, England having lost nearly all its French possessions.

**1378–1417** The Great Schism: rival lines of popes elected, splitting the Church.

**1396** Bulgaria conquered by Ottoman Turks.

**1397** Union of Kalmar: Denmark, Norway and Sweden united under one king.

**1400** Welsh revolt led by Owen Glendower.

**1414** Lollards (heretics) persecuted in England.

**1414–1417** Council of Constance called to heal Great Schism; Martin V elected pope.

| 1415 | Henry V of England renews claim to French throne, and defeats French at Battle of Agincourt. |
| 1420 | Treaty of Troyes: Henry V acknowledged as heir to French throne. |
| 1422 | Deaths of Henry V and of Charles VI of France; renewed struggle for French throne. |
| 1429 | Joan of Arc raises English siege of Orléans; Charles VII crowned king at Rheims. |
| 1431 | Joan of Arc burned as witch. |
| 1437 | Portuguese naval institute founded by Prince Henry the Navigator. |
| *c.*1450 | Invention of printing from moveable type by Johannes Gutenberg. |
| 1453 | Hundred Years War ends, leaving England with Calais as only French possession. |
| 1453 | Ottoman Turks capture Constantinople, ending Byzantine Empire; taken as the end of the Middle Ages. |
| 1455–1485 | Wars of the Roses: civil wars in England between rival families of York and Lancaster. |

△ Ivan the Great (1440–1505), first tsar of Russia.

| 1461–1485 | House of York triumphant in England. |
| 1475 | Edward IV of England invades France; bought off by Louis XI. |
| 1479 | Crowns of Castile and Aragon united, making Spain one country. |
| 1480 | Ivan III, first tsar (emperor) of Russia, makes himself independent of Mongols. |

▽ In 1453 Constantinople was captured by the Turks and the Byzantine Empire came to an end.

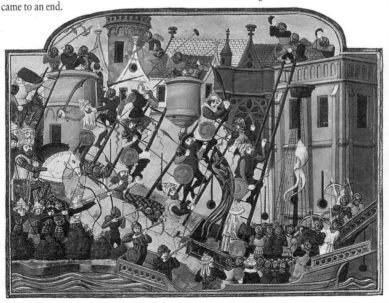

| | |
|---|---|
| **1483** | Boy king Edward V of England deposed and killed by uncle, Richard III. |
| **1485** | Richard III killed at Battle of Bosworth; Henry Tudor brings Lancastrians back to power as Henry VII. |
| **1488** | Bartolomeu Dias, Portuguese navigator, becomes first European to sail round Cape of Good Hope. |
| **1492** | Spaniards finally drive Moors out of Granada, last Muslim province. |
| **1492** | Christopher Columbus discovers West Indies while searching for westward route to eastern Asia. |
| **1493** | Inca empire in Peru at its height. |
| **1497** | John Cabot discovers Newfoundland; claims it for England. |
| **1498** | Vasco da Gama of Portugal discovers sea route to India by way of Cape of Good Hope. |
| **1506** | Work begins on St Peter's Basilica, Rome; Donato Bramante, chief architect. |
| **1508–1512** | Michelangelo paints ceiling of Sistine Chapel in Vatican. |
| **1516** | African slave traffic to Americas begins. |
| **1517** | Beginning of Reformation: monk Martin Luther publishes *95 Theses* at Wittenberg, Germany. |
| **1519–1555** | Reign of Holy Roman Emperor Charles V, who has become king of Spain two years earlier. |
| **1519–1521** | First voyage round world; expedition led by Ferdinand Magellan, who dies during journey. |

△ Title page of Martin Luther's Bible.

| | |
|---|---|
| **1519–1521** | Conquest of Mexico by Spanish adventurer Hernán Cortés. |
| **1520** | Field of Cloth of Gold: meeting between Francis I of France and Henry VIII of England. |
| **1521** | Diet of Worms (church conference) condemns doctrines of Martin Luther. |
| **1524–1525** | Peasants' War: revolt of German peasants. Peasants defeated and punished. |
| **1525** | Battle of Pavia: Imperial forces defeat and capture Francis I of France. |
| **1527** | Sack of Rome by imperial forces; Pope Clement VII taken prisoner. |
| **1529** | Turkish armies advancing through Hungary besiege Vienna. |
| **1530** | Baber, founder of Mogul Empire in India, dies. |
| **1532** | Spaniards under Francisco Pizarro conquer the Incas of Peru. |
| **1533** | Henry VIII of England excommunicated by pope for divorcing Catherine of Aragon. |

◁ Christopher Columbus (1451–1506) pioneered sea routes to the New World.

**1534** Act of Supremacy: Henry VIII assumes leadership of the Church in England, and breaks with Rome.

**1534** Society of Jesus (Jesuits) founded by Ignatius Loyola.

**1541** John Calvin takes Reformation movement to Geneva.

**1545–1563** Council of Trent marks beginning of Counter-Reformation.

**1549** Book of Common Prayer introduced in England.

**1553–1558** Reign of Mary I brings England into reconciliation with Rome.

**1558** French capture Calais, last English possession in France.

**1558–1603** Reign of Elizabeth I in England; return to Protestantism.

**1562–1598** Religious Wars in France between Roman Catholics and Huguenots (Protestants).

**1567** Foundation of Rio de Janeiro.

**1568** Mary, Queen of Scots, driven into exile; imprisoned by Elizabeth I of England.

**1571** Battle of Lepanto: allied Christian fleet defeats Turkish fleet.

**1572** Massacre of St Bartholomew's Day in France; thousands of Huguenots killed.

**1572** Active rebellion of the Netherlands against Spain begins.

**1575** Bengal conquered by Akbar the Great.

**1577–1580** Sir Francis Drake of England sails round the world.

**1582** Pope Gregory XIII introduces reformed Gregorian calendar, which most Roman Catholic countries adopt.

**1585–1589** War of the Three Henrys in France – Henry III, Henry of Navarre, Henry of Guise.

**1587** Elizabeth I of England orders execution of Mary, Queen of Scots, found guilty of treason.

**1587** Sir Francis Drake destroys Spanish fleet at Cádiz.

**1588** Spanish Armada sets sail to invade England; defeated by English fleet.

**1589** Assassination of Henry III of France; succeeded by Huguenot Henry of Navarre, who adopts Roman Catholicism.

**1592** Conquest of Sind by Akbar the Great.

**1598** Edict of Nantes: French Protestants gain political rights.

▽ Religious quarrels led to bloodshed: most terribly in the St. Bartholomew's Day massacre of 1572.

△ Captain John Smith founded the first permanent English colony in America, at Jamestown in Virginia.

△ A contemporary woodcut illustration of the execution by beheading of Charles I in 1649.

**1600** English East India Company founded.

**1602** Dutch East India Company founded.

**1603** French East India Company founded.

**1603** Death of Elizabeth I: James VI of Scotland becomes James I of England, uniting two countries under one crown.

**1607** John Smith founds Colony of Virginia.

**1609** Netherlands win independence from Spain.

**1610** Henry IV of France assassinated; succeeded by Louis XIII, aged nine.

**1610–1611** Henry Hudson discovers Hudson Bay; set adrift by his crew, following a mutiny.

**1611** English and Scottish colonists begin settlement in Ulster.

**1611** Publication of Authorized (King James) Version of the Bible.

**1616** Dutch navigator Willem Schouten makes first ever voyage round Cape Horn.

**1618–1648** Thirty Years War in Europe; begins with revolt by Protestants in Prague.

**1620** Pilgrim Fathers sail to America in *Mayflower*.

**1625–1649** Reign of Charles I in England.

**1626** Dutch colony of New Amsterdam (now New York) founded.

**1629** Massachusetts colony founded.

**1631** First colonists settle in Maryland.

**1631** Sack of Magdeburg by Tilly; defeat of Tilly by Gustavus Adolphus of Sweden at Battle of Leipzig.

**1633** Colonists settle in Connecticut.

**1638** Japanese massacre Christians, and stop all foreign visitors to country.

**1639** Colonists settle in New Hampshire and Maine.

**1640** Financial crisis in England: Charles I summons Long Parliament.

**1641** French colonize Michigan.

**1642–1646** Civil War in England; Parliament in revolt against Charles I.

**1642** Abel Tasman discovers New Zealand.

**1643–1715** Reign of Louis XIV of France.

**1643** Manchu dynasty founded in China.

**1648** Peace of Westphalia: end of Thirty Years War.

**1648** Second Civil War in England; crushed by Parliamentary forces.

**1649** Charles I tried and executed for treason; England a republic.

**1650–1651** Charles II tries to regain throne, but is defeated by Oliver Cromwell.

**1652** Dutch pioneer Jan van Riebeeck founds first European settlement in South Africa.

△ The Great Fire of 1666 destroyed 14,000 buildings in London and burned for seven days.

**1652–1654** War between Dutch and English.
**1653** Oliver Cromwell becomes Lord Protector of England, Scotland, Ireland.
**1660** Charles II restored to thrones of England and Scotland.
**1665–1667** Second Anglo-Dutch War.
**1665** New Jersey colony founded.
**1665** Great Plague ravages London.
**1666** London destroyed by fire.
**1667–1668** War of Devolution between France and Spain.
**1668** Spain recognizes Portuguese independence.
**1672–1674** Third Anglo-Dutch War; France allied to England.
**1685** Louis XIV of France revokes Edict of Nantes; Huguenots flee from France.
**1688–1689** Glorious Revolution in England: Roman Catholic James II deposed; Parliament offers throne to William III of Orange and his wife, James's daughter Mary II.
**1689** France declares war on Spain and England.
**1690** Battle of the Boyne: William III defeats James II, ending Stuart hopes.
**1696–1725** Reign of Peter I, the Great, of Russia.
**1698** Thomas Savery makes first effective steam engine in England.

**1700–1721** Great Northern War: Sweden fights other Baltic states.
**1702** William III dies; succeeded by Anne, the last of the Stuart monarchs.
**1701–1713** War of the Spanish Succession.
**1704** Britain captures Gibraltar.
**1707** Formal union of England and Scotland.

▽ Peter the Great (1672–1725) under whose rule Russia rose to be a power in western Europe.

△ Charles Edward Stuart, the Young Pretender, whose hopes were dashed by the failure of the 1745 Jacobite rebellion.

**1709** Battle of Poltava: Charles XII of Sweden beaten by Peter the Great.

**1714** Elector George of Hanover becomes King George I of England, ensuring Protestant succession.

**1715–1774** Reign of Louis XV of France, great-grandson of Louis XIV.

**1715** Jacobite (Stuart) rebellion in Britain fails.

**1718** Quadruple Alliance of Britain, the Empire, France, and the Netherlands against Spain.

**1721** Robert Walpole, world's first prime minister, becomes First Lord of the Treasury in Britain.

**1733–1735** War of the Polish Succession.

**1739** War of Jenkins' Ear between Britain and Spain.

**1740–1786** Reign of Frederick II, the Great, of Prussia.

**1740–1748** War of the Austrian Succession: dispute over Maria Theresa's right to inherit throne of Austria.

**1745–1746** Second Jacobite rebellion in Britain fails.

**1751** Robert Clive for Britain captures Arcot from French in India.

**1755** Lisbon earthquake: 30,000 people die.

**1756** Start of Seven Years War; Britain, Hanover and Prussia against Austria, France, Russia and Sweden.

**1756** Black Hole of Calcutta; 146 Britons imprisoned in small room – most die.

**1759** British capture Quebec from French.

**1760–1820** Reign of George III of Britain.

**1762** War between Britain and Spain.

**1763** Peace of Paris ends Seven Years War.

**1764** James Hargreaves invents the spinning jenny, marking start of Industrial Revolution in England.

**1767** British government imposes import taxes on North American colonies.

**1770** British navigator James Cook discovers New South Wales.

**1770** Boston massacre: British troops fire on American mob, killing five people.

**1773** Boston Tea Party, protest against tea tax.

**1775–1783** American War of Independence.

**1775** Battles of Lexington, Concord and Bunker Hill.

**1776** Declaration of Independence.

**1777** Battle of Saratoga: a British army surrenders to Americans.

**1778–1779** War of the Bavarian Succession between Austria and Prussia.

**1778** France declares war on Britain to support American colonies.

**1779** Spain joins war against Britain.

**1781** British forces surrender at Yorktown.

◁ Robert Walpole (1676–1745), effectively Britain's first prime minister.

▽ The guillotine was recommended by Dr Joseph Guillotin and was introduced in 1792 during the French Revolution. Louis XVI was beheaded by its blade as was Robespierre, who had himself instituted the bloody Reign of Terror.

| 1783 | Peace of Paris: Britain recognizes independence of United States of America. |
| 1785 | First balloon crossing of English Channel. |
| 1788 | United States adopts its constitution. |
| 1789 | George Washington first president of the United States. |
| 1789–1799 | French Revolution begins with the fall of the Bastille, a prison. |
| 1790 | Washington, DC founded. |
| 1792 | France proclaimed a republic. |
| 1792–1799 | War of the First Coalition: Austria, Britain, the Netherlands, Prussia, Spain against France. |
| 1793 | Louis XVI of France executed; Reign of Terror (to 1794). |
| 1796 | Corsican general Napoleon Bonaparte conquers most of Italy for France. |
| 1798 | Napoleon Bonaparte in Egypt: cut off by Horatio Nelson's naval victory in Battle of the Nile. |
| 1799 | Coup d'état of Brumaire: Napoleon becomes First Consul of France. |
| 1799–1801 | War of the Second Coalition. |
| 1800 | British capture Malta. |
| 1801 | Britain and Ireland united. |
| 1803 | Louisiana Purchase: United States buys Louisiana territory from France. |

| 1804 | Napoleon crowned Emperor of France. |
| 1805–1808 | War of the Third Coalition: Austria, Britain, Naples, Russia, Sweden against France and Spain. |
| 1805 | Battle of Trafalgar: Nelson defeats French and Spanish fleets. |
| 1805 | Battle of Austerlitz: Napoleon defeats Austrians and Russians. |
| 1806 | Napoleon ends Holy Roman Empire, makes his brothers kings of Naples and Holland. |
| 1807 | Britain abolishes slave trading. |
| 1808–1814 | Peninsular War in Spain and Portugal against French invaders. |
| 1809–1825 | Wars of Independence in Latin America. |
| 1812 | Napoleon invades Russia; forced to retreat, losing most of his army. |
| 1812–1815 | War between United States and Britain over searching of neutral shipping. |
| 1813 | Napoleon defeated at Battle of Leipzig; French driven from Spain. |
| 1814 | Napoleon abdicates; exiled to Elba. |
| 1815 | Napoleon tries to regain power; finally defeated at Battle of Waterloo and exiled to St Helena. |

▽ A caricature of Arthur Wellesley, Duke of Wellington (1769–1852), who was known as the Iron Duke.

A WELLINGTON BOOT

△ Simon Bolivar (1783–1830). South American liberator, he led the struggle against Spanish rule.

| | |
|---|---|
| **1818** | Chile becomes independent. |
| **1819** | United States gains Florida from Spain. |
| **1819** | Argentina becomes independent. |
| **1821** | Mexico and Peru gain independence. |
| **1822** | Greece and Brazil declare their independence. |
| **1823** | Monroe Doctrine: United States guarantees Western Hemisphere against European interference. |
| **1825** | First passenger railway opens in England (Stockton to Darlington). |
| **1825** | Bolivia and Paraguay become independent. |
| **1826** | First photograph taken by Nicéphore Nièpce of France. |
| **1830** | July Revolution: Charles X of France deposed; Louis Philippe elected king. |
| **1830** | Belgium and Ecuador become independent. |
| **1833** | Slavery abolished in British colonies. |
| **1836** | Great Trek: Boer colonists move north from Cape Colony in South Africa. |
| **1837–1901** | Reign of Queen Victoria of Britain. |
| **1839** | Guatemala becomes a republic. |
| **1840** | Prepaid adhesive postage stamps introduced in Britain. |
| **1841** | New Zealand becomes British colony. |
| **1841** | Upper and Lower Canada united. |
| **1842** | China yields Hong Kong to Britain. |
| **1846** | Great Famine in Ireland: a million people die, a million emigrate. |
| **1848** | Gold discovered in California. |
| **1848** | Year of Revolutions: in France, Berlin, Budapest, Milan, Naples, Prague, Rome, Venice and Vienna. |

△ Karl Marx (1818–83) German philosopher and founder of modern Communist theory.

| | |
|---|---|
| **1848** | France becomes republic, with Louis Napoleon as president. |
| **1848** | Karl Marx and Friedrich Engels publish *Communist Manifesto*. |
| **1849** | Britain annexes Punjab. |
| **1851** | Australian gold rush begins. |
| **1852** | Napoleon III proclaimed Emperor of the French. |
| **1854–1856** | Crimean War: Turkey, Britain, France, Sardinia against Russia. |
| **1857–1858** | Indian Mutiny; British government takes over rule from East India Company. |
| **1861** | Unification of Italy. |
| **1861–1865** | American Civil War over slavery; southern states secede. |

▽ Abraham Lincoln, a Republican whose party wanted to limit slavery, was elected President of the United States in 1860.

1863  Slavery abolished in United States;
      Battle of Gettysburg.
1865  Confederate General Robert E. Lee
      surrenders at Appomattox Court
      House.
1867  Canada proclaimed a Dominion.
1867  United States buys Alaska from
      Russia.
1867  Luxembourg becomes independent.
1869  Suez Canal opened.
1870–1871  Franco-Prussian War: fall of
      Napoleon III; France a republic
      again; Germany united under
      William of Prussia.
1876  Alexander Graham Bell invents the
      telephone.
1876  France and Britain take joint control
      of Egypt.
1877  Romania becomes independent.
1880–1881  First Boer War; Britain
      defeats Boer settlers in South Africa.
1884  Leopold II of Belgium sets up private
      colony in the Congo.
1887  First motor-cars built in Germany.
1896  Klondyke gold rush begins.
1898  Battle of Omdurman, Sudan: British
      forces defeat the Mahdi and his
      dervishes.
1898  Spanish-American War: United
      States wins Guam, Puerto Rico and
      Philippines; Cuba wins
      independence.
1899–1902  Second Boer War; British
      victory.

△ The Suez Canal was opened in 1869,
opening up a faster sea route between
Europe and the Orient.

1900  Boxer Rebellion in China.
1901  Australia becomes independent
      Commonwealth.
1901  First radio signals sent across
      Atlantic.

▽ In South Africa British regular troops
fought a bitter war against the Boer (Dutch
settlers) guerrilla forces.

△ On 17 December 1903 the Wrights' aeroplane flew for the first time.

▽ Lenin addressing a crowd from a truck during the 1917 Russian Revolution.

**1903** Wright Brothers make first heavier-than-air flight.
**1904–1905** Russo-Japanese War: Japan wins.
**1905** Revolution in Russia: Tsar Nicholas II grants limited reforms.
**1907** New Zealand becomes a Dominion.
**1909** Robert Peary reaches North Pole.
**1910** South Africa becomes a Dominion.
**1911** Roald Amundsen reaches the South Pole.
**1911–1912** Italo-Turkish War: Italy gains Tripoli and Cyrenaica.
**1912** China proclaimed a republic.
**1912–1913** First Balkan War.
**1913** Second Balkan War.
**1914–1918** World War I: begun by assassination of Archduke Ferdinand of Austria at Sarajevo.
**1914** Panama Canal completed.
**1915** Allies fail in Dardanelles campaign against Turkey.
**1916** Easter Rebellion in Ireland fails.
**1916** Battle of Jutland; defence of Verdun; Battle of the Somme; first use of tanks, by the British.

**1917** Revolutions in Russia: Bolsheviks under Lenin seize control; United States enters the war; Battles of Aisne, Cambrai, Passchendaele.
**1918** War ends after final German offensive fails; Germany becomes republic.
**1920** League of Nations meets for first time; Americans refuse to join.
**1920** Civil war in Ireland.
**1921** Southern Ireland becomes a Dominion.
**1922** Russia becomes the Union of Soviet Socialist Republics.
**1922** Fresh civil war in Ireland.
**1923** Turkey becomes a republic.
**1924** First Labour government in Britain.
**1926** General Strike in Britain.
**1927** Charles Lindbergh makes first solo flight across Atlantic Ocean.
**1929** Wall Street crash: start of world depression.

◁ The trench warfare of 1914–18 created appalling conditions for front-line soldiers.

△ Adolf Hitler at a Nazi rally in Germany. His dream of a thousand-year German domination of Europe led to world war.

△ A US B17 bombs Budapest in 1944. World War II was largely dominated by air power.

| | |
|---|---|
| **1933** | Adolf Hitler becomes chancellor of Germany: burning of Reichstag. |
| **1934** | Hitler becomes Führer of Germany. |
| **1935** | Germany regains Saarland. |
| **1935–1936** | Italians conquer Ethiopia. |
| **1936–1939** | Civil War in Spain; Francisco Franco becomes dictator after Nationalists defeat Republicans. |
| **1936** | Germany reoccupies Rhineland. |
| **1938** | The Anschluss: Germany annexes Austria. |
| **1938** | Munich crisis: France, Britain and Italy agree that Germany should take Sudetenland from Czechoslovakia. |
| **1939** | Germans occupy remainder of Czechoslovakia. |
| **1939** | Russo-German treaty. |
| **1939–1945** | World War II: Germany invades Poland; Britain and France declare war. |

| | |
|---|---|
| **1940** | Germans invade Denmark, Norway, Belgium, the Netherlands and France; Britain and Empire left to carry on fight. |
| **1940** | Battle of Britain: German air attack fails. |
| **1941** | Germans invade Greece, Yugoslavia and Russia. |
| **1941** | Japanese attack on Pearl Harbor brings United States into war. |
| **1942** | Japanese capture Malaya, Singapore, Burma and Philippines; Battle of El Alamein in Egypt marks turning point in war. |
| **1943** | Allies invade North Africa, Sicily and Italy; German army surrenders at Stalingrad (now Volgograd). |
| **1944** | Allies land in Normandy, liberating France and Belgium; major Russian attack begins. |
| **1945** | Germany overrun from east and west; Hitler commits suicide; atomic bombs on Japan end war in East. |
| **1946** | First session of United Nations General Assembly. |
| **1947** | India, Pakistan and Burma independent. |
| **1948** | Israel becomes independent. |
| **1948** | Russians blockade West Berlin. |
| **1949** | North Atlantic Treaty Organization formed. |
| **1949** | Communist rule established in China. |
| **1950–1953** | Korean War: United Nations force helps defend South Korea. |

◁ The Allied victory at El Alamein, 1942, turned the tide in North Africa.

1953 New Zealander Edmund Hillary and Sherpa Tenzing Norgay become first men to climb Mount Everest.

1954 French Indochina becomes independent countries of Laos, Cambodia, South Vietnam and North Vietnam after fierce Communist attacks.

1956 Egypt becomes a republic; Suez Canal nationalized.

1956 Russia crushes Hungarian uprising.

◁ Edmund Hillary and Tenzing Norgay, first to climb Mount Everest, in 1953.

1956 Morocco, Tunisia, Sudan all independent.

1957 European Common Market set up.

1957 Russia launches first spacecraft.

1957 Ghana and Malaysia independent.

1958 Guinea becomes independent.

1959 Fidel Castro establishes Communist rule in Cuba.

1960 Year of Independence for Cameroon, Central African Republic, Chad, Congo (Brazzaville), Congo (now Zaïre), Cyprus, Dahomey, Gabon, Ivory Coast, Madagascar, Mali, Niger, Nigeria, Senegal, Somalia, Togo, Upper Volta (now Burkina Faso).

1960 Earthquake destroys Agadir.

1961 First man in space: Yuri Gagarin of the Soviet Union.

1961 Mauretania, Mongolia, Sierra Leone, Tanzania become independent.

1962 Independence of Algeria, Burundi, Jamaica, Rwanda, Trinidad and Tobago, Uganda.

1963 Assassination of US President John F. Kennedy.

▽ The Hungarian uprising of 1956. Russian tanks move into Budapest to quell the people's demand for freedom.

△ Yuri Gagarin, the first man in space, who remained in orbit for 89 minutes. He died in 1968 in an aeroplane crash.

| | |
|---|---|
| **1963** | Kenya and Kuwait become independent. |
| **1964** | Malawi, Malta and Zambia become independent. |
| **1965** | Gambia, Maldive Islands, Singapore become independent; Rhodesia proclaims own independence with white minority rule. |
| **1967** | Six-Day War: Israel defeats Arab countires. |
| **1967** | South Yemen becomes independent. |
| **1968** | Russian troops occupy Czechoslovakia. |
| **1968** | Independence of Nauru, Equatorial Guinea. |
| **1969** | First man on Moon (Neil Armstrong). |
| **1969** | Civil disturbances in Northern Ireland begin to escalate. |
| **1970** | Bloodless coup led by Lon Nol topples Cambodia's Prince Sihanouk. |
| **1970** | Guyana and Fiji become independent. |
| **1971** | East Pakistan rebels and becomes independent as Bangladesh; Qatar, Bahrain also independent. |
| **1973** | American forces end military intervention in Vietnam War. |
| **1973** | Independence of Bahamas. |
| **1973** | The October War: Arab states attack Israel; war halted after five weeks. |
| **1973** | Arab oil-producing states raise oil prices; world economic crisis begins. |
| **1974** | President Richard M. Nixon resigns because of Watergate scandal. |
| **1974** | Portugal's African colonies win independence agreement. |
| **1975** | Communists win decisive victories in Indochina: South Vietnam surrenders to North Vietnam. |
| **1975** | Independence of Papua New Guinea, São Tomé and Príncipe, and Angola. |
| **1975** | Reopening of Suez Canal to shipping after years of closure. |
| **1975** | Death of Spanish dictator Francisco Franco; Prince Juan Carlos crowned King of Spain. |
| **1976** | North and South Vietnam reunified. |
| **1976** | Independence for the Seychelles within the Commonwealth. |
| **1976** | Two earthquakes destroy mining town of Tangshan in China; more than 700,000 die. |
| **1976** | Death of China's Chairman Mao Zedong. |
| **1977** | UN report tells of massacres and murders in Uganda under General Amin's rule (80,000–90,000 killed 1971–1972). |
| **1977** | President Sadat of Egypt and Prime Minister Begin of Israel meet in attempt to gain peace for Middle East. |
| **1979** | Cambodia changes its name to Kampuchea; the capital, Phnom Penh, captured by Vietnamese and rebels. |
| **1979** | Kampala captured by Tanzanian troops and Ugandan exiles; General Amin forced to flee. |
| **1979** | Shah of Iran deposed; exiled Muslim leader, the Ayatollah Khomeini, returns to Iran which is declared an Islamic Republic. |
| **1979** | Margaret Thatcher becomes Britain's first woman Prime Minister after Conservative election victory. |
| **1979** | Russian forces move into Afghanistan. |
| **1980** | Rhodesia becomes independent as Zimbabwe with Black majority rule. |
| **1980** | Gulf War begins between Iran and Iraq. |
| **1981** | Ronald Reagan becomes 40th President of the United States. |
| **1981** | American hostages in Iran freed. |

△ Fans at the Live Aid concert (1985) are cooled down.

**1981** President Sadat of Egypt assassinated.

**1981** Assassination attempts on President Reagan and Pope John Paul fail.

**1982** Argentine annexation of Falkland Islands and South Georgia. Diplomatic solutions fail and a British task force reoccupies the islands.

**1983** Famine hits Ethiopia.

**1983** Yuri Vladimirovich Andropov is elected president of the USSR.

**1984** Yuri Andropov dies; is succeeded as Soviet leader by Konstantin Chernenko.

**1984** Canadian PM Pierre Trudeau resigns.

**1984** IRA bomb intended to kill members of the British Cabinet wrecks Brighton hotel; four die, 30 injured.

**1984** Indian PM Indira Gandhi assassinated by her Sikh bodyguards.

**1984** Chemical leak kills 2,000 and injures 200,000 at Indian town of Bhopal.

**1985** Konstantin Chernenko dies: succeeded as Soviet leader by Mikhail Gorbachev.

**1985** British soccer fans riot in Brussels: England banned from European football.

**1985** International rock concert 'Live Aid' raises £40 million for Ethiopia's starving people.

**1986** Space shuttle *Challenger* explodes on launch, killing its crew of seven.

**1986** Philippines President Marcos is expelled; succeeded by Mrs Corazon Aquino.

**1986** Nuclear reactor at Chernobyl, Ukraine, blazes; fall-out affects much of Europe.

**1987** British car ferry *Herald of Free Enterprise* capsizes at Zeebrugge; 188 people die.

**1987** Nine million trees destroyed, 17 people die as worst storm for 200 years hits England.

**1987** World stock markets crash.

**1987** Soviet leader Mikhail Gorbachev ushers in era of *glasnost* (openness) and reform.

**1988** Piper Alpha oil platform in North Sea explodes, killing 167 people.

**1988** Gorbachev proposes major cuts in nuclear and other weapons.

**1988** Ceasefire halts the Gulf War.

**1988** US resumes space shuttle flights; Soviets launch their first shuttle.

**1988** Earthquake kills 45,000 people in Soviet Armenia, injures 20,000 and destroys three cities making 400,000 people homeless.

**1988** Benazir Bhutto becomes prime minister of Pakistan.

**1988** Soviet astronauts complete a year in space.

**1988** Terrorist bomb wrecks US airliner over Scotland: 269 people killed.

**1989** Emperor Hirohito of Japan dies after a record reign of 62 years.

**1989** George Bush is sworn in as 41st President of the United States.

**1989** Second earthquake in the USSR kills at least 300 people in Tadzhikstan.

**1989** The Rev Barbara Harris becomes Bishop of Massachusetts, first woman Anglican bishop.

**1989** Kampuchea changes its name back to Cambodia.

# SEVEN WONDERS OF THE WORLD*

**Pyramids of Egypt** Oldest and only surviving 'wonder'. Built in the 2000s BC as royal tombs, about 80 are still standing. The largest, the Great Pyramid of Cheops, at el-Gizeh, was 147 m (481 ft) high.

**Hanging Gardens of Babylon** Terraced gardens adjoining Nebuchadnezzar's palace said to rise from 23–91 m (75–300 ft). Supposedly built by the king about 600 BC to please his wife, a princess from the mountains, but they are also associated with the Assyrian Queen Semiramis.

**Statue of Zeus at Olympia** Carved by Phidias, the 12 m (40 ft) statue marked the site of the original Olympic Games in the 400s BC. It was constructed of ivory and gold, and showed Zeus (Jupiter) on his throne.

**Temple of Artemis (Diana) at Ephesus** Constructed of Parian marble and more than 122 m (400 ft) long with over 100 columns 18 m (60 ft) high, it was begun about 350 BC and took some 120 years to build. Destroyed by the Goths in AD 262.

**Mausoleum at Halicarnassus** Erected by queen Artemisia in memory of her husband King Mausolus of Caria (in Asia Minor), who died 353 BC. It stood 43 m (140 ft) high. All that remains are a few pieces in the British Museum and the word 'mausoleum' in the English language.

**Colossus of Rhodes** Gigantic bronze statue of sun-god Helios (or Apollo); stood about 36 m (117 ft) high, dominating the harbour entrance at Rhodes. The sculptor Chares supposedly laboured for 12 years before he completed it in 280 BC. It was destroyed by an earthquake in 224 BC.

**Pharos of Alexandria** Marble lighthouse and watchtower built about 270 BC on the island of Pharos in Alexandria's harbour. Possibly standing 122 m (400 ft) high, it was destroyed by an earthquake in 1375.

*Originally compiled by Antipater of Sidon, a Greek poet, in the 100s BC.*

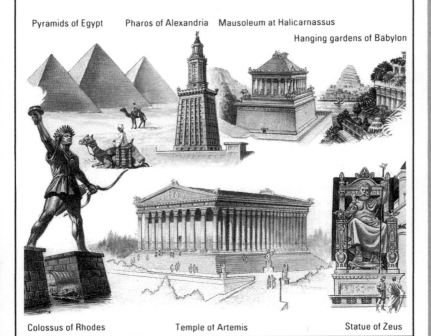

Pyramids of Egypt    Pharos of Alexandria    Mausoleum at Halicarnassus

Hanging gardens of Babylon

Colossus of Rhodes    Temple of Artemis    Statue of Zeus

# Human body

**The human body is a miracle of coordination. The heart beats 70 times a minute pumping blood through the veins and arteries, taking life-giving oxygen to the brain. The body fights off infection and repairs itself: wounds can heal and broken bones knit together. Three billion of the body's cells die every minute and are replaced; only the brain cells cannot be renewed, but these last 100 years. The brain sends messages to our 639 muscles; these respond, moving our 206 bones to command. Our senses keep us in touch with the world, transmitting information, pleasure and pain.**

The body is complicated and finely balanced. It is made up of many different parts; each has its own special job and yet the healthy body is dependent on their all working together.

We need to look after our bodies. We need to supply them with food, sleep and exercise. However, much of the regular maintenance is done by the body itself. Most of the cells of your body are replaced regularly. Around three billion cells die every minute, but they are replaced by three billion new ones. Only the nerve cells, including those of the brain, are not replaced. However, they can live for about 100 years.

▽ The development of the human species has taken millions of years. Our earliest human-like ancestors lived in Africa some 4 million years ago.

Ramapithecus
15 million
years ago

Australopithecus
4-1 million
years ago

Homo habilis
2-1.5 million
years ago

The body is also very good at repairing accidental damage. If cut, it does its best to stop the bleeding, and for all small cuts the normal body can do so without help. The skin heals up, leaving perhaps a small scar. Broken bones knit together to form strong new ones. The body fights off infection, with the help of its immune system.

Often, the work of doctors and surgeons is to give the body the best possible conditions to cure itself. Only when an injury is severe or a particularly virulent set of germs has invaded, are stronger methods needed, such as sewing up wounds, removing diseased tissue or killing micro-organisms.

△ The body of an athlete is like a finely tuned engine. Training helps to develop body strengths and skills to a level far above the average.

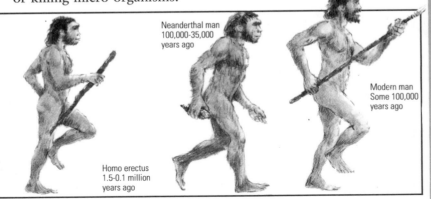

Neanderthal man
100,000-35,000
years ago

Modern man
Some 100,000
years ago

Homo erectus
1.5-0.1 million
years ago

Occasionally, part of the body breaks down completely. Today, we are able to replace some organs by the process of transplant surgery; for example we can give people new hearts and lungs, kidneys or livers.

Groups of organs working together to perform a particular task are called systems. These are the body's seven systems and their functions.

*The skeletal-muscular system* provides a protective framework for the body and the means for moving it about.

*The digestive system* takes in food, processes it to keep the body running and gets rid of waste material.

*The urinary system* balances the body's liquid intake. It plays a major part in clearing the body of waste products.

▽ The urinary system. The two kidneys (one of which has been cut away to show its structure) act as filters removing waste products and excess water from the blood. Urine produced in this way drips down the ureters into the bladder.

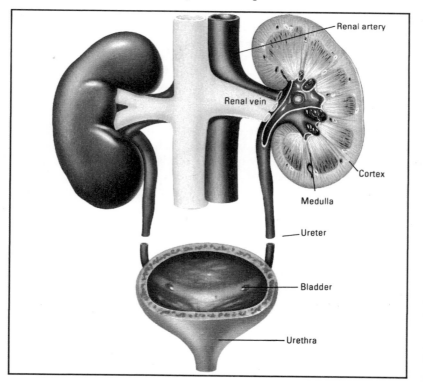

Renal artery

Renal vein

Cortex

Medulla

Ureter

Bladder

Urethra

*The respiratory system* takes in oxygen every time you breathe in. Oxygen is needed by every part of the body. When you breathe out, the gas carbon dioxide (a waste product) is cleared out of your body. The respiratory system also gets rid of some moisture.

*The heart and circulatory system* takes the oxygen from the respiratory system and sends it all round the body in the blood. The blood picks up carbon dioxide and takes it back to the heart, which transfers it to the lungs for disposal.

*The nervous system* is the body's control system. The brain is the control centre, and nerves carry messages, to and from the brain, all over the body.

*The reproductive system* is the means by which babies are produced to carry on the human race. As in other animals, a sperm cell from a male is united with an egg cell in a female to start the reproductive process.

Various organs of the body take part in one or more of these systems. The glands make chemical substances that the body needs in order to keep running. The sense organs – eyes, ears, nose, taste buds and the sense of feeling in the skin – supply the brain with information about the world around the body.

There are still many things about the body that we do not fully understand. One of the most wonderful is the mechanism that controls how we grow and develop as children – and what makes us stop growing when we have reached full size.

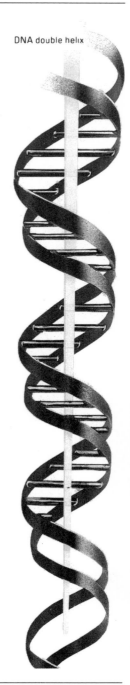
DNA double helix

### HEREDITY

Heredity concerns the inheritance of characteristics from our parents' genes. The nucleus of all human cells (except eggs and sperm) contains 46 thread-like structures called **chromosomes**. These contain a chemical known as **DNA** (deoxyribonucleic acid), of which each molecule has a structure like a twisted ladder called a double helix (see right). The two parts of the 'rungs' of this lader are arranged in lots of different combinations which form coded instructions called **genes**.

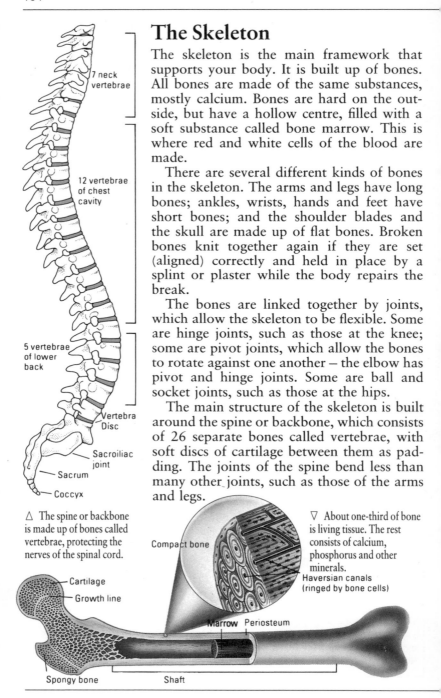

# The Skeleton

The skeleton is the main framework that supports your body. It is built up of bones. All bones are made of the same substances, mostly calcium. Bones are hard on the outside, but have a hollow centre, filled with a soft substance called bone marrow. This is where red and white cells of the blood are made.

There are several different kinds of bones in the skeleton. The arms and legs have long bones; ankles, wrists, hands and feet have short bones; and the shoulder blades and the skull are made up of flat bones. Broken bones knit together again if they are set (aligned) correctly and held in place by a splint or plaster while the body repairs the break.

The bones are linked together by joints, which allow the skeleton to be flexible. Some are hinge joints, such as those at the knee; some are pivot joints, which allow the bones to rotate against one another – the elbow has pivot and hinge joints. Some are ball and socket joints, such as those at the hips.

The main structure of the skeleton is built around the spine or backbone, which consists of 26 separate bones called vertebrae, with soft discs of cartilage between them as padding. The joints of the spine bend less than many other joints, such as those of the arms and legs.

7 neck vertebrae

12 vertebrae of chest cavity

5 vertebrae of lower back

Vertebra

Disc

Sacroiliac joint

Sacrum

Coccyx

△ The spine or backbone is made up of bones called vertebrae, protecting the nerves of the spinal cord.

Compact bone

▽ About one-third of bone is living tissue. The rest consists of calcium, phosphorus and other minerals.

Haversian canals (ringed by bone cells)

Cartilage

Growth line

Marrow   Periosteum

Spongy bone

Shaft

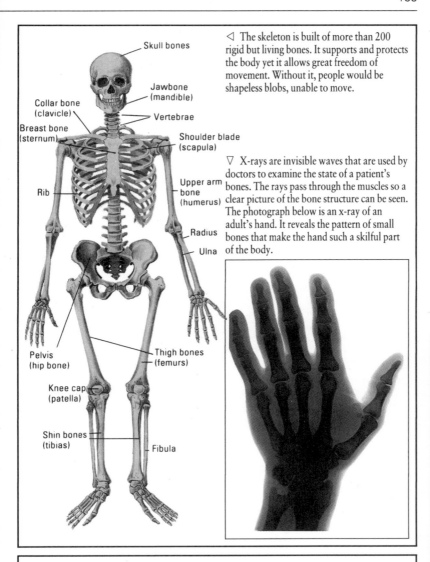

Skull bones

Jawbone (mandible)

Collar bone (clavicle)

Vertebrae

Breast bone (sternum)

Shoulder blade (scapula)

Rib

Upper arm bone (humerus)

Radius

Ulna

Pelvis (hip bone)

Thigh bones (femurs)

Knee cap (patella)

Shin bones (tibias)

Fibula

◁ The skeleton is built of more than 200 rigid but living bones. It supports and protects the body yet it allows great freedom of movement. Without it, people would be shapeless blobs, unable to move.

▽ X-rays are invisible waves that are used by doctors to examine the state of a patient's bones. The rays pass through the muscles so a clear picture of the bone structure can be seen. The photograph below is an x-ray of an adult's hand. It reveals the pattern of small bones that make the hand such a skilful part of the body.

## BONE FACTS

**Number of bones** in the adult human body is 206, but young children have more: the bones fuse together as the children grow.

**Longest bone** in the human body is the femur, or thigh bone. It is also the strongest.

**Long bones** are much stronger and lighter than reinforced concrete.

**Smallest bone** in the human body is the stapes or stirrup bone, one of three tiny bones in each ear.

**Neck bones** in the human body total seven – the same number as in a giraffe, whose neck may be 1.8 m (6 ft) long, or more.

**The skull** contains 22 bones, excluding the six tiny bones in the ears.

△ Striped or skeletal muscles have long striped cells with several nuclei in each cell.

△ Cardiac or heart muscles have shorter, less striped cells, which contain only one nucleus.

△ Smooth muscles are made of short, unstriped cells with one nucleus in each cell.

# Muscles

Joints allow your bones to move, but the actual movements are produced by the muscles. Muscles are attached to your bones by strong bands of tissue called tendons. When muscles contract, they pull your bones. They can only pull, they cannot push, so most muscles come in pairs and work together to pull in turn. The brain sends them the instructions to contract or relax.

Muscle cells can shorten by up to one third of their length. When they contract they always shorten as much as they can. If all the cells in a muscle shorten at the same time the result is a jerky movement, for example when you snatch at something. But usually muscle cells contract in sequence, producing a smooth movement of the whole muscle.

There are three types of muscle in the human body. Most muscles are long and thin, and are made up of many cells arranged in fibres. The kind of muscles that move your arms and legs are called skeletal or striped muscles, because they look striped under a microscope. These are the voluntary muscles under the direct control of the brain, such as those you use when walking.

Other muscles, such as the diaphragm, are flat sheets of tissue. Smooth muscles appear unstriped. These are the involuntary muscles, which work without direct control. They power all sorts of body functions, such as normal breathing and digestion, which must go on all the time whether you are awake or asleep. The third kind of muscle, found only in the heart, is a strong and specialized type called cardiac muscle.

---

### MUSCLE FACTS

**Number of muscles** in the human body totals 639.
**Largest muscle** is the gluteus maximus, found in the buttock. It extends the thigh or the trunk.

**Smallest muscle** is the stapedius, a tiny muscle in the ear which controls movement of the stapes (stirrup bone).
**40 per cent** of your body weight consists of muscles.
**Walking** requires the use of 200 muscles.

## HOW MUSCLES WORK

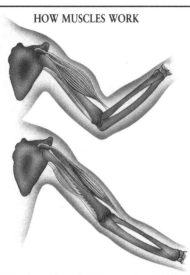

◁ Muscles are made up of bundles of fibres. As the fibres contract, the muscles become shorter and thicker. The muscle fibres are made up of muscle cells. The muscles of the arm work in pairs. As one contracts the other relaxes, straightening and bending the arm.

▽ Beneath the skin many muscles are partially contracted and ready for movement. In the face, short muscles control eye movements, facial expressions, speech and chewing. In addition to the muscles we can control, there are 30 more that work automatically. These are the muscles of the heart, lungs and digestive system.

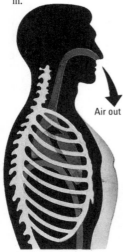

Air in

Diaphragm

Rib cage

△ 1. Breathing in: diaphragm contracts downwards, chest inner space increases so pressure is greater outside than inside lungs. Air is breathed in.

Air out

△ 2. Breathing out: diaphragm arches upwards, chest inner space decreases, so pressure inside lungs is greater than outside. Air is pushed out.

# Lungs, Blood and Heart

One substance that is essential for life is the gas oxygen, which forms about 21 per cent of the air we breathe. Keeping the body supplied with oxygen is the work of the lungs and heart, with the help of the blood. Oxygen is drawn in by the lungs and transferred there to the blood. Blood is pumped around the body by the heart, carrying the oxygen to every living cell in the body.

When a person breathes in, the air is drawn through the nose and mouth. It passes down the trachea (windpipe), which branches into two tubes called bronchi. One bronchus leads to the left lung, the other to the right lung. In the lungs the bronchi branch into a mass of tiny twig-like bronchioles. The smallest bronchioles end in a bunch of tiny alveoli (air sacs). These absorb the oxygen from the air and pass it into the bloodstream.

The heart is a very efficient pump containing four chambers, the left and right atria at the top and the left and right ventricles below. Freshly oxygenated blood coming from the lungs flows into the left atrium. It is pumped through a one-way valve into the left ventricle, and then around the body.

Blood returning from the body has lost its oxygen, but contains a waste product, carbon dioxide gas. This used blood comes into the right atrium, and is pumped through a valve into the right ventricle, and thence to the lungs to have the carbon dioxide removed and more oxygen added.

◁ Valves in the heart and veins control blood flow. Blood flowing forwards forces valve flaps open.

▷ Blood attempting to flow backwards forces flaps to close.

The blood is carried around the body in a series of tubes called blood vessels. Fresh blood from the heart flows through blood vessels called arteries. As with any pipe system, the arteries start large, and branch into smaller and smaller vessels, and finally into thin blood vessels called capillaries. The capillaries have thin walls which allow oxygen and food substances in the blood to pass into the body cells, and waste products to be returned. Finally the blood flows back to the heart through a return system of veins.

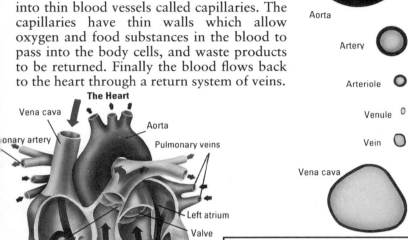

Aorta

Artery

Arteriole

Venule

Vein

Vena cava

**The Heart**

Vena cava

Aorta

onary artery

Pulmonary veins

Left atrium

Valve

Valve

t atrium

Valve

Right ventricle

Valve

Left ventricle

### BLOOD FACTS

**Volume of blood** in an average-sized adult is about 5 litres (1 gallon). Smaller people have less, larger people more.

**Total number of red cells** in the blood of an average man is 25 million million.

**Blood groups** There are four basic blood groups, A, AB, B and O. World wide, Group O is the most common, but other groups are more common in various countries.

**Total length** of the blood vessels in an average-sized adult is about 160,000 km (100,000 miles).

### HEART FACTS

**The heart beats** about 37 million times a year, or 70 times a minute.

**The heart rests** between beats; in a lifetime of 70 years, the total resting time is about 40 years.

**Total weight** of blood pumped every day by the heart is about 13 tonnes, or 13,640 litres (3,000 gallons)

**Weight of the heart** is about 310 g (11 oz) for a man, 260 g (9 oz) for a woman.

**Largest artery** is the aorta, which leaves the left ventricle of the heart. It is 2.5 cm (1 in) across.

### LUNG FACTS

**The alveoli** (air sacs) in the lungs total more than 600 million.

**Walls of the air sacs** cover between 56 and 93 sq m (600–1,000 sq ft).

**Capacity** of an adult's lungs is about 3 litres (5 pints) of air.

**Air is expelled** and breathed in about 15 times a minute, about 0.5 litre (less than 1 pint) at a time.

**The diaphragm** can move as much as 5 cm (2 in) when breathing deeply.

# The Brain and the Senses

The brain, nerves and senses are the great control and communications system of the body. The brain is located in the skull. Messages to it come from the five senses – sight, hearing, smell, taste and feeling. They tell the brain what is happening outside the body. The brain processes this information and issues instructions to the rest of the body in response.

**The Brain**

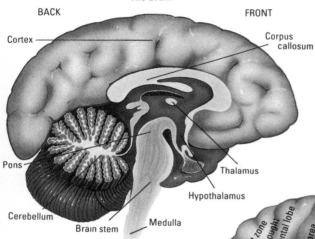

◁ The brain's different areas have different functions. For example, the medulla controls involuntary activities such as breathing. The largest area, the cortex, controls conscious feelings and voluntary movements and is responsible for intelligence and learning.

**The Cortex**

---

**SENSES FACTS**

**Colour vision** is so sensitive that some people can distinguish as many as 300,000 different shades.

**The human ear** can distinguish more than 1,500 different musical tones.

**The spiral canal** of the inner ear is about the size of a pea, but if uncoiled it would be about 38 mm (1½ in) long.

**Taste buds** on the tongue have specialized roles. Those on the tip detect sweet and salt flavours; those at the sides sour flavours; and those towards the back bitter flavours.

△ The cortex is the outer layer of a large, folded area called the cerebrum. The different functions of the cerebrum are shown above. The left side of the cortex controls the right side of the body. The right side controls the left. Sight, hearing, smell and taste are controlled from sensory areas. Motor areas send messages to other parts of the body.

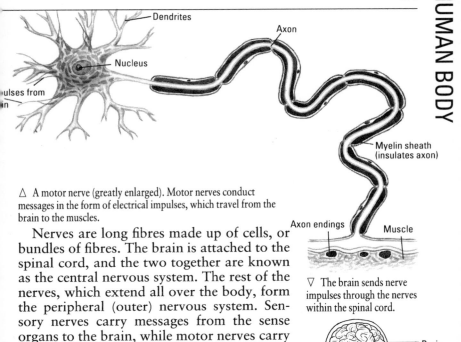

Dendrites

Axon

Nucleus

..ulses from
..in

Myelin sheath
(insulates axon)

Axon endings

Muscle

△ A motor nerve (greatly enlarged). Motor nerves conduct messages in the form of electrical impulses, which travel from the brain to the muscles.

Nerves are long fibres made up of cells, or bundles of fibres. The brain is attached to the spinal cord, and the two together are known as the central nervous system. The rest of the nerves, which extend all over the body, form the peripheral (outer) nervous system. Sensory nerves carry messages from the sense organs to the brain, while motor nerves carry messages from the brain to the muscles.

As you read this page, your brain is combining the letters into words and sentences. Some of this information will be stored as memories. Your brain is also sending messages to control your breathing rate, digestion of your food and many other body functions. Because of your nervous system, you know where you are and what you are doing.

▽ The brain sends nerve impulses through the nerves within the spinal cord.

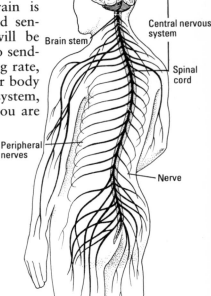

Brain

Central nervous system

Brain stem

Spinal cord

Peripheral nerves

Nerve

### NERVOUS SYSTEM FACTS

**Weight** of an average adult brain is about 1.4 kg (3 lb)

**Total number of nerve cells** in the brain is about 12 billion. Once growing is complete, thousands of cells are lost every day and not replaced.

**Nerve impulses** travel at slightly over 320 km/h (200 mph).

**The spinal cord** is about 430 mm (17 in) long and about 20 mm (¾ in) thick. It weighs about 43 g (1½ oz), and contains 31 pairs of spinal nerves which control the body's muscles.

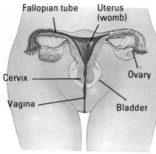

△ The reproductive organs of a woman. From puberty, a mature egg is released from the ovary every 28 days.

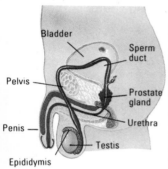

△ The reproductive organs of a man. Sperm are produced in the testes and mature in the epididymus. They travel to the penis in a fluid that is made in the seminal vesicles and prostate gland.

# Reproduction

A baby begins its life when a sperm cell from its father meets an ovum – an egg cell – from its mother inside the mother's body. When the ovum is fertilized by the sperm, the two cells unite to form one cell, which then divides until a ball of 64 cells attaches itself to the lining of the uterus. The baby develops very quickly and has all its organs after about 12 weeks.

The baby takes about nine months to become fully formed and ready to be born. At birth powerful muscles in the uterus (womb) contract and force the baby out through the mother's vagina.

### DID YOU KNOW?

**The uterus** is only about the size and shape of a pear, but during pregnancy it can stretch to about 30 cm (12 in) in length.

**The epididymis** is nearly 6 m (20 ft) long if uncoiled.

**A baby girl** is born with several thousand immature ova in her ovaries. Only a few hundred of these cells mature and are released during her lifetime.

**The testes** are outside the body in the scrotum because a cooler temperature helps the production of sperm.

**An ovum** from the mother and a **sperm** from the father each has 23 DNA-coded chromosomes in its nucleus.

**A mature sperm** is about $\frac{1}{20}$ mm ($\frac{1}{500}$ in) long. Out of hundreds of millions of sperm released together, only one fertilizes the ovum.

▷ A magnified photograph of spermatoza. Each sperm consists of a head and a tail.

## REPRODUCTION GLOSSARY

**afterbirth** The discarded placenta.
**amnion** Protective 'bag' filled with fluid in which the foetus develops.
**cervix** Opening at the bottom of the uterus.
**conception** Fertilization.
**contractions** Regular movements by the muscles of the uterus to push the fully-grown baby out of the mother's body.
**copulation** Sexual intercourse, after which a man's sperm fertilizes a woman's ovum.
**embryo** A baby in its first eight weeks of development.
**epididymis** Coiled tube in which sperm are stored.
**fallopian tubes** Pair of tubes leading from the ovary to the uterus.
**fertilization** Fusion of sperm and ovum.
**foetus** A developing baby after the first eight weeks.
**labour** The period during which the mother experiences contractions.
**menstruation** Monthly discharge of unfertilized egg and blood from the vagina.
**ovaries** Pair of organs in which a woman's egg cells are stored.
**ovum** (plural ova) The female egg cell.
**penis** Male external organ for passing water and copulation.
**placenta** Tissue that forms in the uterus to link the mother's blood supply to her baby.
**pregnancy** Condition in which a woman is carrying a baby.
**scrotum** The pouch of skin outside the body containing a man's testes.
**semen** The mixture of sperm and special fluids produced by a man.
**sperm** The male cells.
**testes** (singular testis) Male organs in which sperm is produced.
**twins** Two children conceived at the same time; identical twins result from the splitting of an embryo at a very early stage; non-identical twins result from the fertilization of two ova.
**umbilical cord** Tube linking foetus to mother through the placenta.
**urethra** Tube inside the penis through which semen leaves a man's body.
**uterus** Hollow female organ where fertilization and development take place.
**vagina** In a woman, the canal leading from the cervix to the exterior of the body.
**womb** The uterus.

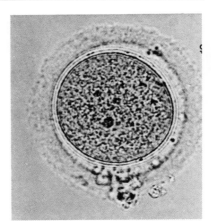

△ An ovum is about 0.1–0.2 mm in diamater. In just nine months, one fertilized ovum will divide to form the two million cells that make up the tissues, organs and fluids of the new-born baby's body.

▽ An ultrasound picture of a baby in the womb. A scan may be given to check the size, health and position of the baby, and to see if the mother is carrying twins. The scan uses waves to pick up the outline of the baby. It is a safer method than an x-ray.

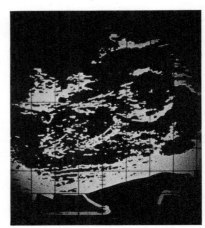

# The Digestive System

The digestive system is the body's fuel processing plant. The food and drink you consume is turned partly into materials to rebuild and replace the body's cells, and partly into energy.

The body produces chemical substances called enzymes, which digest (break down) the food so it can be absorbed. Digestion begins in the mouth, where saliva contains the first of the many enzymes. In the stomach more chemicals are poured on the food to break it down still further. From the stomach the partly digested food goes through the long tube called the small intestine, where most digestion is done. Liquids are processed by the kidneys, which filter out any substances the body still needs.

▽ The stomach squeezes and moves food along, as gastric juices break down the food into a kind of soup. In the small intestine, bile and other juices mix with the soup. Fats, sugars, proteins and vitamins move into the bloodstream. Finally water and waste move into the large intestine. Solid waste is evacuated by way of the rectum.

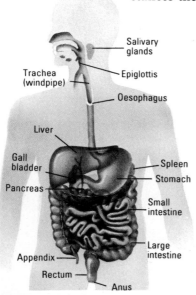

Salivary glands
Trachea (windpipe)
Epiglottis
Oesophagus
Liver
Gall bladder
Pancreas
Spleen
Stomach
Small intestine
Large intestine
Appendix
Rectum
Anus

## DIGESTION FACTS

**The gullet**, or oesophagus, is a tube about 250 mm (10 in) long and 12.5–25 mm (½–1 in) in diameter. It takes food from the mouth to the stomach.

**The stomach** contains the powerful hydrochloric acid, which breaks down food and kills germs; it is protected against the effects of this acid by a lining of mucus (a slimy substance which coats the walls).

**The small intestine** is about 6 m (20 ft) long. It is about 35 mm (1½ in) in diameter. Here food is digested and absorbed. Remaining material passes into the large intestine.

**The large intestine** is about 1.5 m (5 ft) long and 50 mm (2 in) in diameter. Much of the water from the undigested material is absorbed at this point.

**The appendix** is a thin pouch about 90 mm (3½ in) long. It seems to have no function in the human digestive system, though it has an important role in grass-eating animals.

## FOOD FACTS

**Cholesterol**, a fat in eggs and shellfish, can increase the risk of a heart attack.

**Insufficient iron** in the diet can lead to anaemia, a blood deficiency. Iron is found in bread, meat, fruit and vegetables.

**Too much salt** in the diet can lead to high blood pressure.

**Scurvy**, a disease producing swollen gums and inflamed skin spots, can result from not having enough Vitaminc C (found in fruit and vegetables).

# The Dangers of Drugs

Drugs are chemical substances used on the human body, mainly as medicines to cure illnesses. They are made from plants, animal products and minerals. Many of the plant and animal product drugs have been replaced with synthetic versions made in laboratories.

Some drugs, if taken to excess, become addictive – that is, the users cannot do without them. These include many pain-killers and sleeping pills. Unfortunately many people today take some of these addictive drugs to give themselves a temporary feeling of well-being. The problem is that not only do the good feelings wear off but most addictive drugs have harmful effects and can cause serious illnesses and even death.

This drug abuse and its perils is something everyone should be aware of. There is in-creasing anxiety about drug-taking among young people, including schoolchildren. It often begins with alcohol, which is also a mild drug that can become addictive. Young

▽ The physical effects of drug abuse can be severe. Drug addicts can be helped to overcome the often painful effects of withdrawal (ending their addiction).

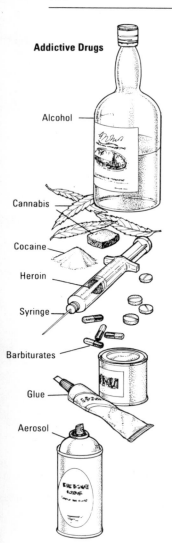

**Addictive Drugs**

Alcohol

Cannabis

Cocaine

Heroin

Syringe

Barbiturates

Glue

Aerosol

△ Some of the substances used by drug addicts: alcohol, cannabis, cocaine, barbiturates and amphetamines, glue (in tins, tubes and aerosols).

people may also be tempted to try glue-sniffing without realizing the harmful effects. Although sniffing substances such as lighter fuel may lead to a good feeling, the gases breathed in can cause serious damage. Glue-sniffers can easily suffocate and die.

The effect of drugs varies widely from person to person. For some, taking even one experimental dose has been known to be fatal. The worst aspect of drug addiction is that prolonged drug-taking can make people lose all will to do anything positive except take another dose of the drug they are hooked on.

## DRUGS FACTS

**amphetamines** Addictive drugs, also called 'pep pills'. After a short period of elation the user feels depressed and persecuted, and may behave violently.

**barbiturates** Sometimes used as sleeping drugs; they can quickly become addictive; they may cause death if used with alcohol.

**cannabis** Also called pot, grass or hash. Produces lethargy, nausea and lack of coordination. It leads to brain, heart and lung damage.

**cocaine** Also called crack, coke or snow; can cause trembling, itching and open sores. Deaths have resulted from injecting, swallowing and 'snorting' cocaine in large doses.

**glue-sniffing** Drug abuse that can cause brain, kidney or liver damage; inhaling may suffocate the user. Substances sniffed include dry-cleaning fluid and aerosol gases.

**LSD (lysergic acid diethylamide)** Known as acid. Produces hallucinations – visions and distortions in sound. For some users, LSD brings a temporary feeling of happiness and relaxation, for others it leads to feelings of anxiety and fear. It can cause sweating and trembling, and heavy users may develop brain damage.

**opiates** Drugs made from opium; heroin (also called H, smack or horse), the most widely used by addicts, produces mental and physical deterioration, loss of appetite, liver failure and death.

## WHERE TO SEEK ADVICE

**Citizens' Advice Bureaus** up and down the country can put people in touch with local organizations that can help with drug addiction.

**The Samaritans** are a group that offers advice and comfort by telephone on a confidential basis at any hour of the day or night. See the local phone book.

**Alcoholics Anonymous** is a self-help organization with groups meeting in all parts of the country. The local phone book will have the number of the nearest contact.

## HUMAN BODY GLOSSARY

**abscess** A painful, swollen area inside the body, caused by bacteria and filled with pus. A gumboil is a type of abscess caused by an infected tooth.

**acne** Spots, blackheads or whiteheads caused by inflammation of the oil glands in the skin. Four out of five teenagers suffer from it.

**Adam's apple** The piece of cartilage which sticks out over the front of the larynx. It is more prominent in men than in women.

**adenoids** Small glands made of lymph tissue at the back of the nasal passages. They help to protect the lungs from infection.

**adolescence** Development from a child to an adult.

**adrenaline** A hormone which stimulates the heart and increases muscular strength and endurance.

**allergy** A reaction, such as a running nose, rash or wheezing, caused when a person is sensitive to certain substances. Hay fever is an allergy to pollen.

**amino acids** The chemical substances which make up proteins. When protein in food is digested (broken down), the amino acids are transported around the body and assembled into new proteins in the cells.

**antibiotics** Drugs which can kill bacteria by preventing them from growing or reproducing.

**antibodies** Substances produced by the body's immune system. They destroy harmful bacteria and viruses.

**antiseptics** Substances which kill certain micro-organisms or slow down their growth.

**arteries** Any blood vessels which carry blood away from the heart to the rest of the body.

**bacteria** Microscopic one-celled organisms found everywhere – in water, in soil, and on and in our bodies. Most are harmless; some are essential, such as those in the intestines; a few cause disease.

**Bacteria come in many shapes and sizes**

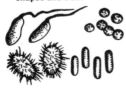

**benign** Word used to describe a tumour or growth which is harmless and not likely to become worse.

**bile** Greenish liquid produced by the liver. It is stored in a sac called the gall bladder and helps to digest fat in the small intestine.

**blood vessel** Any of the many tubes – arteries, veins and capillaries – which carry blood around the body.

**bronchus** One of the branches of the windpipe, leading to the lungs.

**capillaries** The smallest type of blood vessels.

**cardiac** Referring to the heart.

**cartilage** Soft, elastic tissue, often called gristle.

**Two different shapes of epithelial cell**

**cells** The basic living units of the body, sometimes called the 'building blocks' of life. Every part of the body is made up of cells – one million million of them in an average man.

**central nervous system** The brain and spinal cord.

**chromosome** One of 46 structures found in the nucleus of every human cell. Chromosomes carry the genes which determine inherited characteristics, such as sex, hair colour and height.

**colon** Lower part of the large intestine.

**coronary** Referring to the blood vessels that supply the heart. Coronary arteries over the surface of the heart provide oxygen for its cells.

**diaphragm** Flat muscle which separates the chest from the abdomen.

**DNA (Deoxyribonucleic Acid)** Complicated chemical which makes up genes and chromosomes.

**enzymes** Chemical substances which speed up chemical reactions within the body and control processes such as digestion.

**epiglottis** Small flap at the back of the tongue which blocks the windpipe when you swallow and so prevents food 'going down the wrong way'.

**follicle** Small pocket in the skin from which a single hair grows.

**gall bladder** Small sac, about 80–100 mm (3–4 in) long, which stores bile.

**genes** Combinations of DNA which make up the chromosomes in each cell.

**The lymphatic system**

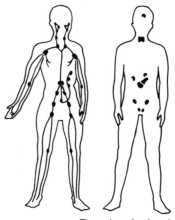

**The main endocrine glands of the body**

**glands** Organs in the body, such as the salivary glands, the kidneys and liver, which produce or work on chemical substances.

**hormones** Sometimes called the body's chemical messengers; produced in certain glands and released into the blood. They control many body processes, such as growth or the amount of sugar in the blood.

**immune system** The body's own defences against infection.

**intestines** The long tube, beginning at the stomach and ending at the anus, in which food is digested.

**keratin** The hard substance found in hair, nails and skin.

**kidneys** Two organs which filter waste from the blood and produce urine, which collects in the bladder. They lie on either side of the spine.

**larynx** The voice box, located at the top of the trachea and containing the vocal cords.

**ligaments** Tough elastic bands of tissue which hold bones together at a joint.

**liver** The body's largest gland; it stores iron and some glucose, processes amino acids and produces bile.

**lymph** Clear liquid which contains white blood cells. It flows through a set of vessels (tubes) called the 'lymphatic system'.

**marrow** Soft, jelly-like substance found in the centre of bones; blood cells are made in some bone marrow.

**membrane** Thin layer of cells which lines or covers various parts of the body.

**micro-organisms** Tiny living things such as bacteria and viruses; often called germs.

**oesophagus** Gullet or food pipe leading from the throat to the stomach.

**Oesophagus**

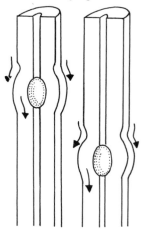

**organ** Group of tissues which work together, for example the heart or the liver.

**pancreas** Gland which produces the hormone insulin, which controls the level of glucose in the blood.

**plasma** Liquid part of blood.

**proteins** Body-building chemicals, made of amino acids.

**pulse** Rhythmic throbbing which can be felt in the arteries as your heart beats.

**pus** Whitish-yellow liquid produced in certain infections.

**reflex actions** Actions which are automatic and cannot be controlled by thinking about them.

**renal** Referring to the kidneys.

**respiration** Breathing; also the use of oxygen in the cells to release energy from glucose, and the release of carbon dioxide.

**saliva** Liquid released by three pairs of glands in the mouth; it starts the process of digestion.

**sebaceous gland** Oil-producing gland in the skin.

**sinuses** Four sets of cavities in the skull, where the air you breathe in is warmed.

**spinal cord** Thick cord of nerves which begins at the base of the brain and extends to the bottom of the back.

**spleen** An organ which is part of the lymphatic system and helps to fight infection.

**tendons** Very strong bands of tissue which connect muscles to bones.

**thymus** Gland in the lower neck, which helps in the immune process.

**thyroid** Gland in the neck that produces a hormone, thyroxine, which controls growth rate and the speed of chemical processes in the body.

**tissues** Groups of similar cells which form various parts of the body, such as nerves or muscles.

**trachea** Windpipe, leading from the larynx to the lungs.

**tumour** Swelling caused by abnormal growth of cells. It may be benign or cancerous.

**ulcer** Open sore on the skin, or on a membrane inside the body.

**ureters** Tubes which carry urine from the kidneys to the bladder.

**urethra** Tube which leads from the bladder to the outside of the body.

**veins** Blood vessels that carry used blood back to the heart.

**viruses** Micro-organisms which cause disease if they invade the body.

**vitamins** Group of about 15 substances found in food. They are needed for good health.

**vocal cords** Two ligaments stretched across the larynx. They vibrate as air passes over them, enabling speech.

▷ The AIDS virus prevents the white blood cells, the body's natural defence mechanism, from working. 1. The virus attaches itself to and 2. móves into a white blood cell. Once inside 3., the core of the virus breaks open and releases DNA to match that of the white blood cell. The blood cell make copies of the virus and dies. When the body has lost a large number of white blood cells it is not protected from even minor infections.

## AIDS

AIDS stands for Acquired Immune Deficiency Syndrome. It is a serious disorder brought about by a virus called Human Immunodeficiency Virus. It has this name because it attacks the white blood cells which form part of the body's immune system. This system otherwise guards the body against disease.

**Cause** is one of two viruses in the group called retroviruses.

**Symptons** include diarrhoea, fever, tiredness, night sweats, loss of appetite and weight, and enlarged lymph glands.

**Transmission** is by intimate sexual contact, or by exposure to infected blood (for example, by sharing hypodermic needles with an infected person). An infected woman who is pregnant can pass the virus to her foetus.

**Treatment** is still a matter of experiment; no cure has yet been found.

AIDS virus

White blood cells

Nucleus with chromosomes

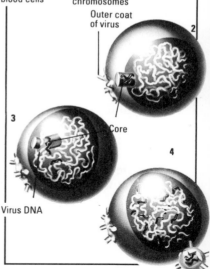

Outer coat of virus

Core

Virus DNA

# Animals

**The last dinosaur died 65 million years ago, the dodo is dead and other animals are in danger of extinction, yet there are still over two million species left on this planet, from the speedy cheetah to the tardy snail, and the egg-laying platypus to the remarkably skilled termite.**

**A**nimals dominate the Earth today. They have done so for only about 500 million years, a fraction of the Earth's 4,600-million-year existence. The number of species (kinds) is probably at least two million, and nobody can calculate how many different individuals there are.

Animal life become possible when the Earth built up a sufficient stock of oxygen, which all animals must breathe in order to live. Some, such as fish, extract oxygen from the waters of the oceans and rivers. Others draw it from the atmosphere. Animals also depend on plants for their food, either directly, as cows do, or indirectly, as flesh-eating animals such as lions and wolves do.

△ Fossils are the preserved remains of plants and animals that died millions of years ago. This spider has been preserved in amber, the hardened resin from pine trees.

The easiest way to divide the many species of animals is into the vertebrates – those with backbones – and the invertebrates – those without.

The vertebrates are the 'higher' animals, those with the most developed brains. They are, in ascending order of development, fishes, amphibians, reptiles, birds and mammals. They include all the large animals which appear to rule the world. But they are not necessarily the most successful.

▽ This fossil is a trilobite. It lived on the sea bed before even dinosaurs were around.

The invertebrates – all the rest – are much simpler creatures. Some, such as amoebas and sponges, are very simple indeed. Others, in particular the insects, are more complex and very successful. There are more kinds and total numbers of insects than of any other land-based creature. They make their

▷ The English naturalist, Charles Darwin (1809–82), put forward the theory that all living things have evolved (developed) over millions of years from primitive forms of life.

homes almost everywhere on land, and if something can be eaten, an insect has evolved that can eat it. Most insects themselves are in danger of being eaten by some other creature.

Large numbers of animals live in the seas, which cover almost three-quarters of the Earth's surface. There are fish, and countless millions of invertebrates such as krill, squid, jellyfish and other smaller creatures. All these animals take their oxygen from water. There are also a few mammals – whales, seals and their relatives – which have moved from land to live in water, though they still breathe air.

One of the big differences between animals and plants is that animals are free to move about. A number of animals move regularly from one place to another, in the process we call migration.

The most obvious migration is that of birds. Many species spend the winter months in the warmer parts of the world, nearer the Equator, and fly north or south to temperate climates to lay their eggs and rear their young. Some insects migrate, notably the monarch butterflies of North America, which fly south to hibernate.

Some mammals also migrate. For example, in East Africa grazing animals – antelopes, zebras, giraffes and others – move from place to place in a huge circle to graze on fresh vegetation. In the north, caribou and reindeer move south in the winter and north in the summer.

At sea, shoals of fish and smaller creatures swim from place to place in search of their food, and they are followed by larger fish, such as sharks, and by whales.

▷ Darwin noticed differences in the finches that lived on several islands in the Pacific, and this led him to his theory of evolution which he called 'natural selection'. It took him another 20 years to work out all the implications.

## THE ANIMAL KINGDOM

▽ The main groups in the animal kingdom. The principal stem includes the lower, but very numerous, groups such as brachiopods, molluscs and arthropods. The vertebrate animals (mammals, birds, reptiles for instance) include the most advanced animals. Some of the classes of worms and other small groups have been omitted.

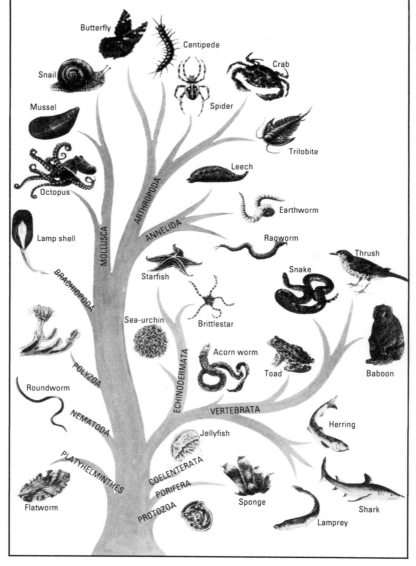

◁ An Arctic tern on its nest.

▽ The swifts include the world's fastest flyer in level flight. Swifts may spend weeks in the air, catching insects and even sleeping on the wing. Their small feet render them virtually helpless on level ground.

## MIGRATION

**Longest bird migration** is by the Arctic tern (*Sterna paradisaea*), which leads a life of perpetual summer. It leaves the Arctic as summer ends and flies 18,000 kilometres (11,000 miles) to Antarctica. At the end of the Antarctic summer it flies back to its breeding ground – so making a round trip of 36,000 kilometres (22,000 miles).

**Longest mammal migration** is by the Alaska seal (*Callorhinus ursinus*), which does a round trip of 9,600 kilometres (6,000 miles).

**Most travelled butterfly** is the monarch butterfly (*Danaus plexippus*) of North America, which migrates 4,000 kilometres (2,500 miles) from Hudson Bay to Florida and back.

◁ The tortoise lives longer than any other animal.

▽ The great ram's horn is a water-dwelling mollusc.

### ANIMAL SPEED RECORDS

|  | km/h | mph |  | km/h | mph |
|---|---|---|---|---|---|
| Spine-tailed |  |  | Greyhound | 63 | 39 |
| swift | 170 | 106 | Rabbit | 56 | 35 |
| Sailfish | 109 | 68 | Giraffe | 51 | 32 |
| Cheetah | 105 | 65 | Grizzly bear | 48 | 30 |
| Pronghorn |  |  | Cat | 48 | 30 |
| antelope | 97 | 60 | Elephant | 40 | 25 |
| Racing |  |  | Sealion | 40 | 25 |
| pigeon | 97 | 60 | Black mamba | 32 | 20 |
| Lion | 80 | 50 | Bee | 18 | 11 |
| Gazelle | 80 | 50 | Pig | 18 | 11 |
| Hare | 72 | 45 | Chicken | 14 | 9 |
| Zebra | 64 | 40 | Spider | 1.88 | 1.17 |
| Racehorse | 64 | 40 | Tortoise | 0.8 | 0.5 |
| Shark | 64 | 40 | Snail | 0.05 | 0.03 |

Spider

Woodlouse

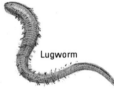

Lugworm

Dahlia Anemone

Starfish

# Animals without Backbones

Animals without backbones are called *invertebrates*. Most of them do not have any form of internal skeleton, though some, such as the cuttlefish, have internal shells. Many have *exoskeletons* (external skeletons). Invertebrates range from sponges to insects, snails and worms. Many of them live in water.

There are more than 20 *phyla* (groups) of invertebrates. Several of them are particularly important. The coelenterates include jellyfish, sea anemones and corals. Molluscs mostly have shells. They include winkles, oysters, limpets, snails, octopuses and squids.

Annelids are worms of various kinds, including the familiar earthworms. Arthropods (the name means 'joint-footed') are very diverse indeed. They include insects, spiders, centipedes, millipedes, and crustaceans such as crabs, lobsters and woodlice. Echinoderms are star-like animals with five limbs. They include starfish and sea urchins.

The chordates are a very mixed bunch. They have some kind of internal rod to support the body, although some lose it when they are adults. There are about 1,300 species which rank as invertebrates, including seasquirts and salps. The most important chordates are the vertebrates, or animals with true backbones.

---

### INVERTEBRATE RECORDS

**Largest spiders** are some of the bird-eating spiders (family Theraphosidae) of South America, whose bodies are more than 75 mm (3 in) long with a leg span of more than 250 mm (10 in).

**Largest centipede** is the giant scolpender (*Scolpendra giganta*) of Central America. Its body is up to 300 mm (12 in) long and 25 mm (1 in) wide. It is large enough to feed on mice and lizards, as well as insects.

**Centipedes with most legs** are those in the order Geophilomorpha. Adults may have up to 177 pairs of legs, or 354 legs altogether.

**Millipedes with most legs** are generally the oldest. Several species are known to have almost 750 legs.

## INVERTEBRATE CLASSIFICATION

| Phylum | Common name, if any | Number of species |
| --- | --- | --- |
| Mesozoa | None | About 50 |
| Porifera | Sponges | About 5,000 |
| Coelenterata | Jellyfish and relatives | About 9,500 |
| Ctenophora | Comb jellies | About 100 |
| Platyhelminthes | Flatworms | About 5,500 |
| Nemertina | Ribbonworms | 750 |
| Aschelminthes | Roundworms and others | 11,800 |
| Gastrotricha | Hairy backs | 175 |
| Kinorhyncha | None | 100 |
| Acanthocephala | Thorny-headed worms | 300 |
| Entoprocta | None | 60 |
| Ectoprocta | Moss animals or bryozoans | 4,000 |
| Brachiopoda | Lamp shells | 260 |
| Annelida | Earthworms and relatives | About 7,000 |
| Arthropoda | Spiders, insects, crustaceans | About 1,150,000 |
| Sipunculoidea | Peanut worms | 250 |
| Echiuroidea | Echiurid worms | 60 |
| Pentastomida | Tongue worms | 70 |
| Tardigrada | Water bears | 180 |
| Mollusca | Molluscs | More than 46,000 |
| Chaetognatha | Arrow worms | 50 |
| Pogohophora | Beard worms | About 80 |
| Echinodermata | Starfish and relatives | About 5,500 |
| Hemichordata | Acorn worms and relatives | 90 |
| Chordata | Chordates | About 1,300 plus back-boned animals |

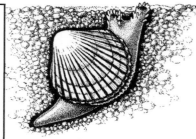

Cockle

Portuguese man of war

Millipede

Edible crab

△ The western marbled white butterfly is found in central and southern Europe and in North Africa.

△ Wood ants make their nests in wooded areas, covering the mounds with leaves and twigs.

△ The common pond skater lives on the surface of still water.

▽ The white-tailed bumblebee often nests in old mouse holes.

# INSECTS

Of all forms of life, the most varied are the insects. More than 1,000,000 species are known, and more are being discovered and classified every year. There are more species of insects than all of the rest of the animal kingdom put together. The number of individual insects is beyond calculation.

An adult insect has six legs, and a body in three sections with a hard outer casing. Most adult insects have wings. They have what are called compound eyes, which may have as many as 30,000 tiny lenses called facets. Each facet conveys a very small part of the whole picture to the insect's brain.

Insects have senses of smell and taste, and many kinds can hear, too. They have cold blood which may be colourless, green or yellow.

Insects are grouped into 33 orders, each containing many families, genera and species. Some orders of insects are little known, and have no common name.

**Apterygote** insects are the simplest kinds. They have no wings, and the young are similar in appearance to the adults, except in size. They include the familiar silverfish, which is often found in houses.

**Exopterygote** insects mostly have wings. They pass through three stages of development – egg, nymph and adult. They include dragonflies, mayflies and stoneflies, which pass their pre-adult life in water; grasshoppers; stick insects; cockroaches; termites; earwigs; lice; and the true bugs, including cicadas and aphids.

**Endopterygote** insects are also winged. They go through four stages of development: egg, larva, pupa and adult. They include beetles, the most numerous of the lot; butterflies and moths; true flies; bees, wasps and ants which, with termites, are called the 'social insects'; and caddis flies, whose larvae live in water.

## Lifecycle of a Butterfly

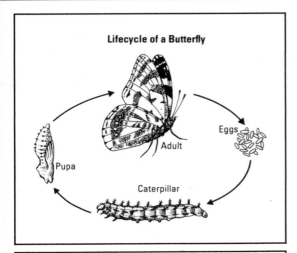

Eggs

Adult

Pupa

Caterpillar

## Lifecycle of a Grasshopper

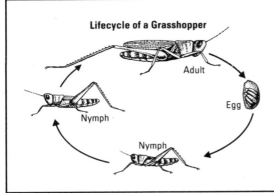

Adult

Egg

Nymph

Nymph

△ The house fly is a pest that carries disease.

△ The great diving beetle is found mainly by ponds and streams.

△ The common wasp builds its nest with paper, which it makes by chewing wood.

▽ The caddis fly is usually seen only at night. Its wings are clothed with hairs.

## INSECT RECORDS

**Largest** insects are several forms of beetles (order Coleoptera). They include the goliath beetles (genus *Goliathus*), the rhinoceros beetle (*Dyastes hercules*) and the longhorned beetle (*Titanus giganteus*), which have all been found at sizes between 125 and 175 mm (5–7 in) long.

**Longest** insects are varieties of stick insects (genera *Palophus* and *Pharnacia*), known to grow more than 300 mm (12 in) long.

**Smallest** insects are the feather-winged beetles (family Ptiliidae), which are less than 0.2 mm (1/100 in) long.

**Most remarkable builders** are various species of termites (order Isoptera). They build nests of soil that may be as much as 7 m (23 ft) tall, with deep cellars as well. Many species build their nests with 'air conditioning', while the compass termites of Australia (*Amitermes meridionalis*) build wedge-shaped mounds with the two short sides facing north-south, so the midday heat strikes as small a surface as possible.

# Animals with Backbones

## FISH

Fish form the largest group of vertebrates.
There are altogether about 13,000 species.
They fall into three groups: jawless fishes,
fishes with skeletons of cartilage (gristle) and
bony fishes.

There are two main kinds of jawless fishes
– hagfish and lampreys. Instead of jaws they
have circular mouths with rasping teeth. The
cartilaginous fishes, of which there are about
575 species, include chimaeras (better known
as ratfishes or elephantfishes), sharks and
rays.

The bony fishes are the most numerous.
They include well-known species such as eels,
herring and salmon, as well as a large and
bewildering variety of lesser-known species.

△ The sea horse, despite its
name, is a fish.

▽ Lampreys and hagfishes
fasten onto other fishes with
their sucker mouths.

---

### FISH RECORDS

**Longest bony fish** is the beluga (*Huso huso*), a kind of sturgeon
found in the Caspian Sea. It has been known to grow up to
7.2 m (23 ft 7 in) in length, and to reach a weight of 1,360 kg
(3,000 lb).

**Heaviest bony fish** is the ocean sunfish (*Mola mola*), which can
weigh up to 2 tonnes.

**Smallest fish** and also the smallest vertebrate is the dwarf goby
(*Pandaka pygmaea*), found in fresh water in the Philippines and
the Marshall Islands. The maximum size for these fish is
12.5 mm (½ in).

**Largest shark** (and largest fish) is the whale shark (*Rhincodon
typhus*), which can reach a length of 15–18 m (50–60 ft), and
weigh 15 tonnes or more.

**Largest rays** are the devil rays in the family Mobulidae, which
measure up to 6 m (20 ft) across. They 'fly' through the water by
flapping their pectoral fins like wings. Some can even leap
quite high into the air.

---

▽ The South American piranha is small but a ferocious feeder.

Vast and deep blue sea,

# FISH CLASSIFICATION

| Order | Common name | No. of species |
|---|---|---|
| **Class Agnatha: jawless fishes** | | |
| Cyclostomata | Lampreys and hagfishes | 45 |
| **Class Chondrichthyes: fishes with a cartilage skeleton** | | |
| Selachii | Sharks | 200 |
| Batoidea | Rays and skates | 350 |
| Chimeriformes | Chimaeras | 25 |
| **Class Osteichthyes: fishes with a bony skeleton** | | |
| Polypteriformes | Bichirs | 12 |
| Acipenseriformes | Sturgeons | 22 |
| Amiiformes | Bowfin | 1 |
| Semionotiformes | Garpikes | 7 |
| Crossopterygii | Coelacanth | 1 |
| Dipnoi | Lungfishes | 5 |
| Elopiformes | Tarpons | 12 |
| Anguilliformes | Eels | 300 |
| Notacanthiformes | Spiny eels | 20 |
| Clupeiformes | Herring and relatives | 350 |
| Osteoglossiformes | Bony tongues | 16 |
| Mormyriformes | Mormyrids | 150 |
| Salmoniformes | Salmon, trout | 500 |
| Myctophiformes | Lantern fish | 300 |
| Ctenothrissiformes | Macristid fish | 1 |
| Gonorhynchiformes | Milk fish | 15 |
| Cypriniformes | Carp and relatives | 350 |
| Siluriformes | Catfishes | 200 |
| Percopsiformes | Pirate perch | 10 |
| Batrachoidiformes | Toadfishes | 10 |
| Gobiesociformes | Clingfishes | 100 |
| Lophiiformes | Angler fishes | 150 |
| Gadiformes | Cod and relatives | 450 |
| Beryciformes | Whalefishes, squirrelfishes | 150 |
| Atheriniformes | Flying fishes, killifishes | 600 |
| Zeiformes | John Dory | 60 |
| Lampridiformes | Ribbonfish | 50 |
| Gasterosteiformes | Seahorses and relatives | 150 |
| Channiformes | Snakeheads | 5 |
| Synbranchiformes | Swamp eels and cuchias | 7 |
| Scorpaeniformes | Gurnards and relatives | 700 |
| Dactylopteriformes | Flying gurnards | 6 |
| Pegasiformes | Sea moths, dragonflies | 4 |
| Tetraodontiformes | Triggerfishes, puffer fishes | 250 |
| Pleuronectiformes | Flatfishes | 500 |
| Perciformes | Perch and relatives, e.g. tuna, mackerel, sea bass | 6,500 |

△ Flatfish, such as plaice, are important commercial food fish. Young flatfish flip over on their sides during development, the mouth twisting and one eye moving across to adapt to a bottom-dwelling existence.

△ Sting rays have whip-like tails armed with poisoned spines.

**Life Cycle of a Frog**
1. Eggs (spawn) are laid in springtime.
2. The tadpole hatches out in two weeks.
3. Front and back legs have grown after nine weeks.
4. The frog is fully formed in about eleven weeks.

## AMPHIBIANS AND REPTILES

Amphibians – animals with backbones that can live both in water and air – are the last survivors of the first true land vertebrates that ever existed. They have cold blood – that is, they take their body temperatures from their surroundings.

There are three orders of amphibians, with a total of about 3,000 species. They are caecilians (simple wormlike creatures); newts and salamanders; and toads and frogs. Most amphibians lay their eggs in water. The eggs hatch into a larval form called a tadpole.

Reptiles are animals with backbones that live by breathing air. They also have cold blood. The 5,000 species alive today are all that remain of a group of animals that once dominated the Earth, dinosaurs and other giant forms.

Reptiles vary in size from 50 millimetres (2 in) long to more than nine metres (30 ft). They usually have scaly skins and most of them lay eggs. A few give birth to live young. They have lungs, like mammals, and most of them are carnivores.

There are four living orders of reptiles: alligators and crocodiles; tuataras (of which only one species exists); tortoises, terrapins and turtles; and lizards and snakes.

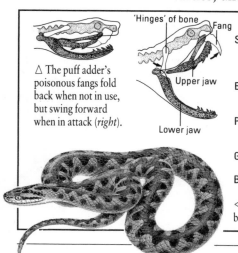

△ The puff adder's poisonous fangs fold back when not in use, but swing forward when in attack (*right*).

'Hinges' of bone Fang

Upper jaw

Lower jaw

### SNAKE NOTES

**Skin** is changed several times a year by a process known as moulting. The snake slips out of its old skin, leaving it lying like a dummy. The new skin is underneath.
**Breathing** for most snakes is done on one lung only. The left lung is either greatly reduced in size or missing altogether.
**Pit vipers** have sense organs that can detect heat. These organs help them detect their prey.
**Gastric juices** in a snake can digest bones and teeth – but not hair and fur.
**Burrowing snakes** burrow into the ground. They feed largely on ants and termites.
◁ The adder has a zig-zag pattern along its back.

## AMPHIBIAN AND REPTILE RECORDS

**Largest amphibians** are the giant salamanders (genus *Megalobatrachus*) of China and Japan, specimens of which have been known to grow up to 1.5 m (5 ft).

**Longest-lived amphibians** are probably Japanese giant salamanders (*Megalobatrachus japonicus*), specimens of which have lived up to 60 years in captivity.

**Largest frog** is the goliath frog (*Gigantorana goliath*) of Africa. This amphibian habitually grows to a body length of 300 mm (12 in), but many specimens have been reported considerably larger.

**Largest reptile** is the estuarine crocodile (*Crocodylus porosus*), which can grow up to 6 m (20 ft).

**Largest marine turtle** is the leathery or leatherback turtle (*Dermochelys coriacea*), whose shell may be 1.8 m (6 ft) long, with a flipper-to-flipper stretch of 3.6 m (12 ft), and a weight of more than 725 kg (1,600 lb).

**Largest land tortoise** is the giant tortoise (*Testudo gigantea*), which may have a shell 1.8 m (6 ft) long, and a weight of 225 kg (500 lb) or more.

**Largest lizard** is the Komodo dragon (*Varanus komodoensis*), which can grow up to 3 m (10 ft) long and weigh 113 kg (250 lb).

**Largest snakes** are the anaconda (*Eunectes murinus*) and the reticulated python (*Python reticulatus*), both of which are reported to grow up to 9 m (30 ft) long.

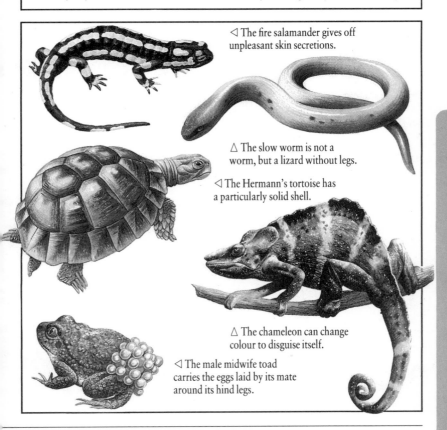

◁ The fire salamander gives off unpleasant skin secretions.

△ The slow worm is not a worm, but a lizard without legs.

◁ The Hermann's tortoise has a particularly solid shell.

△ The chameleon can change colour to disguise itself.

◁ The male midwife toad carries the eggs laid by its mate around its hind legs.

## BIRDS

Birds are animals with feathers, wings and beaks. Nearly all of them can fly. They are warm-blooded – they make their heat from the food they eat.

There are nearly 11,000 species of birds, and they are grouped into 27 orders. Birds can be classified in many different ways. Water-birds spend their lives on or near water. They include wildfowl – ducks, geese and swans – waders, gulls, albatrosses and penguins.

Perching birds are land-based birds that spend their lives in trees or other high places when they are not flying. Game birds include chicken, guinea fowl, partridges and turkeys. Birds of prey hunt other birds and small mammals. They include eagles, hawks and vultures. Owls, which are mostly night-flying, also hunt game.

Birds are directly descended from reptiles. They have some links with their ancestors: many birds have scales on their legs, like those of reptiles, while their feathers are made of the same substance – keratin – as scales.

△ Contour feathers, like the one shown here, cover the outer body of the bird and give it a smooth shape.

Barb

Barbule

Shaft

A bird makes full use of its wings in flight. On take-off the wings and feet are used to lift the bird off the ground. On landing, the fully-spread flight feathers act like a brake, the tail is kept low, and the feet are pushed out to check speed.

Feathers grow unevenly on a bird's body. Some parts are well covered, others are lightly protected. Flight feathers grow on the wings, contour feathers cover the body, and downy feathers are found on the breast. A bird may have between 1,300 and 12,000 feathers. The skeleton is very light; this makes flight easier.

## BIRD RECORDS

**Largest** bird is the male African ostrich (*Struthio camelus*), which grows to a height of about 2.5 m (8 ft). Specimens have been found weighing as much as 155 kg (340 lb).

**Heaviest flying** bird is the Kori bustard (*Choriotis kori*) of eastern and southern Africa, which may weight as much as 18 kg (40 lb).

**Smallest** bird is the bee hummingbird (*Calyptae helenae*) of Cuba. It is about 60 mm (2¼ in) long and weighs only about 2 g (0.07 oz). Its nest would fit into half a walnut shell.

**Greatest wingspan** belongs to the male wandering albatross (*Diomedea exulans*) which has an average wingspan of 3 m (10 ft). It can stay in the air for days.

**Fastest fliers** are various species of spine-tailed swifts (family Apodidae), which fly at about 100 km/h (60 mph). Duck hawks and golden eagles dive at speeds estimated at up to 290 km/h (180 mph).

**Fastest runner** is the ostrich, which can maintain a speed of 55 km/h (34 mph), with bursts up to 80 km/h (50 mph).

▽ The ostrich is the world's largest living bird. Although it cannot fly, it is faster on land than any other bird, and its height enables it to see danger approaching from a long way off.

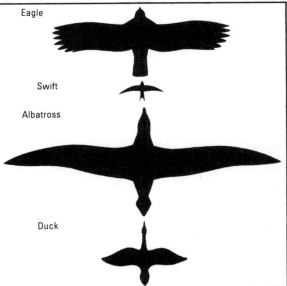

The broad wings of an eagle allow it to soar high up in the sky.

The narrow, pointed wings of a swift enable it to fly and turn quickly.

Albatrosses can glide for days with the help of their long wings.

The short, wide and powerful wings of a duck give it plenty of lift, so it can leave the water quickly if disturbed.

Eagle

Swift

Albatross

Duck

## BIRD CLASSIFICATION

| Order | Common name | No. of species | Order | Common name | No. of species |
|---|---|---|---|---|---|
| Passeriformes | Perching birds; passerines | 5,000 | Gruiformes | Cranes and relatives | 197 |
| Piciformes | Woodpeckers and relatives | 400 | Galliformes | Game birds | 151 |
| Coraciformes | Kingfishers and relatives | 190 | Falconiformes | Birds of prey | 271 |
| Coliformes | Mousebirds | 6 | Anseriformes | Ducks and relatives | 148 |
| Trogoniformes | Trogons | 36 | Ciconiiformes | Storks and relatives | 120 |
| Apodiformes | Swifts and relatives | 387 | Pelecaniformes | Pelicans and relatives | 59 |
| Caprimulgiformes | Nightjars and relatives | 94 | Procellariiformes | Albatrosses and relatives | 91 |
| Strigiformes | Owls | 130 | Sphenisciformes | Penguins | 18 |
| Cuculiformes | Cuckoos and relatives | 147 | Gaviformes | Divers | 5 |
| Psittaciformes | Parrot family | 315 | Podicipediformes | Grebes | 21 |
| Columbiformes | Pigeons and relatives | 305 | Tinamiformes | Tinamous | 50 |
| | | | Cassuariiformes | Emu and cassowaries | 4 |
| Charadriformes | Gulls and relatives (mainly waders) | 295 | Rheiformes | Rheas | 2 |
| | | | Struthioniformes | Ostrich | 1 |
| | | | Apterygiformes | Kiwis | 3 |

**Birds' Beaks**

Blue tit

Heron

Blackbird

Avocet

Tree creeper

△ Bills for various purposes. The eagle's hooked bill is for plucking and tearing the flesh of prey. The blue tit (*above*) feeds on seeds and fruit. The heron is a fish-eater, while the wading avocet skims the mud for small creatures. Blackbirds catch worms and insects. The tree creeper uses its bill to extract insects and spiders from the bark.

▽ The pelican uses the pouch beneath its large bill to store fish caught at sea.

△ The kingfisher dives into ponds and rivers to catch small fish.

Small perching bird

Eagle

Duck

Woodpecker

Grebe

△ Different birds' feet. From top, clockwise – perching, hunting, partly webbed (grebes and divers), climbing, fully webbed for swimming.

△ A Gentoo penguin. Penguins are flightless, but excellent swimmers.

▽ The owl is a nocturnal hunter, with superb hearing and night vision.

△ The sparrow is found worldwide, usually close to human settlement.

# Mammals

Mammals are animals whose females feed their young on milk from their *mammary glands* (breasts). Most mammals retain their young inside their bodies for a period of development. A few, called the monotremes – platypuses and echidnas – lay eggs. Some, known as the marsupials, such as kangaroos and wombats, give birth to young that are only partly developed and have to crawl into a pouch on the mother's belly to carry on growing.

Even among the other mammals, the young vary in how developed they are when they are born. Some newly-born animals, such as antelopes and horses, can get to their feet and walk within an hour or so of being born. Others, such as puppies and kittens, can do nothing for themselves for some days.

The basic mammal type is an animal with four legs, breathing air, and having warm blood. But there are exceptions. Besides the monotremes and the marsupials, there are two groups of sea mammals. Seals have four flippers instead of legs, while whales and porpoises have just one pair of flippers.

△ Bats are the only mammals that truly fly. Their wings are delicate membranes stretched between the 'fingers' of their forelimbs. This Horseshoe bat flies within a metre (3 ft) of the ground and its flight is slow, almost like that of a butterfly.

Curiosity

Happiness

Fear

Excitement

△ Chimpanzees are highly developed social animals. Each individual has a personality, and a chimp's facial expression reveals its emotions. Four typical expressions are shown here.

## MAMMAL RECORDS

**Largest mammal** is the blue whale (*Balaenoptera musculus*), which can be up to 30 m (100 ft) in length.

**Largest land mammal** is the African elephant (*Loxodonta africana*), which can be up to 3.5 m (11 ft 6 in) tall and weigh 7 tonnes.

**Smallest mammal** is Savi's pygmy shrew (*Suncus etruscus*), which has a head and body length of 38 mm (1½ in) and a tail about 25 mm (1 in) long. Its weight is less than 2.8 gm (⅒ oz).

**Tallest mammal** is the giraffe (*Giraffa camelopardis*), which can be as much as 5.5 m (18 ft) tall, and can weigh up to 1 tonne.

△ Wild rabbit. Hares and rabbits belong to the order Lagomorpha.

△ The red squirrel is the only native tree squirrel in Europe.

## CLASSIFICATION OF MAMMALS

There are about 4,000 species of mammals, grouped into 19 orders and about 120 families.

| Order | Animals | No. of species |
|---|---|---|
| Monotremata | Egg-laying mammals – the platypus and echidnas | 6 |
| Marsupialia | Pouched mammals, including kangaroos, opossums, koalas | 238 |
| Insectivora | Insect-eating animals including hedgehogs, moles and shrews | 293 |
| Chiroptera | Bats, the only mammals that can really fly | 690 |
| Primates | Lemurs, monkeys, apes, humans | 171 |
| Edentata | Anteaters, armadillos, sloths | 30 |
| Pholidota | Pangolins (scaly anteaters) | 7 |
| Dermoptera | Flying lemurs | 2 |
| Rodentia | Rodents, gnawing animals, including beavers, capybara, hamsters, mice, porcupines, rats, squirrels | 1792 |
| Lagomorpha | Hares, pikas, rabbits | 64 |
| Cetacea | Whales, dolphins, porpoises | 82 |
| Carnivora | Flesh-eating animals such as bears, cats, dogs, pandas, raccoons | 245 |
| Pinnepedia | Seals, sea lions, walrus | 32 |
| Artiodactyla | Hoofed mammals with an even number of toes, including antelopes, camels, cattle, deer, giraffe, hippopotamuses, pigs | 377 |
| Perissodactyla | Hoofed mammals with an odd number of toes – rhinoceroses, horses and zebras, tapirs | 15 |
| Sirenia | Water mammals – dugong, manatees | 4 |
| Tubulidentata | The aardvark | 1 |
| Hyracoidea | Hyraxes | 6 |
| Proboscidea | Elephants | 2 |

40

15

10

3

1   Birth

▽ Elephants grow slowly and are among the longest-lived of animals. They are classed in an order of their own.

△ The red fox is an adaptable animal and is found in both the town and countryside.

▽ Wolves live in open country and forests. They work closely together when hunting for food.

# DOGS

The dog is probably the favourite companion of human beings. For thousands of years dogs have guarded people's homes, herded their cattle and sheep, helped with hunting for food and played with their children.

All the members of the dog family, Canidae, belong to the carnivores, the flesh-eaters. They tend to hunt in packs. The domestic dog, *Canis familiaris*, is the best known member of the family. There are more than 100 breeds of domestic dogs.

Wild dogs are found in India, Siberia, southeastern Asia, southern and eastern Africa, Brazil and the Guianas. The Australian dingo is a semi-wild dog, which may have been domesticated a long time ago. Other members of the dog family include the North American coyote, fennecs, foxes, jackals and wolves.

Domestic dogs are divided into sporting and non-sporting groups. Sporting groups include gundogs, such as pointers, retrievers, setters and spaniels; and hounds, such as Afghans, beagles and bloodhounds; and terriers. Non-sporting dogs include working dogs such as collies and German shepherds; and utility dogs include all the others.

## DOG RECORDS

**Heaviest domestic dog** is the St Bernard, which weighs up to 100 kg (220 lb) and stands 70 cm (27 in) high at the shoulders.

**Tallest domestic dog** is the Irish wolfhound, which is 79 cm (31 in) high at the shoulders, and well over 1.8 m (6 ft) when standing on its hind legs.

**Smallest domestic dogs** are miniature breeds of the chihuahua, poodle and Yorkshire terrier, which weigh 0.45 kg (1 lb) or less.

**Largest wild dogs** are timber wolves (*Canis lupus*), which stand 79 cm (31 in) high at the shoulders and weigh up to 56 kg (125 lb).

**Fastest domestic dogs** are the saluki, timed at speeds up to 69 km/h (43 mph) and the greyhound 60 km/h (37 mph).

▽ West highland terriers were traditionally used for hunting.

◁ Wild cape dogs stand by their prey.

▷ Greyhounds are the fastest dogs on flat ground.

▽ The toy poodle is the smallest breed of poodle.

◁ The dog, Laika was the first living creature in space, sent by the Soviets in Sputnik 2 in 1957.

## THE CAT FAMILY

Cats are the most purely carnivorous carnivores. They have teeth for stabbing and slicing, but not for chewing. Their lithe bodies are built for speed, and their sharp claws are further formidable weapons. Except for differences in size, all kinds of cats are very similar animals indeed. The lioness roaming through the African shrubland is only a larger version of the small domestic cat. Because of these similarities all cats belong to one family, Felidae.

The cat family also includes tigers, jaguars, leopards, cheetahs, pumas, caracals, lynxes, servals, ocelots and several small wild cats.

Domestic cats fall into two main groups — short-haired and long-haired. Short-haired cats include Burmese, Manx, Abyssinian and Siamese. Siamese were originally bred in Thailand where they were royal sacred cats. The penalty for stealing one was death. Long-haired cats include the different kinds of Persian and Angora cats.

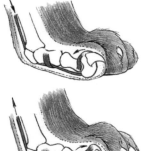

△ Cats are unique among carnivores in having retracting claws. The claws are shown above retracted and (*lower picture*) extended.

▽ Members of the cat family: lion, domestic cat, wild cat, caracal, black leopard, snow leopard and tiger.

The Americas are particularly rich in cat species, some of which are found nowhere else in the world. The jaguar (*Panthera onca*) of South America is the largest and fiercest of the American cats. It is quite untameable and may attack humans. The puma (*Felis concolor*), also called cougar or mountain lion, is another cat found only in America. Smaller than these two is the ocelot (*Felis pardalis*) of South America.

Cats cannot see in total darkness, but they can see far better in the dark than people. At the back of their eyes there is a reflecting layer which sends light back through the sensitive cells, so increasing the effect of minute amounts of light on the brain.

Iris closed

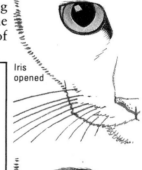

Iris opened

---

### CAT RECORDS

**Largest** member of the cat family is the Siberian tiger (all tigers are *Panthera tigris*). Males have been found up to 3.2 m (10 ft 6 in) long, standing 91 cm (3 ft) tall at the shoulder.

**Smallest wild cat** is probably the rusty-spotted cat (*Felis rubiginosa*) which lives in Sri Lanka and southern India. Males have a body length which may be as little as 40 cm (16 in), plus a tail of 23 cm (9 in).

**Rarest** of the cats is probably the Java tiger, now found in only two areas of the Indonesian island of Java. About a dozen are thought to survive.

**Longest lived** of the big cats is probably the lion (*Panthera leo*), which is known to live more than 25 years in captivity.

---

▷ The European wild cat is larger and heavier than its domestic cousin, and considerably more fierce.

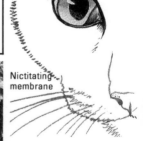

Nictitating membrane

△ Cats' eyes are adapted for night vision, with pupils that expand or contract to slits, according to whether the in-coming light is weak or strong. Cats also have a third eyelid, called the nictitating membrane.

◁ The extinct sabre tooth cat *Smilodon* had enlarged teeth used for hunting large prey.

# Miscellany

## BATS

Bats (order Chiroptera) are the only mammals that have mastered the art of powered flight, though several other animals, such as flying squirrels and flying phalangers, can glide. Bats' hands have greatly lengthened fingers, connected with thin membranes of skin to form wings. There are two main kinds of bats. Fruit bats are the largest bats; they fly by day. Insect-eating bats are mostly small and feed at night, catching insects on the wing. They use a form of sonar to detect and catch their prey.

△ The long-eared bat has large ears to make its sonar system very efficient. Bats do not interfere with each other's signals, even when many are flying at the same time.

▷ The physical structure of a bat. The wings are membranes of skin which stretch from the tips of the bat's 'fingers' down to its feet. The wings are supported by the bat's legs, and tail.

Tail membrane
Shin
Calcar
4th Finger-tips
3rd
5th
2nd finger
Thumb
Forearm

---

### BAT RECORDS

**Largest bat** is the kalong or Malay fruit bat (*Pteropus vampyrus*), which has a wing-span of up to 1.5 m (5 ft). Its weight is about 900 g (2 lb). It is also called the flying fox.

**Smallest bats** are the pipistrelles, several species of which are 80 mm (3 in) or less in length; they include the European pipistrelle (*Pipistrellus pipistrellus*) and the Eastern pipistrelle (*Pipistrellus subflavus*).

**Most dangerous bats** are the blood-sucking vampires (family Desmodontidae) of tropical America, because they can transmit rabies and possibly other diseases.

▽ Bats use 'echo-location' to navigate and find flying insects. They emit an ultrasonic signal which bounces off objects in their path. Some species of moth can send out their own signals to 'block' the bats' sonar.

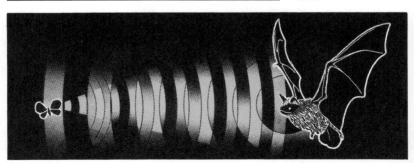

## BEARS

Bears may look friendly and cuddly; in fact they are among the most ferocious of animals. Although they do not usually attack people, they can be dangerous if provoked.

Brown bears live in Europe and Asia. Their close relatives are the large grizzly bears (*Ursus horribilis*) and Kodiak bears (*Ursus middendorffi*) of North America. Polar bears (*Thalarctos maritimus*) live around the coasts of the Arctic Ocean. The American black bears belong to the species *Euarctos americanus*. Spectacled bears (*Tremarctos ornatus*) live in the Andes, while the Himalayan, Malay and sloth bears (*Selenarctos thibetanus, Helarctos malayanus,* and *Melursus ursinus*) live in Asia.

△ Brown bears are true omnivores: they enjoy a varied diet that includes roots and berries, small animals and fish.

▷ Polar bears are excellent swimmers and often travel far out to sea. They eat seals, fish, birds and will even attack walruses. Males move southward in winter, but the females build dens in the snow where they give birth to their cubs.

▽ Kodiak bears live on Kodiak Island, off Alaska. When standing on their hind legs, Kodiak bears may reach the height of 4 m (13 ft).

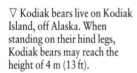

### BEAR RECORDS

**Largest bears** are the Kodiak and Kenai bears of Alaska. They stand more than 2.7 m (9 ft) and may weigh up to 750 kg (1,650 lb).

**Smallest bears** are the Malay bears, some of which stand only 1 m (3 ft 4 in) tall.

**Best swimmer** is the Polar bear, which is often found several miles out to sea.

# CUD-CHEWING ANIMALS

Most of the hoofed animals with even numbers of toes belong to the group known as the ruminants, or cud-chewers. They have a digestive system with a four-part stomach, which can cope with such difficult foodstuffs as grass. They include antelopes, cattle, deer, giraffes, goats, sheep and yaks.

▽ The giraffe is the world's tallest animal, and can measure up to 5.5 m (18 ft) in height.

## RUMINANT RECORDS

**Largest deer** is the Alaskan bull moose (*Alces americana*), which stands about 2.4 m (8 ft) high at the shoulder and weighs 800 kg (1,800 lb).

**Largest antelope** is the Giant eland, or Lord Derby's eland (*Taurotragus oryx*), which is about 1.8 m (6 ft) high at the shoulder and weighs a tonne.

**Largest wild ox** is the gaur (*Bibos gaurus*) of India and southeastern Asia. It stands 2 m (6 ft 4 in) at the shoulder.

**Largest wild sheep** is the argali (*Ovis ammon*) of central Asia. It stands 1.2 m (4 ft) high and weighs over 140 kg (300 lb).

**Largest wild goat** is the markhor (*Capra falconeri*) of Afghanistan, which stands about 1 m (40 in) high at the shoulders and weighs more than 90 kg (200 lb).

**Smallest ruminants** are the hornless little chevrotains (genus Tragulus) which hide in the forests of India and Indonesia. Some species are only 200 mm (8 in) tall at the shoulder.

△ The moose is the largest living deer. It can have an antler spread of up to 2 m (6 ft). The moose is found in the forests of North America, northern Europe and Asia.

# ELEPHANTS

The largest of all animals that live on land is the elephant. Fully grown it may be as much as 3.5 m (11½ ft) tall and weigh up to 7 tonnes. There are two kinds of elephants — the Asian elephant (*Elephas maximus*) and the larger African elephant (*Loxodonta africana*). Elephants live in herds of about ten to fifty and move quietly through the forests in single file, travelling at about 10 km (6 mph). Elephants are vegetarian — an adult male may eat about 270 kg (600 lb) of fodder a day.

▽ The elephant's closest relative is the tiny hyrax, which is about 30 cm (1 ft) long. Like an elephant, it has hoofed toes and a two-chambered stomach for digesting a vegetable diet. It is found in the Middle East and Africa.

---

**ELEPHANT RECORDS**

**Largest elephant** recorded stood about 3.8 m (12 ft 6 in) tall.

**Heavest known tusk** weighs 102.7 kg (226½ lb).

**Smallest elephant** is the Pygmy elephant (*Loxodonta africana cyclotis*) a variety of African elephant. The males are only about 2 m (6 ft 4 in) high at the shoulder.

---

▽ Indian elephants can be used for transport.

△ The largest and most aggressive hyaena is the spotted hyaena. It grows up to 1.5 m (5 ft) long. As well as eating carrion, hyaenas also hunt for food, chasing their prey at speeds up to 60 km/h (37 mph).

## HYAENAS

Hyaenas (family Hyaenidae) have a bad reputation as cowardly, ugly animals. This is partly because they eat the left-overs of bigger predators such as lions. But, like all scavengers, hyaenas perform a useful function, helping to clear up meat that would otherwise turn rotten. There are four species. The spotted hyaena makes a strange laughing cry.

### HYAENA RECORD

**Largest hyaena** is the spotted or laughing hyaena (*Crocuta crocuta*), which may have a body length of 1.4 m (4 ft 6 in), with a short tail.

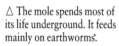

▷ The pygmy shrew is the smallest mammal of all.

△ The mole spends most of its life underground. It feeds mainly on earthworms.

▽ Tenrecs live on the island of Madagascar. The common tenrec may be the most prolific of all mammals having up to 25 babies in a litter.

## INSECT-EATERS

Insectivores are mostly small animals and include such familiar types as shrews and hedgehogs.

Hedgehogs (family Erinaceidae), are animals with a forest of prickly spines all over their backs and sides.

True shrews (family Soricidae) are small animals which work and rest on a three-hour shift pattern, day and night.

Moles (family Talpidae) are the master burrowers of the insectivores. The mole weighs from 40 to 140g (1½–5 oz) and eats about its own weight each day. A mole can dig through 14 m (45 ft) of soil in an hour.

### INSECTIVORE RECORDS

**Largest insectivore** is the Common tenrec (*Centetes ecaudatus*), which may be as much as 400 mm (16 in) in body length.
**Smallest insectivore** is Savi's pygmy shrew (*Suncus etruscus*), the smallest mammal, which has a head and body length of 38 mm (1½ in).

# THE POUCHED MAMMALS

Marsupials are mammals whose females have a *marsupium*, a pouch in which to carry their young while they finish developing. They are found only in Australia, New Guinea and South America, with a few – The Virginia opossums – in North America. They include bandicoots, kangaroos and wallabies, koalas, numbats and wombats.

---

### MARSUPIAL RECORDS

**Largest marsupial** is the red kangaroo (*Macropus rufus*). Its body is about 1.5 m (5 ft) long, and its tail may be up to 1.07 m (3 ft 6 in) long. It is also the fastest and can bound along at more than 48 km/h (30 mph) for short distances.

**Smallest marsupial** is the planigale, a kind of marsupial mouse. It is about 90 mm (3½ in) long, including the tail.

**Most fussy eater** is the koala. It lives only on the leaves of eucalyptus trees – and only on the leaves of five out of the 350 species of eucalyptus at that.

**Least thirsty marsupial** is the mulgara, or crest-tailed marsupial mouse. It gets all its moisture from the insects it eats and needs no drinking water.

---

△ A young koala bear will ride on its mother's back after leaving the pouch.

▽ When threatened, the skunk raises its tail to disclose a pair of musk glands which can squirt foul-smelling liquid a distance of about 3 m (10 ft). This spray can cause temporary blindness.

# THE WEASEL FAMILY

The weasel family (Mustiladae) contains not only weasels and stoats, but also badgers, ferrets, martens, otters, polecats, skunks and gluttons (wolverines). The family includes animals with beautiful furs such as mink and sable. Most of its members have a strong and unpleasant smell.

---

### WEASEL RECORDS

**Largest member** of the weasel family is the glutton or wolverine (*Gulo luscus*), which is 1.2 m (4 ft) long, including a 300 mm (12 in) tail.

**Smallest weasel** is the Least weasel (*Mustela rixosa*) of North America, which is less than 20 cm (7½ in) long.

---

▷ The marten is a carnivore that preys on squirrels and birds.

# Names and Homes

Over the centuries, sportsmen have developed specialized terms for animals – their males, females and young – and the groups in which they are found. Here is a selection. There are also names for animal tracks (such as a fox's *print* and a fallow deer's *view*); beds (a badger's *earth*, a hare's *form*); and cries (a bittern's *boom*, a panther's *saw*).

Many animals are extremely skilled in making homes for themselves and their young to live in. They weave, build and dig. The remarkable thing is that all this work is done by instinct – the animals can do it even if they have never seen other animals constructing their homes.

▷ The hummingbird makes a delicate, round nest.

▷ The oven bird builds a mud nest.

▷ A hornet's paper nest is made from chewed wood pulp.

▽ The beaver builds a dam to raise the water level in its lodge.

△ Swallows often nest in farm buildings and sheds.

## ANIMALS: LONGEVITY AND SPECIALIZED NAMES

| | Average life span (years) | Male | Female | Young | Group |
|---|---|---|---|---|---|
| Antelope | 10 | buck | doe | fawn | herd |
| Bear | 15–50 | boar | sow | cub | sleuth |
| Cat | 15 | tom | queen | kitten | cluster |
| Cattle | 20 | bull | cow | calf | herd |
| Deer | 10–20 | buck, hart, stag | doe hind | fawn | herd |
| Dog | 12–15 | dog | bitch | puppy | kennel |
| Donkey | 20 | jack | jenny | foal | herd |
| Duck | 10 | drake | duck | duckling | team |
| Elephant | 60 | bull | cow | calf | herd |
| Fox | 10 | dog-fox | vixen | cub | skulk |
| Giraffe | 10–25 | bull | cow | calf | herd |
| Goat | 10 | billy-goat | nanny-goat | kid | herd |
| Goose | 25 | gander | goose | gosling | skein, gaggle |
| Hippopotamus | 30–40 | bull | cow | calf | herd |
| Horse | 20–30 | stallion | mare | foal | herd |
| Kangaroo | 10–20 | buck | doe | joey | mob |
| Lion | 25 | lion | lioness | cub | pride |
| Ostrich | 50 | cock | hen | chick | flock |
| Pig | 10–15 | boar | sow | piglet | drove |
| Rabbit | 5–8 | buck | doe | kit | warren |
| Rhinoceros | 25–50 | bull | cow | calf | crash |
| Sheep | 10–15 | ram | ewe | lamb | flock |
| Tiger | 10–25 | tiger | tigress | cub | |
| Whale | 20 | bull | cow | calf | school, pod |
| Zebra | 20–25 | stallion | mare | foal | herd |

# A DICTIONARY OF ANIMAL LIFE

**adaptation** Any characteristic that a species of plant or animal has developed which helps it to survive in its environment. The thick coats, small ears and short tails of Arctic mammals are adaptations to cold living conditions.

**ageing** Process by which an adult animal or plant wears out. An ageing animal cannot make enough new body cells to replace all the old ones that die off. Also wastes collect in the body and affect it.

**amoeba** Group of one-celled jelly-like animals that constantly change shape. They reproduce by simply splitting into two.

**amphibians** Cold-blooded vertebrates usually with four limbs and soft moist skins. Their shell-less unprotected eggs are generally laid in water, and when the young larvae hatch out they usually spend some time in water before they become adults and live on land. Frogs, toads, salamanders and newts are amphibians.

**antelopes** Cud-chewing mammals with bony horns. Among them are the eland, the springbok, the hartebeeste and the gnu. Most species are found in Africa.

**arachnids** Class of arthropods which includes spiders, scorpions, ticks and mites. Most have four pairs of legs.

**arthropods** Largest phylum of all the many-celled animals. The phylum consists of invertebrates with jointed legs and an external skeleton. All insects and spiders are arthropods; so are shrimps, crabs and lobsters.

**birds** Warm-blooded feathered vertebrates with light, hollow bones and with their two fore-limbs developed as wings. Most of them can fly, but a few, such as penguins and ostriches, are flightless.

**carnivores** Animals that feed wholly or mainly on flesh. Dogs, lions, tigers, and sharks are typical carnivores.

**crustaceans** Class of arthropods with hard shells. Most of them, such as crabs, lobsters, shrimps and water-fleas, live in water.

**ecology** Study of all the plants and animals in any particular habitat, and the relationships between them.

**family** An order of animals is divided into groups called families. The members of a family are all closely related and usually quite alike. All cats, for example, belong to one family in the order Carnivora.

**genus** Many families of animals are divided into a number of genera. The cat family, for example, contains several genera, but all the small cats, including the domestic cat, belong to the genus *Felis*. Each genus is made up of very similar animals.

**habitat** A creature's natural environment. Four very different habitats are seashores, hot, sandy deserts, coniferous forests and grasslands.

**herbivores** Animals that feed entirely on plants. Cows, giraffes and sheep are herbivores.

**hibernation** Animals' winter sleep. When an animal hibernates, its body temperature falls, slowing down all the chemical changes that go on in the body, and making the animal sleepy and inactive.

**insects** Largest class of arthropods. Adults have three pairs of legs, and three distinct parts of the body (head, thorax and abdomen). Many of them have wings. Earwigs, bees, ants, fleas and butterflies are insects.

**invertebrates** Animals without even a rudimentary backbone. Cockles, mussels, snails, insects, spiders, starfish and worms are all invertebrates.

**kingdom** Major division of living things. Most biologists recognize three kingdoms: Protista, single-celled organisms; Metaphyta or Plantae, plants; and Metazoa or Animalia, animals. Some zoologists add two more: Monera, bacteria; and Mycota, fungi.

**larva** Stage that many animals pass through between hatching from an egg and becoming adult. The larva is very different from the adult, as a tadpole is from a frog, or a caterpillar from a butterfly.

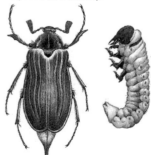

△ The cockchafer, or May-bug and its larva.

**lizards** Reptiles that have long, slender, scaly bodies, a tail and usually four five-toed limbs.

**mammals** Warm-blooded vertebrates with hair and a well-developed brain. All feed their young with their own milk. They range in size from the tiny shrew to the giant blue whale.

**marsupials** Mammals such as kangaroos and koalas, whose young are very underdeveloped when born. They spend a period of development in a pouch on the mother's body. Most of the world's marsupials live in Australia, but opossums live in North and South America.

**metamorphosis** Drastic change that many animals undergo between the stages of being a larva and being an adult, as when a tadpole becomes a frog or a caterpillar becomes a butterfly.

**mimicry** Device by which many harmless and otherwise defenceless animals are shaped and coloured very much like poisonous or dangerous ones. This makes it more likely that predators will be confused and will therefore not attack them.

**molluscs** Soft-bodied invertebrates, most of which have a hard shell. They include snails, oysters and octopuses.

**monotremes** Primitive mammals that do not give birth to live young ones but lay eggs instead. The duck-billed platypus and the two species of echidna (spiny anteater) are the only monotremes.

**mutualism** An association between two different kinds of living creature that brings advantages to both. Mutualism is another word for *symbiosis*.

**nematodes** Eel-worms, roundworms and thread-worms. Some nematodes live as parasites in plants or on other animals but other nematodes live independent lives. There are millions in the soil.

**nocturnal animals** Animals which are active by night and rest during the day. Owls and bats are almost all nocturnal, and so are most moths.

**parasites** Creatures that live on or in the bodies of other creatures (called their 'hosts'). A parasite obtains food from its host but gives nothing in return. Parasites are not always dangerous to their hosts but are often a nuisance to them. It is not in the parasite's interest to kill its host, for by doing so it would lose its home and its food supply.

**phylum** Biologists divide the Animal Kingdom into major groups called phyla. All the animals in the same phylum have important features in common. Among the phyla of the Animal Kingdom are coelenterates, rotifers, molluscs, arthropods, echinoderms and chordates.

**placental mammals** The largest group of mammals. Their young ones become well-developed inside the mother's body before they are born. They are nourished by an organ in the womb called a placenta.

**predators** Animals that live by preying on other animals. Many birds are predators of caterpillars; sharks are predators of various fishes.

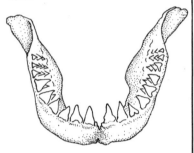

△ The predator's weapons. The teeth of a shark are arranged in overlapping rows. As the outer row wears out, it is replaced by the next row. The rows of teeth are renewed throughout the shark's life.

**primates** The order of mammals that includes monkeys and apes, and also human beings. They have large brains, good eye-sight, usually nails instead of claws, and fingers, thumbs and toes that are specially useful for grasping things.

**protozoans** Organisms that consist of only a single cell with a nucleus. They are found in the Kingdom Protista.

**reptiles** Class of cold-blooded vertebrates with tough, horny or scaly skins. Most lay eggs protected by a shell. They include turtles, tortoises, snakes, lizards and crocodiles. Most of them live on land though some, such as crocodiles, turtles and sea snakes, live in water.

**rodents** Gnawing mammals, such as rats, mice, beavers and squirrels. Rodents have chisel-like front teeth that grow continually, so that they are never worn down.

**roundworms** Large group of simple worms that have no sign of rings or segments on their bodies. Many are parasites, living inside other animals.

**scavengers** Animals that feed on dead plants, dead animals, or animal droppings. By doing so they help to keep a habitat clean. Vultures are useful and important scavengers in many tropical countries.

**snakes** Long, cylindrical limbless reptiles with scaly skins which they shed from time to time. Snakes can swallow prey larger than their own heads. They do this by 'unhinging' their jaws. Many snakes secrete poison in their salivary glands. The bite of some species can swiftly kill a person.

△ Bees are social insects. No individual can survive alone outside the organization of the hive.

**social insects** Insects that live in communities, with different individuals doing different jobs to help the rest. Honeybees are typical. The queen's only job is to lay eggs. The worker bees have many tasks – gathering food, feeding the larvae, tidying the hive and beating their wings to fan and ventilate it. Other social insects are wasps, ants and termites.

**species** Every genus of animal consists of one or more species. For example, the genus *Equus* includes the horse, three species of zebra and two kinds of wild ass. These six species are alike in their basic structure, but they differ in certain details. Only male and female animals of the same species can produce young capable of breeding.

**symbiosis** 'Living together'. Used mainly to describe an association between two different kinds of living creature that brings advantages to both, for example the relationship between oxpeckers and buffalo. Symbiosis is another word for *mutualism*.

**tadpole** Fish-like larva of an amphibian such as a frog or toad. Having no legs or lungs, a tadpole swims in water and breathes through gills. In time it develops legs and lungs; it then loses its tail and gills, and lives on land.

**territory** Specific area that an animal has marked out as its own home and that it is prepared to defend against other animals of its own kind. For example, a dog may bark at another dog that sniffs at the garden gate, but ignore a hedgehog that ambles across the lawn. A robin may chase other robins away from a wide area around its nest, but pay little or no attention to sparrows.

**warm-blooded animals** Animals that control their own body temperatures, so that they do not become too hot in hot surroundings or too cold in cold surroundings.

**ungulates** Herbivorous (plant-eating) hoofed mammals. Horses, camels and cows are ungulates.

△ Modern sheep have been selectively bred for wool and meat.

**vertebrates** Animals with true back-bones and skulls. Fishes, amphibians, reptiles, birds and mammals are all vertebrates.

**womb** Organ in a female mammal in which a baby develops.

**zooplankton** All the tiny animals, larvae and eggs that drift along on or near the surface of the world's seas and lakes.

# Classifying Animals

Names for animals differ widely from one language to another. For example, the English *bear* is the French *ours*, the German *Bär*, the Italian *orso* and the Spanish *osa*. For this reason, zoologists use Latin names for describing animals in order to be quite sure what animal they are talking about. For example, scientists all over the world know exactly what is meant by the family name for bears, *Ursidae*.

Another reason for having an international Latin 'code' is that the same common name is often used for different animals. To a Briton, a robin is a small songbird, *Erithacus rubecula*. To an American, a robin is a larger bird in the same family, *Turdus migratorius*, while to an Australian, a robin is a kind of flycatcher, genus *Petroica*.

Equally, the same name is used for several similar creatures. For example, there are about 2,500 different species of horse fly.

Zoologists classify animals in seven ranks. Kingdom is the highest, followed by Phylum (plural phyla), Class, Order, Family, Genus and finally Species. Species is a group of animals of the same kind which can breed together. By convention, the names for the genus and species are always printed in *italics* with a capital letter for the genus but not for the species.

△ The Swedish naturalist Karl von Linné (1707–78), known as Linnaeus, developed the Latin-name system of animal nomenclature that is now generally used.

▽ Wolves are members of the dog family. The varieties of wolf belong to the same species (*lupus*), differing only in colour, size and geographical location.

## CLASSIFYING WOLVES

The American timber wolf and the European wolf are varieties of the same species of animal. A complete classification of the animal is as follows:

**Kingdom:** Animalia
**Phylum:** Chordata
**Subphylum:** Vertebrata
**Class:** Mammalia
**Order:** Carnivora
**Family:** Canidae
**Genus:** *Canis*
**Species:** *lupus*

▽ Dinosaurs came in all shapes and sizes, from the horned *Triceratops*, to giant sauropods such as *Diplodocus*, about 27 m (88 ft) long. *Tyrannosaurus*, a fierce meat-eater, stood up to 6 m (20 ft) high.

# Dinosaurs

In the long course of evolution, many more species of animals have come and gone than are alive today. The most fascinating were the dinosaurs, the huge reptiles which dominated the Earth for about 135 million years, until they all died out about 65 million years ago.

## A GLOSSARY OF DINOSAURS

**Allosaurus** Huge meat-eating dinosaur over 9 m (30 ft) long which ran on powerful hind legs.

**Ankylosaurus** One of the most heavily armoured dinosaurs, with bony plates and spikes.

**Brachiosaurus** Dinosaur which resembled Brontosaurus but was even larger. It was the biggest land animal ever to live on Earth.

**Brontosaurus** Huge plant-eating dinosaur.

**Camptosaurus** Ornithopod about 6 m (20 ft) long which fed mainly on juicy leaves of trees.

**Diplodocus** The longest of the dinosaurs. It measured 30 m (100 ft) from head to tail.

**Hadrosaurs** A group of dinosaurs with broad, toothless beaks which have earned them the name 'Duckbills'.

**Iguanodon** A plant-eating ornithopod about 9 m (30 ft) long which ran on its hind legs.

**Ornithischians** formed one of the two great groups of dinosaurs. All were plant-eaters.

**Ornithomimus** was the shape and size of an ostrich. It was a nimble reptile which probably stole eggs from the nests of other reptiles.

**Ornithopods** A group of plant-eating dinosaurs which walked on their hind legs.

**Saurischians** formed one of the two great groups of dinosaurs. They included the gigantic sauropods, such as Brachiosaurus, and the fearsome flesh-eaters, such as Tyrannosaurus.

**Sauropods** A group of gigantic plant-eating dinosaurs with huge bodies, long necks and tiny heads, such as Brontosaurus and Diplodocus.

**Stegosaurus** Armoured dinosaur about 7 m (23 ft) long. It had bony plates on its back and spikes on its tail.

**Triceratops** Armoured dinosaur with three long horns on its head and a bony frill round its neck.

**Tyrannosaurus** Largest of the fearsome flesh-eating dinosaurs. It stood 6 m (20 ft) high on its powerful hind legs.

# Animals in Danger

One of the big problems facing the world today is the number of species of animals that are in danger of becoming extinct. A number have already died out over the past few hundred years. There are many reasons for such losses, but human activities are mainly to blame.

The most obvious cause of extinction is hunting, which brought about the end of animals such as the dodo and the passenger pigeon. The dodo was found on just one small island, Mauritius, where it flourished happily for hundreds of years until Europeans discovered the island in the 1500s. Seamen killed the birds for food. By 1681 there were no dodos left.

It is not only comparatively rare animals that can be extinguished in this way. The passenger pigeon existed in huge numbers in North America when Europeans first went there. Some of the flocks are said to have been two billion strong. Hunters began killing them for food on a large scale in the 1800s, and the last passenger pigeon died in a zoo in 1914.

Today, animals are being threatened by the destruction of their habitats, such as the felling of tropical rain forests. However, zoos are saving many animals that are already extinct in the wild.

△ Moas were hunted for food by early Polynesian settlers until they became extinct. They were flightless birds but very fast runners.

▽ The American bison nearly became extinct in the 19th century, when they were hunted for their meat and skins. They have since been protected, and there are today several thousand in the United States alone.

△ The dodo of Mauritius became extinct in the late 17th century.

## ANIMALS RECENTLY EXTINCT

| Animal | Where last seen | When last seen |
| --- | --- | --- |
| Great Auk | N. Atlantic coasts | 1840s |
| Aurochs (wild ox) | Europe | 1627 |
| Burchell's Zebra | South Africa | 1910 |
| Dodo | Mauritius | 1681 |
| Elephant Bird | Madagascar | c.1600 |
| Heath Hen | Martha's Vineyard, USA | 1932 |
| Moa (flightless bird) | New Zealand | 1600s |
| Carolina Parakeet | United States | 1904 |
| Passenger Pigeon | North America | 1914 |
| Quagga (zebra) | South Africa | 1883 |
| Schomburk's Deer | Thailand | 1932 |
| Tasmanian wolf | Tasmania | 1930* |

*Paw marks have been seen since.*

◁ Przewalski's horse nearly became extinct, but is now protected.

## ANIMALS IN DANGER

| Animal | Where last seen | Estimated numbers |
| --- | --- | --- |
| Asiatic Buffalo | India, Nepal | 2,200 |
| Blue Whale | World oceans | 7,500 |
| Bontebok (antelope) | South Africa | 800 |
| Crested Ibis (wading bird) | Japan | Under 12 |
| European Bison | Poland | Over 1,000* |
| Everglades Kite | Florida | 100 |
| Florida Panther | Florida | Under 300 |
| Giant Panda | China | 200 |
| Imperial Eagle | Spain | 100 |
| Indian Rhinoceros | India, Nepal | Under 600 |
| Java Rhinoceros | Indonesia | Under 100 |
| Kakapo (parrot) | New Zealand | Under 100 |
| Key Deer | North America | 600 |
| Mediterranean Monk Seal | Mediterranean Sea | 500 |
| Orang-utan | Borneo, Sumatra | 5,000 |
| Père David's Deer | China | 600* |
| Polar Bear | Arctic | 8,000 |
| Przewalski's Horse | Central Asia | 40–60* |
| Siberian Tiger | USSR, China, Korea | Under 200 |
| Southern Bald Eagle | North America | 600 |
| Whooping Cranes | North America | About 50 |

*Saved from extinction by zoos.*

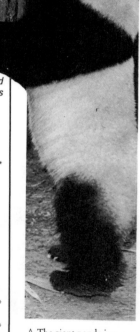

△ The giant panda is a protected species, and is the symbol of the World Wide Fund For Nature, a leading conservation organization.

# Plants

**The plant kingdom extends all over the Earth, in steaming jungles, lush pastures and the surface waters of the oceans; there are plants that survive in parched deserts and on bleak mountain tops. Plants play a vital part in the ecosystem of the Earth. They protect the land from erosion by wind and water; they give cover to wildlife and provide people and animals with food and oxygen. Trees are one of the most valuable assets of this planet, yet we are cutting down tropical rainforests at the rate of 30 acres a minute, day and night.**

Plants belong to the plant kingdom, called either *Plantae* or *Metaphyta*. Plant life is found on all parts of the Earth – even in the sea. Floating about in the upper layers of the oceans is a mass of tiny plants and animals, together known as plankton (from a Greek word meaning 'floating'). These plants and animals are so small they are like dust. The plants of the plankton are eaten by the animals of the plankton, and both provide food for larger sea creatures, such as fish.

When biologists discuss the 'who eats whom' of wild life, they refer to food chains. The reason that plants always come at the beginning of all food chains is that, unlike animals, green plants can make their own food. They draw in carbon dioxide from the air, and water and minerals from the ground, and convert them into fats, proteins, starches and oxygen.

△ In dicotyledon plants such as this sunflower, the stem thickens with each year's growth. In monocotyledon plants such as grasses, the stem lengthens with age but does not thicken.

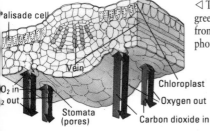

◁ The leaf cells of green plants make food from sunlight by photosynthesis.

Palisade cell

Vein

O₂ in
₂ out

Chloroplast

Oxygen out

Stomata
(pores)

Carbon dioxide in

▽ The main branches of the plant kingdom. The dicotyledons are flowering plants with broad leaves and seedlings having two tiny leaves. Monocotyledons have narrower leaves and seedlings with a single leaf. Bacteria, shown here with the simplest plants, are sometimes classified as animals.

For this work plants need energy. They draw their energy from light. The light is absorbed and processed by *chlorophyll*, a pigment which colours plants green. Fungi – such as mushrooms and toadstools – which do not have chlorophyll, have to draw their food from other plants.

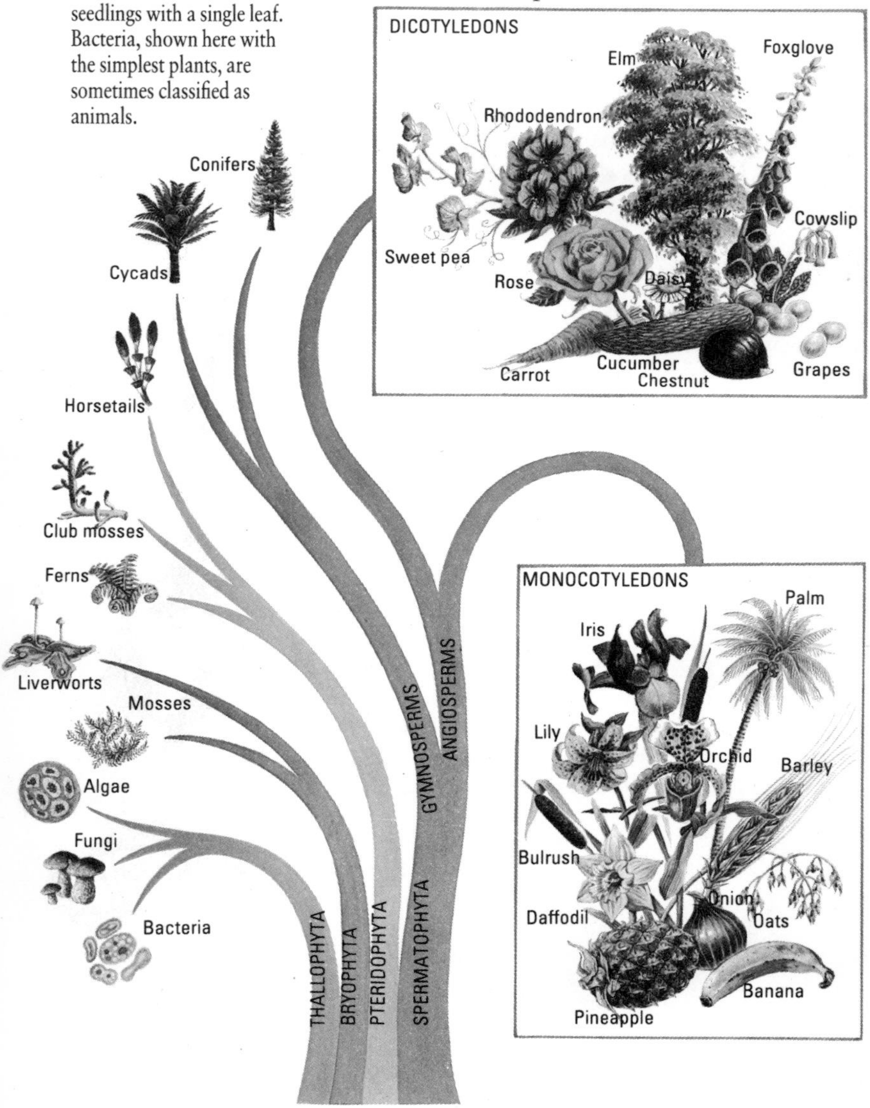

DICOTYLEDONS

Elm
Foxglove
Rhododendron
Sweet pea
Rose
Daisy
Cowslip
Carrot
Cucumber
Chestnut
Grapes

Conifers
Cycads
Horsetails
Club mosses
Ferns
Liverworts
Mosses
Algae
Fungi
Bacteria

MONOCOTYLEDONS

Palm
Iris
Lily
Orchid
Barley
Bulrush
Daffodil
Onion
Oats
Pineapple
Banana

THALLOPHYTA
BRYOPHYTA
PTERIDOPHYTA
SPERMATOPHYTA
GYMNOSPERMS
ANGIOSPERMS

▽ Plants use various ingenious methods of seed dispersal, including the wind, animals and birds. The poppy has a 'sprinkler' system. The ripe ovary swells into a hollow container with holes around the lip. The wind shakes the seeds out through the holes.

When plants have finished making their food they release oxygen into the atmosphere. In this way they perform a valuable service to animal life, because animals must have oxygen to live. In turn, animals perform an essential service for flowering plants (and some other plants too) by pollinating them — that is, transferring *pollen*, the male cells of flowers, to the *stigmas*, the female parts of flowers. Most pollination is done by insects.

As well as emitting oxygen into the atmosphere, plants release a great deal of water. They draw this water from the ground through their roots and pump it up through their stems to the leaves, where it is given off in a process called transpiration.

Plants also help to keep the soil together. Their roots bind it and help to hold water in the ground. Without plant cover, exposed land is at the mercy of wind and water. The wind blows loose dry soil away and water washes the soil down hill. Ignorant or wasteful farming practices and the removal of the

Ash seeds

Thistle seeds

Burdock

Poppy

Bird

Mouse

Blackberries

Dandelion seeds

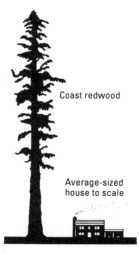

△ Uncontrolled forest clearance can lead to ecological disaster. Rains can wash away fragile forest soil.

▽ The world's tallest trees dwarf most human constructions.

Coast redwood

Average-sized house to scale

natural plant cover created the Dust Bowl of America's Great Plains area during the 1930s. In a similar way, clearing large areas of Amazonian rain forest in Brazil in the 1980s damaged the soil of the region.

### Diversity of plant life

Plants include the largest and oldest living things on Earth. The largest is a huge tree, a giant sequoia known as 'General Sherman' which stands in Sequoia National Park, California, in the United States. It has been estimated that it contains about 1,400 cubic metres (1,800 cubic yards) of timber.

By contrast, the plants of the plankton are so small that one drop of water can hold as many as 500 of them. Some land plants are also very tiny.

The 'General Sherman' is thought to be about 3,500 years old, but it is barely middle-aged compared with the oldest known living tree. That is a bristlecone pine, named 'Methuselah', which is also growing in California. 'Methuselah' is 4,600 years old.

Plants can flourish in all sorts of extreme

conditions. There are plants growing in the cold of the Arctic, Antarctica and high in the Himalayas of central Asia. Other plants can survive in all but the hottest deserts. Most desert plants are small or medium-sized, but the saguaro cactus of America's California and Arizona deserts can reach a height of more than 15 metres (50 feet).

Plants can survive even when they seem to be dead. For example, when the apparently bare deserts of Israel receive a welcome shower of rain, plants spring up overnight from seeds lying in the soil, and soon provide the land with a rare carpet of flowers. Every year the frozen tundra of northern Canada and Siberia thaws out for a few weeks in the summer sunshine, and plants have a brief period of life.

The richest plant life is in the warm, wet tropical regions of Africa, Central and South America and South-East Asia. The rain forests which flourish there contain more diverse species of plants than any other parts of the world. Some of these forests have flourished for more than 40 million years.

△ Cacti are desert plants which store water. Some have swollen stems, others extra-long roots.

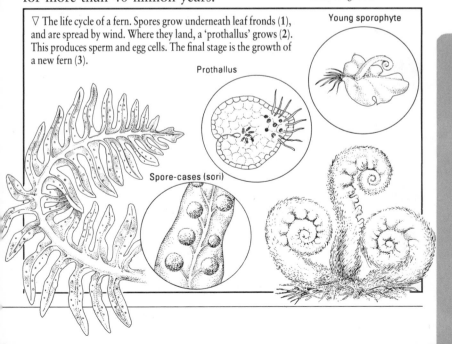

▽ The life cycle of a fern. Spores grow underneath leaf fronds (1), and are spread by wind. Where they land, a 'prothallus' grows (2). This produces sperm and egg cells. The final stage is the growth of a new fern (3).

Young sporophyte

Prothallus

Spore-cases (sori)

## Plants and people

Earth's plant life is the most valuable asset that the human race possesses. Just over 10,000 years ago people found out how to grow plants. As a result of this discovery, they no longer had to move about from place to place, gathering fruit and seeds and hunting animals, but could settle down. This was the beginning of civilization (literally 'living in cities') and the start of life as we know it today.

It also marked the beginning of human changes to the plants they grew. By selecting the best seeds and plants, people were able to grow larger crops. In recent years they have produced some amazing changes. The so-called 'Green Revolution', which started in the 1960s, produced some very high-yielding crops, especially of corn, rice and wheat. The new crops greatly reduced food shortages, especially in southern Asia.

But human influence on plant life has not always been good. People need huge quantities of wood for fuel, to build furniture, houses and boats, and to make paper. As a

△ Maize and sugar beet are two important food crops. The world's chief cereal crops are wheat, oats, barley and rye (cooler climates); and rice, millet and maize (warm climates).

◁ The world consumes vast quantities of timber and wood pulp, produced from temperate and tropical forests. Most softwoods come from the cool coniferous forests of temperate lands.

△ A tea-picker at work.

▽ Rubber is made from the latex oozing from cuts in the rubber trees.

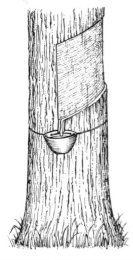

result there has been wholesale destruction of the forests that once covered the Earth.

Europe and North America were the first continents to lose large areas of forests. But people in South America and Africa are now cutting down their trees at a great rate – 12 hectares (30 acres) a minute, day and night. Since 1945 more than 40 per cent of the world's great tropical forests have been destroyed.

Apart from the loss of trees, cutting down forests also destroys the habitats (living places) of many animals and some humans. The tropical rain forests in particular are a serious loss, because they contain many valuable plants. Some of these plants have been discovered and turned to good use, for food and for medicines. Although there are many more to be discovered and exploited, some species have already become extinct because of the destruction of their forest habitats.

# Flowering Plants

Flowering plants are not only the most beautiful plants; they are the most important. They provide food for herbivores – plant-eating animals – and for humans. There are about 285,000 species of flowering plants, against 148,000 for all other plants. Flowering plants form two groups. *Monocotyledons* produce a single seed leaf when they begin to grow; *dicotyledons* start with two seed leaves.

When a flower has been fertilized it produces a fruit. Some fruits dry out as they ripen. Examples of these are peas, beans and nuts. Others are fleshy fruits, such as bananas, grapes, marrows and tomatoes.

The scientific name for flowering plants is angiosperms, meaning 'cased seeds', because their seeds are enclosed in the fruits. Some seeds are quite small, such as those of apples and oranges. Fruits of this type are pomes or berries according to how they are formed.

Cherries, peaches and plums have a hard inner stone, inside which is the seed. Fruits of this type are called drupes. Many fruits that are known as berries, such as blackberries and raspberries, are actually several small drupes joined together.

△ A dicotyledon seedling (*top*) with two seed-leaves, and a monocotyledon. Examples of these two kinds of plants are shown on the facing page.

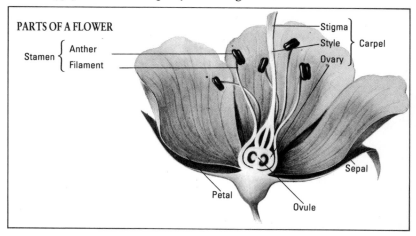

**PARTS OF A FLOWER**

Stamen { Anther
Filament

Stigma
Style } Carpel
Ovary

Petal

Ovule

Sepal

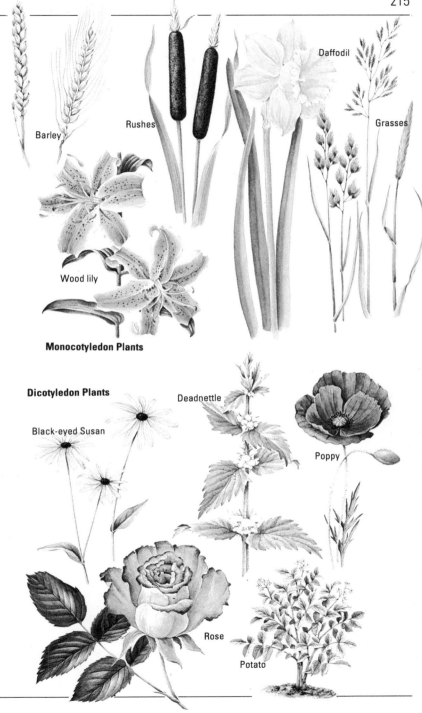

Barley

Rushes

Daffodil

Grasses

Wood lily

**Monocotyledon Plants**

**Dicotyledon Plants**

Deadnettle

Black-eyed Susan

Poppy

Rose

Potato

△ Prickly juniper.

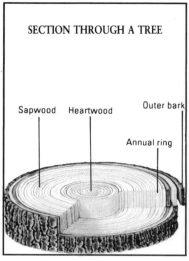

## SECTION THROUGH A TREE

Sapwood  Heartwood  Outer bark

Annual ring

## FAMILIES OF FLOWERING PLANTS

There are more than 140 families (related groups) of flowering plants. Some families have only one or two species in them. Others have dozens. Quite often you would not expect some plants to be related – for example, the rose and the raspberry, or the cabbage and the wallflower. Here are some of the more important families, with examples of the plants in them:

**Amaryllis family:** daffodil, onion, snowdrop, narcissus.
**Arum family:** arum, jack-in-the-pulpit.
**Banana family:** banana, Bird-of-Paradise flower.
**Beech family:** beech, chestnut, oak.
**Birch family:** alder, birch, hazel.
**Borage family:** Virginia cowslip, forget-me-not.
**Buckwheat family:** dock, rhubarb, sorrel.
**Cactus family:** cactus, prickly pear.
**Cashew family:** mango, pistachio nut, sumac.
**Composite family:** artichoke, chrysanthemum, daisy, dandelion, lettuce, sneezewort, thistle.
**Crowfoot family:** anemone, larkspur, peony.
**Ebony family:** ebony, persimmon.
**Figwort family:** foxglove, toadflax.
**Ginger family:** cardamom, turmeric.

**Grass family:** bamboo, rice, rye, wheat.
**Heath family:** azalea, briar, heath, rhododendron.
**Laurel family:** avocado, baytree, laurel.
**Lily family:** asparagus, crocus, lily, tulip.
**Madder family:** bedstraw, coffee.
**Mallow family:** cotton, hollyhock.
**Mint family:** basil, lavender, rosemary.
**Morning-glory family:** bindweed, dodder.
**Mulberry family:** fig, hop, mulberry.
**Mustard family:** cabbage, sweet alyssum, turnip, wallflower.
**Myrtle family:** clove, eucalyptus, pimento.
**Nightshade family:** eggplant, henbane, nightshade, potato, tobacco, tomato.
**Olive family:** ash, jasmine, privet.
**Palm family:** coconut palm, date palm.
**Parsley family:** carrot, dill, parsnip.
**Pea family:** bean, brazilwood, clover, ground nut, laburnum, licorice, soya bean, vetch.
**Pink family:** carnation, pink.
**Primrose family:** European cowslip, pimpernel.
**Rose family:** rose, apple, bramble, nectarine, plum, raspberry, strawberry.
**Rue family:** grapefruit, lemon, lime, orange.
**Saxifrage family:** currant, gooseberry, hydrangea.
**Spurge family:** cassava, rubber, teak.
**Tea family:** camellia, tea.
**Willow family:** aspen, osier, poplar.

# Trees and Shrubs

Trees and shrubs differ from other plants in having woody stems. These stems support the plants and enable them to grow tall. A few plants, such as lianas and other creepers, have woody stems which are not strong enough to allow them to stand alone.

There are two main kinds of trees. Conifers are trees with needle-like leaves. They produce their seeds in cones. Most of them are evergreens – that is, they do not lose their leaves in the autumn, but shed and renew a few all the year round.

Broadleaved trees have wide leaves. They have flowers and produce their seeds in fruits. Most of them are deciduous – that is, they shed their leaves in the autumn and grow new ones in the spring. But some, such as holly, rhododendron and many trees of the rain forests, are evergreens.

△ Sequoia

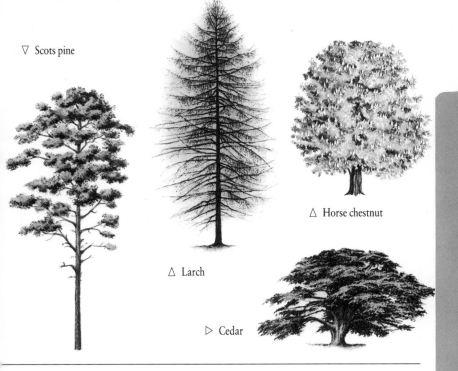

▽ Scots pine

△ Larch

△ Horse chestnut

▷ Cedar

△ The South American bromeliads are epiphytic plants, growing on other plants but able to make their own food.

▷ The Amazon rain forest supports different animal life within each layer.

## THE MULTI-STOREY RAIN FOREST

The Amazon rain forest has five main layers as shown in the diagram (right). The layers and their characteristics are:

**Emergent layer:** A few trees grow high above the others.

**Canopy layer:** A thick mass of treetops which break the heavy rain into fine spray. Many plants and animals live here on nuts and fruit.

**Middle layer:** This layer, sometimes called the understorey, is dark. Lianas (creepers) and climbing plants grow and young trees struggle towards the light.

**Lower layer:** Some shrubs and young trees. Tall trees have buttress roots. Dark.

**Ground layer:** Little light but very damp. Seedlings, herbs and fungi grow in the fragile soil.

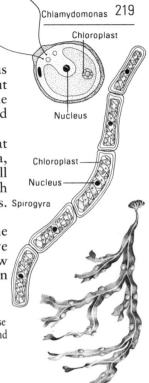

# The Protists

Some living things are difficult to classify as animals or plants. Today many biologists put them into a third kingdom, the 'Protista'. The name Protista comes from a Greek word meaning 'the very first'.

The protists include all the organisms that consist of one cell only, such as bacteria, some of the smaller algae, amoebas and small sea-dwelling creatures in the plankton such as diatoms, radiolarians and sun animals. Many single-celled animals live in colonies.

Some biologists include the fungi in the Protista. Others list them with plants or give them their own kingdom, the Mycota. A few biologists put the bacteria and the blue-green algae in yet another kingdom, the Monera.

▷ Simple plants such as chlamydomonas and spirogyra reproduce either by cell division or sexually (producing separate male and female cells which combine to make a new part).

Bladderwrack is a seaweed growing on rocky shores. These plants cling tightly to rocks, and have rubbery exteriors to prevent them drying out when exposed at low tide.

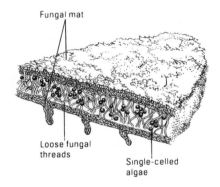

△ Cross-section through a crusty lichen. The fungal threads make a dense mat on the outside, while inside the threads are looser, with green algal cells making food.

▷ Two edible fungi: field mushroom and shaggy ink cap.

# DICTIONARY OF PLANTS

**annual** A plant which completes its life cycle in one season and then dies.

**anther** The part of the stamen that contains the pollen.

**asexual reproduction** Any form of reproduction that does not involve the fusing of male and female sex cells (gametes).

**bark** The outer layer of a woody stem.

**berry** A fleshy fruit with no hard inner layer and usually with several seeds, for example orange, gooseberry.

**biennial** A plant which completes its life cycle in two seasons and then dies.

**bud** An undeveloped shoot.

**bulb** An enlarged underground bud with fleshy leaves in which food is stored.

**calyx** The name for the sepals of a flower.

**carbohydrate** A food, for example sugar and starch, made up of carbon, hydrogen and oxygen, produced in a plant by photosynthesis. Carbohydrate is 'burned' to provide energy.

**carpel** The female reproductive organ of a flower, it is made up of stigma, style and ovary.

**cell** Minute living unit. All living matter is made up of cells.

**chlorophyll** The green pigment which enables green plants to use the energy from light to make food (photosynthesis).

**chromosome** Minute thread-like structure in the nucleus of a cell containing the genes.

**clone** A group of plants with identical chromosomes and features, produced by vegetative reproduction, for example clusters of bulbs.

**compound leaf** One in which the blade is divided into separate leaflets.

**corm** A short fleshy underground stem in which food is stored.

**cotyledon** A seed leaf. The first leaf or pair of leaves of the embryo plant in a seed, often providing a food store.

**deciduous** Shedding all leaves at the end of each growing season.

**dicotyledon** (or dicot). A member of the class of flowering plants with two cotyledons in each seed.

**drupe** A fruit with a fleshy outer layer and a hard inner layer, for example peach, cherry.

**ecology** The study of the relations between living things and their environment.

**embryo** The young plant in the seed.

**fertilization** The combining of the male reproductive cell with the ovule to form a seed.

**fruit** A ripened carpel or group of carpels. It protects and helps in the dispersal of seeds.

**gene** Part of a chromosome, containing the coded hereditary information for a particular characteristic. Most characteristics involve many genes.

**germination** The beginning of growth of a seed or spore.

**glucose** The simple sugar produced in photosynthesis, and stored as a food reserve by some plants.

**herb** or **herbaceous plant** A non-woody seed plant in which the aerial parts (those exposed to the air) die (or die down) at the end of each growing season.

**humus** Decaying organic matter in the soil.

**hybrid** A plant produced when pollen from one species fertilizes the flower of different but usually very closely related species. Hybrids are usually sterile.

# PLANT RECORDS

**Oldest surviving species of tree** is the ginkgo or maidenhair tree of China. It first appeared about 160 million years ago.

**Largest seeds** are those of the coco-de-mer, a palm growing in the Seychelles. The nuts may weigh as much as 23 kg (50 lb).

**Longest seaweed** is the Pacific Giant Kelp, which can grow nearly 61 m (200 ft) long.

**Tallest grasses** are the Thorney bamboos of India, which reach a height of 37 m (120 ft).

**Largest flowers** are those of the Southeast Asian plant *Rafflesia*, which reach more than 90 cm (3 ft) across. Their smell gives them the popular name of stinking corpse lily.

**Tallest trees** are the coast redwoods of California. The tallest living specimen is over 111 m (364 ft) high.

**Earliest fossil land plants** were of a primitive type called *Cooksonia*, which flourished in Ireland about 415 million years ago.

**Earliest fossil flowers** so far known were found at Scania, Sweden, in 1981 in deposits more than 65 million years old.

**legume** (or pod) A type of dry fruit formed from a single ovary, which splits down two sides when ripe, for example pea.

**monocotyledon** A member of the class of flowering plants with only one cotyledon (seed leaf) in each seed.

**nectar** The sweet liquid, produced in glands called nectaries, that attracts insects to a flower.

**nucleus** The part of a cell containing the chromosomes.

**nut** A one-seeded fruit with a hard woody wall.

**organic** Living; also used of material which was once part of a living thing.

**osmosis** The process whereby a solvent such as water diffuses through a semi-permeable membrane, tending to equalize the strengths of the solutions on each side of the membrane.

**ovary** The hollow part of the carpel which contains the ovules. It may also be formed from the cavities of several carpels joined together.

**ovule** A structure inside the ovary which contains the female reproductive cell and which, after fertilization, develops into the seed.

**parasite** A living thing which lives on or in another living thing (the host), and which obtains all its food from the host.

**perennial** A plant that lives on from year to year.

**photosynthesis** The process by which green plants use the energy of light to make glucose from carbon dioxide and water.

**pistil** Another word for the female part of the flower – the carpel or group of carpels.

**pollen** Mass of grains produced in the stamens of a flower, carrying the male reproductive cells.

**pollination** The transfer of pollen from stamen to stigma.

**rhizoid** Hair-like structure which anchors mosses in the ground.

**rhizome** A horizontal underground stem, sometimes containing stored food.

**runner** A creeping stem by which plants such as the strawberry reproduce.

**self-pollination** Transfer of pollen from the stamens to the stigma of the same flower.

**sepals** The outermost parts of a flower. They are usually green and protect the petals before the flower opens.

**shrub** A fairly short woody plant with many branches and no main trunk.

**spore** A single-celled reproductive body which grows into a new plant; found in algae, fungi, ferns and mosses.

**stamen** Male reproductive part of a flower, made up of the pollen-producing anther and its supporting filament (stalk).

**starch** A type of carbohydrate food often stored in plants.

**stigma** The tip of the carpel which receives the pollen.

**style** Stalk-like part of the carpel with the stigma at its tip.

**symbiosis** A close association between two organisms in which both organisms benefit.

**taproot** The main root of the plant.

**tendril** A modified stem, leaf or leaflet used by some climbing plants. It is very thin, and coils round any support that it meets.

**tuber** A swollen stem (such as a potato) or root (for example a dahlia) used to store food.

◁ Plant fossils, like these of an ancient *Segillaria* discovered in South Wales, reveal much about the ecology of the prehistoric Earth. Plants are the planet's oldest life-forms.

# Science

**The study of science is a quest for knowledge and the origins of life. By observation, measurement and assessment of facts, scientists aim to discover answers to the questions How? and Why? Their research penetrates back into time, down into the depths of the ocean, and even beyond the reaches of our planet into outer space.**

Science is the study of the physical side of the universe. It is based on observation, measurement and experiment. It is concerned with facts and with the methodical study of them.

Science may be divided into two disciplines: pure science, the study of things for their own sake; and applied science, using science for practical purposes. One aspect of applied science is technology, which is discussed in more detail on pages 242–243.

The story of science began long ago, before people could read and write. One of the earliest scientific discoveries was how to make and use fire. Even something as simple as the discovery that a sloping roof throws off the rain better than a flat one ranks as an early scientific advance.

When people began to settle down and build themselves cities to live in, science progressed by leaps and bounds. More than 5,000 years ago the ancient Babylonians developed early mathematics and a calendar, and studied the stars. The Egyptians added geometry and surgery. At the same time the Chinese people made similar advances in science, but there was no exchange of scientific knowledge between China and Europe.

The biggest advances in science in ancient times were made by the Greeks, who not only learned a great deal but were able to write it down. One of the greatest Greek scientists, the philosopher Aristotle, developed the skills of observation and classifying knowledge in

△ Sumerian cuneiform writing. Writing enabled knowledge to be permanently recorded.

△ Aristotle (384–322 BC) laid the foundations of many of the modern sciences. He defined and classified the branches of knowledge.

the 300s BC, while Archimedes, a century later, established the principle of conducting experiments.

The Romans did not advance science much, and during the early Middle Ages people in Europe studied it hardly at all. However, the Arabs preserved much of the ancient Greek knowledge. In the Americas, the Aztec, Inca and Maya Indians developed their own independent scientific knowledge but, like the Chinese, they had no influence on Europe.

The revival of science came in the 1500s, during the period which we call the Renaissance − 'rebirth' − because there was a renewed interest in learning. The Greek books preserved by the Arabs were revived and studied. Since then science has progressed very fast.

We are now living at a most exciting time in the story of science. Modern methods of research have enabled us to understand many things that were mysteries to our ancestors. With the aid of telescopes and space probes we are increasing our understanding of the universe. Special deep-sea submarines are enabling us to penetrate the secrets of the oceans and so add to our knowledge of our own planet and the origin of life.

But the more we find out, the more we realize how much there is still to learn. The main branches of science today are listed on the next page.

△ A model of an early reflecting telescope. Invented in the 1600s, it was an enormous advance in scientific instrumentation. For the first time, scientists could study the stars and planets in detail.

▽ Ancient stone circles, such as Stonehenge, may have been used to observe movements of the stars and planets. Astronomers used these observations to work out calendars.

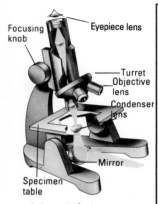

Focusing knob

Eyepiece lens

Turret
Objective lens
Condenser lens

Specimen table

Mirror

△ An optical microscope, with three lenses – each magnifying to a different degree. The microscope revolutionized the life sciences from the 1600s.

▽ A lead-acid accumulator battery, with six wet cells connected in series. The accumulator can be recharged and reused repeatedly.

## BRANCHES OF SCIENCE

| Science | Study of |
|---|---|
| **Earth Sciences** (See section 2, Planet Earth) | |
| geology | Rocks, earthquakes, volcanoes and fossils |
| meteorology | The atmosphere and weather |
| oceanography | Waves, tides, currents, trenches and ocean life |
| palaeontology | Plant and animal fossils |

**Life Sciences**

| | |
|---|---|
| anatomy | Structure, form and arrangement of the body |
| bacteriology | Bacteria; their growth and behaviour |
| biology | Animals and plants; origin, morphology and environment |
| botany | The plant world |
| ecology | Relationship between living things and environment |
| medicine | Cause, prevention and cure of disease |
| nutrition | Supply of adequate and correct foods to satisfy the body's requirements |
| pharmacology | Drugs; their preparation, use and effects |
| physiology | The function of living things |
| psychology | Behaviour of humans and animals; working of the brain |
| zoology | Animal life |

**Mathematical Sciences**

| | |
|---|---|
| computing | The use of computers in mathematics and statistics |
| logic | Reasoning by mathematics; used by computers |
| mathematics | The application of geometry, algebra and arithmetic to concrete data |
| statistics | Numerical information and its analysis |

**Physical Sciences**

| | |
|---|---|
| astronomy | Heavenly bodies and their motions |
| chemistry | Properties and behaviour of substances |
| electronics | Behaviour of electrons in a vacuum, in gases and semiconductors |
| engineering | Application of scientific principles to industry |
| mechanics | The invention and construction of machines; their operation and the calculation of their efficiency |
| metallurgy | The working of metals; smelting and refining |
| physics | Nature and behaviour of matter and energy |

**Social Sciences**

| | |
|---|---|
| anthropology | Origin, culture, development and distribution of human beings |
| archaeology | Remains and monuments left by earlier people |
| economics | Use of natural resources to the best advantage |
| geography | Location of Earth's features and our relation to them |
| linguistics | Languages and their relationship to each other |
| political science | Function of states and governments |
| sociology | Relationship between groups and individuals |

## KEY DATES IN SCIENCE

**c.400BC** Hippocrates devises the code of medical ethics – now the 'Hippocratic oath'.

**1543** Nicolaus Copernicus argues that the Sun is at the centre of the solar system.

**c.1600** Galileo Galilei develops and uses the scientific method.

**1687** Sir Isaac Newton publishes his book, *Principia*, setting out the laws of mechanics.

**1789** Antoine Lavoisier writes *Elements of Chemistry*, the first modern textbook of chemistry.

**1839** Matthias Schleiden and Theodor Schwann suggest that living things are made up of cells.

**1858** Charles Darwin and Alfred Russel Wallace set out their theory of evolution.

**1869** Dmitri Mendeleyev classifies the elements into the Periodic Table.

**1900** Max Planck puts forward the quantum theory.

**1905** Albert Einstein advances his Special Theory of Relativity.

**1911** Ernest Rutherford discovers the nucleus and formulates the atomic theory.

**1942** Enrico Fermi and others achieve the first successful nuclear chain reaction.

**1953** Francis Crick and James Watson discover that DNA – 'the molecule of life' – is a double helix, resembling a twisted ladder.

**1957** Arthur Kornberg grows DNA in a test-tube.

**1963** F.J. Vine and D.H. Matthews revolutionize geology by proving that the sea-floor spreads, so confirming the theory of continental drift.

**1969** Neil Armstrong and Edwin Aldrin become the first men to explore the Moon.

**1986** Spacecraft *Voyager 2* flies past Uranus, the planet seventh from the Sun, and takes the first close-up pictures of it.

▽ Much of the equipment used in a modern chemistry laboratory has changed little over the years, though computers are now used widely to store the results of experiments. Some of the more common items found in a chemistry laboratory are shown here. They are 1. Chemical balance; 2. Bottles with ground glass stoppers; 3. Centrifuge; 4. Microscope; 5. Burette; 6. Conical flask; 7. Filter funnel; 8. Measuring cylinder; 9. Long-necked flask; 10. Pipette; 11. Flat-bottomed flask; 12. Beaker; 13. Test tube and holder; 14. Bunsen burner; 15. Mortar and pestle; 16. Condenser; 17. Tripod stand.

△ Many heavy atoms have unstable nuclei, which break down spontaneously in radioactive decay. As it breaks down, this heavy nucleus is emitting an alpha particle, which comprises two protons and two neutrons.

△ Here the heavy unstable nucleus, in breaking down, emits a beta particle, identical with an electron. This form of radiation is more penetrating than alpha-particle radiation. More penetrating still is gamma radiation.

# Chemistry

Chemistry is the study of matter. Matter is made up of chemical elements – substances which differ from one another. The elements are made up of atoms, and the atoms of each element are different, too.

Each atom has a nucleus, or centre, containing a number of protons – particles carrying a positive electrical charge. The atomic number of each element in the periodic table on pages 228–229 is the number of protons in the nucleus. Whirling around the nucleus are as many electrons (negatively charged particles) as there are protons.

In addition, the periodic table shows the elements arranged in periods (rows) according to their atomic numbers. The vertical columns contain elements that have similar characteristics; for example, the end column on the right contains a group of inert gases which are called the 'noble gases'.

Two groups of elements appear at the bottom of the table: the 'Lanthanides' or rare-earth elements, and the 'Actinides', which are all radioactive. Elements 1 (hydrogen) to 92 (uranium) are found in nature. Those from 93 onwards are called transuranium elements, which have been made in laboratories.

## HOW TO READ A CHEMICAL FORMULA

Chemists use a form of shorthand when writing out the formula of a chemical compound. It is very precise, and tells them exactly what is in each molecule (unit) of the compound. It is based on standard abbreviations, which you will find in the periodic table.

A simple example is the formula for water, $H_2O$. H stands for hydrogen and O stands for oxygen. The subscript (lower) number after the letter H shows how many atoms of that element there are in each water molecule. So we know that each molecule of water contains two atoms of hydrogen and one of oxygen. Many compounds consist of chains or webs of atoms. For example, ethanoic acid, better known in its dilute form as vinegar, has the formula $CH_3COOH$.

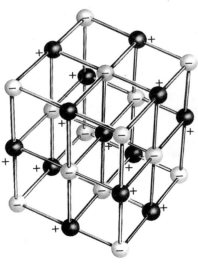

$\triangledown$ The arrangement of ions in a crystal of sodium chloride (common salt). Chlorine and sodium ions are held together by electric attraction.

## CHEMICAL NAMES OF EVERYDAY SUBSTANCES

Many chemical substances have common names such as we use every day. However, chemists have more precise names for them which describe exactly what they are. Here is a selection:

| Substance | Chemical name |
|---|---|
| Baking soda | Sodium bicarbonate |
| Blue vitriol | Copper sulphate |
| Borax | Sodium borate |
| Caustic soda | Sodium hydroxide |
| Chalk | Calcium carbonate |
| Common salt | Sodium chloride |
| Corrosive sublimate | Mercuric chloride |
| Epsom salts | Magnesium sulphate |
| Glauber's salt | Sodium sulphate |
| Hydrochloric acid | Hydrogen chloride |
| Lime | Calcium oxide |
| Magnesia | Magnesium oxide |
| Plaster of Paris | Calcium sulphate |
| Prussian blue | Ferric ferrocyanide |
| Red lead | Triplumbic tetroxide |
| Saltpetre | Potassium nitrate |
| Sal volatile | Ammonium carbonate |
| Vinegar | Dilute ethanoic (acetic) acid |
| Washing soda | Crystalline sodium carbonate |
| Water glass | Sodium silicate |

## CHEMICAL INDICATORS

Indicators are chemicals which show how a chemical change is progressing, or whether a substance is an acid or a base (alkali). Two examples are litmus and methyl orange:

|  | Litmus | Methyl Orange |
|---|---|---|
| Acid | Turns red | Turns red |
| Base | Turns blue | Turns yellow |

## CHEMICAL RECORDS

**Lightest element** is the gas hydrogen.
**Lightest metal** is lithium, which is half the weight of an equal volume of water.
**Hardest element** is carbon when it occurs in the form of diamond.
**Commonest element** in the universe is hydrogen; in the atmosphere it is nitrogen; and in the Earth's crust it is oxygen.

# Periodic table of elements

The elements, listed with their symbols and atomic numbers, lie horizontally in order of their atomic numbers. Those with chemically similar properties fall under one another in the columns. Elements with atomic numbers of 93 and over are man-made.

| | | | | | | | | |
|---|---|---|---|---|---|---|---|---|
| 1<br>Hydrogen<br>H | | | | | | | | |
| 3<br>Lithium<br>Li | 4<br>Beryllium<br>Be | | | | | | | |
| 11<br>Sodium<br>Na | 12<br>Magnesium<br>Mg | | | | | | | |
| 19<br>Potassium<br>K | 20<br>Calcium<br>Ca | 21<br>Scandium<br>Sc | 22<br>Titanium<br>Ti | 23<br>Vanadium<br>V | 24<br>Chromium<br>Cr | 25<br>Manganese<br>Mn | 26<br>Iron<br>Fe | 27<br>Cobalt<br>Co |
| 37<br>Rubidium<br>Rb | 38<br>Strontium<br>Sr | 39<br>Yttrium<br>Y | 40<br>Zirconium<br>Zr | 41<br>Niobium<br>Nb | 42<br>Molybdenum<br>Mo | 43<br>Technetium<br>Tc | 44<br>Ruthenium<br>Ru | 45<br>Rhodium<br>Rh |
| 55<br>Caesium<br>Cs | 56<br>Barium<br>Ba | 57–71<br>Lanthanide<br>series | 72<br>Hafnium<br>Hf | 73<br>Tantalum<br>Ta | 74<br>Wolfram<br>W | 75<br>Rhenium<br>Re | 76<br>Osmium<br>Os | 77<br>Iridium<br>Ir |
| 87<br>Francium<br>Fr | 88<br>Radium<br>Ra | 89–103<br>Actinide<br>series | 104<br>Rutherfordium<br>Rf | | | | | |

| | 57<br>Lanthanum<br>La | 58<br>Cerium<br>Ce | 59<br>Praseodymium<br>Pr | 60<br>Neodymium<br>Nd | 61<br>Prometheum<br>Pm | 62<br>Samarium<br>Sm | 63<br>Europium<br>Eu |
|---|---|---|---|---|---|---|---|
| | 89<br>Actinium<br>Ac | 90<br>Thorium<br>Th | 91<br>Protactinium<br>Pa | 92<br>Uranium<br>U | 93<br>Neptunium<br>Np | 94<br>Plutonium<br>Pu | 95<br>Americium<br>Am |

◁ Dalton's chart of elements, their atomic weights and models of their atoms.

| | | | | | | | | 2<br>Helium<br>He |
|---|---|---|---|---|---|---|---|---|
| | | | 5<br>Boron<br>B | 6<br>Carbon<br>C | 7<br>Nitrogen<br>N | 8<br>Oxygen<br>O | 9<br>Fluorine<br>F | 10<br>Neon<br>Ne |
| | | | 13<br>Aluminium<br>Al | 14<br>Silicon<br>Si | 15<br>Phosphorus<br>P | 16<br>Sulphur<br>S | 17<br>Chlorine<br>Cl | 18<br>Argon<br>Ar |
| 28<br>Nickel<br>Ni | 29<br>Copper<br>Cu | 30<br>Zinc<br>Zn | 31<br>Gallium<br>Ga | 32<br>Germanium<br>Ge | 33<br>Arsenic<br>As | 34<br>Selenium<br>Se | 35<br>Bromine<br>Br | 36<br>Krypton<br>Kr |
| 46<br>Palladium<br>Pd | 47<br>Silver<br>Ag | 48<br>Cadmium<br>Cd | 49<br>Indium<br>In | 50<br>Tin<br>Sn | 51<br>Antimony<br>Sb | 52<br>Tellurium<br>Te | 53<br>Iodine<br>I | 54<br>Xenon<br>Xe |
| 78<br>Platinum<br>Pt | 79<br>Gold<br>Au | 80<br>Mercury<br>Hg | 81<br>Thallium<br>Tl | 82<br>Lead<br>Pb | 83<br>Bismuth<br>Bi | 84<br>Polonium<br>Po | 85<br>Astatine<br>At | 86<br>Radon<br>Rn |

| 64<br>Gadolinium<br>Gd | 65<br>Terbium<br>Tb | 66<br>Dysprosium<br>Dy | 67<br>Holmium<br>Ho | 68<br>Erbium<br>Er | 69<br>Thulium<br>Tm | 70<br>Ytterbium<br>Yb | 71<br>Lutecium<br>Lu |
|---|---|---|---|---|---|---|---|
| 96<br>Curium<br>Cm | 97<br>Berkelium<br>Bk | 98<br>Californium<br>Cf | 99<br>Einsteinium<br>Es | 100<br>Fermium<br>Fm | 101<br>Mendelevium<br>Md | 102<br>Nobelium<br>No | 103<br>Lawrencium<br>Lr |

▷ Albert Einstein, one of the greatest scientists, put forward the theory of relativity which was a new way of looking at time, space, matter and energy. His explanations made possible many developments, one of which was nuclear energy and through it the atomic bomb. Despite this, he also campaigned passionately for world peace.

◁ Russian chemist Dmitri Mendeleyev (1834–1907) laid the foundation for the modern periodic classification of the chemical elements, shown above. He allowed gaps in the table to represent undiscovered elements.

# Physics

Physics is the study of matter and energy. It is basic to the study of many other branches of science, including chemistry and the Earth sciences. Knowledge of its laws has enabled people to put satellites into orbit around the Earth, land men on the Moon and send space probes to the most distant planets.

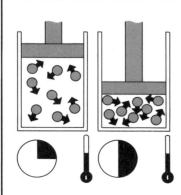

△ Boyle's law describes the behaviour of gases under pressure.

## LAWS AFFECTING GASES

**Boyle's Law** At a constant temperature, the volume of a gas is inversely proportional to its pressure – that is, the higher the pressure, the smaller the space occupied by the gas (described by the Irish physicist Robert Boyle in 1662).

**Charles's Law** At a constant pressure, the volume of a gas is proportional to its absolute temperature - that is, the higher the temperature, the greater the volume (described by the French chemist Jacques Charles in 1787).

**Avogadro's Law** states that equal volumes of different gases, at the same pressure and temperature, all contain the same number of molecules (described by the Italian scientist Amedeo Avogadro in 1811).

## NEWTON'S LAWS OF MOTION

The movement of all objects, both in space and on Earth, was explained by the English scientist Sir Isaac Newton in 1687, in the following three laws of motion:

**The first law** states that a stationary object remains still, and a moving object continues to move in a straight line, unless some external force acts on them.

**The second law** states that how much a force makes an object accelerate depends on the mass of the object and the strength of the force. The same force will move an object of twice the mass at half the acceleration.

**The third law** states that for every action there is an equal and opposite reaction. This is the law that governs rocket motors: when the burning gases escape from the back end of the rocket, they press against the rocket, driving it forward.

△ Sir Isaac Newton (1642–1727).

## THE LAWS OF THERMODYNAMICS

The study of the relationship between heat and work, and how one can be transformed into the other, is called 'thermodynamics'. There are four laws, numbered from 0 to 3:

**Law 0** states that no heat will flow between two bodies at the same temperature.

**Law 1** states that energy cannot be created or destroyed. So energy, in the form of heat, may be transformed into another form of energy, such as motion, as in a motor-car engine, but the amount of energy stays the same.

**Law 2** says that heat can never pass spontaneously from a colder body to a hotter one.

**Law 3** states that it is impossible to cool anything down to absolute zero, the lowest possible temperature, because heat from it would have to be transferred to an even colder body.

▽ By bending light rays, refraction causes images to be displaced. This paintbrush seems to bend because light from it is refracted as it passes from the air into water. The brush also looks enlarged, since the glass gives the water a curved shape, like a magnifying lens.

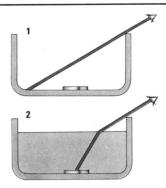

△ A coin invisible in a dish becomes visible when the dish is filled with water – because the light from it bends.

## BRANCHES OF PHYSICS

**acoustics** The study of sound and sound waves
**atomic physics** The study of the behaviour, properties and structure of atoms
**biophysics** The physics of biological processes
**crystallography** The study of the formation, structure and properties of crystals
**cryogenics** The study of very low temperatures
**electrodynamics** The study of the relation between electrical and mechanical forces
**fluid physics** The study of gases and liquids
**geophysics** The study of the physical properties of the Earth

**mechanics** The study of bodies in motion and at rest
**nuclear physics** The study of the atomic nucleus and nuclear reactions
**optics** The study of light
**rheology** The study of the flow of matter
**solid-state physics** The study of the effect of such things as temperature and pressure on properties of solid materials
**thermodynamics** The study of work and energy
**tribology** The study of friction and lubrication

△ Electronically controlled robots that duplicate human actions are now widely used in industrial processes.

# Electricity and electronics

Electricity is a form of energy. In addition to the electricity we are familiar with as power in the home and at work, it is a part of everything. Each atom contains electrically-charged particles, including protons with a positive charge and electrons with a negative charge.

Electronics is an important part of the study of electricity. It deals with the way in which electrons control the flow of electricity. It is largely a matter of pulses of current. The current is controlled by devices such as semiconducting transistors.

These days electronics is involved in many of our daily activities. It is found in factories controlling robot machines; in the home, in the form of radio and TV sets, and controlling dish-washers and washing machines; in transport, controlling railway signals and electric trains, regulating car engines and controlling the engines of aeroplanes. An important application of electronics is the production of new and increasingly powerful calculators and computers.

## MODERN TRENDS IN ELECTRONICS

**1982** Capacity of the most powerful memory chips is increased to 256 kilobits (256,000 bits).
**1983** Compact discs (CDs) come on to the market.
**1984** Capacity of memory chips is increased to 1 megabit (a million bits).
**1986** A two-way wrist radio weighing only 57 g (2 oz) is developed in Japan.
An electronic pacemaker which can vary the heartbeat rate to suit a patient who is taking exercise is developed in the United States.
**1987** Memory chips with capacities of 4 megabits and 16 megabits are developed in Japan.
'Smart cards' – credit cards with built in computers to prevent forgery and overspending – are tested in the USA.
First 3-D video systems are introduced.
**1988** First pocket-sized colour television sets are marketed.

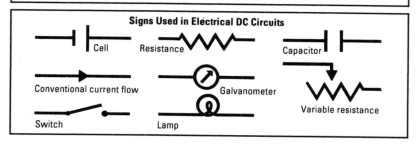

**Signs Used in Electrical DC Circuits**

Cell  Resistance  Capacitor

Conventional current flow  Galvanometer

Variable resistance

Switch  Lamp

# Computers

The first working electronic computer was built at the University of Pennsylvania in 1945. It was called ENIAC (Electronic Numeral Integrator And Calculator). It weighed 30 tonnes and occupied a large hall of 140 square metres (1,500 square feet). It contained more than 18,000 valves. Today's personal computers occupy just a small amount of desk space, and have as much power as ENIAC.

## COMPUTER LANGUAGE

**access** To connect to a remote computer database (usually by telephone line).

**A.I.** Artificial Intelligence; used of software, but true artificial intelligence has yet to be attained.

**ALGOL** A mathematically-oriented programming language; short for ALGOrithmic Language.

**analog** A representation of numerical or physical quantities by means of physical variables such as voltage or resistance.

**ASCII** Short for American Standard Code for Information Interchange, a system of codes used by most computers to represent the alphabet, the numbers 0 to 9, and some punctuation.

**assembler** A program that translates an assembly language into machine language.

**assembly language** A computer language that uses symbols as well as words, more difficult to use than a high-level language.

**backup** A copy of a program or file, made for safety.

**BASIC** Beginner's All-purpose Symbolic Instruction Code: a computer programming language using common English terms.

**binary** A number system with a base of 2, using the symbols 0 and 1; it can be represented electronically by a current on or off in a computer.

**bit** Binary DigiT: A numeral in binary notation, that is 0 or 1.

**bug** An error in a program, causing it to fail.

**byte** A space in a computer's memory occupied by one character.

**COBOL** COmmon Business Orientated Language: a programming language designed for business and commercial use.

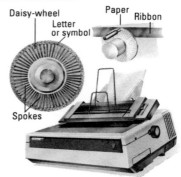

Daisy-wheel
Letter or symbol
Paper
Ribbon
Spokes

△ A daisywheel printer has letters and symbols at the end of the wheel's spokes.

**compatible** Used to describe a computer or program able to work with another computer.

**compiler** A program that translates a high-level language into machine language.

**continuous stationery** A continuous sheet of paper folded into pages.

**CP/M** Control Program for Microcomputers: an operating system used by some computers.

**cursor** An area of highlighting on screen which picks out the character or block which is being worked on.

**daisywheel** A kind of printer which has the characters arranged on a daisy-like wheel.

**data** General term for information processed by a computer.

**debug** To remove the bugs from a program.

**default** The drive, program or other material that is entered automatically if there is no other command.

**desk-top publishing** Producing material for commercial printing using a micro-computer.

**disk** The most commonly used means of storing programs and data; a hard disk is rigid, a floppy disk is not.

**dot matrix** A kind of printer in which the characters are built up from a system of dots.

**draft quality** Low-quality text produced at high speed by a dot-matrix printer, using only a relatively few dots.

**drive** Part of a computer that accepts disks, writes to them and reads from them.

**field** A specific set of characters treated as a whole, or the recording area used for some particular kind of data.

**file** A collection of data or the contents of a document, as stored in memory or on disk.

**file-name** A collection of characters which an operating system identifies as the file.

**format** Electronically marking up a disk so that it will receive data, and erasing any previously entered data.

**FORTRAN** FORmula TRANslation: a programming language for scientific use.

**graphics** Pictures or diagrams on screen and printed out; as distinct from text.

**hacker** A person who does programming as a hobby, often breaking into other people's programs and computer systems.

**hard copy** A print-out of a document held in a computer.

**hardware** The physical working units of a computer system.

**high-level language** Any computer language which enables the user to write instructions in everyday terms, such as 'read' or 'stop'.

**highlighting** Also called reverse video: a method of reversing light and dark areas of a screen to show something up.

**high quality** The best quality of print produced by a dot matrix printer, using more dots at a slower speed than draft quality.

**K** Short for kilobytes: 1 K = 1024 bytes.

**language** A defined set of characters for communication with a computer.

**loop** Repeated execution of a series of commands.

▽ These children are using a computer to draw. Graphics are used to make designs, maps and graphs.

△ Microminiaturization has made the silicon chip smaller and smaller, as this comparison with an ant demonstrates.

**machine language** The language of binary digits – representing codes and symbols – which a computer works with.

**mainframe computer** A powerful high-speed computer, usually with a large storage capacity, to which one or more work stations have access.

**memory** Storage of data or programs within the computer.

**micro** Abbreviation for micro-computer, a small computer for individual use.

**micro chip** A small silicon chip which provides memory for a computer.

**modem** A device that enables one computer to communicate with another over a telephone line; from MOdulator-DEModulator.

**monitor** A cathode ray tube similar to a television set, on which data are displayed.

**mouse** A small pointing device which, when rolled across the desktop, causes a pointer to move across the computer screen.

**MSDOS** An operating system for business micro-computers.

**NLQ** Near Letter Quality: another term for high quality on dot matrix printers.

**printer** A typewriter-like machine that produces printed copy from a computer.

**print-out** The output of a printer.

**program** A complete sequence of instructions for a task to be carried out by a computer.

**programming** Writing a program to carry out a specific task.

**RAM** Random Access Memory, the computer's memory in which both a program and data are held ready for processing. Whatever is stored in it is lost when the computer is switched off.

**ROM** Read Only Memory: permanent instructions or programs kept in the computer's memory, retained when the computer is switched off.

**screen** The visible part of a monitor.

**software** Programs for use in a computer to simplify programming and operations, usually available on disk.

**string** A sequence of zero or more characters.

**terminal** Another name for a work station.

**VDU** Visual Display Unit: a monitor for use with a computer.

**window** Small section of the screen that has a separate display from the main section.

**word processor** A program to store and edit text typed on a computer's keyboard, effectively a superior form of typewriter; the machine itself.

**work station** A set-up of screen, keyboard and printer linked to a mainframe computer.

**zero suppression** Elimination of non-significant zeros either on screen or in a print-out.

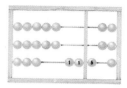

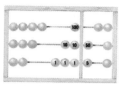

△ The abacus has been used in calculation since ancient times, and is still in use today.

# Mathematics

Mathematics is the science of numbers. It plays an important part in all the other sciences. There are three basic branches of mathematics.

**Pure mathematics** studies what mathematics can do without any particular practical use.

**Applied mathematics** relates mathematics to other activities.

**Statistics** deals with collecting large numbers of figures and analysing them — for example, taking the United Kingdom census every ten years and looking at what its figures tell us about our country.

## NUMERATION

The three types of numbers in common use today are the decimal or Arabic system, with the base 10 and using the symbols 0–9; the Roman system, based on the letters I, V, X, L, C, D and M; and the binary system used by computers, with the base two and using just two symbols, 0 and 1.

In the Roman system I stands for 1, and is repeated to make 2 (II) and 3 (III). V stands for 5, X for 10, L for 50, C for 100, D for 500, and M for 1,000. These letters are combined to make other numbers. A lower symbol before a higher one subtracts from it; a lower symbol after a higher one adds to it; for example XL is 40, while LX is 60. Lines over the top are used for higher figures in the thousands.

In binary, the base of the system is two (written as 10). And, just as 10 to the power of three is written as 1 followed by three zeros (1,000), so two to the power of three (8 in decimal) is written 1000 in binary. In other words, to write any number in binary, using just the symbols 0 and 1, you break it up into powers of two. Computers can read binary numbers very quickly indeed because these contain just the two symbols.

| 0 | Ø Ø Ø Ø |
|---|---------|
| 1 | Ø Ø Ø 1 |
| 2 | Ø Ø 1 Ø |
| 3 | Ø Ø 1 1 |
| 4 | Ø 1 Ø Ø |
| 5 | Ø 1 Ø 1 |
| 6 | Ø 1 1 Ø |
| 7 | Ø 1 1 1 |
| 8 | 1 Ø Ø Ø |

△ Computers work on information in binary code form using only 1s and 0s, indicated by electrical pulses: 0 = no pulse, 1 = a pulse. This table shows the binary forms for 0 to 8.

## EQUIVALENT NUMBERS

| Arabic | Roman | Binary | Arabic | Roman | Binary |
|---|---|---|---|---|---|
| 1 | I | 1 | 50 | L | 110010 |
| 2 | II | 10 | 60 | LX | 111100 |
| 3 | III | 11 | 64 | LXIV | 1000000 |
| 4 | IV | 100 | 90 | XC | 1011010 |
| 5 | V | 101 | 99 | XCIX | 1100011 |
| 6 | VI | 110 | 100 | C | 1100100 |
| 7 | VII | 111 | 128 | CXXVIII | 10000000 |
| 8 | VIII | 1000 | 200 | CC | 11001000 |
| 9 | IX | 1001 | 256 | CCLVI | 100000000 |
| 10 | X | 1010 | 300 | CCC | 100101100 |
| 11 | XI | 1011 | 400 | CD | 110010000 |
| 12 | XII | 1100 | 500 | D | 111110100 |
| 13 | XIII | 1101 | 512 | DXII | 1000000000 |
| 14 | XIV | 1110 | 600 | DC | 1001011000 |
| 15 | XV | 1111 | 900 | CM | 1110000100 |
| 16 | XVI | 10000 | 1,000 | M | 1111101000 |
| 17 | XVII | 10001 | 1,024 | MXXIV | 10000000000 |
| 18 | XVIII | 10010 | 1,500 | MD | 10111011100 |
| 19 | XIX | 10011 | 2,000 | MM | 11111010000 |
| 20 | XX | 10100 | 4,000 | MV̄ | 111110100000 |
| 21 | XXI | 10101 | 5,000 | V̄ | 1001110001001 |
| 30 | XXX | 11110 | 10,000 | X̄ | 10011100010000 |
| 32 | XXXII | 100000 | 20,000 | X̄X̄ | 100111000100000 |
| 40 | XL | 101000 | 100,000 | C̄ | 11000011010100000 |

## DECIMAL MULTIPLES

| Prefix | Symbol | Multiplication factor |
|---|---|---|
| tera | T | $10^{12}$ | 1,000,000,000,000 |
| giga | G | $10^9$ | 1,000,000,000 |
| mega | M | $10^6$ | 1,000,000 |
| kilo | k | $10^3$ | 1,000 |
| hecto | h | $10^2$ | 100 |
| deca | da | 10 | 10 |
| deci | d | $10^{-1}$ | 0.1 |
| centi | c | $10^{-2}$ | 0.01 |
| milli | m | $10^{-3}$ | 0.001 |
| micro | μ | $10^{-6}$ | 0.000001 |
| nano | n | $10^{-9}$ | 0.000000001 |
| pico | p | $10^{-12}$ | 0.000000000001 |
| femto | f | $10^{-15}$ | 0.000000000000001 |
| atto | a | $10^{-18}$ | 0.000000000000000001 |

## ANGLES

second (″)
60″ = 1 minute (′)
60′ = 1 degree (°)
90° = 1 quadrant, or right-angle
4 quadrants = 1 circle = 360°
1 radian = 57.2958° = 57°17′44.8″
$2\pi$ radians = 1 circle = 360°
1° = 0.017453 radian

| 1 | 2 | 3 | 4 | 5 | 6 | 7 | 8 | 9 | 10 | Arabic |
|---|---|---|---|---|---|---|---|---|---|---|
| ▼ | ▼▼ | ▼▼▼ | ▼▼▼▼ | ▼▼▼▼▼ | ▼▼▼▼▼▼ | ▼▼▼▼▼▼▼ | ▼▼▼▼▼▼▼▼ | ▼▼▼▼▼▼▼▼▼ | ◄ | Babylonian |
| A | B | Γ | Δ | E | Z | H | Θ | I | K | Greek |
| I | II | III | IV | V | VI | VII | VIII | IX | X | Roman |
| — | = | ≡ | 四 | 五 | 六 | 七 | 八 | 九 | 十 | Chinese |
| • | •• | ••• | •••• | — | ·̣ | ·̣· | ·̣·· | ·̣··· | = | Mayan |
| ۱ | ۲ | ۳ | ۴ | ۵ | ۶ | ۷ | ۸ | ۹ | ○ | Indian |

◁ The Romans had no zero, so their numbers were difficult to work with. The zero was introduced in India some 1,500 years ago.

## MATHEMATICAL FORMULAE

**Note:** $r$ = radius, $h$ = height; $\pi$ = 3.14159

### Circumference

| | |
|---|---|
| Circle | $2\pi r$ |

### Area

| | |
|---|---|
| Circle | $\pi r^2$ |
| Surface of sphere | $4\pi r^2$ |
| Ellipse, semi-axes $a$, $b$ | $\pi ab$ |
| Triangle, base $b$ | $\frac{1}{2}bh$ |
| Rectangle, sides $a$, $b$ | $ab$ |
| Trapezium, parallel sides $a$, $c$ | $\frac{1}{2}h(a+c)$ |
| Regular pentagon, side $a$ | $1.721a^2$ |
| Regular hexagon, side $a$ | $2.598a^2$ |
| Regular octagon, side $a$ | $4.828a^2$ |

### Volume

| | |
|---|---|
| Sphere | $\frac{4}{3}\pi r^3$ |
| Cylinder | $h\pi r^2$ |
| Cone | $\frac{1}{3}h\pi r^2$ |
| Rectangular prism, sides $a$, $b$, $c$ | $abc$ |
| Pyramid, base area $b$ | $\frac{1}{3}hb$ |

### Algebraic

$$a^2 - b^2 = (a + b)(a - b)$$
$$a^2 + 2ab + b^2 = (a + b)^2$$
$$a^2 - 2ab + b^2 = (a - b)^2$$

For quadratic equation $ax^2 + bx + c = 0$,

$$x = \frac{-b \pm \sqrt{b^2 - 4ac}}{2a}$$

△ The kitchen measuring jug is customarily marked in cu cm/litres and fluid ounces/pints.

# Weights and measures

There are two main systems of weights and measures in use in the world: the metric system, based on the number ten, and an older system, called 'imperial' in Britain, where it originated, and 'customary' in the United States. The imperial system is more difficult to use because the units are so varied.

The revolutionary government of France devised the metric system in the 1790s. It is now used by people in most countries of the world and by scientists everywhere.

## LENGTH

**Metric units**
millimetre (mm)
10 mm = 1 centimetre (cm)
100 cm = 1 metre (m)
1,000 cm = 1 kilometre (km)

1 micron ($\mu$) = $10^{-6}$m (i.e. 1 micrometre)
1 millimicron (m$\mu$) = $10^{-9}$m (i.e. 1 nanometre)
1 ångstrom (Å) = $10^{-10}$m (i.e. 100 picometres)

**Imperial units**
inch (in)
12 in = 1 foot (ft)
3 ft = 1 yard (yd)
1,760 yd = 1 mile = 5,280 ft
1 link = 7.92 in
100 links = 1 surveyor's chain = 22 yd
1 rod, pole, or perch = 5½ yd
4 rods = 1 chain
10 chains = 1 furlong = 220 yd
8 furlongs = 1 mile

## AREA

**Metric units**
square millimetre (sq mm)
100 sq mm = 1 square centimetre (sq cm)
10,000 sq cm = 1 square metre (sq m)
100 sq m = 1 are (a) = 1 square decametre
100 a = 1 hectare (ha) = 1 square hectometre
100 ha = 1 square kilometre (sq km)

**Imperial units**
square inch (sq in)
144 sq in = 1 square foot (sq ft)
9 sq ft = 1 square yard (sq yd)
4,840 sq yd = 1 acre
640 acres = 1 square mile (sq mile)

625 square links = 1 square rod
16 square rods = 1 square chain
10 square chains = 1 acre
36 square miles = 1 township (US)

## WEIGHT

**Metric units**
milligram (mg)
1,000 mg = 1 gram (g)
1,000 g = 1 kilogram (kg)
100 kg = 1 quintal (q)
1,000 kg = 1 metric ton, or tonne (t)

**Imperial units (Avoirdupois)**
grain (gr); dram (dr)
7,000 gr = 1 pound (lb)
16 dr = 1 ounce (oz)
16 oz = 1 lb
14 lb = 1 stone
28 lb = 1 quarter
112 lb = 1 hundredweight (cwt)
20 cwt = 1 ton = 2240 lb

**Troy weight**
24 gr = 1 pennyweight (dwt)
20 dwt = 1 (Troy) ounce = 480 gr

**Apothecaries' weight**
20 gr = 1 scruple
3 scruples = 1 drachm
8 drachms = 1 (apoth) ounce = 480 gr

## CAPACITY

**Metric units**
millilitre (ml)
1,000 ml = 1 litre (l)
100 l = 1 hectolitre (hl)

**Imperial units**
gill
4 gills = 1 pint
2 pints = 1 quart
4 quarts = 1 gallon = 277.274 cu in

**Dry**
2 gallons = 1 peck
4 pecks = 1 bushel
8 bushels = 1 quarter
36 bushels = 1 chaldron

**Apothecaries' fluid**
minim (min)
60 min = 1 fluid drachm (fl dr)
8 fl dr = 1 fluid ounce (fl oz)
5 fl oz = 1 gill
20 fl oz = 1 pint

## VOLUME

**Metric units**
cubic millimetre (cu mm)
1,000 cu mm = 1 cubic centimetre (cu cm)
1,000 cu cm = 1 cubic decimetre (cu dm)
= 1 litre
1,000 cu dm = 1 cubic metre (cu m)
1,000,000,000 cu m = 1 cubic kilometre (cu km)

**Imperial units**
cubic inch (cu in)
1,728 cu in = 1 cubic foot (cu ft)
27 cu ft = 1 cubic yard (cu yd)
5,451,776,000 cu yd = 1 cubic mile (cu mile)

## HISTORICAL UNITS

| Where used | Current equivalent |
|---|---|
| **Cubit** (elbow to finger tip) | |
| Egypt (2650 BC) | 52.4 cm (20.6 in) |
| Babylon (1500 BC) | 53.0 cm (20.9 in) |
| Hebrew | 45 cm (17.7 in) |
| Black Cubit | |
| (Arabia AD 800s) | 54.1 cm (21.3 in) |
| Mexico (Aztec) | 52.5 cm (20.7 in) |
| Ancient China | 53.2 cm (20.9 in) |
| Ancient Greece | 46.3 cm (18.2 in) |
| Ancient Rome | 44.4 cm (17.4 in) |
| England | 45.7 cm (18.0 in) |
| Northern Cubit | 67.6 cm (26.6 in) |
| (c.3000 BC–AD 1800s) | |

| Where used | Current equivalent |
|---|---|
| **Foot** (length of foot) | |
| Athens | 31.6 cm (12.44 in) |
| Rome | 29.6 cm (11.66 in) |
| Northern | 33.5 cm (13.19 in) |
| England (Medieval) | 33.5 cm (13.19 in) |
| France | 32.5 cm (12.79 in) |
| **Ancient Roman units** | |
| 1 digitus | 1.85 cm (0.73 in) |
| 4 digiti = 1 palmus | 7.4 cm (2.9 in) |
| 4 palmi = 1 pes | 29.6 cm (11.7 in) |
| 5 pes = 1 passus | 1.48 m (4.86 ft) |
| 125 passus = 1 stadium | 185 m (202.3 yd) |
| 8 stadia = 1 milliar | 1480 m (0.92 mi) |

## CONVERSION FACTORS

If measurements are in imperial, multiply by the conversion factors given below to find the metric equivalent; if they are in metric, divide by the conversion factors to find imperial.

1 acre = 0.4047 hectares
1 bushel (imp.) = 36.369 litres
1 centimetre = 0.3937 inch
1 chain = 20.1168 metres
1 cord = 3.62456 cubic metres
1 cubic centimetre = 0.0610 cubic inch
1 cubic decimetre = 61.024 cubic inches
1 cubic foot = 0.0283 cubic metre
1 cubic inch = 16.387 cubic centimetres
1 cubic metre = 35.3146 cubic
   feet = 1.3079 cubic yards
1 cubic yard = 0.7646 cubic metre
1 fathom = 1.8288 metres
1 fluid oz (apoth.) = 28.4131 millilitres
1 fluid oz = 28.4 millilitres
1 foot = 0.3048 metre = 30.48 centimetres
1 foot per second = 0.6818 mph =
   1.097 km/h
1 gallon (imperial) = 4.5461 litres
1 gallon (US liquid) = 3.7854 litres
1 gill = 0.142 litre
1 gram = 0.0353 ounce = 0.002205
   pound = 15.43 grains = 0.0321 ounce
   (Troy)
1 hectare = 2.4710 acres

1 hundredweight = 50.80 kilograms
1 inch = 2.54 centimetres
1 kilogram = 2.2046 pounds
1 kilometre = 0.6214 mile = 1093.6 yards
1 knot (international) = 0.5144 metres/
   sec = 1.852 km/h
1 litre = 0.220 gallon (imperial) = 0.2642
   gallon (US) = 1.7598 pints
   (imperial) = 0.8799 quarts
1 metre = 39.3701 in = 3.2808 ft =
   1.0936 yd
1 metric tonne = 0.9842 ton
1 mile (statute) = 1.6093 kilometres
1 mile (nautical) = 1.852 kilometres
1 millimetre = 0.03937 inch
1 ounce = 28.350 grams
1 peck (imperial) = 9.0922 litres
1 pennyweight = 1.555 grams
1 pica (printer's) = 4.2175 millimetres
1 pint (imperial) = 0.5683 litre
1 pound = 0.4536 kilogram
1 quart (imperial) = 1.1365 litres
1 square centimetre = 0.1550 square inch
1 square foot = 0.0929 square metre
1 square inch = 6.4516 square centimetres
1 square kilometre = 0.3860 square mile
1 square metre = 10.7639 square
   feet = 1.1960 square yards
1 square mile = 2.5900 square kilometres
1 square yard = 0.8361 square metre
1 ton = 1.0160 square metre
1 yard = 0.9144 metre

## TIME

Second (s, or sec)
60 s = 1 minute (min)
60 min = 1 hour (h or hr)
24 h = 1 day (d)
7 days = 1 week
365¼ days = 1 year
10 years = 1 decade
100 years = 1 century
1,000 years = 1 millennium
1 mean solar day = 24 h 3 min 56.555 s
1 sidereal day = 23 h 56 min 4.091 s
1 solar, tropical, or equinoctial
   year = 365.2422 d (365 d 5 h 48 min 46 s)
1 sidereal year = 365.2564 d (365 d 6 h
   9 min 9.5 s)
1 synodic (lunar) month = 29.5306 d
1 sidereal month = 27.3217 d
1 lunar year = 354.3672 d = 12 synodic
   months

## INTERNATIONAL PAPER SIZES*

|  | mm | in |
|---|---|---|
| A0 | 841 × 1189 | 33.11 × 46.81 |
| A1 | 594 × 841 | 23.39 × 33.11 |
| A2 | 420 × 594 | 16.54 × 23.39 |
| A3 | 297 × 420 | 11.69 × 16.54 |
| A4 | 210 × 297 | 8.27 × 11.69 |
| A5 | 148 × 210 | 5.83 × 8.27 |
| A6 | 105 × 148 | 4.13 × 5.83 |
| A7 | 74 × 105 | 2.91 × 4.13 |
| A8 | 52 × 74 | 2.05 × 2.91 |
| A9 | 37 × 52 | 1.46 × 2.05 |
| A10 | 26 × 37 | 1.02 × 1.46 |

*The sizes are based on a rectangle of area 1 sq metre (A0), with sides in the ratio 1: √2.

## MISCELLANEOUS MEASURES

**Nautical**
1 span = 9 in = 23 cm
8 spans = 1 fathom = 6 ft
1 cable's length = $\frac{1}{10}$ nautical mile
1 nautical mile (old) = 6080 ft
1 nautical mile (international) =
    6076.1 ft = 1.151 statute miles ( =
    1852 metres)
60 nautical miles = 1 degree
3 nautical miles = 1 league (nautical)
1 knot × 1 nautical mile per hour
1 ton (shipping) = 42 cubic feet
1 ton (displacement) = 35 cubic feet
1 ton (register) = 100 cubic feet

**Crude oil (petroleum)**
1 barrel = 35 imperial gallons
    = 42 US gallons

**Paper (writing)**
24 sheets = 1 quire
20 quires = 1 ream = 480 sheets

**Printing**
1 point = $\frac{1}{72}$ in
1 pica = $\frac{1}{6}$ in = 12 points

**Timber**
1,000 millisteres = 1 stere = 1 cu m
1 board foot = 144 cu in (12 × 12 × 1 in)
1 cord foot = 16 cu ft
1 cord = 8 cord feet
1 hoppus foot = $4/\pi$ cu ft (round timber)
1 Petrograd standard = 165 cu ft

**Cloth**
1 ell = 45 in
1 bolt = 120 ft = 32 ells

**Brewing**
4½ gallons = 1 pin
2 pins = 9 gallons = 1 firkin
4 firkins = 1 barrel = 36 gallons
6 firkins = 1 hogshead = 54 gallons
4 hogsheads = 1 tun

**Horses (height)**
1 hand = 4 in = 10 cm

## TEMPERATURES

The following table shows comparative temperatures in the Celsius (Centigrade) scale and in the Fahrenheit scale. Note that freezing point in Celsius is 0°, and in Fahrenheit is 32°, while boiling point in the two scales is respectively 100° and 212°. The scales coincide on just one temperature – minus 40°.

Maximum and minimum thermometers (*right*) are of the alcohol type, with metal markers. The bimetal thermometer (*below*) relies on the different expansion rates of two metals.

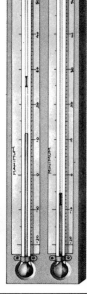

| °Celsius | °Fahrenheit |
|---|---|
| 100 | 212 |
| 90 | 194 |
| 80 | 176 |
| 70 | 158 |
| 60 | 140 |
| 50 | 122 |
| 40 | 104 |
| 30 | 86 |
| 20 | 68 |
| 10 | 50 |
| 0 | 32 |
| −10 | 14 |
| −20 | −4 |
| −30 | −22 |
| −40 | −40 |
| −50 | −58 |

# Technology

△ James Watt's steam engine (1761) was more efficient than earlier designs. It was quickly adopted in factories to drive machinery, such as looms in textile mills.

Technology is defined as the application of practical science to industry. We live in the age of technology. Its benefits are everywhere – in the home, the factory, the office, at school, in hospital.

The most obvious benefits of modern technology are the public services – suppliers of water, gas and electricity; modern sewage and refuse disposal; telephone, radio and television services. To travel from home to school or work there are cars, trains and buses – even the humble bicycle is a technological achievement.

Modern factories are equipped with a range of machines, many of them controlled by computers. Offices have such business machines as typewriters, photocopiers, word-processors and computers. Schools are equipped with laboratories, computers, television and video. Hospitals have a range of equipment to detect disorders and treat them, ranging from electrocardiographs, which monitor heart conditions, to X-ray machines and ultrasonic scanners which can peer inside a person's body.

This technology is mostly very recent. It all began in the 1700s in what is known as the Industrial Revolution – a peaceful revolution which is still going on. The revolution began in Britain, where conditions were right – a period of internal peace and prosperity.

The start was in the textile industry, with machines to spin thread and weave cloth. Early factories were set up beside rivers, which provided power through water-wheels to drive the new machines. At the same time the steam engine was being developed and, by the end of the 1700s, steam was driving much of the machinery. It became easier to build machines because iron was now freely available.

Although the Industrial Revolution began in Britain, it spread almost at once to the rest of Europe and to North America. Inventors in these lands were quick to help the revolution along.

The French contributed new ways of bleaching cotton cloth and of weaving intricate patterns; cheaper supplies of cotton for the busy textile mills came about through the genius of an American inventor, Eli Whitney. Other American inventors contributed harvesting machines to make farming easier.

The combination of steam and iron made railways and fast steamships possible in the 1800s, thus speeding up communications. During that century the electric telegraph, the telephone and radio made their appearance, and aeroplanes followed early in the 1900s. The latest revolution has been brought about by the computer which has speeded up work in offices and factories since the 1950s.

But all these technological advances have been bought at a price: damage to the environment in which we live by pollution of air, water and soil – especially from factories and cars. Chemicals released into the atmosphere are even damaging the layer of ozone high above us which protects us from the more harmful rays of the Sun. Now we are having to harness the resources of technology to preserve the Earth we live on, before it is too late.

▽ Wave power is one projected answer to future 'clean energy' requirements. Each 'beak' of the nodding boom or 'duck' contains a small generator. As the waves move the 'beak' up and down (inset) the generator turns to produce electricity.

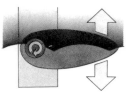

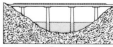

Beam

Arch

Suspension

△ Three common bridge designs. The beam is the simplest, with the weight borne on vertical piers. Suspension bridges have the longest individual spans.

# Engineering

Engineering is the term used to cover construction of all kinds. There are several branches of it.

**Mechanical engineering** is concerned with the making of machines, from aeroplanes to power stations.

**Civil engineering** covers the construction of buildings, canals, dams, highways, railways and tunnels.

**Mining engineering and metallurgy** includes the construction of mines, the extraction of minerals, and refining metals.

**Chemical engineering** includes all the manufacturing processes which involve chemicals, such as making medicines, plastics and soap.

**Electrical and electronic engineering** is concerned with any processes using electricity, and more and more those using electronic equipment, such as computers, radio and television.

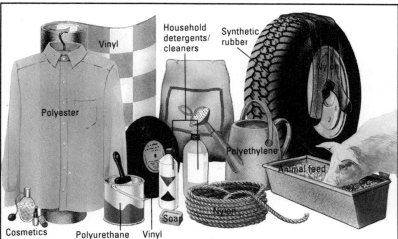

△ Oil-based chemicals are used in the manufacture of thousands of products – among them, the items illustrated here. Plastics, (vinyl, polyester, polyurethane and polyethylene for example) are all by-products of the petro-chemical industry, which relies on oil (and to a lesser extent coal) as its raw material.

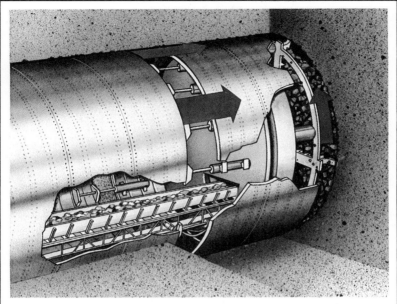

## HOW TUNNELS ARE BUILT

Many tunnels are dug with special machines called moles, which are like huge drills that push slowly through the ground. At the head of the mole, rotating cutters dig out the rock or soil, which is carried away along a conveyor belt.

Powerful jacks act like springs to force the mole forward as it digs away the rock and soil. As the mole advances, engineers fix lining panels in place to form the walls of the tunnel. For both power and safety, the mole is driven by electric motors and hydraulic jacks, which are supplied with high-pressure fluid along lines from the surface.

In good conditions, a mole can burrow through the ground at 5 m (16 ft) an hour for a train-sized tunnel. To prevent waterlogged soil from slowing down the rate of progress, the head of the mole is contained in a sealed compartment.

## ENGINEERING RECORDS

**First successful solar furnace** was built in the 1960s at Odeillo, in the French Pyrenees. It produces a heat of 3,500°C – enough to melt a steel plate in one minute.

**World's biggest hydroelectric plant** is the Itaipu power plant, on the Paraná River between Brazil and Paraguay. It produces enough power to supply a city twice the size of London.

**Largest man-made hole** is the Bingham Canyon Copper Mine near Salt Lake City, Utah, in the USA. It is 775 m (2,543 ft) deep and covers more than 7.2 sq km (2¾ sq miles).

**Deepest mine** is the Western Deep Levels gold mine at Carletonville, South Africa. It is 3,777 m (12,390 ft) deep.

**Largest moveable flood barrier** is the Thames Barrier at Woolwich, completed in 1983. It is 520 m (1,706 ft) wide.

**Most massive vehicles** are the two Marion 'Crawler' transporters used to carry US space shuttles to their launch pads. They measure 40 m by 34.7 m (131 ft × 114 ft) and travel at 1.6 km/h (1 mph).

**Largest radio telescope** is the VLA (Very Large Array) at Socorro, New Mexico, USA. It consists of 27 dish aerials each 25 m (82 ft) across, spaced out on a Y-shaped track 21 km (13 miles) long.

## LONGEST TUNNELS

**Railway***

| | | | |
|---|---|---|---|
| Seikan (Japan) | 53.9 km | 33 miles 862 yds | Opened 1988 |
| Eurotunnel (England/France) | 49.94 km | 31 miles 53 yds | Due to open 1993 |
| Oshimizu (Japan) | 22.2 km | 13 miles 1,397 yds | ** |
| Simplon II (Switz/Italy) | 19.823 km | 12 miles 559 yds | Opened 1922 |

**Road**

| | | | |
|---|---|---|---|
| St Gotthard (Switzerland) | 16.32 km | 10 miles 246 yds | Opened 1980 |
| Arlberg (Austria) | 14.0 km | 8 miles 1,232 yds | Opened 1978 |
| Mont Blanc (France/Italy) | 11.59 km | 7 miles 350 yds | Opened 1965 |

**Underwater**

| | | | |
|---|---|---|---|
| Seikan (Japan)† | 23.3 km | 14 miles 880 yds | Opened 1988 |
| Shin Kanmon (Japan) | 18.7 km | 11 miles 1,073 yds | Opened 1974 |

*Longest continuous rail tunnel is the Belyaevo-Medvedkovo stretch of the Moscow Metro subway, opened in 1979: it is 30.7 km (19 miles 123 yds) long.*
** Under construction.*
† Length of the underwater section of the tunnel.*

## LONGEST BRIDGE SPANS

| | Location | Longest span | | Opened |
|---|---|---|---|---|
| | | (m) | (ft) | |
| **Suspension** | | | | |
| Akashi-Kaiko | Japan | 1,980 | 6,496 | * |
| Humber Estuary | England | 1,410 | 4,626 | 1980 |
| Verrazano Narrows | NY, USA | 1,298 | 4,260 | 1964 |
| Golden Gate | Calif., USA | 1,280 | 4,200 | 1937 |
| **Cantilever** | | | | |
| Quebec Railway | Canada | 549 | 1,800 | 1917 |
| Forth Rail | Scotland | 521 | 1,710 | 1890 |
| **Steel Arch** | | | | |
| New River Gorge | W. Va., USA | 518 | 1,700 | 1977 |
| Bayonne | NJ, USA | 504 | 1,652 | 1931 |
| Sydney Harbour | Australia | 503 | 1,650 | 1932 |
| **Cable-Stayed** | | | | |
| Vancouver | Canada | 465 | 1,526 | 1986 |
| St Nazaire | Loire, France | 404 | 1,325 | 1975 |
| Sunshine Valley | Florida, USA | 366 | 1,200 | 1986 |
| **Continuous Truss** | | | | |
| Astoria | Oregon, USA | 376 | 1,232 | 1966 |
| **Concrete Arch** | | | | |
| Gladesville | Australia | 305 | 1,000 | 1964 |
| **Longest bridge** (total length) | | | | |
| Pontchartrain Causeway | Louisiana, USA | 38.4 km | 23.9 miles | 1969 |

*Under construction.*

## TALLEST TOWERS

| Name | Location | Height (m) | Height (ft) | Date |
|---|---|---|---|---|
| Warszawa Radio Mast | Konstantynow, Poland | 646 | 2,120 | 1974 |
| KTHI-TV Mast | Fargo, USA | 628 | 2,063 | 1963 |

*There are many other TV masts in excess of 1,000 ft (305 m) tall.*

## TALLEST BUILDINGS

| Name | Location | Height (m) | Height (ft) | Date |
|------|----------|-----------|------------|------|
| CN Tower | Toronto, Canada | 553 | 1,815 | 1976 |
| Sears Tower | Chicago, USA | 443 | 1,454 | 1974 |
| World Trade Center | New York City | 411 | 1,350 | 1973 |
| Empire State Building | New York City | 381 | 1,250 | 1931 |
| Chrysler Building | New York City | 319 | 1,046 | 1930 |
| Woolworth Building | New York City | 241 | 792 | 1913 |

## DAMS: HIGHEST AND LARGEST

| Highest | Location | Type | (m) | (ft) | Completed |
|---------|----------|------|-----|------|-----------|
| Nurek | USSR | earthfill | 317 | 1,040 | 1980 |
| Grande Dixence | Switzerland | gravity | 284 | 932 | 1962 |
| Inguri | USSR | arch | 272 | 892 | * |
| Vaiont | Italy | multi-arch | 262 | 858 | 1961 |
| Mica | Canada | rockfill | 242 | 794 | 1973 |
| Mauvoisin | Switzerland | arch | 237 | 777 | 1958 |

| Largest | Location | (cu m) | (cu yd) | Completed |
|---------|----------|--------|---------|-----------|
| Syncrude Tailings | Canada | 540,000,000 | 706,000,000 | * |
| Chapetón | Argentina | 296,200,000 | 387,400,000 | * |
| Pati | Argentina | 238,180,000 | 311,527,000 | * |
| New Cornelia Tailings | Arizona, USA | 209,506,000 | 274,026,000 | 1973 |
| Tarbela | Pakistan | 105,570,000 | 138,100,000 | 1979 |
| Fort Peck | Montana, USA | 96,050,000 | 125,630,000 | 1940 |
| Lower Usuma | Nigeria | 93,000,000 | 121,650,000 | * |

*Under construction.

△ An arch dam curves so the weight of water pushes against the sides of the valley.

▽ A gravity dam of concrete or stone is usually massive.

▽ Earth embankment dams are triangular in section with a skin of concrete.

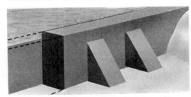

△ Buttress dams have relatively thin walls strengthened by buttress supports.

## INVENTIONS

7000 BC **Pottery** – in Iran
6000 BC **Bricks** – at Jericho, Palestine
4000 BC **Writing** – in Mesopotamia
3750 BC **Cosmetics** – in Egypt
3200 BC **The wheel** – in Mesopotamia
3000 BC **Glass** – in Egypt
2600 BC **Geometry** – in Egypt
 747 BC **Calendar** – by the Babylonians
 700 BC **Dentures** – by the Etruscans of Italy
 100s BC **Paper** – in China
AD 767 **Printing** – in Japan
 950 **Gunpowder** – in China
1280 **Cannon** – in China
1280s **Spectacles** – in Italy
1440s **Printing press and metal type** –
 Johannes Gutenberg (Ger)

△ Gutenberg's printing press. A wine press
provided the first screw mechanism.

1589 **Knitting machine** – William Lee (Eng)
1590 **Microscope** – Hans and Zacharias
 Janssen (Neth)
1592 **Thermometer** – Galileo (It)
1608 **Telescope** – Hans Lippershey (Neth)
1620 **Submarine** – Cornelius van Drebbel
 (Neth)
1644 **Barometer** – Evangelista Torricelli (It)
1679 **Pressure cooker** – Denis Papin (Fr)
1698 **Steam pump** – Thomas Savery (Eng)
1712 **Steam engine** – Thomas Newcomen
 (Eng)
1733 **Flying shuttle** – John Kay (Eng)
1752 **Lightning conductor** – Benjamin
 Franklin (US)
1767 **Spinning jenny** – James Hargreaves
 (Eng)
1783 **Parachute** – Louis Lenormand (Fr)
1785 **Power loom** – Edmund Cartwright (Eng)
1792 **Cotton gin** – Eli Whitney (US)
1800 **Battery** – Alessandro Volta (It)
1816 **Camera** – Nicéphore Niépce (Fr)

△ Pressure cooker, 1930. The device was
first tried in the late 1600s.

1823 **Electromagnet** – William Sturgeon
 (Eng)
1827 **Friction matches** – John Walker (Eng)
1831 **Dynamo** – Michael Faraday (Eng)
1834 **Reaping machine** – Cyrus McCormick
 (US)
1838 **Single-wire telegraph** – Samuel F. B.
 Morse (US)
1839 **Bicycle** – Kirkpatrick Macmillan (Scot)
1841 **Vulcanization** – Charles Goodyear
 (US)
1845 **Sewing machine** – Elias Howe (US)
1849 **Safety pin** – Walter Hunt (US)
1852 **Gyroscope** – Léon Foucault (Fr)
1852 **Elevator** – Elisha Otis (US)
1858 **Washing machine** – Hamilton Smith
 (US)
1862 **Rapid-fire gun** – Richard Gatling (US)
1866 **Dynamite** – Alfred Nobel (Swe)

▽ Hargreaves's spinning jenny was hand-
operated but spun eight threads
simultaneously.

1868 **Motorcycle** – Michaux brothers (Fr)
1872 **Typewriter** – Christopher Scholes (US)
1873 **Barbed wire** – Joseph Glidden (US)

△ Baird's televisor (1930) lost out to the Marconi-EMI electronic television system.

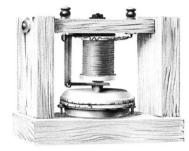

△ Bell's first telephone.

1876 **Telephone** – Alexander Bell (Scot/US)
1876 **Carpet sweeper** – Melville Bissell (US)
1877 **Phonograph** – Thomas Edison (US)

1898 **Tape recorder** – Valdemar Poulson (Den)
1901 **Vacuum cleaner** – Herbert Booth (Eng)
1903 **Aeroplane** – Wright brothers (US)
1924 **Frozen food process** – Clarence Birdseye (US)
1925 **TV** – John L. Baird (Scot) and others
1928 **Electric shaver** – Jacob Schick (US)
1930 **Jet engine** – Frank Whittle (Eng)
1935 **Nylon** – Wallace Carothers (US)
1938 **Ball point pen** – Ladislao Biro (Hung)
1945 **Electronic computer** – J. Presper Eckert (US) and John W. Mauchly (US)
1947 **Polaroid camera** – Edwin Land (US)
1948 **Transistor** – John Bardeen (US), Walter Brattain (US) and William Schockley (US)
1948 **Long-playing record** – Columbia (US)
1960 **Laser** – Theodore Maiman (US)
1961 **Silicon chip** – Texas Instruments (US)
1971 **Microprocessor** – Intel Corp (US)
1973 **Teletext** – BBC and ITA (UK)
1981 **Space shuttle** – NASA (US)

▽ The Polaroid camera.

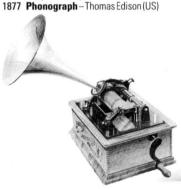

△ Edison's original phonograph played cylindrical records.

1878 **Microphone** – David Hughes (Eng/US)
1879 **Incandescent lamp** – Thomas Edison (US)
1884 **Fountain pen** – Lewis Waterman (US)
1885 **Motor-car engine** – Karl Benz (Ger) and Gottlieb Daimler (Ger), independently
1885 **Transformer** – William Stanley (US)
1892 **Vacuum flask** – James Dewar (Scot)
1892 **Diesel engine** – Rudolf Diesel (Ger)
1893 **Slide fastener** – Whitcomb Judson (US)
1895 **Radio** – Guglielmo Marconi (It)
1895 **Safety razor** – King C. Gillette (US)

# SCIENCE GLOSSARY

**absolute zero** Lowest temperature possible in theory; zero on absolute scale is −273·15°C (−459·67°F).

**acceleration** Rate of change of velocity; measured in distance per second per second.

**acid** Chemical substance that when dissolved in water produces hydrogen ions, which may be replaced by metals to form salts.

**alkali** Base consisting of a soluble metal hydroxide.

**alloy** Metal composed of more than one element; e.g. brass (copper and zinc).

△ Bronze, an alloy of tin and copper, was widely used in the ancient world. These bronze-tipped spears are nearly 2,000 years old and the bronze vessel was made in China in about 1100 BC.

**alternating current** Electric current that rapidly goes from maximum in one direction through zero to maximum in the other direction.

**ampere** (A) Unit of electric current equivalent to flow of $6 \times 10^{18}$ electrons per sec (i.e. 6 million million million electrons).

**anode** Positive electrode through which current enters an electrolytic cell or a vacuum tube.

**Archimedes' principle** When a body is immersed or partly immersed in a fluid, the apparent loss in weight is equal to the weight of the fluid displaced.

**atom** Smallest fragment of an element that can take part in a chemical reaction. See also isotope.

**base** Substance that reacts chemically with an acid to form a salt and water.

**battery** Device that converts chemical energy into electrical energy.

**boiling point** Temperature at which liquid turns into vapour throughout its bulk.

**calorie** Unit of heat equal to amount needed to raise the temperature of one gram of water through one degree C.

**catalyst** Substance that markedly alters the speed of a chemical reaction without appearing to take part in it.

**cathode** Negative electrode through which an electric current leaves an electrolytic cell or a vacuum tube.

**Celsius** Temperature scale on which 0°C is the melting point of ice and 100°C is boiling point of water; often called centigrade.

**circuit, electrical** The complete path taken by an electric current.

**combustion** (burning) Chemical reaction in which a substance combines with oxygen and gives off heat and light.

**compound** Substance consisting of two or more elements in chemical combination in definite proportions.

**condensation** Change of vapour into liquid that takes place when pressure is applied to it or the temperature is lowered.

**conductor, electric** Substance that permits the flow of electricity; e.g. metal.

**crystal** Substance that has been solidified in a definite geometrical form. Some solids do not form crystals.

**current** Flow of electrons along a conductor.

**decibel** Unit for comparing power levels or sound intensities.

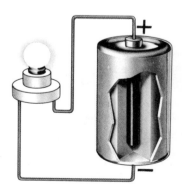

△ A dry battery wired to a bulb makes a simple electrical circuit.

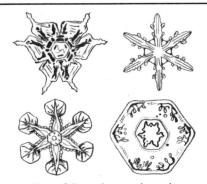

△ All snowflakes are hexagonal crystals.

**diffraction** The spreading out of light by passing it through a narrow slit or past the edge of an obstacle.

**direct current** Current that always flows in the same direction.

**elasticity** Property of a material that makes it go back to its original shape after a force deforming it is removed.

**electrode** Metal plate through which electric current enters or leaves an electrolysis cell, battery or vacuum tube. See anode and cathode.

**electron** Negatively charged subatomic particle.

**element** Substance made up entirely of exactly similar atoms (all with the same atomic number).

**energy** Capacity for doing work.

**evaporation** Phenomenon in which liquid turns into vapour without necessarily reaching the boiling point.

**fission** (splitting) In atomic or nuclear fission, the nuclei of heavy atoms split and release vast quantities of energy.

**fluid** Substance (liquid or gas) that takes the shape of part or all of the vessel that contains it.

**focus** The point at which converging rays of light meet.

**force** Anything that can act on a stationary body and make it move, or make a moving body change speed or direction.

**frequency** Of a wave motion, the number of oscillations, cycles, vibrations or waves per second.

**friction** Force that resists sliding or rolling of one surface in contact with another.

△ The tread on a tyre increases friction, and so reduces slipping or skidding.

**fulcrum** The point of support of a lever when it is lifting something.

**fusion, nuclear** The joining of nuclei of light atoms together with the release of vast amounts of energy; this is the process that occurs in stars.

**gas** A fluid that, no matter how little there is, always takes up the whole of the vessel containing it.

**gravitation** Force of attraction between any two objects because of their masses.

**inclined plane** Simple machine consisting of smooth plane sloping upwards; used for moving heavy loads with a relatively small force.

**inertia** Property of an object that makes it resist being moved or its motion being changed.

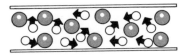

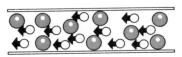

△ In a flowing current, all the electrons in the wire move in the same direction – from negative terminal to positive terminal.

**infra-red rays** Electromagnetic radiation of wavelengths just longer than those of visible light; invisible heat radiation.

**insulator** Substance that does not conduct electricity.

**ion** Atom or group of atoms carrying an electrical charge.

**isotope** One of two or more forms of an element with the same atomic number (i.e. number of protons in the nucleus), but different relative atomic masses (due to different numbers of neutrons in the nucleus).

**joule** Unit of work or energy.

**laser** Device that produces an intense, thin beam of light; abbreviation for **l**ight **a**mplification by **s**timulated **e**mission of **r**adiation.

Crystal or gas — Light bounces to and fro and gains energy

Mirror — Energy source — Beam of laser light

△ A laser consists of a crystal or a tube of gas. The laser absorbs incoming energy, amplifies it and releases a beam of laser light.

**latent heat** Heat absorbed, without a rise in temperature, when a substance is changed from solid to liquid or liquid to gas.

**lens** Device that affects light passing through it by converging (bringing together) or diverging (spreading apart) the rays.

**lever** Simple machine consisting of a rigid beam pivoted at one point, called the fulcrum; effort applied at one point on the beam can lift a load at another point.

**liquid** Substance that without changing its volume takes up the shape of all, or the lower part of, the vessel containing it.

**mass** Amount of matter in an object.

**melting point** Temperature at which solid turns to liquid; equal to freezing point of the liquid.

**metal** Element or alloy that is a good conductor of heat and electricity and has a high density.

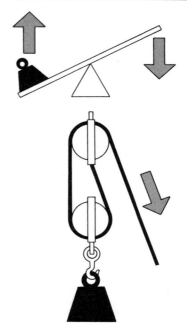

△ The lever (*top*) and pulley are two of the most important simple machines.

**mixture** More than one element or compound together, but not in chemical combination.

**molecule** Smallest amount of chemical substance that can exist alone; it is made up of two or more atoms.

**momentum** The product of the mass and velocity of a moving body.

**motion, Newton's laws of** (1) A stationary object remains still or a moving object continues to move in a straight line unless acted on by an external force. (2) The force producing acceleration in an object is proportional to the product of the object's mass and its acceleration. (3) Every action has an equal and opposite reaction.

**neutron** Uncharged atomic particle found in the nuclei of all atoms except hydrogen.

**nucleus, atomic** The positively charged centre of an atom; consists of one or more protons and, except for hydrogen, one or more neutrons. See also atom.

**ozone** Form of oxygen containing three atoms in each molecule; $O_3$.

**proton** Positively charged atomic particle found in the nuclei of all atoms.

**radiation, heat** Transfer of heat by means of waves; infra-red rays.

**radioactivity** Emission of radiation, such as alpha-particles, beta-particles, and gamma-rays, from unstable elements by the spontaneous splitting of their atomic nuclei.

**refraction** Bending of a light ray as it crosses the boundary between two media of different optical density.

**salt** Chemical compound formed, with water, when a base reacts with an acid; a salt is also formed, often with the production of hydrogen, when a metal reacts with an acid.

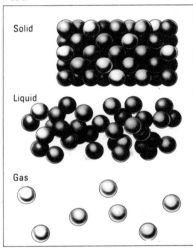

△ The three states of matter. In each state, molecules are arranged differently.

**solid** State of matter that has a definite shape and resists having it changed; a crystalline solid melts to a liquid on heating above its melting point.

**solubility** Quantity of a substance (solute) that will dissolve in a solvent to form a solution.

**speed** Distance travelled by a moving object divided by the time taken. Speed in a particular direction is velocity.

**static electricity** Electricity at rest (not flowing), in contrast to current.

**superconductor** Material which conducts current at very low temperatures with virtually no resistance.

**surface tension** Property of the surface of a liquid that makes it behave as though it were covered with a thin elastic skin.

**ultrasonic waves** 'Sound' waves beyond the range of human hearing.

**ultraviolet rays** Electromagnetic radiation of wavelengths just shorter than those of visible light. The Sun's radiation is rich in ultraviolet rays.

**vacuum** In practice, a region in which pressure is considerably less than atmospheric pressure.

**vapour** Gas that can be turned into a liquid by compressing it without cooling.

**velocity** Rate of change of position equal to speed in a particular direction.

**volt (V)** Unit of electromotive force; (emf).

**volume** Measurement of the space occupied by an object.

**watt (W)** Unit of electrical power, defined as the rate of work done in joules per second; equal to the product of current in amperes (A) and potential difference in volts (V). $W = AV$.

**wavelength** Of a wave motion, the distance between crests (or troughs) of two consecutive waves.

**waves** Regular disturbances that carry energy. Light and radio travel as electromagnetic waves.

**X-rays** Very short wavelength electro-magnetic waves.

△ Ultraviolet rays from the Sun tan pale skin. Most UV light is absorbed by the atmosphere.

# Transport

One of the world's greatest inventions is the wheel, most likely developed from the notion of transporting heavy loads on rolling logs. Logs floating downstream probably provided inspiration for the first rafts and boats. A man watching steam lift the lid off a kettle got the idea for a steam engine, which revolutionized transport in the 1700s. Since then, people have discovered how to fly and have penetrated the ocean depths and outer space, but in many parts of the world we still rely on faithful beasts of burden to get us and our belongings from one place to the next.

Transport and the need for it have grown up together over the centuries. At first, people had to rely on their own two feet for moving from place to place, and had to carry any loads themselves.

Water was probably the first means of transport that people used. Logs floating in rivers would have put the idea into their heads. It seems likely that river transport has been used for hundreds of thousands of years because, when migrating over the land, people must have had to cross streams many times.

The first craft to be used were undoubtedly rafts – logs lashed together with vines, or bundles of reeds tied together. By 6,000 years ago, people were building boats and had invented sails.

▽ Ancient Egyptian boat made from bundles of reeds.

The big change in land transport came with the domestication of animals, which began less than 10,000 years ago. The most important animal for carrying loads and riders was the horse, in use in the Middle East more than 5,000 years ago. Horses remained the chief means of transport until the development of railways in the early 1800s.

△ An early submarine: David Bushnell's *Turtle* of 1776. This tiny one-man craft tried to sink a British warship during the American Revolutionary War.

Important as horses were for carrying people and loads, as draught animals – that is, animals used for pulling loads – oxen of various kinds were preferred because with the primitive harness then in use they could draw larger and heavier weights.

The harness consisted of a wooden yoke attached to the shoulders and neck of the ox. An ox pulls with its head whereas a horse uses the base of its neck. Therefore, the yoke tended to throttle horses. When the horse collar came into use in Europe, from about 500 BC onwards, the full power of the horse for pulling heavy loads could be exploited.

△ Leonardo da Vinci sketched this helicopter-like flying machine in the early 1500s. It never flew, for there was no engine able to power it.

Horses are not suited to desert conditions. There the camel is the most important beast of burden. It can travel for days without water and can feed on plants that other animals reject, such as thorn trees. Its feet are large and do not sink into soft sand. The main disadvantage is that camels seem to have a grudge against everything, even other camels, and especially work!

In the 1980s researchers in Egypt, Israel, Pakistan, Saudi Arabia and Syria were studying camels with the idea of extending their use in areas of Africa and Asia where severe drought and famine are common, and other animals such as horses and cattle do not manage well.

▽ An ordinary bicycle, or penny-farthing, of the 1880s.

### The Industrial Revolution
The Industrial Revolution, which began in Britain in the 1700s, changed the methods and speed of transport. In the 1700s people began constructing networks of canals, es-

**Liner Lengths**

*Great Western* (1837)

*Great Eastern* (1858)

*Mauretania* (1906)

*Normandie* (1932)

*United States* (1952)

*France* (1962)

*Queen Elizabeth 2* (1968)

△ The evolution of the ocean liner: as engine power increased, so did the size, speed and luxury of passenger ships.

pecially in Britain and continental Europe. Canal travel was cheap and ideal for shipping heavy loads.

However, the development of the steam engine led quickly to the development of railways. Canals became less important in Britain, although they are still a major means of transport in continental Europe and the Soviet Union, where they link with the extensive system of rivers.

Railways dominated land travel until the advent of the car, in the late 1800s and early 1900s. Today, cars and trucks form the main means of transport for millions of people.

At sea, steam, and later diesel engines, made sea travel faster. For the first 50 years of the 20th century, the oceans were dominated by the giant passenger liners, such as Britain's *Queen Mary* and *Queen Elizabeth*, which made regular journeys across the Atlantic and other oceans.

Although the great liners have had their heyday, giant ships still ply the seas, but now they are bulk carriers for oil and other freight.

Air transport developed rapidly after World War II and now most long-distance passenger traffic and some freight is carried by air.

**Modern transport**

Transport today is a combination of many means of travel and freighting. On land, roads provide the basic means of transport, because they run from door to door. All over North America and Europe, trucks carry freight, while cars and buses carry passengers.

Other means of transport provide a service only to and from certain places – seaports, airports, railway stations – and depend on road vehicles to carry people and loads to their final destinations. The modern transport network is a miracle of organization.

## MILESTONES IN TRANSPORT

**BC**
**4000** Earliest known canals were constructed in Mesopotamia (modern Iraq).
***c*. 3200** First wheeled vehicles, with solid disc wheels, are used in Mesopotamia.
***c*. 2000** Spoked wheels come into use.
**1800** Hittites develop war chariots.
**540** Chinese begin the Grand Canal, from Beijing to Hangzhou (completed AD 1327).
**312** Roman engineers build the Appian Way from Rome to Capua.
***c*. 200** China develops a system of roads.

**AD**
***c*. 1100** Magnetic compass comes into use.
**1400s** The first three-masted ships are built.
**1474** Four-wheeled coaches are built in Germany.
**1662** Blaise Pascal (France) invents the first (horse-drawn) omnibus.
**1783** Marquis Jouffroy d'Abbans (France) builds the first successful steamboat.
**1802** First paddle steamer, the *Charlotte Dundas*, sails on the Forth and Clyde Canal.

△ Cugnot's steam carriage of 1769 had a top speed of 5 km/h (just over 3 mph).

**1852** Henri Giffard (France) flies first airship.
**1863** First underground railway opens in London.
**1869** Suez Canal opens.
**1869** US transcontinental railway completed.
**1876** Nikolaus Otto improves the four-stroke gasoline engine.
**1890** First electric-powered tube railway.

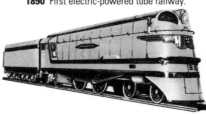

△ Last of its line: Atlantic 4-4-2 steam locomotive of US railways.

**1897** First diesel engine built.
**1903** First power flight in heavier-than-air craft.
**1914** Panama Canal is opened.
**1925** First diesel locomotive goes into regular service in the US.
**1936** Prototype helicopter successfully tested.
**1939** First jet aircraft.
**1954** First nuclear-powered submarine (US).
**1961** First man in space.
**1968** First supersonic airliner (USSR).
**1987** Work begins on the Channel Tunnel.

▽ A nuclear submarine, showing the reactor and the steam turbine engines.

△ An early raft constructed from logs tied together with reeds.

**1815** John L. McAdam (Scotland) develops macadam paving for roads.
**1819** First iron passenger vessel, the barge *Vulcan*, goes into service on the Forth and Clyde Canal.
**1821** First iron-hulled merchant ship, the *Aaron Manby* (UK).
**1831** First passenger railway opens (UK).
**1835** Screw propeller invented.
**1839** First pedal-driven bicycle.

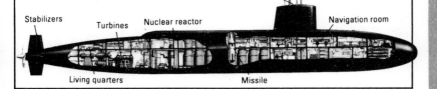

Conning tower

Stabilizers

Turbines    Nuclear reactor

Navigation room

Living quarters    Missile

Notchback

Fastback

Estate

Hatchback

Convertible

△ The modern motor car is manufactured in various shapes, the commonest being saloon, hatchback and estate.

▷ How a petrol engine works. *Induction*: Piston moves downwards and petrol/air mixture is drawn into cylinder. *Compression*: Piston rises, compressing mixture. *Ignition*: Sparking plug sparks, igniting compressed mixture. Gases force piston downwards. *Exhaust*: Piston moves upwards, forcing out burnt gases.

△ Electric trams (1890) provided cheap urban transport.

# Travel by Road

In 1769 the *Fardier*, the world's first horse-less carriage, rumbled on to the road. The brain-child of Capitaine Nicolas Cugnot of the French army, it was a steam cart designed to haul guns. Its top speed was 5 km/h (3 mph), and it had to stop every 15 minutes to take in water and raise steam pressure. It was not a success.

From such unlikely beginnings came the modern motor car and truck. Steam proved unreliable and it was not until nearly a century later, after the invention of the internal combustion engine, that Karl Benz in 1885 and Gottlieb Daimler in 1886 produced

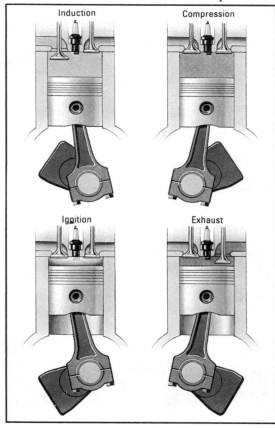

Induction

Compression

Ignition

Exhaust

the first successful cars. Mass production of cars was begun in the United States by Eli Ransom Olds, whose Oldsmobiles began rolling off the production lines in 1901.

Today, there are more than 411 million vehicles on the world's roads. The United States has about 40 per cent of them.

## DATES IN ROAD TRAVEL HISTORY

**1888** First successful electric tramcars run in Richmond, Virginia, in the United States.
**1901** A car with front-wheel drive, the Korn and Latil Voiturette, is built in France.
**1901** A new model Daimler is named the Mercedes, after the daughter of one of the firm's agents. The name has persisted to this day.
**1902** A nine horsepower Napier car is built in Britain with an all-steel body.
**1902** Belgium's Dechamps cars are built with an electric starter as standard.
**1902** Renault of France introduces drum brakes, and Frederick Lanchester of Britain experiments with disc brakes.
**1903** A Dutch Spyker is the first car to be fitted with four-wheel drive and brakes.
**1904** The Hon Charles Rolls and Henry Royce found the firm of Rolls-Royce.
**1904** First car with a silencer is built in the United States.
**1905** Petrol-driven buses are introduced in London.
**1908** Henry Ford produces his first Model T – over the next 19 years he sells 15,007,033 of them.
**1916** First automatic windshield wipers are fitted to a Willys Knight in the United States.
**1919** The world's first traffic lights are installed in Detroit in the United States.

∇ The Ford Model T, known as the 'Tin Lizzie'.

△ Lead-free petrol and catalytic converters reduce pollution from car exhausts.

**1921** The first hydraulic brakes are fitted to an American Duesenberg.
**1924** The world's first motorway is opened, an *autostrada* between Milan and Varese, Italy.
**1926** The Soviet Union builds its first car, the 'Nami 1'.
**1927** White lines down the centre of the road are first used in Britain.
**1928** The first transcontinental bus service in the United States begins a San Francisco– New York service.
**1929** An American Cadillac is the first production car to be fitted with a synchromesh gearbox.
**1934** Citroen of France introduces monocoque construction – building body and chassis in one.
**1934** Percy Shaw invents 'Cat's eyes' – reflecting road studs – in England.
**1938** Automatic direction signalling is introduced.
**1948** Tubeless tyres are introduced.
**1967** First car with a Wankel rotary engine is built in Germany.
**1980** General Motors begin fitting computers in some cars to reduce fuel consumption.
**1988** Lead-free petrol is introduced in the European Community.

## BADGES AND MASCOTS

Badges and mascots are not so common as they used to be. Mascots on the top of car bonnets are now considered dangerous, as they can cause additional injury in an accident. Manufacturers do not always put a badge on every car they build, though there are sometimes badges for special models. Here are a few of the best-known badges, with something about the famous makers to whom they belong.

Alfa-Romeo

**Alfa-Romeo** use a heraldic badge of which the serpent on the right comes from the arms of Milan, Italy, where the cars are made.

**Cadillac** named after Antoine de la Mothe Cadillac, founder of Detroit where the cars are made, also have a heraldic badge.

**Fiat's** badge stands for Fabbrica Italiana Automobile Torino, the name of an Italian company.

**Ford** have always used a script badge; older Fords bore it on their radiators.

**Peugeot's** lion comes from the arms of the Peugeot family's home city, Belfort, France.

**Renault** have used a diamond badge since 1924; before that their cars carried the firm's name on a round badge.

**Rolls-Royce** use two capital Rs, the initials of the firm's founders. For many years the lettering was red, but it was changed to black in 1933 on the death of Sir Henry Royce.

**Chevrolet** have a simple design incorporating the name. The firm was founded by Louis Chevrolet in 1911, but was sold to General Motors in 1917.

**Mercedes-Benz's** three pointed star in a circle was the house emblem of the motoring pioneer Gottlieb Daimler, whose Mercedes company merged with Benz in 1926.

**Volkswagen's** distinctive 'VW' badge stands for the initials of the name, which means 'People's Car.' The first VW, the 'Beetle', was designed to the order of the German dictator Adolf Hitler just before World War II.

**Volvo** use a symbol for iron, for which Sweden, where the cars are made, is famous.

Cadillac

Ford

Renault

Mercedes

Volkswagen

Peugot

## MOTORCYCLES

The motorcycle was actually made before the car, because Gottlieb Daimler built one of hickory wood to serve as a test bed for the gasoline engine he was planning to use for his first car. After 1903 motorcycles developed into useful machines, prized for their cheapness to buy and run, and for their ease in manoeuvring.

Between the world wars the United States and Britain led the world in the production of motorcycles, with the American Harley-Davidson and Indian, and the British BSA and Norton among the leading makes. After World War II the American and British motorcycle industries collapsed and Japan became the leading manufacturer, with Honda, Suzuki, Yamaha and Kawasaki the chief firms.

△ Streamlining of motorcycles reduces wind resistance and increases stability.

### MOTORCYCLING MILESTONES

**1868** Ernest and Pierre Michaux of Paris, France, make the first motorcycle, powered by steam.
**1885** Daimler of Germany builds his first motorcycle, with a four-stroke engine.
**1887** James Butler of Britain builds a motorcycle with a two-stroke engine.
**1894** Hildebrand and Wolfmüller of Munich, Germany, manufacture the first commercially-produced motorcycle.
**1895** The French firm of De Dion-Bouton makes a high-speed, lightweight engine for motorcycles.

△ Honda's VFR 750F machine, has a powerful 750cc engine.

**1896** Car Club de France holds the first motorcycle race, from Paris to Nantes.
**1901** The Indian motorcycle company is formed.
**1903** Harley-Davidson machines are first made.
**1914** Georges Gauthier of France makes the first motor scooter.
**1915** Britain's Post Office begins using motorcycles to deliver mail.
**1926** Front-wheel brakes are introduced.
**1929** The Golden Helmet, the oldest surviving speedway race, is founded in Czechoslovakia.
**1948** Honda begins making motorcycles in Japan.

△ The 1885 Daimler was the first motorcycle. It had no brakes and no gears.

# INTERNATIONAL IDENTIFICATION LETTERS

| | | | | | | |
|---|---|---|---|---|---|
| A | Austria | GCA | Guatemala | RC | Taiwan |
| ADN | Yemen PDR | GH | Ghana | RCA | Central African Rep. |
| AFG | Afghanistan | GR | Greece | RCB | Congo |
| AL | Albania | GUY | Guyana | RCH | Chile |
| AND | Andorra | H | Hungary | RH | Haiti |
| AUS | Australia | HK | Hong Kong | RI | Indonesia |
| B | Belgium | HKJ | Jordan | RIM | Mauritania |
| BD | Bangladesh | I | Italy | RL | Lebanon |
| BDS | Barbados | IL | Israel | RM | Malagasy Rep. |
| BG | Bulgaria | IND | India | RMM | Mali |
| BH | Belize | IR | Iran | RO | Romania |
| BR | Brazil | IRL | Ireland, | ROK | South Korea |
| BRN | Bahrain | | Republic of | ROU | Uruguay |
| BRU | Brunei | IRQ | Iraq | RP | Philippines |
| BS | Bahamas | IS | Iceland | RSM | San Marino |
| BUR | Burma | J | Japan | RU | Burundi |
| C | Cuba | JA | Jamaica | RWA | Rwanda |
| CDN | Canada | KWT | Kuwait | S | Sweden |
| CH | Switzerland | L | Luxembourg | SCV | Vatican |
| CI | Ivory Coast | LAO | Laos | SD | Swaziland |
| CL | Sri Lanka | LAR | Libya | SF | Finland |
| CO | Colombia | LB | Liberia | SGP | Singapore |
| CR | Costa Rica | LS | Lesotho | SME | Surinam |
| CS | Czechoslovakia | M | Malta | SN | Senegal |
| CY | Cyprus | MA | Morocco | SU | USSR |
| D | West Germany | MAL | Malaysia | SWA | Namibia |
| DDR | East Germany | MC | Monaco | SY | Seychelles |
| DK | Denmark | MEX | Mexico | SYR | Syria |
| DOM | Dominican Rep. | MS | Mauritius | T | Thailand |
| DY | Benin | MW | Malawi | TG | Togo |
| DZ | Algeria | N | Norway | TN | Tunisia |
| E | Spain | NA | Netherlands | TR | Turkey |
| EAK | Kenya | | Antilles | TT | Trinidad and |
| EAT | Tanzania | NIC | Nicaragua | | Tobago |
| EAU | Uganda | NIG | Niger | USA | United States |
| EC | Ecuador | NL | Netherlands | VN | Vietnam |
| ES | El Salvador | NZ | New Zealand | WAG | Gambia |
| ET | Egypt | P | Portugal | WAL | Sierra Leone |
| F | France | PA | Panama | WAN | Nigeria |
| FJI | Fiji | PE | Peru | WD | Dominica |
| FL | Liechtenstein | PK | Pakistan | WL | St Lucia |
| FR | Faroe Islands | PL | Poland | WS | Western Samoa |
| GB | United Kingdom | PNG | Papua | WV | St Vincent |
| GBA | Alderney C I | | New Guinea | YU | Yugoslavia |
| GBG | Guernsey C I | PY | Paraguay | YV | Venezuela |
| GBJ | Jersey C I | RA | Argentina | Z | Zambia |
| GBM | Isle of Man | RB | Botswana | ZA | South Africa |
| GBZ | Gibraltar | | | ZRE | Zaïre |
| | | | | ZW | Zimbabwe |

◁ A US licence plate publicizes the owner's home state.

# THE MIGHTY ENGINE

The heart of the car is the internal combustion engine, whose development in the 19th century made the car possible. Here are some of the terms used in describing the working of an engine.

**accelerator** Pedal that regulates engine speed by controlling the flow of fuel.

**air-cooled engine** Engine cooled by air drawn into the engine compartment by a fan.

**choke** Means of enriching the fuel/air mixture going to the cylinder.

**crankshaft** Shaft that is turned by the connecting rods from the pistons. The up-and-down motion of the pistons is converted into rotary motion.

**cylinder** Broad tube in the engine in which each piston moves up and down.

**dipstick** Rod for measuring the amount of oil in the sump or gear-box.

**distributor** Unit that distributes high-voltage current from the coil to each of the sparking plugs in turn.

**exhaust system** Pipes that carry exhaust gases away from the engine.

**fan belt** Belt that drives the cooling fan from a pulley on the crankshaft.

**four-stroke cycle** Operating cycle of the internal combustion engine. The strokes (up or down movements of the piston) are induction, compression, power and exhaust.

**ignition** Firing of the fuel/air mixture in the cylinders.

**radiator** Device for cooling the water in the car's cooling system.

**spark plug** Device that, using high-voltage current from the distributor, generates a spark to ignite the fuel/air mixture in the cylinder.

Air filter

Flywheel: heavy wheel fixed to the crankshaft to help the engine run smoothly

Carburettor

Oil filter

Sump, full of oil

Dipstick, to check the oil level

Petrol pump, to pump petrol from the tank to the carburettor

△ Cutaway of a car engine. The engine may have as many as 150 moving parts. The flywheel ensures that the engine runs smoothly throughout the cylinder-firing sequence.

# Travel by Rail

Railways first came into use in the 1500s in Britain and other parts of Europe, where they were used to haul coal from underground mines. The wagons were drawn by horses or people, women as well as men.

The steam locomotive was developed in Britain in the 18th and 19th centuries. The first practical steam railway was built by Richard Trevithick, a Cornish inventor and professional wrestler.

The first public railway, the Stockton and Darlington Railway, opened in the north of England in 1825. It was engineered by George Stephenson, and carried coal and freight, hauled by the engine *Locomotion No 1*. The first passenger line ran between Liverpool and Manchester; it opened in 1830. Again it was engineered by Stephenson, whose locomotive, the *Rocket*, won trials at Rainhill, near Liverpool the year before, in a contest with four other locomotives.

▽ The *Rocket*, victor in the 1829 Rainhill trials for steam locomotives. It had a multitube boiler, enabling steam to be raised more quickly with less fuel, and was a rugged, reliable design.

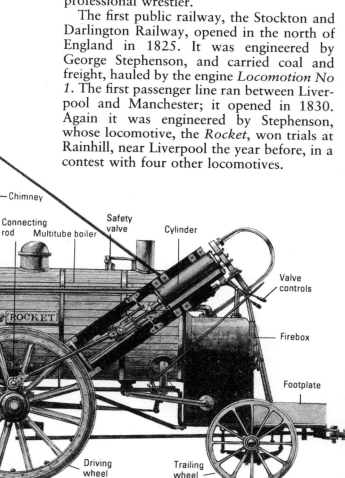

Chimney

Connecting rod

Multitube boiler

Safety valve

Cylinder

Valve controls

Firebox

Footplate

ROCKET

Driving wheel

Trailing wheel

## RAILWAY TERMS

**arrester** Trackside device to slow or stop shunted vehicles.

**brake van** Van manned by a guard and containing a screw brake, marshalled at the rear of a goods train.

**buffers** Sprung metal 'studs' at the ends of a vehicle to absorb the shocks of minor collisions in shunting.

**bufferstop** Set of buffers mounted at the end of a length of track.

**chair** U-shaped metal casting that holds rail to sleepers.

**coupling** Hooking device for joining railway vehicles to a train.

**double-heading** Using two locomotives to pull one train.

**fishplate** Metal plate used to join rails end to end.

**footplate** Part of locomotive on which the crew work.

**frog** X-shaped casting that allows rails to 'cross' at points.

**gauge** Width of track, measured between the inside edges of the rails.

**goods train** Train of vans or wagons for carrying freight.

**hump shunting** Using a downgrade after a hump in the track to move railway vehicles.

**light engine** Locomotive travelling without pulling a train.

**loading gauge** Maximum permitted height of a railway vehicle.

**marshalling** Sorting vehicles into the correct order for a train.

**permanent way** Railway track.

**points** Set of movable rails laid where trains need to switch from one track to another.

**shoe** Steel collector on electric train for collecting electricity from a third rail.

**shunting** Pushing uncoupled vehicles along the track.

**siding** Branch track for holding stationary vehicles.

**sleeper** Wood or concrete tie across and beneath the rails to form the track.

**standard gauge** In Britain, most of Europe and North America, 1.44 m (4 ft 8½ in).

**vacuum brake** Type of railway vehicle brake held *off* by low air pressure (vacuum).

**welded rail** Rail made continuous by welding together shorter lengths.

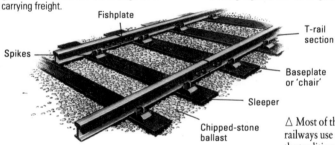

Fishplate · T-rail section · Spikes · Baseplate or 'chair' · Sleeper · Chipped-stone ballast

△ Most of the world's railways use track laid in the traditional manner.

## GOING UNDER

**London Underground** has the longest route in the world, 408 km (254 miles), serving 272 stations. It carries about 770 million passengers a year, more than 350 thousand commuters being carried each working day. The Victoria Line can carry 50 thousand people per hour in trains spaced at two-minute intervals. Its Northern Line from Morden to East Finchley has 28 km (17½ miles) of tunnel, the longest in Britain. The longest route without changing trains is 54.8 km (34 miles) between Epping and West Ruislip. The world's first underground railway, operated by steam locomotives, was the 6-km (3¾-mile) section between Paddington and Farringdon Street. It opened in 1863.

**The Moscow Metro** carries about two billion passengers a year, making it the world's busiest. It has 198 km (123 miles) of track and 123 spacious stations finished in black and white marble.

**The New York City Subway** has more stations – 458 – than any other underground railway in the world. It runs for a total of 373 km (232 miles). It carries approximately 1,100 million passengers a year.

# Travel by Sea

Today, when people fly everywhere, it is hard to realize that until recently it was necessary to travel by ship for any journey overseas. Before the days of rail it was often quicker, if you were near the coast, to sail along it than to travel overland.

It is still often easier to send freight along the coast and, for all except perishable freight, which must be transported quickly, the sea is still the most satisfactory means of transporting goods long distances across the world.

▽ A supertanker (*foreground*) and a container ship, loaded with containers destined for onward movement by road or rail.

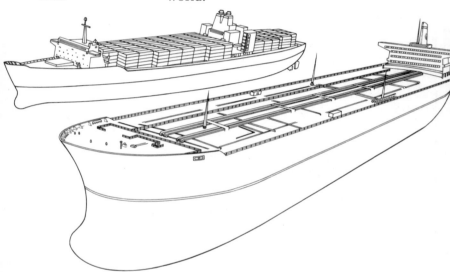

## SHIP'S LOG

A ship's log book is a day-by-day account of everything that happens during a voyage, including her course, speed and weather encountered. This 'log' is a chronology of the sea.

**pre-8000BC** Old Stone Age people use form of dug-out canoe.

**c. 7250BC** Earliest form of seafaring – trade in Mediterranean between Melos and Greek mainland.

**c. 3000BC** First known ships – Egyptian galleys.

**c. 1000BC** Phoenicians develop bireme, galley with two rows of oars on each side.

**c. 200BC** Romans build huge galleys, with as many as 200 oars.

**c. AD1100** Sailors in the Mediterranean and in the China Seas navigating by means of magnetic compass.

**1400s** Portuguese develop three-masted ship; facilitates sailing against wind.

**1620** Dutch scientist Cornelius van Drebbel demonstrates 'submarine', a leather-covered rowing boat, in England.

△ A Viking longship of around 900.

**1822** First iron-built steamship, the *Aaron Manby*; also first prefabricated ship.
**1839** British steamer *Archimedes* first to use screw propeller successfully.
**1845** *Rainbow* (US), first true clipper ship.
**1897** Charles Parsons (UK) demonstrates first turbine-driven ship, *Turbinia*.
**1912** First ocean-going diesel-driven ships.
**1955** First nuclear-powered submarine, *Nautilus* (US).
**1959** First hovercraft, SR-N1, invented by Christopher Cockerell (UK).
**1959** First nuclear-powered surface ship, Russian ice-breaker *Lenin*.
**1962** *Savannah* (US) goes into service as first nuclear-powered merchant ship.
**1962** First public hovercraft service, inaugurated in Britain.
**1979** First helicopter-carrying patrol vessel in operation with Danish Fisheries Protection.
**1986** World's largest dry cargo ship, the Norwegian *Berge Stahl*, launched.
**1988** Catamaran *Jet Services 5* makes fastest Atlantic crossing under sail.

**1783** Steam propulsion first achieved, by Marquis Jouffroy d'Abbans (France), with 180-ton paddle-steamer *Pyroscaphe*.
**1790s** Sailing ships built with iron hulls.
**1801** Robert Fulton (US) builds 6.4 m (21 ft) submarine *Nautilus*.
**1801** First successful power-driven vessel, the *Charlotte Dundas,* built by William Symington (UK).
**1807** Robert Fulton (US) builds the *Clermont*, first regular passenger steamer.

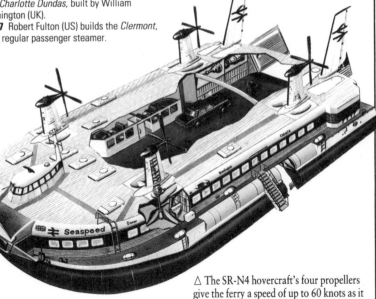

△ The SR-N4 hovercraft's four propellers give the ferry a speed of up to 60 knots as it skims over the sea on its cushion of air.

## SAILING TERMS

The great days of sailing ships began thousands of years ago and came to an end only in the 19th century. Over that time sailors built up a language all their own Some of its terms have passed into everyday use ashore. For example, the phrase 'by and large', meaning 'generally speaking', originally meant sailing just off the wind when a vessel was sailing as near as possible into the wind. These are some common sailing terms.

**aft** Toward the rear of a vessel.
**amidships** Near the middle of a vessel.
**barque** Sailing vessel with three or more masts, all but the last square-rigged; the third mast is rigged fore-and-aft.
**beam** Width of vessel's hull.
**bow** The front of a vessel.

△ Early Egyptian sea-going vessel, with steering oars and a single sail.

**foresail** Lowermost sail on the foremast.
**jib** Triangular sail between the foremast and the bowsprit.
**keel** The main structural member running lengthwise along the bottom of a ship's hull.
**knot** Unit of speed for boats and ships. One knot equals one nautical mile per hour.
**lateen** A triangular sail suspended from a sloping yard attached to a mast.
**mainmast** Mast second from the front; the middle mast on a three-masted vessel.
**mainsail** Lowermost sail on mainmast.
**mizzen** Lateen sail on mizzen mast.
**mizzen mast** Third mast towards the rear of a vessel.
**overall length** Length of a vessel's hull.
**poop** Raised deck towards the stern of a vessel.

△ A paddle steamer of the 1800s. Early steamships had sails as well as engines.

**bowsprit** Long projection from the bow that supports rigging and possibly a jib or spritsail.
**crow's nest** Look-out position near the top of a mast.
**deck** The planked or plated-over 'floor' across a ship's hull. A small vessel has only one deck.
**displacement** Weight of water (generally expressed in tonnes) displaced by a floating vessel.
**draught** Amount of a ship's hull below the waterline, i.e. the minimum depth of water in which a vessel will float.
**fo'c'sle** (forecastle) Raised deck at the front of a vessel.
**fore** (or for'ard) Toward the front of a vessel.
**foremast** Mast at the front of a vessel.

△ The carrack of the 1400s retained the raised stern and forecastle, originally used as fighting platforms.

△ An example of the popular sternwheelers that plied the Mississippi River.

**rudder** Vertical control surface in the water at the rear of a vessel, by means of which it is steered.

**royal** Sail above the topgallant.

**schooner** Two-masted sailing vessel with mainly fore-and-aft sails.

**sheet** Rope or cable attached to the end of a yard for controlling the angle of the sail to the mast.

**spanker** Fore-and-aft sail on the rearmost mast.

**spritsail** Square sail on yard suspended from the bowsprit.

**stay** Thick cable sloping down from a mast, generally to the base of the mast in front of it.

**staysail** Triangular sail between two masts.

**stern** The rear of a vessel.

**topgallant** Sail above the topsail.

**topsail** Sail above the foresail or mainsail, etc.

**yard** A spar, generally horizontal and pivoted to a mast, from which a sail is suspended.

△ A three-masted schooner, with a combination of sails. Such vessels were common trading ships into the early 1900s.

▷ The square-rigged windjammer *Herzogin Cecilie*, 1902. Originally designed for the Atlantic passenger trade, she ended her days in 1936 carrying cargo.

△ *Sirius* (*left centre*) was the first ship to cross the Atlantic under steam, followed into New York harbour in April 1838 by Brunel's *Great Western* (*centre*).

## VOYAGES AND DISASTERS

Many of the most exciting voyages were those made by the explorers. They needed courage, too, because they were often setting off into the unknown. When Bartolomeu Dias and Vasco da Gama sailed south down the coast of Africa, many of their crews had a real fear that they would fall off the edge of a flat Earth.

| SEA DISASTERS | | |
|---|---|---|
| *Date* | *Ship and nature of accident* | *Deaths* |
| 1852 | **Birkenhead,** British troopship, ran aground off Port Elizabeth, South Africa and broke in two on the rocks | 455 |
| 1865 | **Sultana,** Mississippi River steamer, blew up (boiler explosion) | 1,450 |
| 1872 | **Mary Celeste,** American half-brig, found abandoned in Atlantic with no sign of life; great mystery of the sea | |
| 1904 | **General Slocum,** an excursion steamer, burned in New York harbour | 1,021 |
| 1912 | **Titanic,** British liner, struck iceberg in Atlantic | 1,500 |
| 1914 | **Empress of Ireland,** Canadian steamer, sank after collision in St Lawrence River | 1,204 |
| 1915 | **Lusitania,** British liner, torpedoed by German submarine off Ireland | 1,198 |
| 1939 | **Thetis,** British submarine, sank in Liverpool Bay | 99 |
| 1942 | **Curacao,** British cruiser, sank after collision with liner, *Queen Mary* | 335 |
| 1945 | **Wilhelm Gustloff,** German liner, torpedoed by Russian submarine off Danzig | 700 |
| 1954 | **Toya Maru,** Japanese ferry, sank in Tsugaru Strait | 1,172 |
| 1963 | **Thresher,** American nuclear submarine, sank in Atlantic | 129 |
| 1987 | **Herald of Free Enterprise,** cross-Channel ferry, capsized off Zeebrugge, Belgium | 193 |
| 1987 | **Doña Paz,** Philippines ferry, collided with tanker, *Victor*, off Marinduque Island | 1,500 |

## FAMOUS VOYAGES

**1487** Bartolomeu Dias of Portugal sailed south in search of a route to India and discovered the Cape of Good Hope.

**1492** Christopher Columbus sailed from Spain hoping to find a westward route to the Indies, but landed instead on a Caribbean island.

△ Columbus's *Santa Maria* may have looked like this.

**1497–1499** Vasco da Gama of Portugal found the sea route to India around the Cape of Good Hope. The round trip took him two years and two months.

**1519–1521** Ferdinand Magellan of Portugal, sailing with Spanish backing, found the way westward into the Pacific Ocean by sailing through the Magellan Strait. He died on the voyage, but 18 members of his expedition led by Sebastián Del Cano completed the first voyage round the world.

**1577–1580** Francis Drake of England made the second voyage around the world, leaving with five ships and returning with one.

**1642** Abel Janszoon Tasman of the Netherlands sailed southwards from Java and discovered Tasmania and New Zealand.

**1768–1779** James Cook of Britain made three voyages to explore the Pacific and discovered Hawaii.

**1895–1898** Joshua Slocum of America made the first single-handed voyage around the world.

**1947** Thor Heyerdahl of Norway with five companions sailed a balsa wood raft, the *Kon-Tiki*, from Peru to the Tuamoto Islands in Polynesia, to prove that some Pacific Islands could have been settled by people from America.

△ Columbus's first voyage to the New World, 1492. He landed on a Caribbean island.

△ Vasco da Gama was the first European to sail around Africa to India, 1497–99.

△ Magellan's voyage (1519–21) ended with his death in the Philippines. One ship completed the circumnavigation.

△ Blanchard and Jeffries flew across the English Channel in 1785. Their balloon was fitted with 'oars' in a vain attempt at aerial steering.

# Travel by Air

People have been trying to fly for thousands of years. The ancient legend of Daedalus and his son Icarus, who set out to fly from Crete to Sicily, may well have a foundation in experiments with artificial wings and gliding. The 16th century artist Leonardo da Vinci designed several flying machines, which were never built.

People first sailed through the skies in 1783 when two French brothers, the Montgolfiers, made a balloon. Balloons are at the mercy of the wind, and it was not until the Wright brothers made their historic flight in 1903 that people conquered the air. And man-powered flight came in the 1970s. *Gossamer Albatross*, with a pedal-driven propeller powered by biologist and cyclist Bryan Allen, made the first flight across the English Channel.

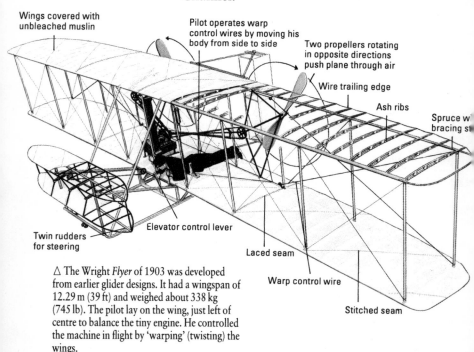

Wings covered with unbleached muslin

Pilot operates warp control wires by moving his body from side to side

Two propellers rotating in opposite directions push plane through air

Wire trailing edge

Ash ribs

Spruce w bracing s

Twin rudders for steering

Elevator control lever

Laced seam

Warp control wire

Stitched seam

△ The Wright *Flyer* of 1903 was developed from earlier glider designs. It had a wingspan of 12.29 m (39 ft) and weighed about 338 kg (745 lb). The pilot lay on the wing, just left of centre to balance the tiny engine. He controlled the machine in flight by 'warping' (twisting) the wings.

## FIRSTS IN FLIGHT

**1783** First human ascent, made in a captive Montgolfier hot air balloon by J. F. Pilâtre in Paris.

**1783** First flight in a hydrogen balloon, made by J. A. C. Charles and M. Roberts.

**1785** First air crossing of the English Channel, in a hydrogen balloon, by J. P. Blanchard and J. Jeffries.

**1852** First (steam) powered airship, flown by Henri Giffard (France).

**1853** First successful aeroplane (glider), built by Sir George Cayley (UK).

**1890s** First successful glider flights, made by Otto Lilienthal (Germany).

**1903** First controlled flights in a heavier-than-air machine, made by Wilbur and Orville Wright (US).

**1909** First flight across the English Channel, by Louis Blériot (France).

**1919** First transatlantic flight by flying-boat by Albert C. Read (US).

**1919** First non-stop transatlantic aeroplane flight, by J. Alcock and A. W. Brown (UK).

**1923** First autogyro, flown by Juan de la Cierva (Spain).

**1927** First non-stop transatlantic solo flight, by Charles Lindbergh (US).

△ Alcock and Brown after their first non-stop transatlantic flight.

**1928** First transatlantic passenger flight, by a German airship.

**1930** First patented design for jet aircraft engine, by Frank Whittle (UK).

**1930** Amy Johnson becomes first woman to fly solo from England to Australia.

**1933** First solo round-the-world flight, made by Wiley Post (US).

**1939** First transatlantic passenger service begun by Pan American Airways.

**1939** First jet-propelled plane, built by Heinkel (Germany).

**1939** First flight of a single-rotor helicopter, made by Igor Sikorsky (US).

**1947** First supersonic flight by Charles Yeager (US).

**1949** First non-stop round-the-world flight, in a Boeing *Superfortress* bomber.

**1979** Bryan Allen (US) in *Gossamer Albatross* makes first man-powered cross-Channel flight.

**1986** Richard Rutan and Jeana Yeager (US) make first non-stop round-the-world flight without refuelling.

▽ The round-the-world aircraft *Voyager* of Rutan and Yeager.

# MILITARY AIRCRAFT

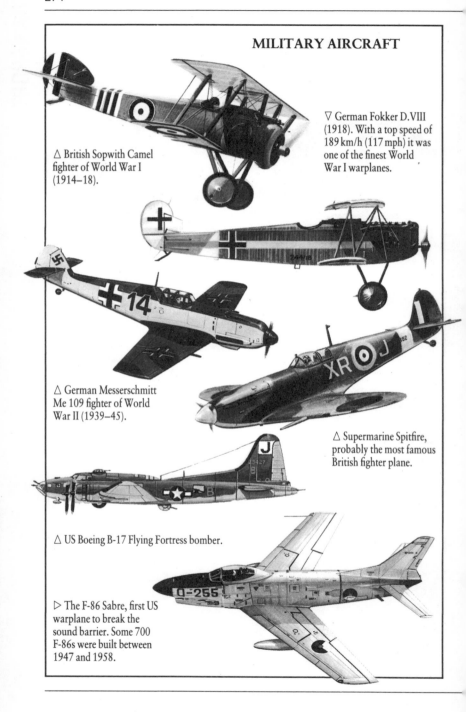

△ British Sopwith Camel fighter of World War I (1914–18).

▽ German Fokker D.VIII (1918). With a top speed of 189 km/h (117 mph) it was one of the finest World War I warplanes.

△ German Messerschmitt Me 109 fighter of World War II (1939–45).

△ Supermarine Spitfire, probably the most famous British fighter plane.

△ US Boeing B-17 Flying Fortress bomber.

▷ The F-86 Sabre, first US warplane to break the sound barrier. Some 700 F-86s were built between 1947 and 1958.

▷ The US F-111 was the first swing-wing combat aircraft (1964). The F(B)-111 variant (illustrated) is a strategic bomber.

◁ The Soviet Tupolev TU-28 (NATO code-named Fiddler) is the world's largest fighter, 26 m (85 ft) long with a 20 m (65 ft) wingspan.

▷ Israel's Kfir (Lion Cub) is based on the French Mirage 5, but is faster with a top speed of 2,440 km/h (1,516 mph).

▽ The Harrier was the first V/STOL warplane in service. This is the RAF GR3 variant.

## INTERNATIONAL MARKINGS

All civil aircraft must be entered on the International Aeronautical Register, which was begun in 1926. Each country has a two-letter (sometimes more) prefix which precedes the aircraft's own code.

| | | | | | |
|---|---|---|---|---|---|
| A2- | Botswana | EP- | Iran | LZ- | Bulgaria |
| A40- | Oman | ET- | Ethiopia | N- | United States |
| A7- | Qatar | F- | France, colonies and | OB- | Peru |
| AN- | Nicaragua | | protectorates | OD- | Lebanon |
| AP- | Pakistan | G- | Great Britain, | OE- | Austria |
| B- | Taiwan (Formosa) | | Gibraltar, | OH- | Finland |
| C- | Canada | HA- | Hungary | OK- | Czechoslovakia |
| C2- | Nauru | HB- | Switzerland, | OO- | Belgium |
| CC- | Chile | | Liechtenstein | OY- | Denmark |
| CCCP- | USSR | HC- | Ecuador | PH- | Netherlands |
| CF- | Canada | HH- | Haiti | PI- | Philippines |
| CN- | Morocco | HI- | Dominican Republic | PJ- | Netherlands Antilles |
| CP- | Bolivia | HK- | Colombia | PK- | Indonesia |
| CR- | Portuguese overseas | HL- | South Korea | PP-, PT- | Brazil |
| | provinces | HP- | Panama | PZ- | **Surinam** |
| CS- | Portugal | HR- | Honduras | S2- | Bangladesh |
| CU- | Cuba | HS- | Thailand | SE- | **Sweden** |
| CX- | Uruguay | HZ- | Saudi Arabia | SP- | Poland |
| D- | West Germany | I- | Italy | ST- | Sudan |
| DM- | East Germany | JA- | Japan | SU- | Egypt |
| DQ- | Fiji | JY- | Jordan | SX- | Greece |
| EC- | Spain | LN- | Norway | TC- | Turkey |
| EI-, EJ- | Republic of Ireland | LQ-, LV- | Argentina | TF- | Iceland |
| EL- | Liberia | LX- | Luxembourg | TG- | Guatemala |
| | | | | TI- | Costa Rica |
| | | | | TJ- | Cameroon |
| | | | | TL- | Central African |
| | | | | | Republic |
| | | | | TN- | Congo |
| | | | | TR- | Gabon |

▽ The curious *Safety* aeroplane of 1909 probably never flew. It had a sturdy frame, circular biplane wings and three propellers.

## STRANGE AIRCRAFT

These illustrations show some very unusual experiments; not all of them were disasters. For example, in 1954 the Lockheed/Rolls-Royce Thrust Measuring Rig (below) was an early machine capable of flying forwards and backwards. This facility was built into the Harrier combat aircraft.

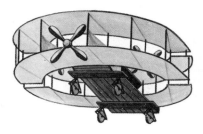

| | | | | | |
|---|---|---|---|---|---|
| TS- | Tunisia | XT- | Upper Volta | 5N- | Nigeria |
| TT- | Chad | XU- | Cambodia | 5R- | Madagascar |
| TU- | Ivory Coast | XV- | Vietnam | 5T- | Mauritania |
| TY- | Benin | XW- | Laos | 5U- | Niger |
| TZ- | Mali | XY-, XZ- | Burma | 5V- | Togo |
| VH- | Australia | YA- | Afghanistan | 5W- | Western Samoa |
| VP-B | Bahamas | YI- | Iraq | 5X- | Uganda |
| VP-F | Falkland Islands | YJ- | New Hebrides | 5Y- | Kenya |
| VP-H | Belize | YK- | Syria | 6O- | Somalia |
| VP-L | Antigua | YR- | Romania | 6V-, 6W- | Senegal |
| VP-P | Western Pacific | YS- | El Salvador | 6Y- | Jamaica |
| | High Commission | YU- | Yugoslavia | 7O- | Yemen PDR |
| VP-V | St Vincent | YV- | Venezuela | 7P- | Lesotho |
| VP-X | Gambia | ZA- | Albania | 7QY- | Malawi |
| VP-Y, | | ZK-, ZL-, | New Zealand | 7T- | Algeria |
| VP-W | Malawi, | ZM- | | 8P- | Barbados |
| | Zimbabwe | ZP- | Paraguay | 8R- | Guyana |
| VQ-G | Grenada | ZS-, ZT-, | | 9G- | Ghana |
| VQ-H | St Helena | ZU- | South Africa | 9H- | Malta |
| VQ-L | St Lucia | 3A- | Monaco | 9J- | Zambia |
| VQ-S | Seychelles | 3B- | Mauritius | 9K- | Kuwait |
| VR-B | Bermuda | 3C- | Equatorial Guinea | 9L- | Sierra Leone |
| VR-H | Hong Kong | 3D- | Swaziland | 9M- | Malaysia |
| VR-O | Sabah (Malaysia) | 3X- | Guinea | 9N- | Nepal |
| VR-U | Brunei | 4R | Sri Lanka | 9Q- | Zaïre |
| VR-W | Sarawak (Malaysia) | 4W- | Yemen | 9U- | Burundi |
| VT- | India | 4X- | Israel | 9V- | Singapore |
| XA-, | | 5A- | Libya | 9XR- | Rwanda |
| XB-, | | 5B- | Cyprus | 9Y- | Trinidad and Tobago |
| XC- | Mexico | 5H- | Tanzania | | |

◁ Northrop's futuristic Flying Wing of the 1940s.

△ The 'Flying Mattress' (1956) had an inflatable wing.

▽ The Italian Caproni Ca-60 multi-wing seaplane of 1919.

XK776

## AIR DISASTERS

| Date | Aircraft and nature of accident | Deaths |
|---|---|---|
| 24.8.21 | ZR-2 dirigible (UK) broke in two, near Hull | 62 |
| 3.9.25 | *Shenandoah* dirigible (US) broke up, Caldwell, Ohio | 14 |
| 4.4.33 | *Akron* dirigible (US) crashed, New Jersey coast | 73 |
| 6.5.37 | *Hindenburg* zeppelin (Ger) burned at mooring, Lakehurst, NJ | 36 |
| 23.8.44 | US Air Force B-24 hit school, Freckelton, England | 76* |
| 28.7.45 | US Army B-25 hit Empire State Building NY, in fog | 19* |
| 1.11.49 | DC-4 airliner (US) rammed by Bolivian P-38 fighter, Washington, DC | 55 |
| 20.12.52 | US Air Force C-124 fell and burned, Washington | 87 |
| 18.6.53 | US Air-Force C-124 crashed and burned near Tokyo | 129 |
| 30.6.56 | Super-Constellation and DC-7 airliners collided over Grand Canyon | 128 |
| 6.2.58 | Elizabethan airliner (UK) crashed on take-off at Munich, W Germany | 23‡ |
| 16.12.60 | DC-8 and Super-Constellation airliners collided over New York | 134* |
| 15.2.61 | Boeing 707 (Belgian) crashed near Brussels | 73§ |
| 3.6.62 | Boeing 707 (French) crashed on take-off, Paris | 130 |
| 22.6.62 | Boeing 707 (French) crashed in storm, Guadeloupe | 113 |
| 20.5.65 | Boeing 720B (Pakistani) crashed at Cairo airport | 121 |
| 24.1.66 | Boeing 707 (Indian) crashed on Mont Blanc (France) | 117 |
| 4.3.66 | Boeing 727 (Jap) plunged into Tokyo Bay | 133 |
| 5.3.66 | Boeing 707 (UK) crashed on Mt Fuji (Japan) | 124 |
| 20.4.67 | Britannia turboprop (Swiss) crashed at Nicosia (Cyprus) | 126 |
| 16.3.69 | DC-9 (Venezuelan) crashed on take-off, Maracaibo | 155* |
| 30.7.71 | Boeing 727 (Jap) collided with F-86 fighter, Japan | 162 |
| 14.8.72 | Ilyushin-62 (E Ger) crashed on take-off, Berlin | 156 |
| 13.10.72 | Ilyushin-62 (USSR) crashed near Moscow | 176 |
| 4.12.72 | Spanish charter jet airliner crashed on take-off, Canary Is. | 155 |
| 22.1.73 | Boeing 707 (chartered) crashed on landing at Kano, Nigeria | 176 |

△ The German airship *Hindenburg* was completed in 1936. Hailed as a turning

point in passenger transport,
its fiery crash in May 1937
ended an era in aviation.

| Date | Aircraft and nature of accident | Deaths |
|------|----------------------------------|--------|
| 3.6.73 | TU-144 (USSR) exploded in air, Goussainville, France | 14¶ |
| 3.3.74 | DC-10 (Turk) crashed in forest, Ermenonville, France | 346 |
| 10.9.76 | British Trident 3 and Yugoslavian DC-9 collided in mid-air near Zagreb (Yugoslavia) | 176 |
| 27.3.77 | Two Boeing 747s (American and Dutch) collided on ground at Tenerife's Los Rodeos airport (Canary Islands) | 582 |
| 1.1.78 | Boeing 747 (Indian) crashed into the sea off Bombay (India) | 213 |
| 15.11.78 | DC-8 (Iceland) crashed while attempting to land, Sri Lanka | 262 |
| 14.3.79 | Trident (China) crashed near Beijing | 200 |
| 28.11.79 | DC-10 (NZ) crashed into Mount Erebus, Antarctica | 257 |
| 19.8.80 | Lockheed Tristar (Saudi) destroyed by fire after emergency landing, Riyadh | 301 |
| 13.1.82 | Boeing 737 (US) struck bridge over Potomac River, Washington DC | 78* |
| 9.7.82 | Boeing 727 (US) crashed in strong winds into a housing estate, Kenner, Louisiana | 153* |
| 7.12.83 | Two jet liners (Spain) collided in fog on the runway at Madrid airport | 93 |
| 28.10.84 | Soviet military aircraft crashed after take-off from Kabul | 240 |
| 23.6.85 | Boeing 747 (Indian) blown up by bomb over Atlantic | 329 |
| 2.8.85 | Delta Airlines jumbo crashed on landing at Fort Worth, Texas | 140 |
| 12.8.85 | Boeing 747 (Japan) crashed into Mt Otusaka, Japan | 520 |
| 22.8.85 | Boeing 737 (UK) caught fire on take-off at Manchester | 54 |
| 12.12.85 | Charter jet (US) crashed at Gander, Canada | 256 |
| 6.11.86 | Helicopter (UK) crashed into North Sea | 45 |
| 28.11.87 | South African jumbo jet crashed into Indian Ocean | 159 |
| 21.12.88 | Boeing 747 (US) blown up by bomb over Scotland | 258 |
| 9.1.89 | Boeing 737 (UK) crashed on motorway in England | 46 |

*Total includes deaths on ground or in buildings.
‡Mostly players (8) and officials (3) of England football champions
Manchester United and 8 journalists.
§Including skaters (17) and officials of US world championships team.
¶First supersonic airliner crash.

# Communications

All living creatures communicate with one another – whales sing, bees dance and cats scent-mark their territory. People communicate by speech, laughter, gesture and touch. They advanced further by inventing the written word, and this has formed the basis of our civilization. Today's technology means that words and pictures, in the form of electronic signals, can be transmitted across continents and bounced from satellites in outer space. The method is there – the message is up to us!

All animals communicate in one way or another – dogs bark, birds sing to mark out their territories, female moths emit pheromones (scent-like chemical messengers) to lure males from many kilometres away. But human beings have developed the art of communication far beyond that of animals.

△ Written Chinese uses 80,000 characters, traditionally painted with a brush.

We can communicate with one another not only from city to city, but across the oceans and out into space. We can send and receive messages from far out in space. Communications can be instant: someone in London can chat by telephone to a friend in California as readily as to a friend in the next street. Interesting events such as a royal wedding can be seen as they happen on television in every country in the world.

Perhaps the most important way in which we communicate is by storing and sharing knowledge. If you go into a big library, you will find books containing the knowledge and experience collected over thousands of years.

People invented writing only about 5,500 years ago. They had accumulated knowledge and passed it on to others long before that. They passed on their news and knowledge orally – that is, by word of mouth. Bards used to memorize and chant stories of bygone days. The great poems the *Iliad* and the

*Odyssey*, attributed to the Greek minstrel Homer who lived around 2,800 years ago, were undoubtedly passed on in this way for a long time before they were written down.

The earliest visual form of communication that has survived is the paintings we see on the walls of caves, particularly those in France and Spain. Some of those paintings are more than 30,000 years old. Writing gradually evolved from just such paintings.

People have always been travellers. From their beginnings in Africa they spread first through Europe and Asia, and then to the Americas and across the ocean to the islands of the Pacific. Wherever they went, they carried with them their knowledge and the ability to communicate it.

Modern methods of communication developed only in the past 500 years or so. The first real breakthrough was the invention of printing in the 1400s. Books and, later, newspapers, have poured off the presses ever since. The next breakthrough came less than 200 years ago, when the discovery of electricity enabled people to send messages instantly over long distances. The telegraph and the telephone made possible quick communication between distant places.

The importance of sending news quickly is shown by the War of 1812 between Britain and the United States. The cause of the quarrel was British interference with US shipping during war with France. The British agreed on June 16, 1812, to end this interference, but because Congress did not know this it declared war on Britain on June 18. The peace treaty ending that war was signed on December 24, 1814. The news took so long to reach America that the Battle of New Orleans, which cost 1,500 British lives, took place 15 days after the treaty was signed.

Now, thanks to radio, television and satellite link-ups, it would be much more difficult for this kind of tragic error to happen.

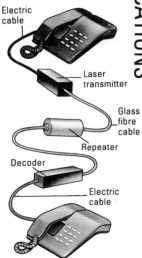

▽ Two electric wires are needed for each telephone conversation, whereas one glass fibre can transmit nearly 1 million calls at the same time.

Electric cable

Laser transmitter

Glass fibre cable

Repeater

Decoder

Electric cable

# Writing

The earliest way in which people tried to write was by drawing pictures. The cave paintings of the Stone Age showed the animals the men were hunting, possibly as an indication to the gods that the hunters needed help to find their prey.

Soon people started using drawings to describe not just things but ideas, such as 'front' and 'God'. From there it was a step to make the drawings stylized – symbols or signs rather than pictures. People used signs for words, as in written Chinese. Then they used them to stand for syllables. Finally our alphabet, where the signs stand for sounds, came into being.

△ In the Middle Ages, before the invention of printing, books were written by hand. Many hours of painstaking work went into the elaborate decoration of illuminated manuscripts.

## TERMS IN THE HISTORY OF WRITING

**alphabet** A set of letters used in writing; the name comes from the first two letters of the Greek alphabet, alpha and beta.

**cuneiform** Wedge-shaped writing inscribed with a stylus on clay tablets. It was invented by the Sumerians about 3000 BC.

**Cyrillic** Form of alphabet used in Russian and Bulgarian, derived from the Greek alphabet.

**Greek** Form of alphabet was adapted about 1000 BC from the writing systems of the Middle East. Modern alphabets are derived from it.

**hieroglyphics** Picture writing, especially the picture writing used by the ancient Egyptians and by early American Indians, such as the Aztec.

**letter** A symbol representing a sound.

**logogram** A symbol representing a complete word or phrase; the sign £, pound sterling, is a logogram.

**pictographs** Pictures of objects; used in the ancient Middle East and by the Aztec and Maya of North America.

**quipu** Knotted strings used by the Inca of Peru, mostly for keeping accounts.

**rebus** A mixture of words and pictures, the pictures representing syllables or words.

**runes** Letters of an alphabet used by the Teutonic peoples of northern Europe before AD 1000.

**stylus** Tool made from a reed for impressing cuneiform characters into clay tablets.

**syllabary** A set of symbols representing syllables, as in Japanese writing.

**tally** Split stick used for keeping accounts, according to the number of notches cut in it.

▷ A Sumerian clay table with cuneiform writing, about 2800 BC, and a reed 'pen'.

▷ The first pencil, 1565, contained a lead of pure graphite.

| Greek | | | Hebrew | | | Russian | | |
|---|---|---|---|---|---|---|---|---|
| Letter | Name | Transliteration | Letter | Name | Transliteration | Letter | | Transliteration |
| A α | alpha | a | א | aleph† | ʼ | А | а | a |
| Β β | beta | b | ב | beth | b | Б | б | b |
| | | | | | | В | в | v |
| Γ γ | gamma | g | ג | gimel | g | Г | г | g |
| Δ δ | delta | d | ד | daleth | d | Д | д | d |
| E ε | epsilon | e | ה | heh | h | Е | е | e, ye |
| | | | | | | Ж | ж | zh |
| Z ζ | zeta | z | ו | waw | w | З | з | z |
| Η η | eta | ē | ז | zayin | z | И | и | i |
| Θ θ | theta | th | ח | heth | ḥ | Й | й | ĭ |
| Ι ι | iota | i | ט | teth | ṭ | К | к | k |
| | | | | | | Л | л | l |
| Κ κ | kappa | k | י | yod | y | М | м | m |
| Λ λ | lambda | l | כך* | kaph | k, kh | Н | н | n |
| Μ μ | mu | m | ל | lamed | l | О | о | o |
| | | | | | | П | п | p |
| Ν ν | nu | n | מם* | mem | m | Р | р | r |
| Ξ ξ | xi | x (ks) | נן* | nun | n | С | с | s |
| Ο ο | omicron | o | ס | samekh | s | Т | т | t |
| | | | | | | У | у | u |
| Π π | pi | p | ע | ayin | ʼ | Ф | ф | f |
| Ρ ρ | rho | r | פף* | peh | p, ph | Х | х | kh |
| Σ σ,ς* | sigma | s | צץ* | sadhe | ṣ | Ц | ц | ts |
| | | | | | | Ч | ч | ch |
| Τ τ | tau | t | ק | qoph | q | Ш | ш | sh |
| Υ υ | upsilon | u, y | ר | resh | r | Щ | щ | shch |
| Φ φ | phi | ph | שׁ | shin | sh | | ы | i |
| Χ χ | chi | kh, ch | שׂ | sin | ś | | ь | ʼ |
| Ψ ψ | psi | ps | ת | taw | t | Э | э | e |
| Ω ω | omega | o | | | | Ю | ю | yu |
| | | | | | | Я | я | ya |

▷ Steel nib pen, 1800s.

▷ Ball point pen, mid 1900s.

△ Fountain pen, late 1800s.

△ Printing by letterpress using inked, raised type.

# Printing

Printing was one of the world's most important inventions because it brought knowledge within the reach of ordinary people. For thousands of years before printing, books were made by scribes laboriously writing out each copy by hand. Such books were rare and expensive. Modern printing began in Europe in the 1440s.

Inked rollers

Water rollers

Printing plate

Offset blanket cylinder

▷ In offset lithography, inked rollers transfer ink to the large cylinder holding the printing plate. Ink is then transferred or 'offset' from the plate to a rubber blanket and onto the paper.

---

## PRINTING GLOSSARY

**electrotype** A copy of engravings and type made by an electroplating process.

**engraving** A plate engraved for printing, or a printed illustration.

**halftone** A printing process in which a picture is made up of tiny dots; varying sizes of black dots create an illusion of different shades of grey.

**intaglio** Printing from a design cut into a metal plate; ink stays in the cutaway part when the rest of the plate is wiped clean.

**lithography** A form of planographic printing.

**photogravure** A form of intaglio printing from a plate made photographically.

**planographic printing** Printing from a flat surface with the design in a greasy medium; the ink clings only to the greasy part.

**relief printing** Printing from an inked design which is raised above the background.

**stereotype** A copy of a page of type made with the aid of a mould.

△ The collation process of a modern newspaper press.

## CHRONOLOGY OF PRINTING

**c 1320 BC** The Chinese use inked engraved seals to stamp documents.

**AD 868** The earliest known printed book is produced in China, using a carved wood block.

**c 1040** The Chinese alchemist Pi Sheng invents moveable type made of pottery.

**1403** T'ai Tsung, king of Korea, establishes a foundry for casting metal type.

**1423** The earliest known European printed picture is produced from a wood block.

**c 1440** Johannes Gutenberg, a goldsmith of Mainz, Germany, invents a system of casting type, a printing press, and suitable ink.

**1451** Gutenberg prints his first book, a Latin grammar, using a black-letter (Gothic) type.

**1457** First book printed in two colours, black and red, is produced in Mainz.

**1470** Nicolas Jensen, a French printer working in Venice, invents Roman type.

**1475** William Caxton sets up the first printing press in England.

**1477** Intaglio printing from engraved metal plates is introduced.

**1501** Francesco Griffo of Bologna, Italy, invents *italic* type.

**1719** Full colour printing is pioneered in Frankfurt, Germany.

**1727** William Ged invents stereotyping in Scotland.

**1798** Bavarian actor Alois Senefelder invents lithography.

**1800** Earl Stanhope, an English amateur printer, makes the first iron-framed press.

**1810** German printer Friedrich König, working in London, makes a steam-powered press.

**1839** Electrotyping is invented in the United States, Britain and Russia.

Keyboard

Computer

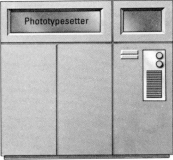

Phototypesetter

△ Computerized phototypesetting system.

▽ Linotype composing machine, 1886.

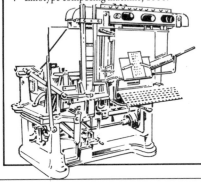

**1845** Richard Hoe of New York makes the first high-speed rotary press.

**1880** The first half-tone picture is printed in the New York *Daily Graphic*.

**1886–7** Linotype and Monotype machines speed up typesetting, hitherto done by hand.

**1895** Photogravure comes into use.

**1939** American William C. Huebner invents the first photocomposition machine.

**1965** Computer typesetting is introduced in Germany.

**1980s** Complete pages are produced by computers, transferred to paper by laser, and then photographed on to a printing plate.

△ Daguerreotype camera, 1839.

△ Powell's stereoscopic camera, 1858, produced 3-D photographs.

△ The cheap Brownie camera, 1900, made the snapshot universal.

△ Leitz camera, 1925, was the first reliable hand-held camera using fast film.

# Photography

There is an old Chinese saying that a picture is worth a thousand words, but before the advent of photography pictures were expensive and not always accurate. Pictures depended on the ability of the artist – and only a few people can draw and paint well.

Since the first photograph was taken in 1826 that has changed. Anyone can take a photograph. Communication by pictures has proved of immense importance in science and education as well as in everyday life.

Photography has many applications in industry, including the production of the miniature circuits needed for the silicon chips in computers and pocket calculators. In medicine it has enabled doctors to examine the interior of the body from the outside by means of X-ray photography, and to photograph inside by inserting long tubes incorporating fibre optics.

▽ How a camera works. Opening the shutter lets light from the object through a lens, which directs the light through an aperture (the iris). The light is focused onto the film by a second set of lenses, forming an inverted (upside-down) image.

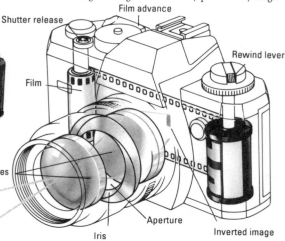

Shutter release
Film advance
Rewind lever
Film
Lenses
Iris
Aperture
Inverted image
Object

## GLOSSARY

**aperture** Opening of variable size made by the diaphragm. It helps to control the amount of light entering the camera.

**exposure** The amount of light reaching the film, controlled by the aperture size and the shutter speed.

**f-number (or f-stop)** One of a collection of numbers on a camera showing the aperture size after adjusting the diaphragm.

**focus** To make an image clear and sharp on the viewing screen and the film.

**image** The upside-down picture captured on the film when the shutter is released.

**lens** Several specially shaped pieces of glass focusing the image.

**negative** An image fixed on a film. Light tones appear dark; dark tones appear light.

**reflex camera** Camera with a mirror or mirrors inside to reflect light entering through the lens onto a viewing screen.

**transparency** A true-to-life colour picture made on transparent film.

▽ Inside a twin-lens reflex camera.

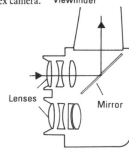

▽ Inside a single-lens reflex camera.

## KEY DATES IN PHOTOGRAPHY

**c1000** Arab astronomers use the camera obscura, a tiny aperture in a darkened room.

**1725** Johann Schulze of Germany discovers that some silver compounds darken on exposure to light.

**1826** Joseph Nicéphore Niépce, a French inventor, takes the earliest known surviving photograph.

**1839** Louis Jacques Daguerre, a French artist, invents a process of making photographs on copper plates.

**1839** William Henry Fox Talbot, an English scientist, produces the Calotype negative, from which prints can be made.

**1851** Frederick Scott Archer, an English sculptor, invents the wet glass plate.

**1855** Roger Fenton of England photographs the Crimean War.

**1858** First aerial photograph is taken from a captive balloon.

**1860s** Experiments on colour photography in England and France prove unsuccessful.

**1861** Matthew Brady begins photographing the American Civil War.

**1873** Bromide printing paper is introduced.

**1888** George Eastman introduces flexible paper roll film and the Kodak camera in which to use it.

**1889** Eastman replaces the paper film by celluloid.

**1895** X-ray photography is introduced.

**1903** French brothers Louis and Auguste Lumière invent the first practical three-colour process.

**1914** Panchromatic black and white film, sensitive to all colours, comes into use.

**1925** A German firm, Leitz, produces the first miniature camera, the Leica.

**1931** Harold Edgerton of the United States invents electronic flash.

**1935** Kodak introduces the Kodachrome process.

**1942** Agfa in Germany and Kodak in the United States introduce colour prints.

**1945** The zoom lens is introduced.

**1947** Edwin Land of the United States invents the Polaroid camera, producing instant black and white prints.

**1963** Polaroid produces instant colour film.

**1963** Holography – three-dimensional photography – is introduced in the United States.

**1970s** Automatic focusing is introduced.

**1989** Ultra high speed flash, producing an output of 40 joules in 1/250,000 second, becomes commercially available.

△ Carrier pigeons were used to carry the news of the Battle of Waterloo to London in 1815. Pigeons were still useful message-carriers during World War II.

▽ Many letters are still sorted by hand (*below*). Automatic sorting machines scan coded phosphorescent dots on envelopes and direct each letter to the correct destination box.

# Postal Services

The world's earliest postal services were set up by kings to send messages to distant parts of their lands. One of the most efficient was that of the Persian ruler Darius the Great in the 500s BC. He had couriers galloping along specially built post roads, carrying his orders. Similar services were organized by the Mongol emperors of China, Genghis Khan and his grandson Kublai Khan.

In Europe the first Roman emperor, Augustus, organized an efficient postal system during the first century AD. After the end of the Roman empire, postal services lapsed. They were revived in Russia in the 1200s, and in England and France in the 1400s. England's post office as a service available to the public began in the 1600s. The first American postal service was started in Massachusetts in 1639.

Today every country has a postal service, linked by the Universal Postal Union, which is now an agency of the United Nations.

## MILESTONES IN POSTAL SERVICES

**1635** Charles I sets up England's first public postal service.
**1680** English merchant William Dockwra sets up a short-lived penny postal service in London.
**1775** Benjamin Franklin sets up the United States federal postal service.
**1784** First British mail coaches run.
**1809** Australia's first postal service begins in New South Wales.
**1838** First travelling post office runs on British railways.
**1840** First adhesive postage stamp (the 'Penny Black') is issued in Britain, with the introduction of a universal penny post.

△ A US mail box. Postal services have become an indispensable part of modern life.

△ A collection of British stamps, from Queen Victoria to Queen Elizabeth II.
**1847** First adhesive postage stamps in the United States.
**1848** France introduces adhesive stamps and universal postal rates.
**1860** Pony Express mail service between St Joseph, Missouri, and Sacramento, California, is started; it lasts only 17 months, killed by the telegraph.

**1869** First postcard is introduced in Austria.
**1874** Universal Postal Union formed.
**1911** First experimental British airmail service.
**1919** First regular airmail service between London and Paris begins.
**1929** England-India airmail service begins.
**1935** Transpacific airmail service is started between San Francisco, California, and the Philippines.
**1939** Transatlantic airmail service starts.
**1959** British Post Office introduces experimental post codes in Norwich.
**1960** Mechanized sorting office opens at Providence, Rhode Island.

## SPECIAL POSTAL SERVICES

**C.O.D.** (collect on delivery) enables a person to pay the postman for goods when they are delivered.
**Datapost** provides a guaranteed service, either same day or next day, for important items.
**Metered post** Large users can hire franking machines which print the postage directly on envelopes or on adhesive labels.
**Postal order** A form of cheque that can be bought at a post office and posted to a named person, who must prove identity when cashing it.

**Poste restante** Mail may be sent to a post office to be called for – particularly useful for travellers.
**Registered** letters or packets are charged extra: they must be signed for by the receiver, and compensation is paid if they are lost.
**Savings bank** A banking service for small deposits available at any post office in the United Kingdom.
**Special delivery** Packets and letters sent special delivery are guaranteed to be delivered to their destinations next day.

# Long-distance Signalling

For thousands of years, people have sent pre-arranged signals by means of hilltop beacon fires. But detailed long-distance communications began only in the 1790s when Claude Chappé, a French engineer, built a semaphore telegraph. Moving mechanical arms on a tall tower signalled messages in code and, following the same principle, signals are still sometimes sent by flag-waving today. A series of such towers sent messages swiftly from one to the next down the line over hundreds of kilometres.

Modern electronic communications began a few years later with the invention of the electric telegraph, perfected in 1838 by an American portrait painter, Samuel Morse, and his colleagues Professor Leonard D. Gale and Alfred Vail.

▽ Samuel Morse's electric telegraph, 1882. The key C was used to send messages in Morse code. The recorder A registered incoming signals as dots and dashes on a paper tape.

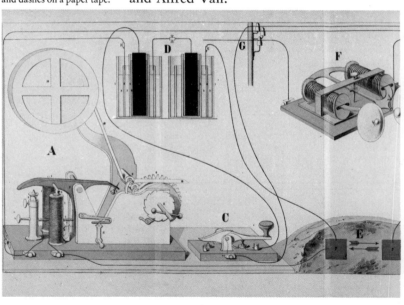

| | | | | | |
|---|---|---|---|---|---|
| A ·— | G ——· | M —— | S ··· | Y —·—— | 5 ····· |
| B —··· | H ···· | N —· | T — | Z ——·· | 6 —···· |
| C —·—· | I ·· | O ——— | U ··— | 1 ·———— | 7 ——··· |
| D —·· | J ·——— | P ·——· | V ···— | 2 ··——— | 8 ———·· |
| E · | K —·— | Q ——·— | W ·—— | 3 ···—— | 9 ————· |
| F ··—· | L ·—·· | R ·—· | X —··— | 4 ····— | 0 ————— |

# IMPORTANT DATES IN TELEGRAPHY

△ Chappé's semaphore used relay stations like this.

**1794** First semaphore telegraph, 225 km (140 miles) from Lille to Paris, is built by Claude Chappé.
**1804** Francisco Salva of Barcelona sends messages up to 1 km (900 yards) by electric telegraph, using one wire for each letter of the alphabet.
**1837** William Cooke and Charles Wheatstone of Britain patent a five-wire telegraph system.
**1838** Samuel Morse perfects his single-wire telegraph system and the Morse code.
**1844** Morse sends the first long-distance message, 'What hath God wrought', from Washington DC to Baltimore, Maryland.
**1845** A railway telegraph message sent over 32 km (20 miles) from Slough to London, leads to the arrest of a murderer.

**1851** Submarine cable is laid under the English Channel between Britain and France.
**1855** British professor David E. Hughes, working in the United States, invents a printing telegraph machine.
**1856** Formation of Western Union Telegraph Company leads to unified telegraph service in the United States.
**1858** Wheatstone patents a punched-tape system for faster transmission.
**1861** Telegraph service is extended from the east to the west coast of America.
**1866** First successful transatlantic cable is laid.
**1872** Duplex telegraphy is invented in the United States and multiplex telegraphy is invented in France.
**1927** Teleprinter services come into general use.
**1935** First facsimile telegraph service opens in the United States.

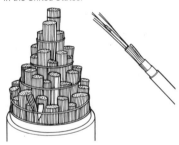

△ Optical fibre and conventional electric cables. The smaller optical cable has much greater capacity.

# LONG-DISTANCE SIGNALLING GLOSSARY

**cablegram** A telegram sent by an undersea cable.
**duplex system** A method of sending two messages simultaneously in opposite directions over the same cable.
**flag-hoist signalling** Signalling between ships by displaying different coloured flags on ships' masts.
**hand-signal flags** Two flags used in a simple method of semaphore signalling (see diagram on p.281).
**heliograph** A system of sending signals by flashing sunlight from a mirror, used by the British and other armies in the 1800s.

**international flag code** The code used for flag-hoist signalling at sea.
**multiplex system** Sending several messages simultaneously over the same cable.
**pyrotechnic signals** Signals made with rockets, flares and smoke.
**semaphore** Signalling by means of two flags or mechanical arms, held in various positions to represent letters.
**telegram** A message transmitted by telegraph.
**wireless telegraphy** Telegraphy by means of signals transmitted by radio.

# Radio and Television

Radio and television are the two quickest means of communication. They depend on electromagnetic waves, which travel through space as fast as light. There are several kinds of electromagnetic waves, including radio waves (the longest), infrared rays, visible light, ultraviolet light, X-rays and gamma rays (the shortest). Radio and television both use radio waves. These were discovered by the German physicist Heinrich Hertz in 1887, though their existence had been predicted by James Clerk Maxwell, a Scottish scientist, 23 years earlier.

△ Radio pioneer Guglielmo Marconi with his 1901-style transmitter.
▽ An early radio receiver.

The first radio signals for communications were transmitted in 1895 by the Italian inventor Guglielmo Marconi. Radio was used for communicating to ships at sea from 1903 onwards, and first saved lives in 1909 when two ships collided in the Atlantic.

Radio telephones came into use in the 1920s to cross the Atlantic Ocean, before the first permanent cable was laid in 1956. From 1962 radio signals relayed by satellites carried phone calls and radio programmes all over the world. Soon after, citizens' band radio began, first in North America and then in Europe. In the 1980s, radio came into use for mobile telephones.

Television received its first practical demonstration in 1926 from a Scottish inventor, John Logie Baird, though Baird's system

Aerial

▷ A huge radio telescope reflecting dish.

◁ A VCR records the incoming signal in a diagonal pattern of strips across the tape.

Video cassette recorder

Videotape

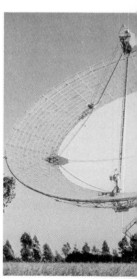

△ John Logie Baird pioneered TV with a mechanical system that produced flickering images. Light from the object (a doll's head) passed through holes in a spinning disc and was turned into electrical signals. These signals were then turned back into a light beam projected onto a screen to produce pictures.

was not the one finally adopted. Regular broadcasting began in the 1930s. Television's main use in communications is in bringing into people's homes news and pictures of events as they happen. It is also used for surveillance purposes by police and shop-keepers.

Both radio and television have an important role in communicating what is loosely called 'entertainment' direct to people's homes. This ranges from popular music to comedy shows, drama and informative talks. They also have an important part in education, beaming learning material to schools, colleges and people's homes. Britain's Open University, and similar institutions, provide higher education with radio and TV help.

---

### RADIO AND TV FACTS

**Biggest TV manufacturer** is Japan, producing around 13 million sets a year.

**Biggest radio manufacturer** is Hong Kong, making about 42 million sets a year.

**The Coronation** of Queen Elizabeth II in 1953 was the first major international TV broadcast.

**Earliest transatlantic radio transmission** was the Morse signal for 'S', sent in 1901.

**Earliest transatlantic TV transmission** was made in 1928 by Baird to a liner at sea; it was picked up in Hartsdale, New York State.

**First public radio broadcast** was by Professor Reginald A. Fessenden in Massachusetts in 1906.

**First stereo broadcasts** on radio were made in the United States in 1961.

**Geostationary satellites** – those which orbit the Earth in step with Earth rotation – came into use in 1963, making constant radio links possible.

**The ionosphere**, a region of electrified air between 130 km and 160 km (80–100 miles) above the Earth, 'bounces' radio waves around the world.

**Most TV sets in use** China claimed 600 million sets in use in 1988.

**Ninety-eight per cent** of United States households owned at least one TV set in 1988.

**Satellite TV** began in Europe in 1989, with signals beamed via the Astra satellite to home receivers.

**Teletext**, transmission of pages of information by television using spare lines not normally seen, was pioneered in Britain in 1973.

**Telstar**, launched in 1962, was the first successful communications satellite.

**Videotape recording** was first demonstrated in 1956.

△ A teletext machine.

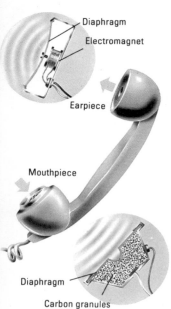

Diaphragm

Electromagnet

Earpiece

Mouthpiece

Diaphragm

Carbon granules

△ How a telephone works. As the caller speaks, a microphone vibrates and the vibrations are turned into electrical signals which travel along cables. At the earpiece, these signals set up vibrations in the diaphragm, which reproduces the sound-patterns of the caller's voice.

# Business Communications

The main advances in communications have come in the realm of business, which can increasingly to be carried on at a distance.

**Electronic mail** is an international series of computer networks, through which a subscriber can send messages to other subscribers by addressing them to mailboxes. A mailbox is an electronic store with a code number. Messages can be sent and stored, or retrieved, at any time.

**Electronic offices** enable staff of a company to work at home or in small branch offices. The basis of the system is either a computer terminal linked to a mainframe (see p.235) at the head office, or personal computers linked by fax or another form of electronic mail.

**Electronic paging** is a radio system which enables key workers to be contacted quickly. It is used extensively in factories and hospitals. Each person on the system carries a small pocket 'bleeper' which can be activated, calling them to the nearest telephone.

**Fax** – short for 'facsimile' – machines enable people to send copies of documents or pictures over telephone lines or radio links. The document to be transmitted is scanned by a photoelectric cell, which turns tones of black and white into electronic signals.

**Telephones** have come a long way since their invention in 1876 and business as we know it would be impossible without them. **Mobile telephones** allow people to be contacted while travelling. One kind operates within a building, enabling the user to move about freely carrying a small telephone receiver. Many countries now have networks of transmitters and receivers enabling people to use telephones in their cars, on trains and even in passenger aircraft.

**Photocopying** is a method of making quick copies of documents. It was invented in 1938. An image of the document is recorded temporarily on an electrically charged plate, which prints it on to paper by means of powder. The image is fixed by heat.

**Telex** is an older system of quick communication, and is an advance on simple telegraph systems. Each subscriber has a teleprinter machine, like a large typewriter. Any message is typed on the machine and recorded on a punched tape. When the tape is fed through the machine it transmits the message to a similar machine at the receiving end at about 100 words a minute. This system is used by newspapers and agencies for transmitting 'copy' quickly.

**Teletext** is a faster form of telex that links word processors through a telephone line. It was developed in Europe in the 1980s. The message is encoded on a floppy disk and is transmitted electronically to the receiving station.

**Viewdata** is a system by which information can be stored at a central point and retrieved by means of a telephone line, linked to word processors. A subscriber to the system can call up thousands of pages of information, ranging from the latest stock market prices to encyclopedia-style reference data.

▽ A photocopier reproduces images electrostatically. Light is reflected from the original onto a light-sensitive material charged with static electricity. An image forms, and is fixed when dusted with powdered ink and heat-transferred onto paper.

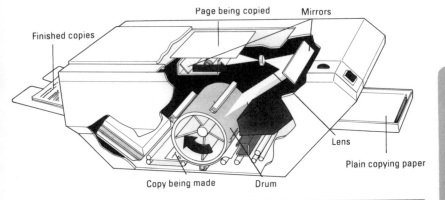

Page being copied    Mirrors

Finished copies

Lens

Plain copying paper

Copy being made    Drum

# Arts and Entertainment

Since the dawn of civilization, people have been moved to express their feelings and relate their experiences in pictures, words, music and dance. Twenty thousand years ago Stone Age people painted on the walls of caves scenes of life at that time; they also made primitive musical instruments. Literature began when stories were told around the hunters' fire; ballet was born in ritual dances to appease or thank the gods. All art is a celebration of life, in sorrow and in happiness. Today we can enjoy art and entertainment in our homes through television, video, radio and compact disc.

Throughout the history of mankind, people have been involved in those activities which we now call 'the arts'. Having met their basic needs for food, warmth and shelter, they have used their creative skills and imagination to satisfy a need for decoration, colour and entertainment in their lives.

The earliest carvings and paintings we know of were produced by Stone Age people over 20,000 years ago. Archaeologists have discovered primitive musical instruments made during the Stone Age. Decorated pottery of baked clay has been found dating from the Neolithic period (6000–3000 BC). The Greeks and Romans had theatres where plays were performed, and the plays and poetry of ancient Greece are considered to be the world's first important literature.

Some 4,500 years ago, the Egyptians built huge stone temples for their gods and tombs (pyramids) for their kings and queens. These are the first major works of architecture, and many can still be seen today.

Across the Atlantic, in Central and South America, Indian civilizations had developed their own types of art, architecture, pottery

△ Roman theatre at Orange, France. Actors wore large masks denoting the character they were playing.

▽ The lute was a popular early stringed instrument. Its name comes from the Arabic al-'ud.

and stone carving by about 1000 BC.

This section covers the traditional arts of painting and sculpture, pottery and porcelain, architecture, classical music, opera and ballet, the theatre and literature. It also includes a new range of media which the scientific advances of the 20th century have brought into being. These are the cinema, radio and television and popular music. They can be seen as arts in their own right, especially the cinema. The use of satellites in space to relay television signals means that events happening in one country can be shown on TV, as they happen, on the other side of the world.

The cinema was developed in the early years of this century and the first film with a sound track came out only in 1927. The development of radio and television came even more recently. The first public radio broadcasting services did not begin until the 1920s and the world's first television service began in Britain in 1936. Very few people in Britain or America had television sets until the 1950s.

In the 1970s video became popular. Video is a way of recording pictures and sounds on magnetic tape, which is simpler to use than film. Many people now have video cassette recorders (VCRs), which enable them to record television programmes and to play video cassettes. Easy-to-use video cameras make it simple for people to make their own home movies.

Towards the end of the nineteenth century, the phonograph (gramophone) was invented by an American, Thomas A. Edison. Soon afterwards the wax-coated, grooved disc which we call 'a record' was invented. The development of the gramophone record and the coming of radio brought about the growth of the huge popular music industry. Now records are being replaced by tapes and, latest of all, by compact discs.

△ *Figure of a Standing Woman* by the Swiss sculptor Alberto Giacometti (1901–66).

▽ A modern hand-held video camera. Video technology has revolutionized visual entertainment in the twentieth century.

△ Egyptian tomb paintings preserve echoes of a vanished civilization.

# Painting

The earliest paintings we know of are cave paintings in France and Spain. Some beautiful wall paintings still survive from ancient Egypt, Greece and Rome. In western Europe, the subjects of medieval paintings were religious. They were followed by the real flowering of art which came with the Renaissance. Painters such as Leonardo da Vinci began to make their subjects more lifelike. Later, Dutch painters such as Rembrandt and Vermeer began to portray everyday scenes. In the late 19th century an important new style of painting called 'Impressionism' developed. Artists such as Monet and Renoir painted from nature, studying the effects of different lights on a subject. Painting in the 20th century became even freer and styles included 'Cubism' and then 'Abstract Art'.

## SOME PAINTING TERMS

**abstract art** Art form that represents ideas (by means of geometric and other designs) instead of natural forms.

**airbush** Device used by artist to spray paint, varnish or fix, worked by compressed air.

**aquarelle** A water-colour painting.

**cave paintings** Pictures (mostly animals) painted by prehistoric artists on the walls of caves.

**chiaroscuro** ('light-dark') Balance of light and shade in a picture.

▽ Picasso's *Guernica* (1937) was inspired by the horrors of war.

**Cubism** Important movement in modern French painting started by Picasso and Braque in 1907. Cubists aimed to reduce objects to basic shapes of cubes, spheres, cylinders and cones.

**distemper** Cheap and impermanent method of painting in which powdered colours are mixed with glue.

**Dutch School** Art and artists of Netherlands in 1600s. Leaders were Rembrandt, Hals, Van der Velde.

**egg tempera** A painting medium in which the colours are ground with pure egg yolk; one of the most permanent media available.

**Expressionism** Movement that aims at expressing the artist's inner feelings and experiences. It began in late 1800s.

**Fauves** ('wild beasts') Group of Parisian painters of early 1900s (Dufy, Matisse, Rouault, Vlaminck, etc) who shocked the critics by their brilliant use of colour.

**finger painting** Chinese water-colour technique using finger instead of a brush.

**fresco** Method of great antiquity but perfected during Italian Renaissance; uses pigments ground in water applied to a fresh lime-plaster wall or ceiling.

**gouache** Non-transparent water-colour paint that provides easy way of obtaining oil-painting effects.

**icon** Religious picture (usually painted on wood or ivory) associated with Eastern Church.

**Impressionism** Important movement that developed among French painters just after mid-1800s. Impressionists were concerned with light and its effects. They included Renoir, Manet, Degas, Monet, Pissarro and Sisley.

**landscape painting** Picture whose main subject is pure landscape without human figures; rare before 1600s.

**miniature** Tiny painting (less than 15 cm, or 6 in, across), usually a portrait.

**mural** Wall-painting, usually executed in fresco, oil or tempera.

**narrative painting** One that tells a story; popular in Victorian England.

**oil painting** Technique of covering a slightly absorbent surface with pigment ground in oil.

**op art** (optical art) Modern technique with which painter creates optical illusions by means of dazzling patterns.

**palette** Range of colours available to a painter; usually arranged on little board for easy mixing, with thumb-hole for holding.

**pastel** Painter's colouring medium consisting of crayon of pure pigment or pigment mixed with chalk and other materials.

**pigments** Dry paints or dyes that are mixed with oil, water, or other material.

**portrait painting** Representation in painting of a human being. First portraits were usually of kings and other leaders.

**Post-impressionism** Work of French painters that followed Impressionism between 1885 and 1905. Typified by Cézanne, Gauguin, Van Gogh and Seurat.

△ *The Scream*, lithograph by Edvard Munch (1893).

**Renaissance** Rebirth in arts and learning that took place in Europe (especially Italy) from 1300s to 1500s. Among the masters of this period were Botticelli, Leonardo da Vinci, Michelangelo, Titian and Raphael.

**representational art** Type of painting that shows objects as nearly as possible as they actually are; the opposite of abstract art.

**rococo** European art style (about 1735–1765) characterized in painting by lavish decoration and extravagant ornament.

**still life** Art form in which subject of picture is made up of inanimate objects; favourite form of Dutch School.

**tempera** Binding medium for powder colours, made up of egg yolk, sometimes thinned with water. Tempera mixtures last longer than oil colours.

**triptych** Series of three painted panels or doors that are hinged or folded.

**Venetian School** Painters who worked in Venice during High Renaissance. They included Titian, Veronese, Tintoretto and Giorgione.

**water-colour** Technique of painting with colours that have been mixed with water-soluble gum; paints are applied to paper with soft, moistened brush. English painters such as Turner, Cozens, Sandby, Cotman and Girtin were supreme at the art.

300

## GREAT ARTISTS

**Botticelli, Sandro** (1444–1510) Italian painter who spent most of his life in Florence. Most of his work consisted of religious pictures.

**Braque, Georges** (1882–1963) French painter and sculptor; one of the founders of Cubism.

**Brueghel, Pieter** (1520?–1569) Flemish artist renowned for lively pictures of village life.

**Cézanne, Paul** (1839–1906) French painter famous for his landscapes and still lifes.

**Constable, John** (1776–1837). One of the greatest English landscape painters.

**Degas, Edgar** (1834–1917) French artist of the Impressionist period, noted for his pictures of ballet dancers.

△ Degas is famous for his paintings of the ballet.

**Dürer, Albrecht** (1471–1528) German artist who made many fine woodcuts and engravings for book illustrations.

**Gauguin, Paul** (1848–1903) French painter who escaped from European civilization to paint in the peaceful Pacific island of Tahiti.

**Giotto** (1266?–1337) Italian painter who greatly influenced Renaissance art. His style was more realistic than that of the formal painters of his time.

**Goya, Francisco** (1746–1828) Spanish court painter representing people realistically rather than in a flattering light.

**Greco, El** (1541–1614) Nickname meaning 'The Greek', born in Crete, but worked in Venice and Spain. His pictures often contain strange, thin, brightly coloured figures.

**Hogarth, William** (1697–1764) English artist who satirized the cruelty and vice which he saw around him in London.

△ Giotto's *The Madonna in Majesty* (early 1300s).

**Holbein, Hans, the Younger** (1497?–1564) German portrait painter who created realistic likenesses of his subjects.

**Leonardo da Vinci** (1452–1519) Italian painter, architect, sculptor and musician, as well as a brilliant inventor and scientist.

**Michelangelo Buonarroti** (1475–1564) Italian painter, sculptor and architect. Possibly his finest work was painted on the ceiling of the Sistine Chapel, in the Vatican.

**Monet, Claude** (1840–1926) French artist who developed the Impressionist technique of using light to change the nature of a painting.

**Picasso, Pablo** (1881–1973) Spanish painter whose early paintings were dominated by the colour blue. In 1907 he introduced the style known as Cubism, that changed the whole course of art.

△ Durer's woodcut *Praying Hands*.

**Raphael** (1483–1520) Italian artist whose pictures are notable for their peaceful beauty and perfect composition.

**Rembrandt van Rijn** (1606–1669) One of the finest Dutch portrait painters; a master at capturing the character of his subjects, and in the dramatic use of light and shade (chiaroscuro).

**Renoir, Pierre Auguste** (1841–1919) French Impressionist painter who used rich colours; particularly known for his nudes.

**Rubens, Peter Paul** (1577–1640) Flemish artist who became court painter in Antwerp after spending eight years in Italy.

**Titian** (1477–1576) One of the greatest Venetian painters. He painted many religious works for churches.

△ Self-portrait, Van Gogh.

**Toulouse-Lautrec, Henri de** (1864–1901) French artist, best remembered for his Parisian cabaret posters and his pictures of music-hall performers.

**Turner, Joseph Mallord William** (1775–1851) English painter especially noted for his water-colours and his magnificent sunsets.

**Van Gogh, Vincent** (1853–1890) Dutch painter whose early pictures were sombre, but in his later work he used bright, swirling colours. His later paintings reflect his growing insanity.

**Velázquez, Diego Rodríguez de Silva** (1599–1660) Spanish court painter; renowned for his portraits of Philip IV and the courtiers.

△ Self-portrait, Rembrandt.

▽ *Chain Pier, Brighton* by Constable.

△ Mysterious stone carved
heads stand on Easter
Island in the Pacific Ocean.
More than 600 statues have
been discovered.

# Sculpture

The earliest pieces of sculpture we know of were carved by Stone Age people some 30,000 years ago. The ancient Egyptians made fine sculptures between 2,000 and 4,000 years ago – many were huge statues of their kings and queens. Some of the world's most beautiful carvings were done by the sculptors of ancient Greece and Rome. All over the world, in China, India, Africa and many other countries, people have made three-dimensional images. During the Renaissance, especially in Italy, the art of sculpture advanced rapidly. Michelangelo carved superb statues, such as his *David*. Today, sculptors work in stone, marble, wood, metal, even fibreglass. They often carve sculptures in which the general shape is more important than the likeness of the figure or object.

## SOME SCULPTURAL TERMS

**armature** Wood or metal framework used to support sculptor's model.

**bronze** Alloy of copper and tin used by sculptors in ancient Greece. Rome, China, and Africa; revived in modern times.

**bust** Sculpture of the upper part of the human body.

**cast** Figure made from mould of original model. See cire perdue; plaster cast, sand cast.

**cire perdue** (French, 'lost wax') Traditional method for casting bronze sculptures: model with wax surface is enclosed in mould; wax is melted and runs out through holes at bottom; molten metal poured through holes at top, filling up space left by wax.

**figurine** Miniature figure.

**free-stone** An easily worked fine-grained limestone or sandstone.

**genre sculpture** Style that reflects everyday or rustic life; hallmark of Etruscan art and of biblical subjects in Middle Ages.

**heroic** Any figure or group of figures carved larger than life.

**maquette** (French, 'small model') Small wax or clay model made by sculptor in preparation for larger work.

**marble** Popular stone for sculpture because of its extreme durability; found in all colours ranging from nearly pure white to nearly pure black.

**mobile** Movable sculpture of shapes cut out of wood or sheet metal, linked by wires or rods in order to revolve easily or move up and down; invented by American sculptor, Alexander Calder (1932).

**modelling** Building-up of forms in three dimensions by means of plastic material such as clay or wax.

**plaster cast** Intermediate stage in bronze sculpture from which final mould is made.

**polychromatic sculpture** Sculpture painted in naturalistic colours to make it more lifelike; mostly pre-1500s.

**relief** Sculpture not free-standing from background; various degrees, from *bas-relief* (low relief) to *alto-relievo* (high relief).

**sand cast** Mould of special sand made from plaster model and from which bronze cast is made.

**sculpture-in-the-round** Sculpture that can be seen from all sides.

**stabile** Sculpture that does not move, as opposed to mobile.

## FAMOUS SCULPTORS

**Bernini, Gianlorenzo** (1598–1680) Italian Renaissance sculptor. As well as owing much to classical tradition, his figures appear almost to be living people.

**Brancusi, Constantin** (1876–1957) Romanian sculptor, most famous for a series of bird sculptures made of different materials, but also for bronzes such as the powerful Prodigal Son.

**Calder, Alexander** (1898–1976) American sculptor, known particularly for his moving sculptures made from flat metal discs suspended from wires. These were given the name 'mobiles'.

**Donatello** (1386–1466) Italian Renaissance sculptor who carved realistic figures. He developed a new form of relief sculpture where the feeling of depth is created without cutting deep into the surface of the marble.

**Epstein, Sir Jacob** (1880–1959) English sculptor influenced by primitive art. At the beginning of his career, people were shocked by the directness of his work.

△ *The Kiss*, by Constantin Brancusi.

**Gabo, Naum** (1890–1977) Russian sculptor who made new use of industrial materials such as glass, metal, plastics and wire.

**Giacometti, Alberto** (1901–1966) Swiss sculptor and painter, best-known for his tall, spindly figures cast in bronze.

**Hepworth, Barbara** (1903–1975) British sculptor, created abstract carvings in wood and stone, huge shapes broken by holes with wires stretched across them.

**Lipschitz, Jacques** (1891–1973) Cubist Lithuanian sculptor, most famous for his powerful, angular animals and figures.

**Michelangelo Buonarroti** (1475–1564) Italian Renaissance sculptor, painter and architect, famous for many fine carvings including the Pietà, David, and a series of slaves who seem to be trying to escape from the rock from which they are carved.

**Modigliani, Amedeo** (1884–1920) Italian sculptor and painter. Influenced by Cézanne and by African art, he carved elongated faces from wood.

**Moore, Henry** (1898–1986) British sculptor best known for his large reclining nudes and for groups of figures. He was influenced by both primitive African and Mexican art.

**Phidias** (c 490–c 417 BC) Influential Greek sculptor. He designed and supervised the Parthenon sculptures, as well as a sculpture of Zeus at Olympia.

**Rodin, Auguste** (1840–1917) French sculptor who worked in bronze and marble. His work includes The Thinker, The Kiss and The Burghers of Calais.

◁ *The Prodigal Son*, by Rodin.

▽ The art of making fine porcelain reached Europe from China in the 18th century.

# Pottery and Porcelain

Objects made from baked clay are called pottery. They include cups, saucers, plates, bowls, pots, jugs, vases and many other useful items. People have made pottery for thousands of years and have gradually learned to make it more efficient and more beautiful. Porcelain is fine pottery made with white china clay — the art of making it was perfected in China — and Chinese porcelain is some of the most beautiful ever produced. Stoneware (also called earthenware) is often made of blue, brown, grey, red or yellow clay. It is thicker and heavier than porcelain, but less hard.

### SOME HISTORIC POTTERY AND PORCELAIN FACTORIES

| | |
|---|---|
| Belleek (Ireland) | 1857– |
| Bennington (US) | 1793–1894 |
| Bow (England) | 1744–1776 |
| Bristol (England) | 1749–1781 |
| Caughley (England) | 1754–1814 |
| Chantilly (France) | 1725–1800 |
| Chelsea (England) | 1745–1784 |
| Coalport (England) | 1796– |
| Copenhagen (Denmark) | 1774– |
| Derby (England) | 1750–1848 |
| Derby, Royal Crown | 1876– |
| Frankenthal (Germany) | 1755–1799 |
| Greenpoint (US) | 1848– |
| Hoechst (Germany) | 1750–1798 |
| Limoges (France) | 1771– |
| Liverpool England) | 1710–c.1800 |
| Ludwigsburg (Germany) | 1758–1824 |
| Meissen (Germany) | 1710– |
| Mennecy (France) | 1735–1785 |
| Nymphenburg (Germany) | 1753– |
| Sèvres (France) | 1756– |
| Spode (England) | 1770– |
| Tucker (US) | 1826–1838 |
| Vincennes (France) | 1738–1756 |
| Wedgwood (England) | 1759– |
| Worcester (England) | 1751– |

### CHINESE DYNASTIES

Chinese pottery and porcelain is dated by the dynasty (royal family) or individual emperor in whose time it was made. Some of the most important are:

| Dynasty | Dates |
|---|---|
| Han | 206 BC–AD 220 |
| Three Kingdoms | 220–265 |
| Six Dynasties | 265–588 |
| Sui | 589–618 |
| T'ang | 618–906 |
| Five Dynasties | 906–959 |
| Sung | 960–1279 |
| Yüan (Mongol) | 1280–1368 |
| Ming | 1368–1644 |
| Ch'ing (Manchu) | 1644–1912 |
| (Emperor Chi'en Lung 1736–1795) | |

▽ The T'ang dynasty is noted for its superb ceramics, like this decorated jar.

## SOME POTTERY AND PORCELAIN TERMS

**biscuit ware** Pottery fired but not glazed.
**bone china** Type of porcelain made in England today, for high-quality tableware.
**ceramics** Term for anything made of baked clay; the potter's art.
**china** (originally 'Chinaware') Chinese porcelain of 16th century; now any Chinese porcelain or western version of it.
**chinoiserie** Decoration on 18th-century European porcelain, depicting Chinese scenes.
**clay** The potter's basic material, found just beneath the topsoil, formed by decomposition of rock; *kaolin*, or *china clay*, a pure white coarse clay; *ball clay*, a highly plastic, fine pure clay; *fireclay*, a dark rough clay, able to stand high temperatures, but not plastic; *buff*, or *stoneware, clay*, a smooth plastic clay hardening at high temperatures.
**creamware** High-quality earthenware perfected by Josiah Wedgwood in Staffordshire (18th century).
**delftware** Tin-enamelled earthenware, mostly blue-and-white, originally made in Delft (Holland) in 17th and 18th centuries.
**earthenware** Pottery fired to relatively low temperature (about 1,100°C), easy to work and having dull finish.
**enamel** Coloured glaze used to decorate pottery already glazed.
**firing** Process of hardening shaped clay by heating it.
**glazing** Process for producing smooth, waterproof finish to pottery; *glaze* is liquid clay-like mixture applied before or after first firing.
**kiln** Chamber in which clay is fired.
**paste** Term for mixture from which porcelain is made; *hard-paste* porcelain made from

Platform
Wheel
Foot-operated treadle
△ A potter's wheel.

kaolin and petuntse, the true porcelain originating in China and rediscovered at Meissen (Germany) in 18th century, fired at very high temperatures; *soft-paste* porcelain made from white clay and fusible silicate, more translucent than hard paste but with softer whiteness.
**porcelain** The finest kind of pottery, white all through and translucent. See *paste*.
**pottery** Strictly, all baked-clay ware except stoneware and porcelain.
**slip** Clay in liquid form, used for casting, joining or decoration.
**stoneware** Hard, strong type of pottery fired at about 1,250°C and able to hold liquid without glazing. Used for items such as pots and heavy dishes.
**terracotta** Brownish-red burnt-clay pottery, baked in moulds and used for architectural mouldings.
**throwing** Shaping wet clay by hand on potter's wheel.
**turning** Final trimming of partially dried pottery on wheel or lathe.

▽ How a pot is made in a factory: molten clay is poured into a mould and water is allowed to seep out until the required thickness of clay has hardened.

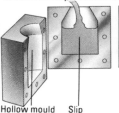

Hollow mould   Slip
Layer of clay

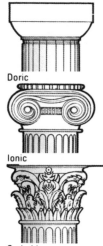

Doric

Ionic

Corinthian

△ The style of Greek capitals (carved column tops) helps to identify a building's architectural style.

# Architecture

Architecture is the art of designing buildings. It began about 4,500 years ago in ancient Egypt, and many of the Egyptians' huge pyramids and tombs still stand. Greek architecture began to take shape about 600 BC. Its beauty is typified by the Acropolis in Athens. The Romans copied Greek architecture, but also discovered how to make an arch, enabling them to construct much stronger buildings. During the Middle Ages many of Europe's most beautiful cathedrals were built in the Gothic style. Then came the Renaissance, which brought new ideas in architecture as it did in the other arts. Later, famous architects such as Sir Christopher Wren (1632–1723) built grander churches, colleges and houses. Today, people still build with brick and stone, but architects are also using new materials such as concrete and steel, 'tinted glass' and plastics.

## SOME ARCHITECTURAL TERMS AND STYLES

**abacus** Slab forming upper part of capital.

**apse** Semicircular (or polygonal) area with domed roof at end of aisle of church.

**arcade** Row of arches supported by columns and carrying roof.

**arch** Curved structure spanning an opening.

**architrave** Lowest section of entablature.

**Art Nouveau** Style (1890–1910) characterized by use of, for example, coloured materials, moulded stonework, tapered wrought-iron brackets and curving motifs of flowers and leaves.

**Baroque** Heavily decorated European style (1600s–1700s) involving flamboyant use of Renaissance forms.

**basilica** Huge vaulted civic hall (Roman) or early Christian church.

**Brutalism** Reforming movement in modern architecture that emerged in Britain in 1950s; based on the work of Le Corbusier and Mies van der Rohe.

**buttress** Projecting support (mass of masonry) built on outside of wall; in *flying-buttress*, masonry is free-standing with half-arch transferring thrust from wall.

**Byzantine** Style that flourished in Eastern Roman Empire (AD 400s to 1453), characterized by ornately domed and vaulted churches, rounded arches, minarets, spires and frequent use of mosaics.

**capital** Broad top part of column, supporting entablature.

**caryatid** Draped female figure used as pillar in classical architecture.

**classical** Style of ancient Greece or Rome, or any style based on these.

**cloisters** Quadrangle surrounded by roofed passages connecting parts of monastery.

**cornice** Top, projecting section of entablature, supporting roof.

**dome** Roof in shape of semi-sphere, usually built over square base.

**dormer** Small gabled window projecting from sloping roof.

**Elizabethan** English style of 1500s marking change from Gothic to Renaissance and featuring sturdy, squared buildings with large windows and ornamentation in Flemish and German styles.

**entablature** Part of building in classical architecture between top of columns and roof; consists of architrave, frieze and cornice.

**façade** Main face of building.

**fenestration** Arrangement of windows in a building.

**fluting** Longitudinal grooves in a column.

**frieze** Middle section of entablature.

**Functionalism** Modern theory that the shape of a building should be decided by its proposed use.

**gable** Triangular end of roof with two sloping sides.

**gargoyles** Projecting stone spouts (usually grotesquely carved) acting as outlets for gutter water on medieval buildings.

**Georgian** English style (1700s), a quiet and dignified classical style.

**Gothic** Style developed in France in 1100s. Characterized by pointed arches, elaborate vaulting, flying-buttresses, slender pillars, large stained-glass windows and intricate tracery. English Gothic is divided into three styles: *Early English* (late 1100s to 1200s), *Decorated* (late 1200s to 1300s), *Perpendicular* (mid-1300s to 1500s).

**Greek** Beautifully proportioned classical style lasting from about 700 BC. until conquest by Romans in mid-100s BC. Graceful buildings, with three orders of columns: *Doric* (stubby columns), the later (from about 400 BC) *Ionic* (longer, slimmer columns on moulded bases with intricately carved capitals) and *Corinthian* (more elaborate, with foliage on capital).

**International Style** Term given to modern style of architecture that evolved in western Europe in 1920s, spread internationally in 1930s and flourished in United States.

**keystone** Locking stone at top of arch.

**lintel** Horizontal stone above doorway or window, supporting wall above.

**minaret** Tower of mosque, with gallery for muezzin to call Muslims to prayer.

**moulding** Decorative edging on architectural surface.

**nave** Main body of church, west of crossing, flanked by aisles.

△ Roman: Arch of Constantine in Rome. The Romans invented the arch.

**Norman** Style brought to Britain by Normans in 1066.

**pagoda** Tower, of Chinese origin, partitioned horizontally with balconies or cornices.

**pedestal** Block used to support column.

**pediment** Triangular end of sloping roof in classical architecture.

**piazza** Open square surrounded by buildings.

**pier** Free-standing vertical support for arch, beam, etc.

**pilaster** Flat, rectangular column attached to or built into wall.

**portico** Area with roof supported by rows of columns.

**post-and-lintel** Construction using vertical elements (posts) and horizontal beams (lintels).

**Regency** English style of the early 1800s.

**Renaissance** Style emerging in Italy in 1400s, based on classical style of Ancient Greece and Rome combined with many current Gothic features.

**Rococo** Light, airy version of baroque style that developed in the 1700s.

**Roman** Style at its height from about 100 BC to AD 300s. Characterized by vaults and semicircular arches.

**rotunda** Circular building, usually domed.

**steel-frame** Skeleton of steel girders that provides framework for buildings such as skyscrapers.

**tracery** Elaborately patterned openwork in Gothic architecture, originally framework of light stone bars dividing large window.

**transept** In church, hall running north-south and crossing nave at right-angles.

**Tudor** English late-Gothic period (1500s).

**vault** Brick or stone ceiling built on arch principle.

△ Ancient Greek: Temple of Artemis.

# FAMOUS ARCHITECTS

**Aalto, Alvar** (1898–1976) Finnish architect whose buildings include the Hall of Residence, Massachusetts Institute of Technology and the church at Imatra. He made wide use of timber.

**Adam, Robert** (1728–1792) British architect, decorator and furniture designer. He used ancient Greek and Roman styles, making them lighter and more romantic.

**Alberti, Leone Battista** (1404–1472) Italian Renaissance architect who built influential churches using classical features in an experimental approach

**Bernini, Gianlorenzo** (1598–1680) Italian architect responsible for the completion of the rebuilding of St Peter's, Rome, designing the piazza in the baroque style.

**Bramante, Donato** (1444–1514) First of the Italian High Renaissance architects. Sticking closely to severe classical design, he had a great influence on later architects.

**Brunelleschi, Filippo** (1377–1446) Italian Renaissance architect, most famous for designing and building the dome of Florence Cathedral. This was used as a model for St Peter's, Rome

**Cortona, Pietro da** (1596–1669) Italian painter and architect whose dramatic church façades are designed almost like stage sets.

**Gaudi, Antoni** – (1852–1926) Spanish architect of the Art Nouveau style. The Casa Milá in Barcelona has a wavy roof line and the apartment rooms have no straight walls or right angles.

**Gropius, Walter** (1883–1969) Great modern German architect known for functional factory and office designs and for refounding the 'Bauhaus' (House of Building) to teach arts and crafts.

△ Wren's masterpiece, St. Paul's Cathedral, London.

**Hardouin-Mansart, Jules** (1646–1708) French architect known for his use of baroque designs in the extensions to the Palace of Versailles.

**Jones, Inigo** (1573–1652) English architect who introduced Palladian style to Britain, greatly influencing later architecture. His buildings include the Queen's House, Greenwich and the Banqueting Hall, Whitehall.

**Le Corbusier** (1887–1965, Charles Edouard Jeanneret) Swiss architect who worked in France. Best-known for designing apartments and houses and for his wide use of reinforced concrete.

△ Temple of the Holy Family, Barcelona, designed by Gaudi in 1905.

**Lutyens, Sir Edwin** (1869–1944) English architect who built country houses.

**Mackintosh, Charles Rennie** (1868–1928) Scottish Art Nouveau architect, and designer of interiors and furniture. Used effects of simplicity and curved lines.

**Michelangelo Buonarroti** (1475–1564) Italian Renaissance architect, painter and sculptor, who rejected the rigid classical rules and introduced novel designs. Best-known for his work on St Peter's, Rome.

**Mies van der Rohe, Ludwig** (1886–1969) German architect and planner. Director of the Bauhaus from 1930 to 1933. His designs were suited to the use of the buildings.

**Nash, John** (1752–1835) English architect, known particularly for his work on the rebuilding of the Royal Pavilion at Brighton, where he used Gothic, Hindu and Chinese forms.

**Nervi, Pier Luigi** (1891–1978) Italian engineer and architect known for his inventive use of reinforced concrete. He built two sports halls for the Olympic Games held in Rome in 1960.

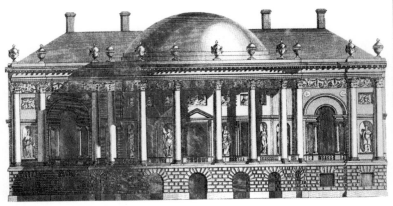

△ Drawing of a mansion by Palladio.

**Niemeyer, Oscar** (1907– ) Inventive Brazilian architect responsible for many buildings in the new capital, Brasília.

**Palladio, Andrea** (1508–80) Probably the most influential Italian architect who returned to classical Roman forms with symmetrical planning and fine proportions.

**Pugin, Augustus** (1812–1852) English architect who promoted Gothic Revival style; worked on the Houses of Parliament.

**Rogers, Richard** (1933– ) English architect who worked on designs for Beaubourg (Georges Pompidou Centre) in Paris and the Lloyds Building in London.

**Saarinen, Eero** (1910–1961) American architect who used interesting new designs on industrial buildings.

**Utzon, Jorn** (1918– ) Famous for his design for the Sydney Opera House whose roof looks like the sails of ships.

**Voysey, Charles** (1857–1941) Architect and furniture designer responsible for a new style of English houses, which fitted into the surroundings.

**Wren, Sir Christopher** (1632–1723) English architect and scientist, responsible for much of the rebuilding of London after the Great Fire in 1666. Also famous for his work on St Paul's Cathedral and Greenwich Hospital.

**Wright, Frank Lloyd** (1869–1959) American architect, best-known for his designs for the Johnson Wax Building which included 21 miles of glass tubing to provide light to the offices and corridors.

△ Lloyd's of London, by Richard Rogers.

## PERIODS OF ARCHITECTURE

**Greek** 600s–100s BC
**Roman** 100s BC–AD 400s
**Byzantine** AD 400s–1453
**Romanesque** late 800s–late 1100s
**Norman** (England) late 1000s–1100s
**Gothic** (France) mid-1100s–1400s
**Renaissance** (Italy) 1400s–1500s
**French Renaissance** 1500s
**Elizabethan** (England) 1500s–1600
**Baroque** (Italy 1600–1750
**Georgian** (England) 1725–1800
**Rococo** (France) mid-1700s
**Regency** (England) 1800–1825
**Art Nouveau** (Europe) 1890–1910
**Expressionism** (Germany) 1910–1930s
**Functionalism** 1920s–
**International Style** 1920s–
**Brutalism** 1950s–

△ One of George
Cruikshank's illustrations
from Dickens' novel *Oliver
Twist*.

# Literature

Literature – the art of the written word – has existed as long as people have been able to express themselves in writing. In western Europe the first great ages of literature were those of ancient Greece and Rome. The works of Homer, Virgil and others, which became known as 'the classics', have influenced writers up to the present day. The Renaissance brought another great explosion of literary activity, with writers such as Chaucer, Dante and, perhaps greatest of all, Shakespeare. Poems and plays are both very ancient forms of literature, but the novel is relatively new. It was only fully developed at the end of the 18th century and reached a peak of popularity in the 19th century.

## SOME LITERARY TERMS

**allegory** A story in which the obvious meaning symbolizes a hidden meaning.

**ballad** A poem describing a historical or legendary event or deed. Ballads were very popular in the late Middle Ages.

**blank verse** A form of poetry based on unrhyming ten-syllable lines with alternate syllables stressed.

**couplet** Two successive lines of verse that rhyme with one another.

**drama** A story written as a dialogue, in conversational form, so that it can be spoken and acted.

**elegy** A poem mourning a death or on some other solemn theme.

**epic** A long narrative poem about heroic, historical or legendary events and people. An example is Homer's *Odyssey*.

**fable** A short tale with a moral lesson in which animals act and talk like people.

**limerick** A kind of comic, nonsense poem in five lines, usually rhyming *a a b b a*. Edward Lear wrote many limericks.

**ode** A medium-length poem, usually in praise of something. It has various forms.

**rhyme** Agreement in sound of two syllables, but with differing preceding consonants.

**romantic** Belonging to the Romantic period, the early 1800s, when writers stressed liberty and chose exotic themes and settings.

**satire** A style using sarcasm or irony to

△ An illustration from *Don Quixote*, one of the earliest novels, by the Spanish writer Cervantes.

attack some form of human behaviour.

**sonnet** A 14-lined poem with various rhyming schemes. Italian sonnets rhyme *abba abba cde cde*. Elizabethan sonnets rhyme *abab cdcd efef gg*.

## GREAT WRITERS

**Andersen, Hans Christian** (1805–75), Danish writer, best known for his fairy tales. Some of the most loved are *The Tinder Box, The Emperor's New Clothes* and *The Snow Queen.*

**Austen, Jane** (1775–1817), English novelist, wrote about comfortably-off country people, who led lives bound by strict rules of behaviour. Her books include *Sense and Sensibility, Pride and Prejudice* and *Emma.*

△ Jane Austen, drawn by her sister.

**Balzac, Honoré de** (1799–1850), French novelist, wrote a series of 90 realistic stories about everyday life in France called the *Human Comedy.*

**Blake, William** (1757–1827), English poet and artist. His *Songs of Innocence* and *Songs of Experience* show the same world from the viewpoints of innocence and disillusioned experience.

**Brontë** Family name of three English novelist sisters: **Charlotte** (1816–55), **Emily Jane** (1818–48), and **Anne** (1820–49). Charlotte included many personal experiences in her most famous novel, *Jane Eyre. Wuthering Heights*, a dramatic love story is probably Emily's best work.

**Bunyan, John** (1628–88), English preacher and religious writer, best known for his allegory *The Pilgrim's Progress.*

**Burns, Robert** (1759–96), Scottish poet who wrote poems in Scottish dialect and composed many songs, including *Auld Lang Syne.*

**Byron, Lord George** (1788–1824), English Romantic poet, wrote several long narrative poems. Probably the finest is *Don Juan.*

△ Danish storyteller, Hans Christian Andersen.

**Carroll, Lewis** (Charles Lutwidge Dodgson 1832–98), best remembered for his stories *Alice's Adventures in Wonderland* and *Through the Looking Glass.*

**Cervantes, Miguel de** (1547–1616), Spanish novelist, playwright and poet, author of the novel *Don Quixote*, story of a gentleman who imagines he can put right all the evil in the world.

**Chaucer, Geoffrey** (1340?–1400), English poet, famous for his *Canterbury Tales*, a collection of stories told by travellers on a journey.

△ Illustration of pilgrims from Chaucer's *Canterbury Tales.*

**Coleridge, Samuel Taylor** (1772–1834), English Romantic poet and friend of Wordsworth, wrote the famous poem *The Rime of the Ancient Mariner*.

**Dante Alighieri** (1265–1321), Italian poet, wrote *Divine Comedy*, a poem in three parts about a man's role on Earth.

**Dickens, Charles** (1812–70), English novelist, wrote stories about the harsh lives of ordinary people in industrial England. The best-known include *Great Expectations, David Copperfield* and *Oliver Twist*.

**Dostoevsky, Fyodor** (1821–81), Russian novelist, wrote powerful stories. Among the finest are *Crime and Punishment, The Idiot* and *The Brothers Karamazov*.

**Eliot, George** (Marian Evans 1819–80), English novelist, wrote *The Mill on the Floss* and several other novels including *Middlemarch*, a story about country people.

**Eliot, T. S.** (Thomas Stearns 1888–1965), American-born British poet, dramatist and critic, wrote poetry expressing his frustration and despair.

▽ Dante, painted amid scenes from the *Divine Comedy*.

△ Charles Dickens, one of Britain's greatest novelists.

**Hemingway, Ernest** (1898–1961), American novelist, wrote stories about adventurous and violent lives. Best-known include *A Farewell to Arms* and *For Whom the Bell Tolls*.

**Homer** (700s BC), great and influential Greek poet, wrote the *Iliad* which tells the story of the siege of Troy, while the *Odyssey* describes the wanderings of the hero Odysseus after the war.

**Johnson, Dr Samuel** (1709–84), English poet and essayist, wrote on English poetry and compiled a *Dictionary of the English Language*.

**Joyce, James** (1882–1941), Irish novelist, wrote stories about people in conflict with their surroundings.

**Keats, John** (1795–1821), English Romantic poet, composed narrative poems. The finest include *Ode to Autumn* and *Ode to a Nightingale*.

▷ Portrait of John Keats by Benjamin Haydon.

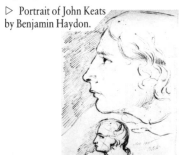

**Kipling, Rudyard** (1865–1936), an Indian-born English novelist, wrote of the British Empire, and adventure stories for children which include *Kim, The Jungle Book* and the *Just So Stories*.

**Lawrence, D. H.** (David Herbert 1885–1930), English novelist; much of his work is about working-class life, including growing up and natural love. He wrote *Sons and Lovers* and *Lady Chatterley's Lover*.

**Milton, John** (1608–74), English poet and religious and political writer. His most important works are the long poems *Paradise Lost* and *Paradise Regained*.

**Poe, Edgar Allan** (1809–49), American short-story writer, poet and critic, is best known for his tales of mystery.

**Rabelais, François** (1494?–1553?), French priest and doctor, poked fun at life in his day in his four books about Gargantua and Pantagruel.

**Scott, Sir Walter** (1771–1832), Scottish novelist and poet, author of romantic adventures often set in the Middle Ages. They include *Waverley* and *Ivanhoe*.

**Shelley, Percy Bysshe** (1792–1822), English Romantic poet, wrote idealistic poems including *Ode to a Skylark* and *The Cloud*.

**Stevenson, Robert Louis** (1850–94), Scottish novelist, wrote *Treasure Island* and *Kidnapped*, both adventure stories, and *Dr Jekyll and Mr Hyde*, a mystery.

**Swift, Jonathan** (1667–1745), Irish clergyman, wrote satirical pamphlets on religion and politics, but is best known for his story *Gulliver's Travels*.

**Tennyson, Alfred, Lord** (1809–92), English poet, wrote *Break, Break, Break, The Charge of the Light Brigade* and *Idylls of the King*.

**Tolstoy, Count Leo** (1828–1910), Russian novelist and playwright, wrote one of the world's greatest novels, *War and Peace*. It traces the lives of several families during Napoleon's invasion of Russia.

**Twain, Mark** (Samuel Langhorne Clemens 1835–1910), American novelist, wrote many books about American life. His best-known, *The Adventures of Huckleberry Finn*, describes life along the Mississippi River.

**Virgil** (Publius Vergilius Maro 70–19 BC), a Roman poet, wrote the *Aeneid*, a long epic poem about the founding of Rome.

**Wordsworth, William** (1770–1850), an English poet, expressed his deep love of nature in poems often written in beautiful, simple language.

▽ William Wordsworth, pioneer of the Romantic Movement in English poetry.

# Music

We know that people have been making some kind of music all through history – for example, paintings of musicians have been found in Egyptian tombs – but we do not know what early music sounded like because there was no way of writing it down. As instruments improved through the centuries, new ones were added to the orchestra. Bach and Handel, both born in 1685, used orchestras with mostly stringed instruments such as violins but they also had flutes, oboes, trumpets and horns. The first man to use the orchestra as a whole was Haydn, who established the symphony. The piano as we know it today was not developed until the early 19th century. Early this century new kinds of music were produced by composers such as Stravinsky. Recently, composers have used electronic systems to produce sounds which are often strange to our ears.

△ J. S. Bach, the greatest of his distinguished musical family.

▽ The Emperor Maximilian I of Germany travelled with an impressive entourage of court musicians.

▷ Illustration of string family of instruments, 1618.

# SOME MUSICAL TERMS

**accelerando** Gradually faster.

**adagio** At a slow pace.

**allegro** At a fast pace.

**alto** Highest adult male voice

**andante** At a quiet, peaceful pace.

**arpeggio** Notes of chord played in rapid succession.

**bar** Metrical division of music bounded by vertical bar-lines.

**baritone** Male voice higher than bass and lower than tenor.

**bass** Lowest male voice.

**brass instruments** Metal instruments sounded by blowing through mouthpiece and altering tension of lips (French horn, trumpet, euphonium, trombone, tuba).

**choir** A body of singers.

**chord** Three or more notes sounded together.

**chorus** Main body of singers in choir; words and music repeated after each stanza of song.

**classical music** Music that aims at perfection of structure and design (period of Bach to Brahms).

**clef** Sign in musical notation that fixes pitch of each note written on the stave.

**concerto** Substantial work for one or more solo instruments and orchestra.

**contralto** Lowest female voice.

**counterpoint** Two or more melodies combined to form a satisfying harmony.

**crescendo** Increasing in loudness.

**descant** The addition of a second melody above a given melody, form of counterpoint.

**diminuendo** Gradually softer.

**flat** Conventional sign showing that pitch of a certain note has been lowered by a semitone.

**forte** Played or sung loudly.

**fortissimo** Very loud (loudest).

**harmony** Combining of chords to make musical sense.

**key** Classification of the notes of a scale.

**largo** At a slow pace.

**lied** German word for 'song' (plural lieder).

**major** One of the two main scales, with semitones between 3rd and 4th and 7th and 8th notes.

**measure** American term for bar.

**melody** A tune; series of musical sounds following each other, as distinct from harmony.

**mezzo** Half or medium.

**mezzo-soprano** Female voice between contralto and soprano.

**minor** One of the two main scales. Harmonic minor scales have a semitone between 2nd and 3rd, 5th and 6th, and 7th and 8th notes.

**movement** Complete section of larger work (such as symphony).

# SYMBOLS AND NOTATION

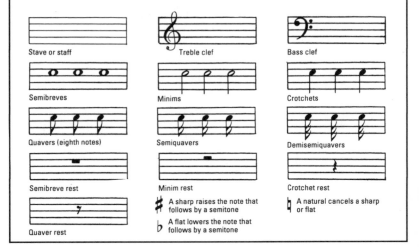

Stave or staff

Semibreves

Quavers (eighth notes)

Semibreve rest

Quaver rest

Treble clef

Minims

Semiquavers

Minim rest

♯ A sharp raises the note that follows by a semitone

♭ A flat lowers the note that follows by a semitone

Bass clef

Crotchets

Demisemiquavers

Crotchet rest

♮ A natural cancels a sharp or flat

**nocturne** A 'night-piece', tuneful but sad.

**octave** Interval made up of eight successive notes of scale, from one note to note of same name, above or below.

**oratorio** Religious musical composition for soloists, chorus and orchestra, but without costume or scenery.

**percussion instruments** Instruments that are struck; they include drums, tambourine, cymbals, bells, glockenspiel, xylophone, vibraphone, marimba, triangle, gong and castanets.

**piano** Played or sung softly.

**pitch** Highness or lowness in sound of one note compared with another.

**plainsong** Unaccompanied vocal melody used in medieval church music.

**presto** At a fast pace.

**romantic music** Music (mainly 19th century) that plays on the emotions.

**scale** Progression of successive notes ascending or descending.

**score** Written music showing all parts (vocal and instrumental) of composition on separate staves.

**semitone** A half-tone; smallest interval commonly used in western music.

▽ Tuba (brass family).

▽ Throughout history, drums have often been regarded as sacred instruments.

**sharp** Conventional sign indicating that note referred to has been raised in pitch by a semitone.

**sonata** Musical piece, usually for one or two players, following the sonata-form; made up of exposition, development, and recapitulation.

**soprano** Highest female voice.

**stave** or **staff** Framework of lines and spaces on which music is usually written.

**stringed instruments** Instruments that are played with a bow (violins, violas, cellos, double basses).

**symphony** Large orchestral piece of music of a serious nature, usually in four movements.

**tempo** Pace or speed of piece of music.

**tenor** Highest natural male voice.

**treble** Upper part of a composition; a high voice, usually of children.

**virtuoso** Musician of outstanding technical skill.

**woodwind instruments** Instruments that are blown and are traditionally, but not always, made of wood; they include flute, oboe, clarinet, piccolo, recorder, saxophone, bassoon and English horn (cor anglais).

## THE TONIC SOL-FA

The tonic sol-fa is a method of musical notation using letters and syllables instead of notes on a stave. It was devised by the English musician John Curwen (1816–1880), who based it on the system known as solmization used in the middle ages.

The eight notes of a major scale are denoted by the syllables doh, re, mi, fah, soh (or sol), lah, te, doh. It works for any scale by just changing the note which represents doh. Sharpened and flattened notes are indicated by changing the vowel sounds (for example, sol sharp is se, and te flat is taw).

## GREAT COMPOSERS

**Bach, Johann Sebastian** (1685–1750)
German composer born at Eisenach; the most
distinguished in a long line of musicians.
Bach's vast output can be divided into three
groups: organ works; instrumental and
orchestral works; and religious choral works.

**Beethoven, Ludwig van** (1770–1827)
German composer, one of the outstanding
figures of Western music. His symphonies,
overtures, concertos, piano sonatas and
string quartets are considered some of the
world's greatest.

▽ Beethoven's early music was influenced
by Mozart and Haydn.

**Brahms, Johannes** (1833–97) German
composer. His works include four
symphonies, two piano concertos, a violin
concerto and a double concerto (violin and
cello), chamber music, piano music and many
songs and choral compositions.

**Britten, Benjamin** (1913–76) One of the
outstanding 20th century British composers,
and a brilliant pianist, Britten was especially
noted for his operas, choral music and songs.

**Chopin, Fryderyk**, or **Frédéric** (1810–49)
Polish piano virtuoso and composer, known
almost entirely for piano music.

**Dvořák, Antonín** (1841–1904) Czech
composer. From 1892–5 was in the United
States as Director of the National
Conservatory in New York, where he wrote
his best-known work, the symphony *From the
New World*.

**Gershwin, George** (1898–1937) American
composer and pianist whose combination of
American styles (jazz and blues) with
impressionist harmony was a major influence
on 20th century American music.

▽ German composer, George Frideric
Handel (1685–1759).

**Handel, George Frideric** (1685–1759)
German-born composer of Italian operas and,
later, oratorios (music dramas) mainly on
religious themes; *Messiah* is the most
famous. Handel also wrote many
instrumental compositions.

**Haydn, Franz Joseph** (1732–1809) Prolific
Austrian composer whose development of
the sonata-symphony form and style earned
him the title of 'Father of the Symphony'.

**Mahler, Gustav** (1860–1911) Bohemian-
born composer noted for his symphonies,
written in late German-romantic style.

**Mozart, Wolfgang Amadeus** (1756–1791)
Austrian composer, born in Salzburg. As a
child prodigy, he toured Europe giving piano
recitals with his sister and father. For speed
and ease of composition Mozart was
unrivalled, producing in his short life over 600
works.

**Schubert, Franz Peter** (1797–1828)
Austrian composer. In a career even shorter
than Mozart's. Schubert achieved a large
output ranging from symphonies and operas
to chamber music and over 500 songs.

**Stravinsky, Igor** (1882–1971) Russian-born
composer and one of the key figures of 20th
century music. Made his reputation with a
series of remarkable ballets, including *The
Firebird*, *Petrushka* and *The Rite of Spring*.

**Tchaikovsky, Peter Ilyich** (1840–93)
Russian composer, the first to become widely
popular outside his country. His work was
notable for its melodic flair, emotional
content and vivid orchestration.

△ Dame Kiri Te Kanawa

# OPERA

An opera is a play with music. The actors are singers who sing all or many of their words. An orchestra accompanies them. The first operas were performed in Italy nearly 400 years ago. Famous composers of serious operas include Mozart (*The Marriage of Figaro, The Magic Flute*); Verdi (*Aida, La Traviata*); Puccini (*Tosca, Madame Butterfly*); Wagner (*The Ring of the Nibelung*).

## SOME OPERATIC TERMS

**aria** (Italian, 'air') A solo.

**ballad opera** Simple kind of opera, made up of popular tunes interspersed with spoken dialogue.

**comic opera** Opera with a farcical plot.

**finale** Closing portion of act or opera; usually whole company sings together.

**folk opera** Opera based on folk music and folk tales.

**grand opera** Opera with libretto entirely set to music.

**intermezzo** Instrumental piece interposed between scenes or acts of opera, also called interlude.

**Leitmotiv** (German, 'leading motive') Short theme in opera that emphasizes by repetition an individual character, object or idea.

**libretto** Text of opera.

**opera buffa** Humorous opera, but not farcical as comic opera; typical is Rossini's *Barber of Seville*.

**opera seria** Serious opera, as distinct from opera buffa.

**operetta** Light opera based on amusing subjects and implying some spoken dialogue; nowadays often synonymous with musical comedy.

**patter song** Comical song made up of string of words and sung at high speed; Gilbert and Sullivan's operas include many songs of this type.

**prima donna** (Italian, 'first lady') Principal female singer in cast; or, more often, most famous or most highly paid; also called diva.

▽ The Opera House, Paris.

# BALLET

The ballet as it is danced today began in France, and during the reign of King Louis XIV (1600s) it was officially recognized as a form of art. Traditional or classical ballet follows strict rules – the five basic ballet positions were devised over 300 years ago. Some of the most famous classical ballets have been danced for many years. *Giselle*, for example, was first performed in 1841. Other long-time favourites are *Swan Lake* and *Sleeping Beauty*. Modern ballets include freer dance steps and often illustrate a mood or theme rather than telling a story.

△ Vaslav Nijinsky in *Le Spectre de la Rose* (1911).

◁ Modern classical ballet enjoys worldwide popularity, despite the high cost of production.

## SOME BALLET TERMS

**arabesque** Position in which dancer stands on one leg with arms extended, body bent forward from hips, while other leg is stretched out backwards.

**attitude** Position in which dancer stretches one leg backwards, bending it a little at the knee so that lower part of leg is parallel to floor.

**ballerina** Female ballet dancer.

**barre** Exercise bar fixed to classroom wall at hip level; dancers grasp it when exercising.

**battement** Beating movement made by raising and lowering leg, sideways, backwards or forwards.

**choreography** Art of dance composition.

**corps de ballet** Main body of ballet dancers, as distinct from soloists.

**entrechat** Leap in which dancer rapidly crosses and uncrosses feet in air.

**fouetté** Turn in which dancer whips free leg round.

**glissade** Gliding movement.

**jeté** Leap from one foot to another.

**pas** Any dance step.

**pas de deux** Dance for two.

**pas seule** Solo dance.

**pirouette** Movement in which dancer spins completely round on one foot.

**pointes** Tips of dancer's toes, on which many movements are executed.

**positions** Five positions of feet on which ballet is based.

**tutu** Short, stiff, spreading skirt worn in classical ballet.

## POPULAR MUSIC

Early popular music was what we now call 'folk music', but 'pop music' as we know it today largely developed from jazz. This was the music which grew mainly from work songs, religious songs and blues songs sung in the United States by Black slaves who came originally from Africa. During the 1940s popular music was 'swing', the music of the big bands. Then, in the 1950s, came 'rock and roll'. Performers such as Elvis Presley and, after him, the Beatles – at their peak from 1962 to 1970 – have influenced the course of popular music ever since.

▽ Jazz developed from marching band music and work songs. Originally played by Blacks, jazz rapidly became popular with Whites and developed into various styles including traditional Dixieland, big band or swing, mainstream and modern.

### SOME POPULAR MUSIC TERMS

**a cappella** In the world of popular music, singing unaccompanied, especially in groups.
**acoustic** Not electrically amplified.
**backing group** Group of singers who sing in support of a soloist.
**big bands** Dance bands of swing era (late 1930s and early 1940s), featuring many musicians and one or more vocalists.
**bluegrass** American country music played with a distinctive beat; line-up includes some or all of following: acoustic guitar, banjo, mandolin, fiddle, string bass.
**blues** Originally Black American folk music using 12-bar melodic section; usually vocal, the music is often slow and sad but it can be fast and exciting.

**calypso** Folk music of West Indies, usually sung, in 4/4 time.
**country and western, country** Topical and traditional rural music, mainly vocal and American, evolved from folk, blues and hillbilly music.
**cover version** Re-issue of a number, often to compete with the original.
**folk music, folk song** Music and ballads of the people, usually handed down from one generation to another.
**gig** One-night musical engagement.
**gospel music** Black American religious music, first sung in the churches of the southern states.
**jitterbugging** Improvised, all-in, athletic dancing, originating in late 1930s.

**jive** A later form of jitterbugging.
**mainstream jazz** Middle-of-the-road jazz that avoids extremes.
**New Wave** Movement beginning in the 1970s which included punk influences, offbeat arrangements, and also heavy rock.
**pop** Currently popular music or song, generally launched and performed with maximum publicity and with an eye to record sales.
**punk rock** Rock music with outrageous, often obscene, words, accompanied by equally outrageous behaviour by its performers.
**ragtime** Essentially Black American piano music based on rigidly syncopated pattern; had some influence on jazz.
**reggae** A West Indian type of rock jazz with simple 2-beat rhythm.
**rhythm and blues** Urban blues performed mainly by Black American musicians.
**rock, rock and roll, rock 'n' roll** Mixture of rhythm and blues with country and western, originating in 1950s with emphasis on the beat and body movements of dancers.
**soul music** Popular, often religious music written and performed by Blacks; used for dancing.
**spiritual** Religious folk song, usually of Black American origin (also white spirituals); generally superseded by gospel music.

△ A pop concert in support of South African black nationalist leader Nelson Mandela.

**steel bands** West Indian percussion bands, originating in Trinidad, that use as instruments the tops of oil drums, tuned to various pitches.
**swing** Commercialized jazz featured by the big bands.
**Tin Pan Alley** Originally 28th Street in New York City, where most of commercial song hits were published; today, term describes any well-known area of the pop publishing business.
**traditional jazz, trad** Jazz that adheres to traditional New Orleans style of highly improvised melodies.

△ The Beatles had 30 million-selling records between 1962 and 1970.

▽ Three of the stars from TV's ever-popular show M*A*S*H. From left to right: Alan Alda, Loretta Swit and Harry Morgan. Filming finished in 1983.

# Radio and Television

Television and radio broadcasting has developed even more recently than the cinema. The first advertised radio broadcast in the United States came in 1906, and in Great Britain in 1920. The world's first television service (from London's Alexandra Palace) did not begin until 1936. Now, nearly every home in Britain and America has both TV and radio, and for many people they are the main source of both news and entertainment.

Television programmes that combine entertainment with education have always been very popular. Special film-making techniques make it possible for us to see things, such as right inside a living colony of ants, that we are unlikely to observe in everyday life.

Most of us enjoy fantasy as entertainment, and absurd antics in cartoon films, such as those featuring Mickey Mouse or Tom and Jerry, are old favourites. In addition, as technology improved rapidly after World

War II, so it became possible to make TV programmes with special effects, for example, Star Trek and Dr Who, so that impossible things seem to happen, transporting us to make-believe worlds.

The use of satellites in space to transmit TV pictures even allows us to receive pictures of events on the other side of the world as they happen. The widespread use of video also means that many more people can make their own recordings to show on the television screen. A series of channels devoted to different subjects is now offered by cable television. Music, sport and natural history programmes are just three of the specialities that we can see on cable TV at any time.

With the advent of television, people probably listen to radio less nowadays. Radio remains, however, very important to people wanting frequent news broadcasts, imaginative programmes like plays or background listening while doing something at home.

△ A clever combination of puppetry and computer graphics produced the irreverent and zany character of Max Headroom – one of television's inanimate superstars.

194m medium wave
95·8 MHz VHF stereo

ALL THE HITS AND MORE

◁ Radio disc jockeys often do much more than just spin pop records. Interviews with performers, commentary on the records, and light-hearted banter all form part of their repertoire.

# Theatre

△ William Shakespeare, probably the greatest playwright in English. Surprisingly little is known about his life.

Actors have been performing plays in theatres since the time of the ancient Greeks, and some of the most famous plays are the tragedies by the Greek writers Aeschylus, Sophocles and Euripides. In Britain there were no proper theatres until the 1500s. Before then, troupes of actors travelled round the countryside performing plays outside churches or in market places. William Shakespeare (1564–1616) is probably England's greatest playwright, and the Elizabethan and Jacobean period in which he lived can be seen as the great age of the theatre in Britain.

## SOME GREAT DRAMATISTS

**Beckett, Samuel** (born 1906), Irish dramatist and novelist, became famous for plays that express the absurdity of human existence. The most important are *Waiting for Godot*, and *Endgame*.

**Chekhov, Anton** (1860–1904), Russian dramatist, whose plays include *Uncle Vanya*, *The Three Sisters* and *The Cherry Orchard*.

**Goethe, Johann Wolfgang von** (1749–1832), German poet, dramatist, and novelist, wrote several plays, including *Egmont* and his most famous work *Faust*, a long poetic drama in two parts. It tells the legendary story of a man who sells his soul to the Devil.

**Ibsen, Henrik** (1828–1906), Norwegian dramatist, known for his realistic, poetic and increasingly symbolic plays about problems of modern life. They include *Ghosts, A Doll's House* and *Hedda Gabler*.

**Molière** (Jean Baptiste Poquelin, 1622–73), French writer of comedies and actor, ran a theatre company for which he wrote many plays. The best include *The Bourgeois Gentleman, Tartuffe, The Misanthropist*.

**O'Neill, Eugene** (1888–1953), American dramatist, wrote a series of successful plays between 1920 and 1934, of which *Mourning Becomes Electra* is the best-known. His later plays include *The Iceman Cometh*.

**Shakespeare, William** (1564–1616), Probably Britain's greatest dramatist, also an actor and a writer of beautiful sonnets. His 36 plays include historical dramas, such as *Henry V* and *Julius Caesar;* comedies, *A Midsummer Night's Dream* and *The Taming of the Shrew;* tragedies, *Hamlet, King Lear,* and *Romeo and Juliet;* and fantasy romances, *The Tempest*.

△ A scene from *Le Bourgeois Gentilhomme*, by Molière.

△ The Globe Theatre, London, about 1600.

# SOME THEATRICAL TERMS

**cabaret** Entertainment performed while audience dines.

**epilogue** Speech made at the end of a play by one of the characters or by an actor representing the author.

**farce** Kind of comic play based on a series of hilariously improbable events. For example the farces of Georges Feydeau and Arthur Wing Pinero.

**kitchen-sink drama** Realistic plays of the mid-1950s about the lives of working-class people. For example Arnold Wesker's *Chicken Soup with Barley.*

**melodrama** Play with a sensational plot and exaggerated emotion. For example *The Bells* by Leopold Lewis.

**mime** Art of acting without words. Marcel Marceau is a famous mime artist.

**music hall** Kind of theatre from the 1850s to World War I, which presented variety entertainment consisting of comic acts, acrobats, songs and dances.

**mystery play** Religious play of the 1300s and 1400s presenting a scene from the Bible. Also called a miracle play.

**pantomime** Christmas entertainment based loosely on a fairy story, such as *Cinderella,* but with modern songs and topical jokes.

**passion play** Religious play about the Crucifixion performed on Good Friday in Middle Ages. A famous passion play is still performed every ten years at Oberammergau in southern Germany.

**prologue** Speech made at the beginning of a play by one of the characters or by an actor representing the author.

**props,** or **properties** Small objects needed on the stage to make a play realistic, such as cups, flowers and newspapers, but not furniture or scenery.

**repertory** Collection of plays that a company performs in a season.

**revue** Theatre entertainment popular since the 1890s and consisting of a series of songs, short acted scenes and dances.

**son et lumière** Open-air entertainment at a place of historical interest. The history of the place is told over loudspeakers while relevant features are lit up.

**theatre-in-the-round** Theatre in which the stage is surrounded by the audience.

**theatre of the absurd** Kind of drama of the 1950s portraying the absurd human existence on Earth, such as plays by Samuel Beckett, Harold Pinter and Eugène Ionesco.

**thriller** Play with an exciting plot, usually including crime with murder.

**tragedy** Play with an unhappy ending.

▽ Cutaway view of a large modern theatre.

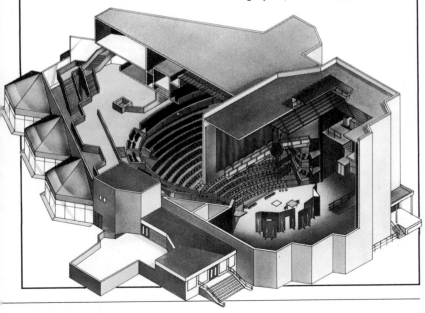

# Cinema

The first moving pictures came from an invention called the kinetoscope, built by an American, Thomas Edison, in 1891. Shortly afterwards, Auguste and Louis Lumière built their cinematographe, which projected pictures from a piece of film on to a screen. Early films were black and white, movements were jerky and they had no sound. At first they showed only real events, but soon filmmakers began to invent their own stories and use actors. By the end of World War I (1914–18), Hollywood in California had become the film-making capital of the world, as it still is today. The first moving picture with sound was the *Jazz Singer* (1927).

△ Charlie Chaplin made film clowning an art.

## SOME FILM-MAKING TERMS

**close-up** Picture taken near the subject.
**dolly** Mobile carriage to carry a camera.
**dubbing** Adding sound to a film.
**freeze** A shot held so that the action seems to stop.
**flash-back** Interruption in the story of a film to recall a past event.
**intercut shots** Two related series of shots shown alternately, such as the heroine tied to the railway lines and the train approaching.
**library shot** Film taken from material already made and in stock.
**long shot** A shot taken from a distance.
**pan** Short for panoramic shot – a sideways sweep by the camera.

**prop** Short for property – an object used by an actor, such as a gun or a telephone.
**rushes** The day's shots, before editing.
**scenario** Scene-by-scene outline of a film script.
**set** Area prepared for a film scene, either in a studio or outside.
**shooting** Filming a scene.
**take** Part of a scene shot without interruption.
**track in, track back** Move a camera on its dolly towards or away from the subject.
**zooming** Using a variable lens to give the effect of tracking in or back.

▽ *Gone with the Wind* starring Clark Gable and Vivien Leigh, broke all box-office records.

## ACADEMY AWARDS

| Year | Best film | Best actor | Best actress | Best director |
|------|-----------|------------|--------------|---------------|
| 1927–28 | Wings | Emil Jannings (The Way of All Flesh and The Last Command) | Janet Gaynor (Seventh Heaven; Street Angel; and Sunrise) | Frank Borzage (Seventh Heaven), Lewis Milestone (Two Arabian Knights) |
| 1928–29 | The Broadway Melody | Warner Baxter (In Old Arizona) | Mary Pickford (Coquette) | Frank Lloyd (The Divine Lady) |
| 1929–30 | All Quiet on the Western Front | George Arliss (Disraeli) | Norma Shearer (The Divorcee) | Lewis Milestone (All Quiet on the Western Front) |
| 1930–31 | Cimarron | Lionel Barrymore (A Free Soul) | Marie Dressler (Min and Bull) | Norman Taurog (Skippy) |
| 1931–32 | Grand Hotel | Frederic March (Dr Jekyll and Mr Hyde), Wallace Beery (The Champ) | Helen Hayes (The Sin of Madelon Claudet) | Frank Borzage (Bad Girl) |
| 1932–33 | Cavalcade | Charles Laughton (The Private Life of Henry VIII) | Katharine Hepburn (Morning Glory) | Frank Lloyd (Cavalcade) |
| 1934 | It Happened One Night | Clark Gable (It Happened One Night) | Claudette Colbert (It Happened One Night) | Frank Capra (It Happened One Night) |
| 1935 | Mutiny on the Bounty | Victor McLaglen (The Informer) | Bette Davis (Dangerous) | John Ford (The Informer) |
| 1936 | The Great Ziegfeld | Paul Muni (The Story of Louis Pasteur) | Luise Rainer (The Great Ziegfield) | Frank Capra (Mr Deeds Goes to Town) |
| 1937 | The Life of Émile Zola | Spencer Tracy (Captains Courageous) | Luise Rainer (The Good Earth) | Leo McCarey (The Awful Truth) |
| 1938 | You Can't Take It With You | **Spencer Tracy** (Boys' Town) | Bette Davis (Jezebel) | Frank Capra (You Can't Take It With You) |
| 1939 | Gone With the Wind | Robert Donat (Goodbye Mr Chips) | Vivien Leigh (Gone With the Wind) | Victor Fleming (Gone With the Wind) |
| 1940 | Rebecca | James Stewart (The Philadelphia Story) | Ginger Rogers (Kitty Foyle) | John Ford (Grapes of Wrath) |
| 1941 | How Green Was My Valley | Gary Cooper (Sergeant York) | Joan Fontaine (Suspicion) | John Ford (How Green Was My Valley) |
| 1942 | Mrs Miniver | James Cagney (Yankee Doodle Dandy) | Greer Garson (Mrs Miniver) | William Wyler (Mrs Miniver) |
| 1943 | Casablanca | Paul Lukas (Watch on the Rhine) | Jennifer Jones (The Song of Bernadette) | Michael Curtiz (Casablanca) |
| 1944 | Going My Way | Bing Crosby (Going My Way) | Ingrid Bergman (Gaslight) | Leo McCarey (Going My Way) |
| 1945 | The Lost Weekend | Ray Milland (The Lost Weekend) | Joan Crawford (Mildred Pierce) | Billy Wilder (The Lost Weekend) |

| Year | Best film | Best actor | Best actress | Best director |
|------|-----------|------------|--------------|---------------|
| 1946 | The Best Years of Our Lives | Frederic March (The Best Years of Our Lives) | Olivia de Havilland (To Each His Own) | William Wyler (The Best Years of Our Lives) |
| 1947 | Gentleman's Agreement | Ronald Colman (A Double Life) | Loretta Young (The Farmer's Daughter) | Elia Kazan (Gentleman's Agreement) |
| 1948 | Hamlet | Laurence Olivier (Hamlet) | Jane Wyman (Johnny Belinda) | John Huston (The Treasure of Sierra Madre) |
| 1949 | All the King's Men | Broderick Crawford (All the King's Men) | Olivia de Havilland (The Heiress) | Joseph L. Mankiewicz (A Letter to Three Wives) |
| 1950 | All About Eve | Jose Ferrer (Cyrano de Bergerac) | Judy Holliday (Born Yesterday) | Joseph L. Mankiewicz (All About Eve) |
| 1951 | An American in Paris | Humphrey Bogart (The African Queen) | Vivien Leigh (A Streetcar Named Desire) | George Stevens (A Place in the Sun) |
| 1952 | The Greatest Show on Earth | Gary Cooper (High Noon) | Shirley Booth (Come Back, Little Sheba) | John Ford (The Quiet Man) |
| 1953 | From Here to Eternity | William Holden (Stalag 17) | Audrey Hepburn (Roman Holiday) | Fred Zinnemann (From Here to Eternity) |
| 1954 | On the Waterfront | Marlon Brando (On the Waterfront) | Grace Kelly (The Country Girl) | Elia Kazan (On the Waterfront) |
| 1955 | Marty | Ernest Borgnine (Marty) | Anna Magnani (The Rose Tattoo) | Delbert Mann (Marty) |

▽ Marlon Brando, in *On the Waterfront*, for which he won an Oscar.

▽ Katherine Hepburn, in *The Philadelphia Story*.

△ The hit musical *My Fair Lady* transferred from the stage to the screen in the 1960s.

| Year | Best film | Best actor | Best actress | Best director |
|------|-----------|------------|--------------|---------------|
| 1956 | *Around the World in 80 Days* | Yul Brynner *(The King and I)* | Ingrid Bergman *(Anastasia)* | George Stevens *(Giant)* |
| 1957 | *The Bridge on the River Kwai* | Alec Guiness *(The Bridge on the River Kwai)* | Joanne Woodward *(The Three Faces of Eve)* | David Lean *(The Bridge on the River Kwai)* |
| 1958 | *Gigi* | David Niven *(Separate Tables)* | Susan Hayward *(I Want to Live)* | Vincente Minnelli *(Gigi)* |
| 1959 | *Ben-Hur* | Charlton Heston *(Ben-Hur)* | Simone Signoret *(Room at the Top)* | William Wyler *(Ben-Hur)* |
| 1960 | *The Apartment* | Burt Lancaster *(Elmer Gantry)* | Elizabeth Taylor *(Butterfield 8)* | Billy Wilder *(The Apartment)* |
| 1961 | *West Side Story* | Maximilian Schell *(Judgment at Nuremberg)* | Sophia Loren *(Two Women)* | Robert Wise & Jerome Robbins *(West Side Story)* |
| 1962 | *Lawrence of Arabia* | Gregory Peck *(To Kill a Mockingbird)* | Anne Bancroft *(The Miracle Worker)* | David Lean *(Lawrence of Arabia)* |
| 1963 | *Tom Jones* | Sidney Poitier *(Lilies of the Field)* | Patricia Neal *(Hud)* | Tony Richardson *(Tom Jones)* |
| 1964 | *My Fair Lady* | Rex Harrison *(My Fair Lady)* | Julie Andrews *(Mary Poppins)* | George Cukor *(My Fair Lady)* |
| 1965 | *The Sound of Music* | Lee Marvin *(Cat Ballou)* | Julie Christie *(Darling)* | Robert Wise *(The Sound of Music)* |
| 1966 | *A Man for All Seasons* | Paul Scofield *(A Man for All Seasons)* | Elizabeth Taylor *(Who's Afraid of Virginia Woolf?)* | Fred Zinnemann *(A Man for All Seasons)* |

△ A scene from the 1979 Oscar-winning movie *Cabaret*.

| Year | Best film | Best actor | Best actress | Best director |
|------|-----------|------------|--------------|---------------|
| 1967 | *In the Heat of the Night* | Rod Steiger *(In the Heat of the Night)* | Katharine Hepburn *(Guess Who's Coming to Dinner)* | Mike Nichols *(The Graduate)* |
| 1968 | *Oliver* | Cliff Robertson *(Charly)* | Katharine Hepburn *(A Lion in Winter),* Barbra Streisand *(Funny Girl)* | Sir Carol Reed *(Oliver)* |
| 1969 | *Midnight Cowboy* | John Wayne *(True Grit)* | Maggie Smith *(The Prime of Miss Jean Brodie)* | John Schlesinger *(Midnight Cowboy)* |
| 1970 | *Patton* | George C. Scott *(Patton)* | Glenda Jackson *(Women in Love)* | Franklin J. Schaffner *(Patton)* |
| 1971 | *The French Connection* | Gene Hackman *(The French Connection)* | Jane Fonda *(Klute)* | William Friedkin *(The French Connection)* |
| 1972 | *The Godfather* | Marlon Brando *(The Godfather)* | Liza Minnelli *(Cabaret)* | Robert Fosse *(Cabaret)* |
| 1973 | *The Sting* | Jack Lemon *(Save the Tiger)* | Glenda Jackson *(A Touch of Class)* | George Roy Hill *(The Sting)* |
| 1974 | *The Godfather Part II* | Art Carney *(Harry and Tonto)* | Ellen Burstyn *(Alice Doesn't Live Here Any More)* | Francis Ford Coppola *(The Godfather Part II)* |
| 1975 | *One Flew Over the Cuckoo's Nest* | Jack Nicholson *(One Flew Over the Cuckoo's Nest)* | Louise Fletcher *(One Flew Over the Cuckoo's Nest)* | Milos Forman *(One Flew Over the Cuckoo's Nest)* |
| 1976 | *Rocky* | Peter Finch *(Network)* | Faye Dunaway *(Network)* | John G. Avildsen *(Rocky)* |
| 1977 | *Annie Hall* | Richard Dreyfus *The (Goodbye Girl)* | Diane Keaton *(Annie Hall)* | Woody Allen *(Annie Hall)* |

| Year | Best film | Best actor | Best actress | Best director |
|---|---|---|---|---|
| 1978 | *The Deer Hunter* | John Voight *(Coming Home)* | Jane Fonda *(Coming Home)* | Michael Cimino *(The Deer Hunter)* |
| 1979 | *Kramer Vs Kramer* | Dustin Hoffman *(Kramer Vs Kramer)* | Sally Field *(Norma Rae)* | Robert Benton *(Kramer Vs Kramer)* |
| 1980 | *Ordinary People* | Robert De Niro *(Raging Bull)* | Sissy Spacek *(Coalminer's Daughter)* | Robert Redford *(Ordinary People)* |
| 1981 | *Chariots of Fire* | Henry Fonda *(On Golden Pond)* | Katharine Hepburn *(On Golden Pond)* | Warren Beatty *(Reds)* |
| 1982 | *Gandhi* | Ben Kingsley *(Gandhi)* | Meryl Streep *(Sophie's Choice)* | Sir Richard Attenborough *(Gandhi)* |
| 1983 | *Terms of Endearment* | Robert Duval *(Tender Mercies)* | Shirley MacLaine *(Terms of Endearment)* | James L. Brooks *(Terms of Endearment)* |
| 1984 | *Amadeus* | F. Murray Abraham *(Amadeus)* | Sally Field *(Places in the Heart)* | Milos Forman *(Amadeus)* |
| 1985 | *Out of Africa* | William Hurt *(Kiss of the Spider Woman)* | Geraldine Page *(The Trip to Bountiful)* | Sydney Pollack *(Out of Africa)* |
| 1986 | *Platoon* | Paul Newman *(The Color of Money)* | Marlee Matlin *(Children of a lesser God)* | Oliver Stone *(Platoon)* |
| 1987 | *The Last Emperor* | Michael Douglas *(Wall Street)* | Cher *(Moonstruck)* | Bernard Bertolucci *(The Last Emperor)* |
| 1988 | *Rain Man* | Dustin Hoffman *(Rain Man)* | Jodie Foster *(The Accused)* | Barry Levinson *(Rain Man)* |

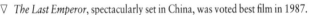

▽ *The Last Emperor*, spectacularly set in China, was voted best film in 1987.

# Sport

**Practising sports gives people a chance to engage in mental or physical combat with one another, to improve their fitness and prowess, or just to exercise and have fun. The first organized sports were the Olympics, where athletes competed for crowns of laurels. Today, with huge money prizes and worldwide fame for the champions, sports are taken every bit as seriously as when they were first thought of as a training for warriors.**

Sports range from baseball to billiards, from boxing to chess. Dozens of different sporting activities can help to make us faster, stronger, more agile or more skilful. The best sportsmen and sportswomen compete for prizes or to break sporting records, but most of us just play for fun. Early on, though, sports were not for amusement. More than 2,000 years ago athletic sports trained men for hunting or war.

Ancient Greeks were the first to hold sports festivals for friendly competition. The original Olympic Games began as early as 776BC. Athletes raced one another on foot. They also

△ Discus-throwing was one of the pentathlon events in the ancient Greek Olympics.

◁ The Olympic flame, carried from Greece, symbolizes the modern Games.

boxed, long-jumped and hurled the discus and javelin. Ancient Greece was the first home of what we now call track and field athletics. But Rome conquered Greece and in AD394 put an end to its Games.

Organized sports stayed almost unknown through Europe's Dark Ages, about AD400–1000. Meanwhile, India or Persia invented chess, and horseracing flourished in the Middle East.

In the Middle Ages, Europe's main sports were archery contests and combat sports between knights fighting on foot or mounted. In the 1400s football began as a game where crowds brawled over a ball, and the Scots played an early form of golf. Germans rolled stones to knock over wooden clubs. The Dutch called the game skittles and took it to North America in the 1600s. In 1841 the original game, played with nine pins, was banned in Connecticut because of gambling. So the players added an extra pin, and tenpin bowling started.

Modern sports truly took shape only in the 1700s and 1800s. In the new Industrial Age millions of people gained the spare time and money to enjoy organized sports. This first

△ A marathon race, traditionally run over 42.19 km (26 miles 385 yards). Major city marathons attract thousands of runners of all levels of ability.

▽ Medieval knights in mock-combat. Jousting at tournaments trained soldiers in warlike skills.

Kendo

Judo

Karate

△ Martial arts, such as judo, karate and kendo, were originally developed for combat, but have been refined for modern sports competition.

▷ Equestrian sports include horse racing, show jumping and eventing. Horse and rider are tested equally.

happened in Great Britain, where the Industrial Age started. By the mid 1800s fast steam trains could carry sports teams to play far-off rivals. As sports became popular, organizations laid down rules for them. In 1863 the Football Association largely fixed the rules for association football (soccer). A year later the MCC (Marylebone Cricket Club) legalized overarm bowling in cricket. Cricket had begun in England, supposedly when shepherds used their *cricc* (crook) as a bat to hit balls bowled at their sheep-pen's wicket gate. By 1900 sports and sports rules invented in Europe or North America had spread to countries around the world.

Some sports were old ones revived. Track and field athletics events reappeared in the modern Olympic Games, first held in Greece in 1896. German schools that taught physical fitness brought back gymnastics. New rules improved many old sports. (Boxers wear gloves and fight rounds with rests in between thanks to rules laid down in 1867.)

Brand new sports appeared, too. In 1823 a boy at Rugby School, England, picked up a football and ran holding it. So rugby football was born. Rugby, in turn, led to American football. In much the same way American

youngsters invented baseball by changing the rules used in cricket and rounders. In the late 1800s old racket games gave rise to badminton, squash and lawn tennis. Figure skating dates from the 1860s and basketball from 1891. By 1900 the French were racing the newly developed cars and motorcycles.

Competition grew stronger once aeroplanes could whisk the world's best sportsmen and women to international contests anywhere on Earth. As standards improved, people broke old sporting records again and again. In 1896 the 1,500 metres (Olympic mile) was run in 4 minutes 33.2 seconds. By 1985 more than a minute had been lopped off that time. In 1896 the long jump record stood at under 21 feet (6.4 metres). Since then the distance has increased by nearly half as much again. Year by year old records tumble to new world champions.

Since 1900 sports of all kinds have become ever more popular. Now, millions of us swim, run, skate, row or play some form of ball game. Millions more watch ball games and races on television or go to sports contests on circuits and in stadiums.

△ American long jumper, Ralph Boston, jumping over 27 ft (8.2 m) in his bid for the world record at the Los Angeles Olympic Games.

▽ Pole vaulters use fibreglass poles to clear the bar.

# Athletics

## MEN'S WORLD RECORDS

| | | | |
|---|---|---|---|
| 100 metres | 9.83 sec | Ben Johnson (Canada) | 30.8.87 |
| 200 metres | 19.72 sec | Pietro Mennea (Italy) | 12.9.79 |
| 400 metres | 43.29 sec | 'Butch' Reynolds (USA) | 17.8.88 |
| 800 metres | 1 min 41.73 sec | Sebastian Coe (GB) | 10.6.81 |
| 1,000 metres | 2 min 12.18 sec | Sebastian Coe (GB) | 11.7.81 |
| 1,500 metres | 3 min 29.46 sec | Saïd Aouita (Morocco) | 23.8.85 |
| 1 mile | 3 min 46.32 sec | Steven Cram (GB) | 27.7.85 |
| 2,000 metres | 4 min 50.81 sec | Saïd Aouita (Morocco) | 16.7.87 |
| 3,000 metres | 7 min 32.1 sec | Henry Rono (Kenya) | 27.6.78 |
| 5,000 metres | 12 min 58.39 sec | Saïd Aouita (Morocco) | 22.7.87 |
| 10,000 metres | 27 min 13.81 sec | Fernando Mamede (Portugal) | 2.7.84 |
| Marathon* | 2 hr 6 min 50 sec | Belayneh Dinsamo (Ethiopia) | 17.4.88 |
| 110 metres hurdles | 12.93 sec | Renaldo Nehemiah (USA) | 19.8.81 |
| 400 metres hurdles | 47.02 sec | Ed Moses (USA) | 31.8.83 |
| 3,000 m steeplechase | 8 min 5.4 sec | Henry Rono (Kenya) | 13.5.78 |
| 4 × 100 metres relay | 37.83 sec | United States | 11.8.84 |
| 4 × 400 metres relay | 2 min 56.16 sec | United States | 20.10.68 |
| High jump | 2.36 m (7 ft 8¾ in) | Gerd Wessig (W Germany) | 1.8.80 |
| Pole vault | 6.06 m (19 ft 10½ in) | Sergey Bubka (USSR) | 10.7.88 |
| Long jump | 8.90 m (29 ft 2½ in) | Bob Beamon (USA) | 18.10.68 |
| Triple jump | 17.97 m (58 ft 11 in) | 'Willie' Banks (USA) | 16.6.85 |
| Shot put | 23.06 m (75 ft 8 in) | Ulf Timmerman (E Germany) | 22.5.88 |
| Discus throw | 74.08 m (243 ft) | Jürgen Schult (E Germany) | 6.6.86 |
| Hammer throw | 86.74 m (284 ft 7 in) | Yuriy Sedykh (USSR) | 30.8.86 |
| Javelin throwt | 87.66 m (287 ft 7 in) | Jan Zelezny (Czech) | 31.5.87 |
| Decathlon | 8847 points | 'Daley' Thompson (GB) | 8–9.8.84 |

## WOMEN'S WORLD RECORDS

| | | | |
|---|---|---|---|
| 100 metres | 10.49 sec | Florence Griffith-Joyner (USA) | 16.7.88 |
| 200 metres | 21.71 sec | Marita Koch (E Germany) | 10.6.79 |
| 400 metres | 47.60 sec | Marita Koch (E Germany) | 6.10.85 |
| 800 metres | 1 min 53.28 sec | Jarmila Kratochvilova (Czech) | 26.7.83 |
| 1,000 metres | 2 min 30.60 sec | Tatyana Providokhina (USSR) | 20.8.78 |
| 1,500 metres | 3 min 52.47 sec | Tatyana Kazankina (USSR) | 13.8.80 |
| 1 mile | 4 min 16.71 sec | Mary Slaney (USA) | 21.8.85 |
| 2,000 metres | 5 min 28.69 sec | Maricica Puica (Romania) | 11.7.86 |
| 3,000 metres | 8 min 22.62 sec | Tatyana Kazankina (USSR) | 26.8.84 |
| 5,000 metres | 14 min 37.33 sec | Ingrid Kristiansen (Norway) | 5.8.86 |
| 10,000 metres | 30 min 13.74 sec | Ingrid Kristiansen (Norway) | 5.7.86 |
| Marathon* | 2 hr 21 min 6 sec | Ingrid Kristiansen (Norway) | 21.4.85 |
| 100 metres hurdles | 12.29 sec | Sally Gunnell (GB) | 17.8.88 |
| 400 metres hurdles | 52.94 sec | Marina Styepanova (USSR) | 17.9.86 |
| 4 × 100 metres relay | 41.37 sec | East Germany | 6.10.85 |
| 4 × 400 metres relay | 3 min 15.17 sec | USSR | 1.10.88 |
| High jump | 2.09 m (6 ft 10¼ in) | Stefka Kostadinova (Bulgaria) | 30.8.87 |
| Long jump | 7.52 m (24 ft 8¼ in) | Galina Chistyakova (USSR) | 11.6.88 |
| Shot put | 22.63 m (74 ft 3 in) | Natalya Lisovskaya (USSR) | 7.6.87 |
| Discus throw | 76.80 m (252 ft) | Gabriele Reinsch (E Germany) | 9.7.88 |
| Javelin throw | 78.90 m (258 ft 10 in) | Petra Felke (E Germany) | 29.7.87 |
| Heptathlon | 7,291 points | Jackie Joyner-Kersee (USA) | 16–17.8.88 |

*World best time (courses vary)*     †*New javelin*

△ Heide Rosendahl (West Germany) competing in the hurdles.

## 1988 OLYMPICS MEDAL TABLE

| | G | S | B | Total | | G | S | B | Total |
|---|---|---|---|---|---|---|---|---|---|
| USSR | 55 | 31 | 46 | 132 | Spain | 1 | 1 | 2 | 4 |
| East Germany | 37 | 35 | 30 | 102 | Switzerland | 0 | 2 | 2 | 4 |
| United States | 36 | 31 | 27 | 94 | Morocco | 1 | 0 | 2 | 3 |
| West Germany | 11 | 14 | 15 | 40 | Turkey | 1 | 1 | 0 | 2 |
| Bulgaria | 10 | 12 | 13 | 35 | Jamaica | 0 | 2 | 0 | 2 |
| South Korea | 12 | 10 | 11 | 33 | Argentina | 0 | 1 | 1 | 2 |
| China | 5 | 11 | 12 | 28 | Belgium | 0 | 0 | 2 | 2 |
| Romania | 7 | 11 | 6 | 24 | Mexico | 0 | 0 | 2 | 2 |
| Great Britain | 5 | 10 | 9 | 24 | Austria | 1 | 0 | 0 | 1 |
| Hungary | 11 | 6 | 6 | 23 | Portugal | 1 | 0 | 0 | 1 |
| France | 6 | 4 | 6 | 16 | Surinam | 1 | 0 | 0 | 1 |
| Poland | 2 | 5 | 9 | 16 | Chile | 0 | 1 | 0 | 1 |
| Italy | 6 | 4 | 4 | 14 | Costa Rica | 0 | 1 | 0 | 1 |
| Japan | 4 | 3 | 7 | 14 | Indonesia | 0 | 1 | 0 | 1 |
| Australia | 3 | 6 | 5 | 14 | Iran | 0 | 1 | 0 | 1 |
| New Zealand | 3 | 2 | 8 | 13 | Dutch Antilles | 0 | 1 | 0 | 1 |
| Yugoslavia | 3 | 4 | 5 | 12 | Peru | 0 | 1 | 0 | 1 |
| Sweden | 0 | 4 | 7 | 11 | Senegal | 0 | 1 | 0 | 1 |
| Canada | 3 | 2 | 5 | 10 | US Virgin Islands | 0 | 1 | 0 | 1 |
| Kenya | 5 | 2 | 2 | 9 | Colombia | 0 | 0 | 1 | 1 |
| Netherlands | 2 | 2 | 5 | 9 | Djibouti | 0 | 0 | 1 | 1 |
| Czechoslovakia | 3 | 3 | 2 | 8 | Greece | 0 | 0 | 1 | 1 |
| Brazil | 1 | 2 | 3 | 6 | Mongolia | 0 | 0 | 1 | 1 |
| Norway | 2 | 3 | 0 | 5 | Pakistan | 0 | 0 | 1 | 1 |
| Denmark | 2 | 1 | 1 | 4 | Philippines | 0 | 0 | 1 | 1 |
| Finland | 1 | 1 | 2 | 4 | Thailand | 0 | 0 | 1 | 1 |

△ The shuttlecock used in competition badminton is made of feathers.

# Badminton

**Court** 13.4 × 6.1 m (44 × 20 ft); *singles* 13.4 × 5.2 m (44 × 17 ft)
**Height of net** 1.55 m (5 ft 1 in)
**Weight of shuttlecock** 4.73–5.50 g
**Scoring** best of 3 or 5 15-pt games (men); best of 3 11-pt games (women)
**Ruling body** International Badminton Federation (IBF)
**World team championships** Thomas Cup (men); Uber Cup (women)
**Major individual competitions** World championships; All-England Championships

# Baseball

**Pitching distance** 18.4 m (60 ft 6 in)
**Side of 'diamond'** 27.4 m (90 ft)
**Max. length of bat** 1.07 m (3 ft 6 in)
**Diameter of ball** 7 cm (2¾ in)
**Weight of ball** 142–149 g (5–5¼ oz)
**Number per side** 9 (substitutes allowed)
**No. of innings** 9 or more (played to finish)

△ A baseball bat is cylindrical, and hitting the ball cleanly demands an excellent eye.

▽ The cue used in billiards and snooker. The modern two-piece cue unscrews in the middle.

# Basketball

**Court** 26 × 14 m (85 × 46 ft)
**Height of baskets** 3.05 m (10 ft)
**Diameter of baskets** 46 cm (18 in)
**Circumference of ball** 75–78 cm (29½–30½ in)
**Weight of ball** 600–650 g (21–23 oz)
**Duration** 40 min actual play (2 × 20) plus periods of 5 min until result is obtained
**No. per side** 5 (usually up to 5 substitutes)
**Ruling body** Fédération Internationale de Basketball Amateur (FIBA)
**Major competitions** World championships (men and women) and Olympic Games

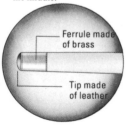

Ferrule made of brass

Tip made of leather

# Billiards and Snooker

**Table** 3.66 × 1.86 m (12 ft × 6 ft 1½ in)
**Diameter of balls** 5.25 cm (2¹/₁₆ in)
**Billiards** red, white, spot white
**Billiards scoring** pot or in-off red 3, white 2; cannon 2
**Snooker balls (value)** black (7), pink (6), blue (5), brown (4), green (3), yellow (2), 15 reds (1 each), white (cue-ball)
**Ruling body** Billiards and Snooker Control Council
**Major competitions** World championships (for both snooker and billiards, professional and amateur)

The 'points' of a cue

Shaft

Length at least 910 mm (3 ft)

Butt

Two part cues screw together here

# Bowls (flat green)

**Rink (max.)** 40.2 × 5.8 m (132 × 19 ft)
**Bowls** diam. (max.) 14.6 cm (5¾ in) biased, weight (max.) 1.59 kg (3½ lb), made of wood, rubber or composition
**Jack** diam. 6.35 cm (2½ in), weight 227–284 g (8–10 oz)
**Ruling body** International Bowling Board
**Events** singles (4 bowls each, 21 *shots* up), pairs (2–4 bowls each, 21 *ends*), triples (2 or 3 bowls each, 18 *ends*), fours (2 bowls each, 21 *ends*)
**World championships** – every 4 years

△ A boxing glove. The sport is banned in some countries.

# Boxing

### Professional

**Ring** 4.88–6.1 m (16–20 ft) square
**Gloves** 170 g (6 oz) fly to welter-weight, 227 g (8 oz) light-middleweight and above
**Duration** 6, 8, 10, 12 or 15 (title) 3-min rounds
**Ruling body** World Boxing Council (WBC)

### Amateur

**Ring** 3.66–6.1 m (12–20 ft) square
**Gloves** 227 g (8 oz)
**Duration** three 3-min rounds (seniors)
**Ruling body** Amateur International Boxing Association (AIBA)

| WEIGHT LIMITS | | | | |
|---|---|---|---|---|
| | WBC | | AIBA | |
| *Division* | *kg* | *st-lb* | *kg* | *st-lb* |
| Light-fly | — | — | 48.0 | 7–07 |
| Fly | 50.80 | 8–00 | 51.0 | 8–00 |
| Bantam | 53.52 | 8–06 | 54.0 | 8–07 |
| Feather | 57.15 | 9–00 | 57.0 | 9–00 |
| Junior light | 58.97 | 9–04 | — | — |
| Light | 61.24 | 9–09 | 60.0 | 9–07 |
| Junior welter | 63.50 | 10–00 | 63.5 | 10–00 |
| Welter | 66.68 | 10–00 | 67.0 | 10–08 |
| Junior middle | 69.85 | 11–00 | 71.0 | 11–02 |
| Middle | 72.58 | 11–06 | 75.0 | 11–11 |
| Light-heavy | 79.38 | 12–07 | 81.0 | 12–10 |
| Heavy | | no limit | 91.0 | 14–03 |

# Chess

**Ruling body** International Chess Federation

| WORLD CHAMPIONS | |
|---|---|
| 1866–1894 | Wilhelm Steinitz (Austria) |
| 1894–1921 | Emanuel Lasker (Germany) |
| 1921–1927 | Jose R. Capablanca (Cuba) |
| 1927–1935 | Alexander A. Alekhine (USSR*) |
| 1935–1937 | Max Euwe (Netherlands) |
| 1937–1946 | Alexander A. Alekhine (USSR*) |
| 1948–1957 | Mikhail Botvinnik (USSR) |
| 1957–1958 | Vassily Smyslov (USSR) |
| 1958–1959 | Mikhail Botvinnik (USSR) |
| 1960–1961 | Mikhail Tal (USSR) |
| 1961–1963 | Mikhail Botvinnik (USSR) |
| 1963–1969 | Tigran Petrosian (USSR) |
| 1969–1972 | Boris Spassky (USSR) |
| 1972–1975 | Bobby Fischer† (USA) |
| 1975–1985 | Anatoli Karpov (USSR) |
| 1985– | Gary Kasparov (USSR) |

*Took French citizenship
†Karpov won title when Fischer defaulted.

△ Chess pieces: (*from left*) Pawn, Rook, Knight, Bishop, Queen, King.

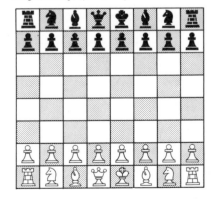

▷ A chess board at the start of play.

# Cricket

△ Cricket bat, ball, stumps and bails (the wicket), and batting pads. In the early years of cricket, bats were curved.

▽ A match in progress at Kent Cricket Club's ground. The batsman has just struck the ball while the wicket keeper covers the bails and fielders crouch in readiness for a catch.

**Pitch** wicket to wicket 20 m (22 yd), bowling crease 2.64 m (8 ft 8 in) wide

**Stumps** 71.1 cm (28 in) high, 22.9 cm (9 in) overall width

**Bat (max.)** 96.5 cm (38 in) long, 10.8 cm (4¼ in) wide

**Ball** circum., 22.4–22.9 cm (8¹³⁄₁₆–9 in), weight 156–163 g (5½–5¾ oz)

**No. per side** 11 (substitutes only for fielding)

**Ruling body** International Cricket Conference (ICC)

## Cricket records – Test matches

**Highest innings** 365* G S Sobers, W Indies (v Pakistan, Kingston, 1958)

**Most runs in series** 974 D G Bradman, Australia (v England, 1930) in **career** – 10,122 S Gavaskar, India

**Most hundreds in career** 34 S Gavaskar, India

**Best bowling in match** 19–90 J C Laker, England (v Aus., Old Trafford, 1956) **in innings** – 10–53 J C Laker, England (v Australia, Old Trafford, 1956)

**Most wickets in series** 49 S F Barnes, England (v S Africa, 1913–14) **in career** 395 R J Hadlee, New Zealand

**Highest partnership** 451 (2nd wkt) W H Ponsford (266) & D G Bradman (244), Australia (v England, Oval, 1934)

**Highest total** 903 (for 7) England (v Australia, Oval, 1938)

**Most wicket-keeping dismissals in career** 355 R W Marsh, Australia

**Most Test appearances** 125 S Gavaskar, India

### TEST MATCHES
(to Sep 1988)

| Country | Played | Won |
|---|---|---|
| Australia | 476 | 196 |
| England | 650 | 230 |
| India | 250 | 41 |
| New Zealand | 189 | 26 |
| Pakistan | 174 | 41 |
| South Africa | 172 | 38 |
| Sri Lanka | 26 | 2 |
| West Indies | 263 | 98 |

### OTHER EVENTS

Benson and Hedges World Series Cup
ICC Trophy
World Cup

**World Cup finals:**
1975 West Indies beat Australia
1979 West Indies beat England
1983 India beat West Indies
1987 Australia beat England

## Cricket records – all matches

**Highest innings** 499 Hanif Mohammad, Karachi (v Bahawalpur, 1959)

**Most runs in season** 3,816 D C S Compton, England and Middlesex, 1947; **in career** 61,237 J B Hobbs, England and Surrey

**Most hundreds in career** 197 J B Hobbs, England and Surrey

**Most runs in over** 36 G S Sobers, Nottinghamshire (v Glamorgan, Swansea, 1968) and R. J. Shastri, Bombay (v. Baroda, India, 1985).

**Best bowling in innings** 10–10 H Verity, Yorkshire (v Nottinghamshire, Leeds, 1932)

**Most wickets in season** 304 A P Freeman, England and Kent, 1928; **in career** 4,187 W Rhodes, England and Yorkshire

**Highest partnership** 577 (4th wkt) V S Hazare (288) and Gul Mahomed (319), Baroda (v Holkar, Baroda, 1947)

**Highest total** 1,107 (all out) Victoria (v NSW, Melbourne, 1926)

**Most wicket-keeping dismissals in career** 1,648 R W Taylor, England and Derbyshire.

*not out

### COUNTY CHAMPIONSHIPS FROM 1948

| | |
|---|---|
| 1948 | Glamorgan |
| 1949 | Middlesex and Yorkshire |
| 1950 | Lancashire and Surrey |
| 1951 | Warwickshire |
| 1952 | Surrey |
| 1953 | Surrey |
| 1954 | Surrey |
| 1955 | Surrey |
| 1956 | Surrey |
| 1957 | Surrey |
| 1958 | Surrey |
| 1959 | Yorkshire |
| 1960 | Yorkshire |
| 1961 | Hampshire |
| 1962 | Yorkshire |
| 1963 | Yorkshire |
| 1964 | Worcestershire |
| 1965 | Worcestershire |
| 1966 | Yorkshire |
| 1967 | Yorkshire |
| 1968 | Yorkshire |
| 1969 | Glamorgan |
| 1970 | Kent |
| 1971 | Surrey |
| 1972 | Warwickshire |
| 1973 | Hampshire |
| 1974 | Worcestershire |
| 1975 | Leicestershire |
| 1976 | Middlesex |
| 1977 | Kent and Middlesex |
| 1978 | Kent |
| 1979 | Essex |
| 1980 | Middlesex |
| 1981 | Nottinghamshire |
| 1982 | Middlesex |
| 1983 | Essex |
| 1984 | Essex |
| 1985 | Middlesex |
| 1986 | Essex |
| 1987 | Nottinghamshire |
| 1988 | Worcestershire |

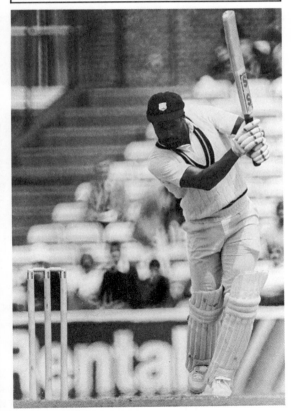

◁ West Indian all-rounder Viv Richards, displays a masterful batting action.

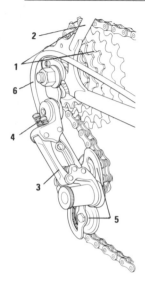

# Croquet

**Ball** Court 32 × 25.6 m (35 × 28 yd)
**Players** 2 or 4
**Balls** 4 (blue and black v red and yellow), diam 9.2 cm (3⅝ in), weight 454 g (1 lb)
**Hoops** 6 (twice each) plus *peg* diam 9.5 cm (3¾ in)
**International team competition** MacRobertson Shield

# Cycle Racing

**Ruling body** Union Cycliste Internationale
**Major competitions** ROAD RACING Tour de France, Olympic 100-km (62-mile) race.
  TRACK RACING Olympics and world championships (sprint, pursuit, 1-km time trial, motor-paced)
**Other cycle sports** six-day racing, cyclo-cross, cycle speedway, bicycle polo, time trials

△ The derailleur gear used on sports cycles: **1.** 5-speed gear block with 5 sprocket wheels. **2.** Rear fork frame. **3.** Selector mechanism. **4.** Tension adjusting screw. **5.** Sprung rollers. **6.** Gear cable.

▷ The Tour de France is the leading road race for professionals. Each day-long stage of the race is a gruelling test of stamina. The race leader wears the coveted yellow jersey.

# Equestrian Sports

**Ruling body** Fédération Equestre Internationale (FEI)
**Major competitions** SHOW JUMPING world championships (men's and women's) every 4 years, alternating with Olympics; President's Cup (world team championship) based on Nations Cup results; 2-yearly European championships (men's and women's); King George V Gold Cup; Queen Elizabeth II Gold Cup
  THREE-DAY EVENT (1 Dressage, 2 Endurance or Cross-country, 3 Show jumping) 4-yearly world championships and Olympics; 2-yearly European championships; Badminton Horse Trials
  DRESSAGE Olympics and world championships

# Fencing

**Ruling body** Fédération Internationale d'Escrimé (FIE)
**Events** foil, épée, sabre (men); foil (women)
**Major competitions** annual world championships (including Olympics)
**Duration of bout** first to 5 hits (or 6 min) men; 4 hits (or 5 min) women

# Football, American

**Pitch** 110 × 49 m (360 × 160 ft)
**Goals** 6 m (20 ft) high, 5.6 m (18½ ft) wide, 3 m (10 ft) off ground, amateur; 9 m (30 ft), professional
**Ball** length 28 cm (11 in), short circum. 54 cm (21¼ in), weight 397–425 g (14–15 oz)
**Duration** 60 min (4 × 15) playing time
**No. per side** 11 (unspecified no. of substitutes)
**Scoring** *touchdown* 6 pts, *extra point* 1, *field goal* 3, *safety* 2

# Football, Association

(pp 344–345)
**Pitch** 91.4–118.9 m (100–130 yd) by 45.7–91.4 m (50–100 yd)
**Goals** 7.3 m (8 yd) wide, 2.4 m (8 ft) high

# Football, Australian

**Pitch** oval 135–185 m (148–202 yd) by 110–155 m (120–170 yd)
**Goal posts** 6.4 m (21 ft) wide, *behind posts* 6.4 m either side of goal posts
**Ball** short circum. 57 cm (22½ in), long circum. 74 cm (29 in), weight 450–500 gm (16–17 oz)
**Duration** 100 min (4 × 25)
**No. per side** 18 (2 substitutes)
**Scoring** *goal* 6 pts, *behind* 1

△ American football is played in the USA at school, college and professional level. It started around 1850 and is rapidly gaining new fans outside the USA.

△ Fencers wear wire mesh masks, thick padded jackets and gloves. A 'hit' is recorded electronically in modern competitions.

△ The FIFA World Cup, played for every four years, is the leading tournament for national soccer teams.

▷ More people play and watch soccer world wide than any other team game.

## FA CUP WINNERS

| | | |
|---|---|---|
| 1930 Arsenal | 1954 West Bromwich Albion | 1972 Leeds United |
| 1931 West Bromwich Albion | 1955 Newcastle United | 1973 Sunderland |
| 1932 Newcastle United | 1956 Manchester City | 1974 Liverpool |
| 1933 Everton | 1957 Aston Villa | 1975 West Ham United |
| 1934 Manchester City | 1958 Bolton Wanderers | 1976 Southampton |
| 1935 Sheffield Wednesday | 1959 Nottingham Forest | 1977 Manchester United |
| 1936 Arsenal | 1960 Wolverhampton | 1978 Ipswich Town |
| 1937 Sunderland | Wanderers | 1979 Arsenal |
| 1938 Preston North End | 1961 Tottenham Hotspur | 1980 West Ham United |
| 1939 Portsmouth | 1962 Tottenham Hotspur | 1981 Tottenham Hotspur |
| 1946 Derby County | 1963 Manchester United | 1982 Tottenham Hotspur |
| 1947 Charlton Athletic | 1964 West Ham United | 1983 Manchester United |
| 1948 Manchester United | 1965 Liverpool | 1984 Everton |
| 1949 Wolverhampton | 1966 Everton | 1985 Manchester United |
| Wanderers | 1967 Tottenham Hotspur | 1986 Liverpool |
| 1950 Arsenal | 1968 West Bromwich Albion | 1987 Coventry City |
| 1951 Newcastle United | 1969 Manchester City | 1988 Wimbledon |
| 1952 Newcastle United | 1970 Chelsea | 1989 Liverpool |
| 1953 Blackpool | 1971 Arsenal | |

## WORLD CUP FINALS

| 1930 | Montevideo, Uruguay (100,000) | Uruguay | 4 | Argentina | 2 |
|------|-------------------------------|---------|---|-----------|---|
| 1934 | Rome, Italy (55,000) | Italy | 2 | Czechoslovakia | 1 |
| 1938 | Paris, France (65,000) | Italy | 4 | Hungary | 2 |
| 1950 | Rio de Janeiro, Brazil (199,850) | Uruguay | 2 | Brazil | 1 |
| 1954 | Berne, Switzerland (55,000) | W Germany | 3 | Hungary | 2 |
| 1958 | Stockholm, Sweden (49,700) | Brazil | 5 | Sweden | 2 |
| 1962 | Santiago, Chile (69,500) | Brazil | 3 | Czechoslovakia | 1 |
| 1966 | Wembley, England (93,000) | England | 4 | W Germany | 2 |
| 1970 | Mexico City, Mexico (110,000) | Brazil | 4 | Italy | 1 |
| 1974 | Munich, W Germany (75,000) | W Germany | 2 | Netherlands | 1 |
| 1978 | Buenos Aires, Argentina (77,000) | Argentina | 3 | Netherlands | 1 |
| 1982 | Madrid, Spain (90,000) | Italy | 3 | W Germany | 1 |
| 1986 | Mexico City, Mexico (114,580) | Argentina | 3 | W Germany | 2 |

## EUROPEAN CUP FINALS

| 1956 | Paris | Real Madrid (Spain) | 4 | Stade de Reims (France) | 3 |
|------|-------|---------------------|---|-------------------------|---|
| 1957 | Madrid | Real Madrid (Spain) | 2 | Fiorentina (Italy) | 0 |
| 1958 | Brussels | Real Madrid (Spain) | 3 | AC Milan (Italy) | 2 |
| 1959 | Stuttgart | Real Madrid (Spain) | 2 | Stade de Reims (France) | 0 |
| 1960 | Glasgow | Real Madrid (Spain) | 7 | Eintracht Frankfurt (W Ger) | 3 |
| 1961 | Berne | Benfica (Portugal) | 3 | Barcelona (Spain) | 2 |
| 1962 | Amsterdam | Benfica (Portugal) | 5 | Real Madrid (Spain) | 3 |
| 1963 | Wembley | AC Milan (Italy) | 2 | Benfica (Portugal) | 1 |
| 1964 | Vienna | Internazionale (Italy) | 3 | Real Madrid (Spain) | 1 |
| 1965 | Milan | Internazionale (Italy) | 1 | Benfica (Portugal) | 0 |
| 1966 | Brussels | Real Madrid (Spain) | 2 | Partizan Belgrade (Yug) | 1 |
| 1967 | Lisbon | Celtic (Scotland) | 2 | Internazionale (Italy) | 1 |
| 1968 | Wembley | Manchester United (England) | 4 | Benfica (Portugal) | 1 |
| 1969 | Madrid | AC Milan (Italy) | 4 | Ajax (Netherlands) | 1 |
| 1970 | Milan | Feyenoord (Netherlands) | 2 | Celtic (Scotland) | 1 |
| 1971 | Wembley | Ajax (Netherlands) | 2 | Panathinaikos (Greece) | 0 |
| 1972 | Rotterdam | Ajax (Netherlands) | 2 | Internazionale (Italy) | 0 |
| 1973 | Belgrade | Ajax (Netherlands) | 1 | Juventus (Italy) | 0 |
| 1974 | Brussels | Bayern Munich (W Ger) | 1 | Atlético Madrid (Spain) | 1 |
| | *Replay* | Bayern Munich (W Ger) | 4 | Atlético Madrid (Spain) | 0 |
| 1975 | Paris | Bayern Munich (W Ger) | 2 | Leeds United (England) | 0 |
| 1976 | Glasgow | Bayern Munich (W Ger) | 1 | St Etienne (France) | 0 |
| 1977 | Rome | Liverpool (England) | 3 | B Mönchengladbach (W Ger) | 1 |
| 1978 | Wembley | Liverpool (England) | 1 | FC Bruges (Belgium) | 0 |
| 1979 | Munich | Nottingham Forest (England) | 1 | Malmö (Sweden) | 0 |
| 1980 | Madrid | Nottingham Forest (England) | 1 | SV Hamburg (W Ger) | 0 |
| 1981 | Paris | Liverpool (England) | 1 | Real Madrid (Spain) | 0 |
| 1982 | Rotterdam | Aston Villa (England) | 1 | Bayern Munich (W Ger) | 0 |
| 1983 | Athens | Hamburg (W Ger) | 1 | Juventus (Italy) | 0 |
| 1984 | Rome | Liverpool (England) | 1 | AS Roma (Italy) | 1 |
| | (Liverpool won 4–2 on penalties) | | | | |
| 1985 | Brussels | Juventus (Italy) | 1 | Liverpool (England) | 0 |
| 1986 | Seville | Steaua Bucharest (Romania) | 0 | Barcelona (Spain) | 0 |
| | (Steaua won 2–0 on penalties) | | | | |
| 1987 | Vienna | FC Porto (Portugal) | 2 | Bayern Munich (W Ger) | 1 |
| 1988 | Stuttgart | PSV Eindhoven (Netherlands) | 0 | Benfica (Portugal) | 0 |
| | (Eindhoven won 6–5 on penalties) | | | | |

△ The three basic types of golf club. A golf driver is called a wood but may be made of metal or plastic.

▽ A gymnast performing an exercise on the rings.

# Golf

**Ball** max. weight 46 g (1.62 oz), min. diam. UK 4.11 cm (1.62 in), US 4.27 cm (1.68 in)

**Hole** diam. 10.8 cm (4¼ in)

**No. of clubs carried** 14 maximum

**Ruling bodies** Royal and Ancient Golf Club of St Andrews; United States Golf Association

**Major competitions** Individual – Open, US Open, US Masters, US PGA

**Team** World Cup (international teams of 2, annual), Eisenhower Trophy (world amateur, teams of 4, 2-yearly), Ryder Cup (US v GB, 2-yearly)

## Golf Records

**Lowest round** 55 A E Smith (GB) 1936

**36 holes** 122 Sam Snead (US) 59–63, 1959

**72 holes** 255 Peter Tupling (GB) 1981

**Most 'Big Four' titles** 18 Jack Nicklaus (US)

**Most British Opens** 6 Harry Vardon (GB)

**Most US Opens** 4 Willie Anderson (US), Bobby Jones (US), Ben Hogan (US), Jack Nicklaus (US)

**Most US Masters** 6 Jack Nicklaus (US)

**Most US PGAs** 5 Walter Hagen (US), Jack Nicklaus (US)

## Golf Terms

BIG FOUR The major individual tournaments: Open and US Open, Masters, and PGA.

BIRDIE One under par for hole.

BOGEY One over par for hole.

DORMIE In match play, leading by numbers of holes left.

DOUBLE BOGEY Two over par for hole.

EAGLE Two under par for hole.

FAIRWAY Smooth turf between tee and green.

FOURBALL Match in which pairs score their 'better ball' at each hole.

FOURSOME Match in which pair play same ball, alternately.

GREEN Specially prepared surface in which hole is situated.

MATCH PLAY In which player or pair play each other and winner is determined by holes won.

MEDAL PLAY In which number of strokes taken determines winner.

PAR Standard score (assessed on first-class play) for hole or holes.

PUTTER Club used to hit ball when on green.

ROUGH Unprepared part of course.

STROKE PLAY Medal play.

TEE Starting place for hole, or peg on which ball is placed.

# Gymnastics

**Ruling body** Fédération Internationale de Gymnastique

**Events** men's – floor exercises, rings, parallel bars, pommel horse, vault (lengthwise), horizontal bar; overall; team; women's – floor exercises (to music), vault, asymmetrical bars, beam; overall; team

**Major competitions** World and Olympic championships, alternately every 4 years

# Hockey

**Goals** 3.66 m (12 ft) wide, 2.13 m (7 ft) high
**Ball** circum. 23 cm (9 in), weight 156–163 g (5½–5¾ oz), made of cork and twine covered in leather
**Duration of game** 70 min (2 × 35)
**No. per side** 11 (2 substitutes in men's game)
**Ruling bodies** men's – Fédération Internationale de Hockey (FIH); women's – Women's International Hockey Rules' Board
**Major competitions** Olympic Games and World Cup (4-yearly)

△ The Great Britain hockey team. At the highest level, such as the Olympics, hockey is now played on all-weather surfaces, rather than on grass pitches.

▽ A lacrosse stick is strung so that the ball cannot get lodged in it, and may not be made of metal.

# Horse Racing

**Major races**
**England** Derby, Oaks, St Leger, 1,000 and 2,000 Guineas (the 5 Classics), King George VI & Queen Elizabeth Stakes, Ascot Gold Cup; Grand National (steeplechase), Cheltenham Gold Cup (steeplechase), Champion Hurdle
**Ireland** Irish Sweeps Derby
**France** Prix de l'Arc de Triomphe
**Australia** Melbourne Cup, Caulfield Cup
**South Africa** Durban July Handicap
**USA** Kentucky Derby, Preakness Stakes, Belmont Stakes (Triple Crown); Washington International

# Lacrosse

**Pitch** 100 × 55 m (110 × 60 yd) men; 110 × 64 m (120 × 70 yd) preferred for women's international matches
**Goals** 1.8 × 1.8 m (6 × 6 ft)
**Ball** circum. 19.7–20.3 cm (7¾–8 in), weight 142–149 g (5–5¼ oz) men; 135–149 g (4¾–5¼ oz) women
**Duration** 60 min (4 × 15) men, 50 min (2 × 25) women
**No. per side** 10 (13 substitutes) men, 12 (1 substitutes) women

# Motor Sport

**Ruling body** Fédération Internationale de l'Automobile (FIA)

**Major events and competitions** Formula One – World Drivers Championship (based on points gained in individual grands prix: 9, 6, 4, 3, 2, 1 for first 6
Sports car racing – Le Mans
Rally driving – Monte Carlo Rally

**Other motor sports** drag racing, karting, hillclimbing, trials, autocross, rallycross, autotests, stock-car racing, vintage-car racing

## Records

**World Drivers Championship** 5 JM Fangio (1951, 1954–57)
**Championship Grand Prix wins** 36 Alain Prost 1980–
**Grand Prix wins in season** 8 Ayrton Senna 1988
**Land Speed Record** 1019.5 km/h (633.5 mph) Richard Noble (GB) in *Thrust 2*, 1983
**Water Speed Record** 511.1 km/h (317.6 mph) Ken Warby (Aus) in *Spirit of Australia*, 1978

▷ A superkart: its streamlined body and rear aerofoils give improved roadholding and higher speeds.

## FORMULA ONE WORLD CHAMPIONS

| | |
|---|---|
| 1950 | Giuseppe Farina (Italy) |
| 1951 | Juan Manuel Fangio (Argentina) |
| 1952 | Alberto Ascari (Italy) |
| 1953 | Alberto Ascari (Italy) |
| 1954 | Juan Manuel Fangio (Argentina) |
| 1955 | Juan Manuel Fangio (Argentina) |
| 1956 | Juan Manuel Fangio (Argentina) |
| 1957 | Juan Manuel Fangio (Argentina) |
| 1958 | Mike Hawthorn (England) |
| 1959 | Jack Brabham (Australia) |
| 1960 | Jack Brabham (Australia) |
| 1961 | Phil Hill (USA) |
| 1962 | Graham Hill (England) |
| 1963 | Jim Clark (Scotland) |
| 1964 | John Surtees (England) |
| 1965 | Jim Clark (Scotland) |
| 1966 | Jack Brabham (Australia) |
| 1967 | Denis Hulme (New Zealand) |
| 1968 | Graham Hill (England) |
| 1969 | Jackie Stewart (Scotland) |
| 1970 | Jochen Rindt (Austria) |
| 1971 | Jackie Stewart (Scotland) |
| 1972 | Emerson Fittipaldi (Brazil) |
| 1973 | Jackie Stewart (Scotland) |
| 1974 | Emerson Fittipaldi (Brazil) |
| 1975 | Niki Lauda (Austria) |
| 1976 | James Hunt (England) |
| 1977 | Niki Lauda (Austria) |
| 1978 | Mario Andretti (USA) |
| 1979 | Jody Scheckter (South Africa) |
| 1980 | Alan Jones (Australia) |
| 1981 | Nelson Piquet (Brazil) |
| 1982 | Keke Rosberg (Finland) |
| 1983 | Nelson Piquet (Brazil) |
| 1984 | Niki Lauda (Austria) |
| 1985 | Alain Prost (France) |
| 1986 | Alain Prost (France) |
| 1987 | Nelson Piquet (Brazil) |
| 1988 | Ayrton Senna (Brazil) |

# Motorcycling Sport

**Ruling body** Fédération Internationale Motocycliste (FIM)
**Classes** 50 cc, 125 cc, 250 cc, 350 cc (junior), 500 cc (senior),
750 cc, unlimited; sidecar
**Major competitions** world championships (based on points
gained in individual grands prix), including Isle of Man TT
**Other motorcycle sports** scrambling (motocross), trials,
grasstrack racing

# Rugby Union

**Pitch (max.)** 69 m (75 yd) wide, 100 m (110 yd) between goals,
23 m (25 yd) behind goals
**Goal posts** 5.6 m (18½ ft) wide, no height limit, crossbar 3 m
(10 ft) above ground
**Ball** length 28 cm (11 in), short circum. 58–62 cm (22¾–24½ in)
weight 400–440 g (14–15½ oz)
**Duration of game** 80 min (2 × 40)
**No. per side** 15 (2 substitutes, for injury only)
**Scoring** *try* 4 pts, *conversion* 2, *penalty goal* 3, *dropped goal* 3
**Ruling body** International Rugby Football Board
**Major competitions** Five Nations Championship (England,
France, Ireland, Scotland, Wales), Ranfurly Shield (New
Zealand), Currie Cup (South Africa)
**Touring sides** British Lions (GB), All Blacks (New Zealand),
Springboks (South Africa), Wallabies (Australia), Tricolors (France)

## Records

**Team score** *touring side* – 125 New Zealand (v Northern New
South Wales, 1962)
*in international* – 106 New Zealand (v Japan, 1987), France (v
Paraguay, 1988)
*in International Championship* 69 England (v Wales, 1881)
**Individual score** *any first-class match* – 80 Jannie van der
Westhuizen, Carnarvon (v Williston, 1972)
*international* – 34 Phil Bennett, Wales (v Japan, 1975)
*international career* – 479, Hugo Porta (Argentina)
*international tries* – 23 Ian Smith (Scotland)
**Attendance** 104,000 Murrayfield, Edinburgh (Scotland v Wales,
1975)

△ The bottle-neck at the
start of a scramble race.
Dust and mud fly as riders
compete for the lead.

▽ Rugby players struggle
for possession of the ball at
a line-out. At all levels,
Rugby Union is officially
amateurs-only.

# Speedway

**Track** 4 laps of 274–411 m (300–450 yd) surface – red shale or granite dust
**Meeting** 20 races, 4 riders in race, each getting 5 rides
**Scoring** 1st 3 pts, 2nd 2, 3rd 1
**Machines** Brakeless 500 cc motorcycles
**Ruling body** Fédération Internationale de Motorcycliste (FIM)
**Major competitions** World Championship (individual), World Team Cup, World Pairs Championship
**Most World Championship wins** 6 Ivan Mauger (NZ)

▽ Needle-sharp spikes on the tyres of ice speedway racers ensure grip on the track. The riders wear heavy leg protection.

## SPEEDWAY WORLD CHAMPIONS

| | |
|---|---|
| **1936** Lionel Van Praag (Australia) | **1968** Ivan Mauger (New Zealand) |
| **1937** Jack Milne (USA) | **1969** Ivan Mauger (New Zealand) |
| **1938** Bluey Wilkinson (Australia) | **1970** Ivan Mauger (New Zealand) |
| **1949** Tommy Price (England) | **1971** Ole Olsen (Denmark) |
| **1950** Freddie Williams (Wales) | **1972** Ivan Mauger (New Zealand) |
| **1951** Jack Young (Australia) | **1973** Jerzy Szczakiel (Poland) |
| **1952** Jack Young (Australia) | **1974** Anders Michanek (Sweden) |
| **1953** Freddie Williams (Wales) | **1975** Ole Olsen (Denmark) |
| **1954** Ronnie Moore (New Zealand) | **1976** Peter Collins (England) |
| **1955** Peter Craven (England) | **1977** Ivan Mauger (New Zealand) |
| **1956** Ove Fundin (Sweden) | **1978** Ole Olsen (Denmark) |
| **1957** Barry Briggs (New Zealand) | **1979** Ivan Mauger (New Zealand) |
| **1958** Barry Briggs (New Zealand) | **1980** Michael Lee (England) |
| **1959** Ronnie Moore (New Zealand) | **1981** Bruce Penhall (USA) |
| **1960** Ove Fundin (Sweden) | **1982** Bruce Penhall (USA) |
| **1961** Ove Fundin (Sweden) | **1983** Egon Müller (W Germany) |
| **1962** Peter Craven (England) | **1984** Erik Gundersen (Denmark) |
| **1963** Ove Fundin (Sweden) | **1985** Erik Gundersen (Denmark) |
| **1964** Barry Briggs (New Zealand) | **1986** Hans Nielsen (Denmark) |
| **1965** Bjorn Knuttsson (Sweden) | **1987** Hans Nielsen (Denmark) |
| **1966** Barry Briggs (New Zealand) | **1988** Erik Gundersen (Denmark) |
| **1967** Ove Fundin (Sweden) | |

# Swimming and Diving

**Standard Olympic pool** 50 m (54.7 yd) long, 8 lanes
**Ruling body** Fédération Internationale de Natation Amateur
(FINA)
**Competitive strokes** freestyle (usually front crawl), backstroke,
breaststroke, butterfly; individual medley (butterfly, backstroke,
breaststroke, freestyle), medley relay (backstroke, breaststroke,
butterfly, freestyle)
**Diving events** men's and women's springboard at 3 m (10 ft),
highboard at 10 m (33 ft) (lower boards also used)
**Major competitions** Olympics and world championships
**Major long-distance swims** English Channel, Cook Strait (NZ),
Atlantic City Marathon (US)

## Swimming

### MEN'S WORLD RECORDS

| **Freestyle** | | | |
|---|---|---|---|
| 50 metres | 22.18 sec | Peter Williams (South Africa) | 10.4.88 |
| 100 metres | 48.74 sec | Matthew Biondi (USA) | 24.6.86 |
| 200 metres | 1 min 47.44 sec | Michael Gross (W. Germany) | 29.7.84 |
| **Breaststroke** | | | |
| 100 metres | 1 min 01.65 sec | Steven Lundquist (USA) | 29.7.84 |
| **Butterfly** | | | |
| 100 metres | 52.84 sec | Pedro Pablo Morales (USA) | 23.6.86 |
| **Backstroke** | | | |
| 100 metres | 55.00 sec | Igor Polyanskiy (USSR) | 16.7.88 |

### WOMEN'S WORLD RECORDS

| **Freestyle** | | | |
|---|---|---|---|
| 50 metres | 24.98 sec | Yang Wenyi (China) | 10.4.88 |
| 100 metres | 54.73 sec | Kristin Otto (GDR) | 19.8.86 |
| 200 metres | 1 min 57.55 sec | Heike Friedrich (GDR) | 18.6.84 |
| **Breaststroke** | | | |
| 100 metres | 1 min 07.91 sec | Silke Hörner (GDR) | 21.8.87 |
| **Butterfly** | | | |
| 100 metres | 57.93 sec | Mary T. Meagher (USA) | 16.8.81 |
| **Backstroke** | | | |
| 100 metres | 1 min 00.59 sec | Ina Kleber (GDR) | 24.8.84 |

# Table Tennis

**Table** 2.74 × 1.52 m (9 × 5 ft), 76 cm (2½ ft) off floor
**Net** height 15.2 cm (6 in), length 1.83 m (6 ft)
**Ball** diam. 37–38 mm (1.46–1.5 in), weight 2.4–2.53 g made of
celluloid-type plastic, white or yellow
**Bat surface** max. thickness 2 mm (0.08 in) pimpled rubber or
4 mm (0.16 in) sandwich rubber
**Scoring** best of 3 or 5 21-pt games
**Ruling body** International Table Tennis Federation
**Major competitions** world championships, Swaythling Cup
(men's team), Corbillon Cup (women's team), all 2-yearly

△ The smaller, modern table
tennis bat was introduced in
the 1920's.

△ At 17, Boris Becker became Wimbledon's youngest-ever men's singles champion in 1985. He was also the first unseeded champion.

▽ The layout of a tennis court. The inner sidelines are for singles, the outer ones for doubles. The surface may be grass, wood, or one of a variety of synthetic materials.

# Tennis

**Ball** diam. 6.35–6.67 cm (2½–2⅝ in), weight 56.7–58.5 g (2–2¹⁄₁₆ oz), made of wool-covered rubber, white or yellow

**Rackets** no limits, wood or metal frames, strung with lamb's gut or nylon

**Scoring** best of 3 or 5 6-up sets, with tiebreaker at 6–6 (or first to lead by 2); games of 4 pts (15, 30, 40, game), 40–40 being *deuce* and 2-pt lead required; tiebreaker game usually first to 7 pts. with 2-pt lead

**Ruling body** International Lawn Tennis Federation (ILTF)

**Major competitions** Wimbledon, Australian Open, US Open, French Open (the four constituting 'Grand Slam'), Davis Cup (world team championship), Federation Cup (Women's World Cup), Wightman Cup (US v GB women)

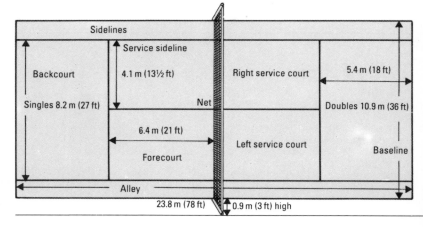

## WIMBLEDON CHAMPIONS
### (since 1946)

| | men | women |
|---|---|---|
| 1946 | Yvon Petra (Fr) | Pauline Betz (US) |
| 1947 | Jack Kramer (US) | Margaret Osborne (US) |
| 1948 | Bob Falkenburg (US) | Louise Brough (US) |
| 1949 | Fred Schroeder (US) | Louise Brough (US) |
| 1950 | Budge Patty (US) | Louise Brough (US) |
| 1951 | Dick Savitt (US) | Doris Hart (US) |
| 1952 | Frank Sedgman (Aus) | Maureen Connolly (US) |
| 1953 | Victor Seixas (US) | Maureen Connolly (US) |
| 1954 | Jaroslav Drobny (Cz) | Maureen Connolly (US) |
| 1955 | Tony Trabert (US) | Louise Brough (US) |
| 1956 | Lew Hoad (Aus) | Shirley Fry (US) |
| 1957 | Lew Hoad (Aus) | Althea Gibson (US) |
| 1958 | Ashley Cooper (Aus) | Althea Gibson (US) |
| 1959 | Alex Olmedo (Peru) | Maria Bueno (Brazil) |
| 1960 | Neale Fraser (Aus) | Maria Bueno (Brazil) |
| 1961 | Rod Laver (Aus) | Angela Mortimer (GB) |
| 1962 | Rod Laver (Aus) | Karen Susman (US) |
| 1963 | Chuck McKinley (US) | Margaret Smith (Aus) |
| 1964 | Roy Emerson (Aus) | Maria Bueno (Brazil) |
| 1965 | Roy Emerson (Aus) | Margaret Smith (Aus) |
| 1966 | Manuel Santana (Sp) | Billie Jean King (US) |
| 1967 | John Newcombe (Aus) | Billie Jean King (US) |
| 1968 | Rod Laver (Aus) | Billie Jean King (US) |
| 1969 | Rod Laver (Aus) | Ann Jones (GB) |
| 1970 | John Newcombe (Aus) | Margaret Court* (Aus) |
| 1971 | John Newcombe (Aus) | Evonne Goolagong (Aus) |
| 1972 | Stan Smith (US) | Billie Jean King (US) |
| 1973 | Jan Kodes (Cz) | Billie Jean King (US) |
| 1974 | Jimmy Connors (US) | Chris Evert (US) |
| 1975 | Arthur Ashe (US) | Billie Jean King (US) |
| 1976 | Bjorn Borg (Swed) | Chris Evert (US) |
| 1977 | Bjorn Borg (Swed) | Virginia Wade (GB) |
| 1978 | Bjorn Borg (Swed) | Martina Navratilova (Cz) |
| 1979 | Bjorn Borg (Swed) | Martina Navratilova (Cz) |
| 1980 | Bjorn Borg (Swed) | Evonne Cawley† (Aus) |
| 1981 | John McEnroe (US) | Chris Evert-Lloyd (US) |
| 1982 | Jimmy Connors (US) | Martina Navratilova (US) |
| 1983 | John McEnroe (US) | Martina Navratilova (US) |
| 1984 | John McEnroe (US) | Martina Navratilova (US) |
| 1985 | Boris Becker (W Ger) | Martina Navratilova (US) |
| 1986 | Boris Becker (W Ger) | Martina Navratilova (US) |
| 1987 | Pat Cash (Aus) | Martina Navratilova (US) |
| 1988 | Stefan Edberg (Swed) | Steffi Graf (W Ger) |

*Formerly Margaret Smith
†Formerly Evonne Goolagong

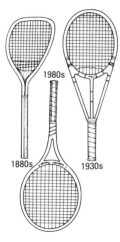

△ The first tennis rackets were wooden, with off-set, pear-shaped heads, strung with natural gut. Most modern rackets use synthetic materials – metal, carbon graphite, glass fibre, or ceramic.

▽ Steffi Graf, likely to dominate women's tennis into the 1990s.

▽ In weightlifting, the discs are marked with their weights and loaded onto the bar with the largest inside. The discs weigh: 25 kg (55 lb); 20 kg (44 lb); 15 kg (33 lb); 10 kg (22 lb); 5 kg (11 lb); 2.5 kg (5½ lb); 1.25 kg (2¾ lb).

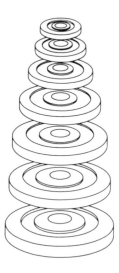

# Volleyball

**Court** 18 × 9 m (59 × 29½ ft)
**Net height** 2.43 m (7 ft 11.7 in) for men, 2.24 m (7 ft 4 in) for women
**Ball** circum. 65–67 cm (25.6–26.4 in), weight 260–280 gm (9–10 oz)
**No. per side** 6 (6 substitutes)
**Scoring** best of 3 or 5 15-pt sets
**Ruling body** Fédération Internationale de Volleyball (FIVB)
**Major competitions** Olympics and world championships, alternately every 4 years (men and women)

# Water Polo

**Pool** 20–30 m (22–33 yd) by 8–20 m (8¾–22 yd), min. depth 1 m (1.8 m for international competitions)
**Goals** 3 × 0.9 m (9¾ × 3 ft) for depths over 1.5 m (4 ft 11 in); for shallower pools, crossbar 2.4 m (7 ft 10 in) above bottom
**Ball** circum. 68–71 cm (26¾–28 in), weight 400–450 gm (14–16 oz)
**Duration of game** 28 min (4 × 7)
**No. per side** 7 (6 substitutes)
**Ruling body** FINA (see SWIMMING)
**Major competitions** as for SWIMMING

# Weightlifting

**Ruling body** International Weightlifting Federation (IWF)
**Lifts** *snatch* (bar pulled overhead in one movement) and *(clean and) jerk* (bar raised to shoulders first, then driven aloft as legs are straightened); (non-Olympic) *bench press, squat, dead lift*
**World championships** annual (including Olympics) Classes – flyweight (52 kg/114½ lb limit), bantam (56 kg/123½ lb), feather (60 kg/132¼ lb), light (67.5 kg/148¾ lb), middle (75 kg/165¼ lb), light-heavy (82.5 kg/181¾ lb), middle-heavy (90 kg/198¼ lb), heavy (110 kg/242½ lb), super-heavy (over 110 kg)

## WEIGHTLIFTING RECORDS
(combined snatch and jerk)

| | | | | |
|---|---|---|---|---|
| Flyweight | 270 kg (595¼ lb) | Sevdalin Marinov | Bulgaria | 1988 |
| Bantamweight | 300 kg (661¼ lb) | Neum Shalamanov | Bulgaria | 1984 |
| Featherweight | 342.5 kg (755 lb) | Naim Suleimanoglu* | Turkey | 1988 |
| Lightweight | 355 kg (782½ lb) | Mikhail Petrov | Bulgaria | 1987 |
| Middleweight | 382.5 kg (843¼ lb) | Aleksandr Varbanov | Bulgaria | 1988 |
| Light-heavywt | 405 kg (892½ lb) | Yurik Vardanyan | USSR | 1984 |
| Middle-heavywt | 422.5 kg (931¼ lb) | Viktor Solodov | USSR | 1984 |
| 100 kg (220½ lb) | 440 kg (970 lb) | Yuriy Zakharevich | USSR | 1983 |
| Heavyweight | 455 kg (1003 lb) | Yuriy Zakharevich | USSR | 1988 |
| Super-heavywt | 472.5 kg (1040½ lb) | Aleksandr Kurlovich | USSR | 1987 |

*Formerly Neum Shalamanov of Bulgaria*

# Winter Sports

### Ice Skating
**Ruling body** International Skating Union (ISU)
**World championships** annual (including Olympics)
**Figure skating events** men's, women's single, pairs, (pairs) dancing (all with compulsory and 'free' sections); two sets of marks, for technical merit and artistic impression
**Speed skating events (on oval 400-m circuits)** men's 500, 1,500, 5,000 and 10,000 m; women's 500, 1,000, 1,500 and 3,000 m; overall titles in world and international events.

△ All ice hockey players, but especially the goal minder, are padded for protection in this fast, rough sport.

### Ice Hockey
**Rink** max. 61 × 30.5 m (200 × 100 ft)
**Surround** max. 1.22 m (4 ft) high boards
**Goals** 1.83 × 1.22 m (6 × 4 ft)
**Puck** diam. 7.62 cm (3 in), thickness 2.54 cm (1 in), weight 156 × 170 g (5½ × 6 oz), made of vulcanized rubber
**Duration** 60 min (3 × 20) playing time
**No. per side** 6 (max. 18 on team)
**Ruling body** International Ice Hockey Federation
**Major competitions (amateur)** annual world championships (incl. Olympics)

### Curling
**Rink** 42 × 4.27 m (138 × 14 ft)
**Houses (targets)** diam. 3.66 m (12 ft), dist. between centres 34.75 cm (114 ft)
**Stones (max.)** circum. 91.4 cm (36 in), thickness 11.4 cm (4½ in), weight 20 kg (44 lb), made of granite or similar
**No. per team** 4 (2 stones each)
**No. of *heads* (or *ends*)** 10 or 12 (or time limit)
**Ruling body** Royal Caledonian Curling Club
**World championships** Silver Broom Trophy (annual)

### Bobsleigh
**Course** min. length 1,500 m (1,640 yd), with at least 15 banked turns; agg. time for 4 descents
**Events** 2- and 4-man bobs
**Ruling body** International Bobsleigh Federation
**World championships** annual (including Olympics)

▽ Competitors in luge tobogganing descend the course feet-first aboard the lightweight skeleton toboggan.

### Luge Tobogganing
**Course** 1,000–1,500 m (1,094–1,640 yd); agg. time for 4 descents
**Events** 1- and 2-man luge, 1-woman luge; ridden in sitting position
**Ruling body** International Luge Federation
**World Championships** annual (including Olympics)

### Cresta Run
**Course** unique to St Moritz 1,213 m (1,326.6 yd); agg. time for 3 descents
**Event** single seater, ridden face down
**Ruling body** St Moritz Tobogganing Club
**Major competitions** Grand National (full course, from Top), Curzon Cup (from Junction, 888 m or 971 yd); Olympic event (full course) 1928 and 1948

△ Nordic skiing is a test of stamina and, as its name suggests, is most popular in Scandinavia.

▽ In downhill skiing, competitors must descend a given course in the fastest possible time.

**Alpine Ski Racing**
Events downhill, slalom, giant slalom, combined
Downhill vert. drop 800–1,000 m (2,625–3,281 ft) men; 500–700 m (1,640–2,297 ft) women
Slalom 55–75 gates men, 40–60 gates women; alternate gates (pairs of poles 4–5 m, 13–16 ft apart) have blue or red flags and are 0.75–15 m (2.5–49 ft) apart
Giant slalom min. 33 gates 4–8 m (13–26 ft) wide, at least 10 m (33 ft) apart
Ruling body Fédération Internationale de Ski (FIS)
Major competitions 2-yearly world championships (including Olympics, which has no combined title), annual World Cup (men's and women's, individuals scoring in 15 of 21 top international events, first 10 scoring 25, 20, 15, 11, 8, 6, 4, 3, 2, 1 pts.), annual Arlberg-Kandahar

**Ski-Bob Racing**
Events downhill, giant slalom, special slalom, combined
Ruling body Fédération Internationale de Skibob (FISB)
World championships two-yearly (men's and women's)

**Nordic Ski Competition**
Events 15, 30, 50 km (9.3, 18.6, 31 miles) men's, 5, 10 km (3.1, 6.2 miles) women's; 4 × 10 km relay (men), 3 × 5 km relay (women); nordic combination (15 km cross-country and ski jumping, men's); men's 70 and 90 m (230 and 295 ft) ski jumping (points awarded for style and distance)
Ruling body Fédération Internationale de Ski (FIS)
Major competitions 2-yearly world championships (including Olympics); 90-m (295 ft) ski jumping and biathlon, annually

**Biathlon**
Course 20 km (12.4 miles), with 4 stops for target shooting men; 10 km (6.2 miles), with 3 stops, women
Events men's individual and relay (4 × 7.5 km)
Scoring on time, with 2-min penalties for shots missing target, 1-min penalty for hit in outer ring of target

# Miscellany

Some fact files do not fall readily into a special section. We present a number of them in the next 18 pages.

## Nobel Prizes

The Swedish chemist Alfred Nobel invented the explosive dynamite in 1867. It made him a multi-millionaire.

When he realized how much death and destruction his invention was causing, he decided to leave his fortune as a fund to give annual prizes for outstanding work in physics; chemistry; physiology and medicine; literature; and — the one most dear to him — peace. The first prizes were awarded in 1901.

A sixth prize, for economics, was set up by the Swedish Central Bank in 1969.

△ Alfred Nobel (1833–96) endowed the prizes that now bear his name.

### PRIZEWINNERS, 1901–1988

**Physics**

| | |
|---|---|
| 1901 | Wilhelm Roentgen (German) |
| 1902 | Hendrik Lorentz & Pieter Zeeman (Dutch) |
| 1903 | Pierre and Marie Curie & Henri Becquerel (French) |
| 1904 | Lord Rayleigh (British) |
| 1905 | Philipp Lenard (German) |
| 1906 | Sir Joseph Thomson (British) |
| 1907 | Albert Michelson (American) |
| 1908 | Gabriel Lippmann (French) |
| 1909 | Guglielmo Marconi (Italian) & Karl Ferdinand Braun (German) |
| 1910 | Johannes van der Waals (Dutch) |
| 1911 | Wilhelm Wien (German) |
| 1912 | Nils Gustav Dalén (Swedish) |
| 1913 | Heike Kamerlingh-Onnes (Dutch) |
| 1914 | Max von Laue (German) |
| 1915 | Sir William H. Bragg & Sir William L. Bragg (British) |
| 1916 | *No award* |
| 1917 | Charles Barkla (British) |
| 1918 | Max Planck (German) |
| 1919 | Johannes Stark (German) |
| 1920 | Charles Guillaume (Swiss) |
| 1921 | Albert Einstein (German/Swiss) |
| 1922 | Niels Bohr (Danish) |

△ Marie and Pierre Curie. She won two Nobel prizes.

| | |
|---|---|
| 1923 | Robert Millikan (American) |
| 1924 | Karl Siegbahn (Swedish) |
| 1925 | James Franck & Gustav Hertz (German) |
| 1926 | Jean Perrin (French) |
| 1927 | Arthur Compton (American) & Charles T. R. Wilson (British) |
| 1928 | Owen Richardson (British) |
| 1929 | Prince Louis Victor de Broglie (French) |
| 1930 | Sir Chandrasekhara Raman (Indian) |

1931 *No award*
1932 Werner Heisenberg (German)
1933 Erwin Schrödinger (Austrian) &
Paul Dirac (British)
1934 *No award*
1935 Sir James Chadwick (British)
1936 Victor Hess (Austrian) & Carl
Anderson (American)
1937 Clinton Davisson (American) &
George Thomson (British)
1938 Enrico Fermi (Italian)
1939 Ernest O. Lawrence (American)
1940–42 *No award*
1943 Otto Stern (American)
1944 Isidor Isaac Rabi (American)
1945 Wolfgang Pauli (Austrian)
1946 Percy Bridgman (American)
1947 Sir Edward Appleton (British)
1948 Patrick M. S. Blackett (British)
1949 Hideki Yukawa (Japanese)
1950 Cecil Frank Powell (British)
1951 Sir John Cockcroft (British) &
Ernest Walton (Irish)
1952 Edward Purcell & Felix Bloch
(American)
1953 Frits Zernike (Dutch)
1954 Max Born (German/British) &
Walther Bothe (German)
1955 Polykarp Kusch & Willis Lamb Jr
(American)
1956 William Shockley, Walter Brattain
& John Bardeen (American)
1957 Tsung Dao Lee & Chen Ning Yang
(Chinese/American)
1958 Pavel Cherenkov, Ilya Frank & Igor
Tamm (Russian)
1959 Emilio Segrè & Owen Chamberlain
(American)
1960 Donald Glaser (American)
1961 Robert Hofstadter (American) &
Rudolf Mossbauer (German)
1962 Lev Landau (Russian)
1963 Eugene Wigner (American), Maria
Goeppert-Mayer (German/
American) & Hans Jensen (German)
1964 Charles Townes (American) &
Nikolai Basov & Alexandr
Prokhorov (Russian)
1965 Richard Feynman & Julian
Schwinger (American) & Sin-itiro
Tomonaga (Japanese)
1966 Alfred Kastler (French)
1967 Hans Bethe (American)
1968 Luis Alvarez (American)
1969 Murray Gell-Mann (American)

△ Italian physicist Enrico Fermi. He produced the first nuclear chain reaction during World War II.

1970 Hannes Allfven (Swedish) & Louis
Néel (French)
1971 Dennis Gabor (British)
1972 John Bardeen, Leon Cooper &
John Schrieffer (American)
1973 Ivar Giaever (American), Leo Esaki
(Japanese) & Brian Josephson
(British)
1974 Sir Martin Ryle & Antony Hewish
(British)
1975 James Rainwater (American), Aage
Bohr & Benjamin Mottelson
(Danish)
1976 Burton Richter (American) &
Samuel Ting (American)
1977 Sir Nevill Mott (British), John Van
Vleck (American) & Philip Anderson
(American)
1978 Peter J. Kapitsa (Russian), Arno
Penzias (American) & Robert W.
Wilson (American)
1979 Sheldon Glashow (American),
Abdus Salam (Pakistan) & Steven
Weinberg (American)
1980 James Cronin & Val Fitch
(American)
1981 Kai Siegbahn (Swedish), Nicolaas
Bloembergen & Arthur Schawlow
(American)
1982 Kenneth G. Wilson (American)
1983 Subrahmanyan Chandrasekhar &
William Fowler (American)

| 1984 | Carlo Rubbia (Italian) & Simon van der Meer (Dutch) |
| 1985 | Klaus von Klitzing (West German) |
| 1986 | Ernst Ruska & Gerd Binnig (West German) & Heinrich Rohrer (Swiss) |
| 1987 | Karl Müller (Swiss) & Johannes Bednorz (West German) |
| 1988 | Leon Lederman, Melvin Schwartz & Jack Steinberger (American) |

**Chemistry**

| 1901 | Jacobus van't Hoff (Dutch) |
| 1902 | Emil Fischer (German) |
| 1903 | Svante Arrhenius (Swedish) |
| 1904 | Sir William Ramsay (British) |
| 1905 | Adolf von Baeyer (German) |
| 1906 | Henri Moissan (French) |
| 1907 | Eduard Buchner (German) |
| 1908 | Ernest Rutherford (New Zealand/British) |
| 1909 | Wilhelm Ostwald (German) |
| 1910 | Otto Wallach (German) |
| 1911 | Marie Curie (French) |
| 1912 | Victor Grignard & Paul Sabatier (French) |
| 1913 | Alfred Werner (Swiss) |
| 1914 | Theodore Richards (American) |
| 1915 | Richard Willstätter (German) |
| 1916–17 | *No award* |
| 1918 | Fritz Haber (German) |
| 1919 | *No award* |
| 1920 | Walther Nernst (German) |
| 1921 | Frederick Soddy (British) |
| 1922 | Francis Aston (British) |
| 1923 | Fritz Pregl (Austrian) |
| 1924 | *No award* |
| 1925 | Richard Zsigmondy (German) |
| 1926 | Theodor Svedberg (Swedish) |
| 1927 | Heinrich Wieland (German) |
| 1928 | Adolf Windaus (German) |
| 1929 | Sir Arthur Harden (British) & Hans von Euler-Chelpin (German/Swedish) |
| 1930 | Hans Fischer (German) |
| 1931 | Carl Bosch & Friedrich Bergius (German) |
| 1932 | Irving Langmuir (American) |
| 1933 | *No award* |
| 1934 | Harold Urey (American) |
| 1935 | Frédéric and Irène Joliot-Curie (French) |

| 1936 | Peter Debye (Dutch) |
| 1937 | Sir Walter Haworth (British) & Paul Karrer (Swiss) |
| 1938 | Richard Kühn (German) |
| 1939 | Adolf Butenandt (German) & Leopold Ružička (Swiss) |
| 1940–42 | *No award* |
| 1943 | Georg von Hevesy (Hungarian/Swedish) |
| 1944 | Otto Hahn (German) |
| 1945 | Artturi Virtanen (Finnish) |
| 1946 | James Sumner, John Northrop & Wendell Stanley (American) |
| 1947 | Sir Robert Robinson (British) |
| 1948 | Arne Tiselius (Swedish) |
| 1949 | William Giauque (American) |
| 1950 | Otto Diels & Kurt Alder (German) |
| 1951 | Glenn Seaborg & Edwin McMillan (American) |
| 1952 | Archer Martin & Richard Synge (British) |
| 1953 | Hermann Staudinger (German) |
| 1954 | Linus Pauling (American) |
| 1955 | Vincent du Vigneaud (American) |
| 1956 | Sir Cyril Hinshelwood (British) & Nikolai Semenov (Russian) |
| 1957 | Lord Todd (British) |
| 1958 | Frederick Sanger (British) |
| 1959 | Jaroslav Heyrovský (Czech) |
| 1960 | Willard Libby (American) |
| 1961 | Melvin Calvin (American) |
| 1962 | Max Perutz & Sir John Kendrew (British) |
| 1963 | Karl Ziegler (German) & Giulio Natta (Italian) |
| 1964 | Dorothy Hodgkin (British) |
| 1965 | Robert Woodward (American) |
| 1966 | Robert Mulliken (American) |
| 1967 | Ronald Norrish & George Porter (British) & Manfred Eigen (German) |
| 1968 | Lars Onsager (American) |
| 1969 | Derek Barton (British) & Odd Hassel (Norwegian) |
| 1970 | Luis Leloir (Argentinian) |
| 1971 | Gerhard Herzberg (Canadian) |
| 1972 | Christian Anfinsén, Stanford Moore, & William Stein (American) |
| 1973 | Ernst Fischer (West German) & Geoffrey Wilkinson (British) |
| 1974 | Paul Flory (American) |
| 1975 | John Cornforth (Australian) & Vladimir Prelog (Swiss) |
| 1976 | William Lipscomb (American) |
| 1977 | Ilya Prigogine (Belgian) |
| 1978 | Peter Mitchell (British) |

| | |
|---|---|
| 1979 | Herbert Brown (American) & George Wittig (German) |
| 1980 | Paul Berg, Walter Gilbert (American) & Frederick Sanger (British) |
| 1981 | Kenichi Fukui (Japanese) & Roald Hoffman (American) |
| 1982 | Aaron Klug (British) |
| 1983 | Henry Taube (American) |
| 1984 | Bruce Merrifield (American) |
| 1985 | Herbert Hauptman & Jerome Karle (American) |
| 1986 | Dudley Herschbach & Yuan Lee (American) & John Polyani (Canadian) |
| 1987 | Charles Pedersen & Donald Cram (American) |
| 1988 | Johann Deisendorfer, Robert Huber & Hartmut Michel (German) |

△ Sir Alexander Fleming, discoverer of penicillin.

## Physiology and Medicine

| | |
|---|---|
| 1901 | Emil von Behring (German) |
| 1902 | Sir Ronald Ross (British) |
| 1903 | Niels Finsen (Danish) |
| 1904 | Ivan Pavlov (Russian) |
| 1905 | Robert Koch (German) |
| 1906 | Camillo Golgi (Italian) & Santiago Ramón y Cajal (Spanish) |
| 1907 | Charles Laveran (French) |
| 1908 | Paul Ehrlich (German) & Elie Metchnikoff (Russian/French) |
| 1909 | Emil Theodor Kocher (Swiss) |
| 1910 | Albrecht Kossel (German) |
| 1911 | Allvar Gullstrand (Swedish) |
| 1912 | Alexis Carrel (French) |
| 1913 | Charles Richet (French) |
| 1914 | Robert Bárany (Austrian) |
| 1915–18 | No award |
| 1919 | Jules Bordet (Belgian) |
| 1920 | August Krogh (Danish) |
| 1921 | No award |
| 1922 | Archibald Hill (British) & Otto Meyerhof (German) |
| 1923 | Sir Frederick Banting (Canadian) & John Macleod (British) |
| 1924 | Willem Einthoven (Dutch) |
| 1925 | No award |
| 1926 | Johannes Fibiger (Danish) |
| 1927 | Julius Wagner-Jauregg (Austrian) |
| 1928 | Charles Nicolle (French) |
| 1929 | Christiaan Eijkman (Dutch) & Sir Frederick Hopkins (British) |
| 1930 | Karl Landsteiner (American) |
| 1931 | Otto Warburg (German) |
| 1932 | Edgar Adrian & Sir Charles Sherrington (British) |
| 1933 | Thomas H. Morgan (American) |
| ·1934 | George Minot, William P. Murphy & George Whipple (American) |
| 1935 | Hans Spemann (German) |
| 1936 | Sir Henry Dale (British) & Otto Loewi (German/Austrian) |
| 1937 | Albert Szent-Györgyi (Hungarian) |
| 1938 | Corneille Heymans (Belgian) |
| 1939 | Gerhard Domagk (Belgian) |
| 1940–42 | No award |
| 1943 | Henrik Dam (Danish) & Edward Doisy (American) |
| 1944 | Joseph Erlanger & Herbert Gasser (American) |
| 1945 | Sir Alexander Fleming, Howard Florey & Ernst Chain (British) |
| 1946 | Hermann Muller (American) |
| 1947 | Carl and Gerty Cori (American) & Bernardo Houssay (Argentinian) |
| 1948 | Paul Mueller (Swiss) |
| 1949 | Walter Hess (Swiss) & Antônio Moniz (Portuguese) |
| 1950 | Philip Hench & Edward Kendall (American) & Tadeus Reichstein (Swiss) |
| 1951 | Max Theiler (S. African/American) |
| 1952 | Selman Waksman (American) |
| 1953 | Fritz Lipmann (German/American) & Hans Krebs (German/British) |
| 1954 | John Enders, Thomas Weller & Frederick Robbins (American) |
| 1955 | Hugo Theorell (Swedish) |
| 1956 | André Cournand & Dickinson Richards Jr (American) & Werner Forssmann (German) |

△ Crick and Watson researched the structure of DNA.

1957 Daniel Bovet (Italian)
1958 George Beadle, Edward Tatum & Joshua Lederberg (American)
1959 Severo Ochoa & Arthur Kornberg (American)
1960 Sir Macfarlane Burnet (Australian) & Peter Medawar (British)
1961 Georg von Békésy (Hungarian/ American)
1962 Francis Crick & Maurice Wilkins (British) & James Watson (American)
1963 Alan Hodgkin & Andrew Huxley (British) & Sir John Eccles (Australian)
1964 Konrad Bloch (German/American) & Feodor Lynen (German)
1965 Francois Jacob, André Lwoff & Jacques Monod (French)
1966 Charles Huggins & Francis Peyton Rous (American)
1967 Ragnar Granit (Swedish) & H. Keffer Hartline & George Wald (American)
1968 Robert Holley, Har Gobind Khorana & Marshall Nirenberg (American)
1969 Max Delbrück, Alfred Hershey & Salvador Luria (American)
1970 Sir Bernard Katz (British), Ulf von Euler (Swedish) & Julius Axelrod (American)

1971 Earl Sutherland Jr (American)
1972 Rodney Porter (British) & Gerald Edelman (American)
1973 Karl von Frisch & Konrad Lorenz (Austrian) & Nikolaas Tinbergen (Dutch)
1974 Albert Claude & Christian de Duve (Belgian) & George Palade (Romanian-American)
1975 David Baltimore & Howard Temin (American) & Renato Dulbecco (Italian)
1976 Baruch Blumberg & Carleton Gajdusek (American)
1977 Rosalyn Yalow, Roger Guillemin & Andrew Schally (American)
1978 Werner Arber (Swiss), Daniel Nathans & Hamilton Smith (American)
1979 Godfrey Hounsfield (British) & Allan McLeod Cormack (American)
1980 George Snell (American), Jean Dausset (French) & Baruj Benacerraf (Venezuelan)
1981 David Hubel & Roger Sperry (American) & Torsten Wiesel (Swedish)
1982 Sune Bergstrom & Bengt Samuelsson (Swedish) & John Vane (British)
1983 Barbara McClintock (American)
1984 César Milstein (British), Georges Köhler (West German) & Niels Jerne (Danish)

| | |
|---|---|
| 1985 | Michael Brown & Joseph Goldstein (American) |
| 1986 | Rita Levi-Montalcini (American/Italian) & Stanley Cohen (American) |
| 1987 | Susumu Tonegawa (Japanese) |
| 1988 | Sir James Black (British) & Gertrude Elion & George Hitchings (American) |

## Literature

| | |
|---|---|
| 1901 | René Sully-Prudhomme (French) |
| 1902 | Theodor Mommsen (German) |
| 1903 | Björnstjerne Björnson (Norwegian) |
| 1904 | Frédéric Mistral (French) and José Echegaray (Spanish) |
| 1905 | Henryk Sienkiewicz (Polish) |
| 1906 | Giosuè Carducci (Italian) |
| 1907 | Rudyard Kipling (English) |
| 1908 | Rudolf Eucken (German) |
| 1909 | Selma Lagerlöf (Swedish) |
| 1910 | Paul von Heyse (German) |
| 1911 | Maurice Maeterlinck (Belgian) |
| 1912 | Gerhart Hauptmann (German) |
| 1913 | Sir Rabindranath Tagore (Indian) |
| 1914 | *No award* |
| 1915 | Romain Rolland (French) |
| 1916 | Verner von Heidenstam (Swedish) |
| 1917 | Karl Gjellerup and Henrik Pontoppidan (Danish) |
| 1918 | *No award* |
| 1919 | Carl Spitteler (Swiss) |
| 1920 | Knut Hamsun (Norwegian) |
| 1921 | Anatole France (French) |
| 1922 | Jacinto Benavente (Spanish) |
| 1923 | William Butler Yeats (Irish) |
| 1924 | Wladyslaw Reymont (Polish) |
| 1925 | George Bernard Shaw (Irish) |
| 1926 | Grazia Deledda (Italian) |
| 1927 | Henri Bergson (French) |
| 1928 | Sigrid Undset (Norwegian) |
| 1929 | Thomas Mann (German) |
| 1930 | Sinclair Lewis (American) |
| 1931 | Erik Karlfeldt (Swedish) |
| 1932 | John Galsworthy (English) |
| 1933 | Ivan Bunin (Russian) |
| 1934 | Luigi Pirandello (Italian) |
| 1935 | *No award* |
| 1936 | Eugene O'Neill (American) |
| 1937 | Roger Martin du Gard (French) |
| 1938 | Pearl S. Buck (American) |
| 1939 | Frans Eemil Sillanpää (Finnish) |

| | |
|---|---|
| 1940–43 | *No award* |
| 1944 | Johannes V. Jensen (Danish) |
| 1945 | Gabriela Mistral (Chilean) |
| 1946 | Hermann Hesse (Swiss) |
| 1947 | André Gide (French) |
| 1948 | Thomas Stearns Eliot (Anglo-American) |
| 1949 | William Faulkner (American) |
| 1950 | Bertrand Russell (English) |
| 1951 | Pär Lagerkvist (Swedish) |
| 1952 | François Mauriac (French) |
| 1953 | Sir Winston Churchill (English) |
| 1954 | Ernest Hemingway (American) |
| 1955 | Halldór Laxness (Icelandic) |
| 1956 | Juan Ramón Jiménez (Spanish) |
| 1957 | Albert Camus (French) |
| 1958 | Boris Pasternak (Russian)–declined |
| 1959 | Salvatore Quasimodo (Italian) |
| 1960 | Saint-John Perse (Alexis Saint-Léger) (French) |
| 1961 | Ivo Andrić (Yugoslavian) |
| 1962 | John Steinbeck (American) |
| 1963 | George Seferis (Giorgios Seferiades) (Greek) |
| 1964 | Jean-Paul Sartre (French)–declined |
| 1965 | Mikhail Sholokhov (Russian) |
| 1966 | Shmuel Yosef Agnon (Israeli) and Nelly Sachs (Swedish) |
| 1967 | Miguel Angel Asturias (Guatemalan) |
| 1968 | Yasunari Kawabata (Japanese) |
| 1969 | Samuel Beckett (Irish) |

▽ Ernest Hemingway, journalist, adventurer and novelist.

△ Soviet writer Alexander Solzhenitsyn was forced into exile for his dissident views.

| | |
|---|---|
| 1970 | Alexander Solzhenitsyn (Russian) |
| 1971 | Pablo Neruda (Chilean) |
| 1972 | Heinrich Böll (West German) |
| 1973 | Patrick White (Australian) |
| 1974 | Eyvind Johnson and Harry Edmund Martinson (Swedish) |
| 1975 | Eugenio Montale (Italian) |
| 1976 | Saul Bellow (American) |
| 1977 | Vicente Aleixandre (Spanish) |
| 1978 | Isaac Bashevis Singer (American) |
| 1979 | Odysseus Alepoudhelis (Greek)– known as Odysseus Elytis |
| 1980 | Czeslaw Milosz (Lithuanian/ American) |
| 1981 | Elias Canetti (Bulgarian) |
| 1982 | Gabriel García Márquez (Colombian) |
| 1983 | William Golding (British) |
| 1984 | Jaroslav Seifert (Czechoslovakian) |
| 1985 | Claude Simon (French) |
| 1986 | Wole Soyinka (Nigerian) |
| 1987 | Joseph Brodsky (Russian) |
| 1988 | Naguib Mahfouz (Egyptian) |

**Peace**

| | |
|---|---|
| 1901 | Henri Dunant (Swiss) & Frédéric Passy (French) |
| 1902 | Elie Ducommun and Albert Gobat (Swiss) |
| 1903 | Sir William Cremer (British) |
| 1904 | Institute of International Law |
| 1905 | Baroness Bertha von Suttner (Austrian) |
| 1906 | Theodore Roosevelt (American) |
| 1907 | Ernesto Moneta (Italian) & Louis Renault (French) |
| 1908 | Klas Arnoldson (Swedish) & Fredrik Bajer (Danish) |
| 1909 | Auguste Beernaert (Belgian) & Paul d'Estournelles (French) |
| 1910 | International Peace Bureau |
| 1911 | Tobias Asser (Dutch) & Alfred Fried (Austrian) |
| 1912 | Elihu Root (American) |
| 1913 | Henri Lafontaine (Belgian) |
| 1914–16 | *No award* |
| 1917 | International Red Cross |
| 1918 | *No award* |
| 1919 | Woodrow Wilson (American) |
| 1920 | Léon Bourgeois (French) |
| 1921 | Karl Branting (Swedish) & Christian Lange (Norwegian) |
| 1922 | Fridtjof Nansen (Norwegian) |
| 1923–24 | *No award* |
| 1925 | Sir Austen Chamberlain (British) & Charles Dawes (American) |
| 1926 | Aristide Briand (French) & Gustav Stresemann (German) |
| 1927 | Ferdinand Buisson (French) & Ludwig Quidde (German) |
| 1928 | *No award* |
| 1929 | Frank Kellog (American) |
| 1930 | Nathan Söderblom (Swedish) |
| 1931 | Jane Addams & Nicholas Butler (American) |
| 1932 | *No award* |
| 1933 | Sir Norman Angell (British) |
| 1934 | Arthur Henderson (British) |
| 1935 | Carl von Ossietzky (German) |
| 1936 | Carlos de Saavedra Lamas (Argentinian) |
| 1937 | Viscount Cecil of Chelwood (British) |
| 1938 | International Office for Refugees |
| 1939–43 | *No award* |
| 1944 | International Red Cross |
| 1945 | Cordell Hull (American) |
| 1946 | Emily Balch & John Mott (American) |

| Year | Recipient | Year | Recipient |
|------|-----------|------|-----------|
| 1947 | Friends Service Council (British) & American Friends Service Committee | 1971 | Willy Brandt (West German) |
| 1948 | *No award* | 1972 | *No award* |
| 1949 | Lord Boyd Orr (British) | 1973 | Henry Kissinger (American); Le Duc Tho (North Vietnamese)– declined |
| 1950 | Ralph Bunche (American) | | |
| 1951 | Léon Jouhaux (French) | 1974 | Sean MacBride (Irish) & Eisaku Sato (Japanese) |
| 1952 | Albert Schweitzer (Alsatian) | | |
| 1953 | George C. Marshall (American) | 1975 | Andrei Sakharov (Russian) |
| 1954 | Office of the UN High Commissioner for Refugees | 1976 | Betty Williams & Mairead Corrigan (British) |
| 1955–56 | *No award* | 1977 | Amnesty International |
| 1957 | Lester Pearson (Canadian) | 1978 | Mohammed Anwar El Sadat (Egyptian) & Menachem Begin (Israeli) |
| 1958 | Dominique Georges Pire (Belgian) | | |
| 1959 | Philip Noel-Baker (British) | | |
| 1960 | Albert Luthuli (South African) | 1979 | Mother Teresa (Albanian/Indian) |
| 1961 | Dag Hammarskjöld (Swedish) | 1980 | Adolfo Pérez Esquivel (Argentinian) |
| 1962 | Linus Pauling (American) | 1981 | Office of the UN High Commissioner for Refugees |
| 1963 | International Red Cross & League of Red Cross Societies | | |
| 1964 | Martin Luther King Jr (American) | 1982 | Alva Myrdal (Swedish) & Alfonso Robles (Mexican) |
| 1965 | UNICEF (UN Children's Fund) | | |
| 1966–67 | *No award* | 1983 | Lech Walesa (Polish) |
| 1968 | René Cassin (French) | 1984 | Bishop Desmond Tutu (South African) |
| 1969 | International Labour Organization | | |
| 1970 | Norman Borlaug (American) | 1985 | International Physicians for the Prevention of Nuclear War |
| | | 1986 | Elie Wiesel (Romanian/American) |
| | | 1987 | Oscar Arias Sánchez (Costa Rican) |
| | | 1988 | United Nations peace keeping forces |

▽ Desmond Tutu called for international action to end apartheid in South Africa.

## Economics (since 1969)

| | | | |
|---|---|---|---|
| 1969 | Ragnar Frisch (Norwegian) and Jan Tinbergen (Dutch) | 1978 | Herbert Simon (American) |
| 1970 | Paul Samuelson (American) | 1979 | Theodore Schultz (American) and Sir Arthur Lewis (British) |
| 1971 | Simon Kuznets (American) | 1980 | Lawrence Klein (American) |
| 1972 | Kenneth Arrow (American) and Sir John Hicks (British) | 1981 | James Tobin (American) |
| 1973 | Wassily Leontief (American) | 1982 | George Stigler (American) |
| 1974 | Gunnar Myrdal (Swedish) and Friedrich von Hayek (Austrian) | 1983 | Gerard Debreu (American) |
| | | 1984 | Sir Richard Stone (British) |
| 1975 | Leonid Kantorovich (Russian) & Tjalling Koopmans (Dutch) | 1985 | Franco Modigliani (American) |
| | | 1986 | James Buchanan (American) |
| 1976 | Milton Friedman (American) | 1987 | Robert Solow (American) |
| 1977 | James E. Meade (British) & Bertil Ohlin (Swedish) | 1988 | Maurice Allais (French) |

# Pronunciation of Surnames

Some British surnames are not pronounced as they are spelled. Here is a list that shows some which do not follow the usual rules of spelling. The sign ' (as in Beech'em) means that the first part is pronounced with more emphasis than the second. The sign - (as in Dee-ell) means that both parts have the same stress.

| Name | Pronounced | Name | Pronounced | Name | Pronounced |
|---|---|---|---|---|---|
| Bartelot | Bart'lett | Drogheda | Dro'heda | Macmahon | Mac-mahn |
| Beauchamp | Beech'em | Dynevor | Din'never | Mainwaring | Man'nering |
| Beauclerc | Bo'clair | Elgin | El'gin** | Marjoribanks | Marshbanks |
| Beaulieu | Bew'ly | Eyre | Air | Maugham | Mawm |
| Belvoir | Beaver | Farquhar | Far'har | Menzies | Meng'is |
| Bethune | Beeton | Featherstone- | | Methven | Meffen |
| Bicester | Bister | haugh | Fan'shaw | Meyrick | Merrick |
| Bohun | Boon | Fiennes | Fynes | Monaghan | Mon-na-han |
| Boleyn | Bullen | Fildes | Fyldes† | Pepys | Peeps |
| Bourchier | Bow'cher | Foulis | Fowls | Powell | Powell or |
| Bough | Boff | Gahagen | Gay'gan | | Pole |
| Campbell | Camble | Gallagher | Gal'laher | Powys, | Powis or Po'is |
| Chandos | Shandos | Geohegan | Gay'gan | Powis | |
| Charteris | Charters | Glamis | Glahmz | Pugh | Pew |
| Cheyne | Chain or | Gough | Goff | Reay | Ray |
| | Cheyney | Grieg | Greeg or Greg | Rees, Rhys | Reece |
| Chisholm | Chizum | Grierson | Greerson | Ruthven | Riven or |
| Chivas, | Chives, | Grosvenor | Gro'venor | | Ruffen |
| Shives | Shee'vus | Hawarden | Har'den | St John | Sin-jun |
| Cholmond- | Chum'ley | Home | Hume | | Strawn or |
| eley | | Iveagh | Ivah | Strachan | Stra-han |
| Cochrane | Cock'ran | Iverach | Eeverach* | Tredegar | Tread-eager |
| Cockburn | Co'burn | Ives | Aivz or Ivz | Urquhart | Ur-chart* |
| Colquhoun | Co-hoon | Ker, Kerr | Kar or Ker | Wemyss | Weems |
| Cowper | Cooper | Kirkby | Ker'by | Wolseley | Wools'ly |
| Dalziel | Dee-ell | Leicester | Lester | Yeats | Yates |
| Derby | Darby | Leigh | Lee | | |
| Donne | Dun | Leman | Lee'man | | |
| Donoghue | Don-no-hew or | Maclean | Mac-lane | | |
| | Dun-no-hew | Macleod | Mac-loud | | |

\* 'ch' is pronounced gutturally, as in Scottish 'loch'.
\*\* Hard 'g' as in 'get'.
† Long 'i' as in 'wild'.

# Ranks in the Peerage

There are five ranks in the British peerage, and there are definite rules about them and how the holders of titles should be addressed. Peers are entitled to sit in the House of Lords.

## THE PEERAGE

**Duke** is the highest rank in the peerage; the wife of a duke is a duchess. Formally, a duke is addressed as 'Your Grace' or 'My Lord Duke'.

**Marquess** is the second rank in the peerage; the wife of a marquess is a marchioness. A marquess is formally addressed as 'The Marquess of So-and-so', and subsequently as 'Lord So-and-so'.

**Earl** is the third rank in the peerage; the wife of an earl is a countess. An earl is formally addressed as 'The Earl of So-and-so' or 'Earl So-and-so' (some earls do not have 'of' in their titles); less formally as 'Lord So-and-so'; a countess as 'Lady So-and-so'.

**Viscount** is the fourth rank in the peerage; the wife of a viscount is a viscountess. A viscount is formally addressed as 'Viscount So-and-so', and subsequently as 'Lord So-and-so'.

**Baron** is the fifth rank in the peerage; the wife of a baron is a baroness. A baron is both formally and informally addressed as 'Lord So-and-so'.

**Peeresses in their own right** take the feminine form of their respective titles. There were about 20 of them in the late 1980s.

**Life peers** have the rank of baron.

**Secondary titles** Dukes, marquesses and earls generally hold one or more secondary titles of lower rank.

## OTHER TITLES

**Baronet** is an hereditary knight. A baronet is addressed as 'Sir John So-and-so,' and when written the abbreviation 'Bart.' or 'Bt.' comes after the name. His wife is addressed as 'Lady So-and-so'.

**Knight** is a title awarded for life only. A knight is addressed as 'Sir John So-and-so'. His wife is addressed as 'Lady So-and-so'.

**Eldest sons** of dukes, marquesses and earls take their fathers' second titles as courtesy titles, but are not eligible to sit in the House of Lords.

**Younger sons** of dukes and marquesses have the courtesy title 'Lord John So-and-so'; they are not eligible to sit in the House of Lords; all sons of viscounts and the younger sons of earls have the courtesy title 'The Hon John So-and-so'.

**Daughters** of dukes, marquesses and earls have the courtesy title 'Lady Mary So-and-so'; daughters of viscounts and barons have the courtesy title 'The Hon Mary So-and-so'.

△ Black Rod, the House of Lords' representative, strikes the door of the House of Commons summoning the members to the upper house to hear a speech from the throne or royal assent being given.

# Poets Laureate

The poet laureate is a court official who is expected to compose odes or other poems in honour of royal and state occasions. The office carries a tiny pension. The first poet laureate was appointed in the reign of James I.

△ The charge of the Light Brigade, 1854, was immortalized by the poem of Alfred Lord Tennyson, longest-serving poet laureate.

### POETS LAUREATE

| | | | |
|---|---|---|---|
| Ben Johnson | 1619–1637 | Henry James Pye | 1790–1813 |
| Sir William Davenant | 1638–1668 | Robert Southey | 1813–1843 |
| John Dryden | 1668–1688 | William Wordsworth | 1843–1850 |
| Thomas Shadwell | 1689–1692 | Lord Tennyson | 1850–1892 |
| Nahum Tate | 1692–1715 | Alfred Austin | 1896–1913 |
| Nicholas Rowe | 1715–1718 | Robert Bridges | 1913–1930 |
| Laurence Eusden | 1718–1730 | John Masefield | 1930–1967 |
| Colley Cibber | 1730–1757 | Cecil Day Lewis | 1968–1972 |
| William Whitehead | 1757–1785 | Sir John Betjeman | 1972–1984 |
| Thomas Warton | 1785–1790 | Ted Hughes | 1984– |

# International Abbreviations

Abbreviations – usually just the initial letters of words – are a quick and easy of writing long or complicated names. Here are some common abbreviations that are used and understood wherever English is read or spoken.

**AA** Autombobile Association
**AC** Alternating current
**A.D.** *Anno Domini*, in the Year of Our Lord.
**adj.** Adjective
**Adm.** Admiral
**adv.** Adverb
**a.m.** *Ante meridiem*, before noon
**AM** Amplitude modulaton
**anon.** Anonymous
**Apr.** April
**assn., assoc.** Association
**Aug.** August
**A.V.** Authorized Version [of the Bible]
**Ave** Avenue
**A.W.O.L.** Absent without official leave

**b.** Born
**BA** Bachelor of Arts
**BBC** British Broadcasting Corporation
**B.C.** Before Christ
**Brig.** Brigadier
**BSc** Bachelor of Science
**BST** British Summer Time

**c.** *Circa*, about; *centum*, one hundred; cent
**C** Celsius, Centigrade
**cap.** Capital; capital letter
**Capt.** Captain
**CB** Citizens' band
**ch., chap.** Chapter
**Chron.** Chronicles
**CIA** Central Intelligence Agency
**CID** Criminal Investigation Department
**cf.** *Confer*, compare
**cm** Centimetre
**co.** Company; county
**c/o** Care of
**CO** Commanding officer
**c.o.d.** Cash (or collect) on delivery
**coll., colloq.** Colloquial

**Con.** Conservative
**conj.** Conjunction
**cont., contd.** Continued
**Cor.** Corinthians
**corp.** Corporation
**Cpl** Corporal

**d.** Died; *denarius*, a penny before 1971
**DC** Direct current
**D.C.** District of Colombia
**dec.** Deceased
**Dec.** December
**Dem.** Democrat
**dept.** Department
**Deut.** Deuteronomy
**Dr** Doctor

**E** East
**Eccl.** Ecclesiastes
**EC** European Community
**ed.** Edition; edited; editor
**EFTA** European Free Trade Association
**e.g.** *Exempli gratia*, for example
**Eph.** Ephesians
**eq.** Equal; equation
**Esth.** Esther
**esp.** Especially
**et al.** *Et alii*, and others
**etc.** *Et cetera*, and so forth
**et. seq.** *Et sequens*, and the following
**Ex., Exod.** Exodus
**Ez.** Ezra
**Ezek.** Ezekiel

**F** Fahrenheit
**FBI** Federal Bureau of Investigation
**Feb.** February
**ff.** Following [pages]
**FM** Frequency modulation
**fig.** Figure
**Fri.** Friday
**ft** Foot

**g** Gram

**Gal.** Galatians
**GB** Great Britain
**Gen.** Genesis; general
**GMT** Greenwich Mean Time
**govt.** Government

**h** Hour
**ha** Hectare
**hi-fi** High fidelity
**HMS** Her (or His) Majesty's Ship
**Hon.** Honourable
**hp** Horsepower
**HQ** Headquarters
**hr.** Hour
**ht** Height
**Hz** Hertz

**I.** Island
**IBA** Independent Broadcasting Authority
**ibid.** *Ibidem*, in the same place
**i.e.** *Id est*, that is
**ill.** Illustrated
**IMF** International Monetary Fund (UN)
**inc.** Incorporated, including
**IQ** Intelligence quotient
**IRA** Irish Republic Army
**Is.** Isaiah; island(s)
**ISBN** International Standard Book Number

**Jan.** January
**Jer.** Jeremiah
**Josh.** Joshua
**Jr** Junior
**Jud.** Judges

**kg** Kilogram
**kHz** Kilohertz
**km** Kilometre
**km/h** Kilometres per hour
**KW** Kilowatt

**£** *Libra*, pound (money)
**I** Litre
**L.** Liberal

**Lab.** Labour
**lat.** Latitude
**lb** *Libra*, pound (weight)
**Lev.** Leviticus
**Lib.** Liberal
**Lieut.** Lieutenant
**log.** Logarithm
**long.** Longitude
**Lt.** Lieutenant
**Ltd** Limited

**m** Metre
**M** Monsieur
**Maj.** Major
**Mar.** March
**Matt.** Matthew
**max.** Maximum
**mg** Milligram
**MHz** Megahertz
**min.** Minute; minimum
**misc.** Miscellaneous
**ml** Millilitre
**Mlle** Mademoiselle
**mm** Millimetre
**Mme** Madame
**Mon.** Monday
**MP** Member of Parliament; military police
**mph** Miles per hour
**Mr** Mister
**Mrs** Mistress
**Ms** Miss or Mrs
**MS** Manuscript
**Mt** Mount

**n.** noun
**N** North
**NASA** National Aeronautics and Space Administration
**NATO** North Atlantic Treaty Organization
**N.B.** *Nota bene*, note well
**NCO** Non-commissioned officer
**no.** *Numéro*, number
**Nov.** November
**NT** New Testament
**Num.** Numbers

**ob.** *Obiit*, died
**Oct.** October
**OK, O.K.** Correct
**op.** *Opus*, work
**op. cit.** *Opere citato*, in the work cited

**OT** Old Testament

**p** Penny, pence
**p.** Page
**pen.** Peninsula
**per cent., %** *Per centum*, by the hundred
**Pet.** Peter
**PhD** Doctor of Philosophy
**pl.** Plural
**plc** Public limited company
**PLO** Palestine Liberation Organization
**p.m.** *Post meridiem*, afternoon
**PO** Post office
**pop.** Population
**POW** Prisoner of war
**pp.** Pages
**Prov.** Proverbs
**PS** *Post scriptum*, postscript
**PTO** Please turn over
**Pvt.** Private (rank)

**QED** *Quod erat demonstrandum*, which was to be shown
**q.v.** *Quod vide*, which see

**R** *Rex*, king; *regina*, queen; river
**RAC** Royal Automobile Club
**RAF** Royal Air Force
**rd.** Road
**ref.** Reference
**Rep.** Republican
**Rev.** Revelations; Reverend
**RIP** *Requiescat in pace*, rest in peace
**RN** Royal Navy
**Rom.** Romans
**rpm** Revolutions per minute
**RSVP** *Répondez, s'il vous plaît* (Fr.) Reply, if you please

**s** Second
**S** South
**s.a.e.** Stamped addressed envelope
**Sat.** Saturday
**sec.** Second
**Sept.** September
**sing.** Singular
**soc.** Society
**Soc.** Socialist
**sp.** Species; spelling

**sq.** Square
**Sr.** Senior
**SS** steamship
**St.** Saint; strait; street
**Sun.** Sunday
**syn.** Synonym

**temp.** Temperature
**Thess.** Thessalonians
**Thur.** Thursday
**TNT** Trinitrotoluene
**tr.** Transpose; translation
**TUC** Trades Union Congress
**Tues.** Tuesday

**UFO** Unidentified flying object
**UK** United Kingdom of Great Britain and Northern Ireland
**UN** United Nations
**UNESCO** United Nations Educational, Scientific and Cultural Organization
**univ.** University
**USA** United States of America
**USSR** Union of Soviet Socialist Republics

**v.** Verb
**v., vid.** *Vide*, see
**v., vs.** Versus
**V** Volt
**VAT** Value-added tax
**VHF** Very high frequency
**VIP** Very Important Person
**viz.** *Videlicet*, namely
**vol.** Volume

**W** West
**W** Watt
**Wed.** Wednesday
**WHO** World Health Organization (UN)
**wt** Weight

**Xmas** Christmas

**YHA** Youth Hostels Association
**YMCA** Young Men's Christian Association
**YWCA** Young Women's Christian Association

**zool.** Zoology

# American English

Over the years the American and British versions of the English language have changed, and today there are many words and phrases which have different meanings, depending on which side of the Atlantic Ocean you are. Here are some of the most common American words with their British meanings.

**apartment** flat
**attorney** lawyer
**automobile** car
**baby carriage** pram
**bill** banknote
**billboard** hoarding
**biscuit** a bread roll or scone
**bit** ⅛ of a dollar (12½ cents)
**bug** any insect
**candy** sweets
**carousel** roundabout
**casket** coffin
**check** cheque
**checkers** draughts
**cookie** sweet biscuit
**clerk** shop assistant
**closet** cupboard
**cracker** savoury or water biscuit
**diaper** baby's nappy
**doughboy** infantry solider
**dove** past tense of dive
**downtown** city centre
**drugstore** chemist's shop, also sells a variety of goods including refreshments.
**elevator** lift
**engineer** engine driver
**fall** autumn
**faucet** tap
**fender** car bumper
**first floor** ground floor
**garbage can** dustbin
**gasoline (gas)** petrol
**given name** Christian name
**grab bag** lucky dip
**greenbacks** paper money
**gridiron** football field
**highway** main road
**hog** pig
**homicide** murder
**hood** car bonnet
**janitor** caretaker
**jumping rope** skipping rope
**line** queue
**lot** plot of ground

**lumber** timber
**major** specialize in a subject
**make out** get along, manage
**mortician** undertaker
**muffler** car silencer
**name for** name after
**notion department** haberdashery in a department store
**of** before – 'He left at ten minutes of six'.
**pants** trousers
**peek-a-boo** hide and seek
**pie** tart
**pocketbook** handbag
**porch** verandah
**purse** handbag
**railroad** railway
**ranch** farm
**realtor** estate agent
**round-trip ticket** return ticket
**row house** terrace house
**sidewalk** pavement
**skillet** frying pan
**slingshot** catapult
**sneakers** gym shoes
**spool** cotton reel
**streetcar** tram
**string** shoelace
**subway** underground railway
**suspenders** braces
**tag day** flag day
**through** 'Tuesday through Thursday' – from Tuesday to Thursday inclusive. Also: finished, ended
**thumb tack** drawing pin
**tightwad** miser
**trash** rubbish
**trunk** car boot
**undershirt** vest
**uptown** residential part of a city
**vest** waistcoat
**washroom** lavatory
**windshield** windscreen

## TRADITIONAL ANNIVERSARY NAMES

| Year | Name |
|---|---|
| 1 | paper |
| 2 | cotton |
| 3 | leather |
| 4 | fruit, flowers |
| 5 | wood |
| 6 | iron, sugar |
| 7 | wool, copper |
| 8 | bronze |
| 9 | pottery |
| 10 | tin, aluminium |
| 11 | steel |
| 12 | silk, fine linen |
| 13 | lace |
| 14 | ivory |
| 15 | crystal |
| 20 | china |
| 25 | silver |
| 30 | pearl |
| 35 | coral |
| 40 | ruby |
| 45 | sapphire |
| 50 | golden |
| 55 | emerald |
| 60 | diamond |
| 70 | platinum |

## GEM CUTS

*Cutting gemstones is a highly skilled craft and the cuts used for different gems include the following.*

Brillant cut

Trap cut

## GEMSTONES

Nearly all gemstones are minerals, as are those in this table. The four non-mineral gems are amber, coral, jet and pearl. The hardness of solid substances is expressed on a scale called the Mohs scale. This ranges from zero, for talc, to ten, for diamond.

| Mineral | Colour | Mohs hardness |
|---|---|---|
| Agate | brown, red, blue, green, yellow | 7.0 |
| Alexandrite | green, red | 8.5 |
| Amethyst | violet | 7.0 |
| Aquamarine | sky blue, greenish blue | 7.5 |
| Beryl | green, blue, pink | 7.5 |
| Bloodstone | green with red spots | 7.0 |
| Chalcedony | all colours | 7.0 |
| Chrysoprase | apple green | 7.0 |
| Citrine | yellow | 7.0 |
| Diamond | colourless, tints of various colours | 10.0 |
| Emerald | green | 7.5 |
| Garnet | red and other colours | 6.5–7.25 |
| Jade | green, whitish, mauve, brown | 7.0 |
| Jasper | dark red, multi-coloured | 7.0 |
| Lapis lazuli | deep blue | 5.5 |
| Malachite | dark green banded | 3.5 |
| Moonstone | whitish with blue shimmer | 6.0 |
| Onyx | various colours with straight coloured bands | 7.0 |
| Opal | black, white, orange-red, rainbow coloured | 6.0 |
| Periodot | green | 6.5 |
| Ruby | red | 9.0 |
| Sapphire | blue and other colours | 9.0 |
| Serpentine | red and green | 3.0 |
| Soapstone | white, may be stained with impurities | 2.0 |
| Sunstone | whitish red-brown flecked with golden particles | 6.0 |
| Topaz | blue, green, pink, yellow, colourless | 8.0 |
| Tourmaline | brown-black, blue, pink, red, violet-red, yellow, green | 7.5 |
| Turquoise | greenish grey, sky blue | 6.0 |
| Zircon | All colours | 7.5 |

## DERIVATION OF DAYS AND MONTHS

| Day/month | Named after | Day/month | Named after |
|---|---|---|---|
| Sunday | the Sun | March | Mars, Roman god of war |
| Monday | the Moon | April | aperire, Latin 'to open' |
| Tuesday | Tiu, Norse god of war | May | Maia, Roman goddess of spring and growth |
| Wednesday | Woden, Anglo-Saxon chief of gods | | |
| Thursday | Thor, Norse god of thunder | June | Juno, Roman goddess of marriage |
| Friday | Frigg, Norse goddess | July | Julius Caesar |
| Saturday | Saturn, Roman god of harvests | August | Augustus, first emperor of Rome |
| | | September | septem, Latin 'seven' |
| January | Janus, Roman god of doors and gates | October | octo, Latin 'eight' |
| | | November | novem, Latin 'nine' |
| February | Februa, Roman period of purification | December | decem, Latin 'ten' |

# Index

In this index the figures in *italics* denote illustrations in the book. In a work of this kind it is not possible to index every entry; otherwise the index would be almost as long as the book itself. For entries not found in the index, look in the relevant charts and alphabetically arranged glossaries.

# Acknowledgements

The publishers wish to thank the following for supplying photographs for this book:

Page 24 Novosti; 35 Camera Press; 49 ZEFA; 51 Hulton Picture Company; 110 Mansell Collection; 118 Camera Press; 122 Camera Press; 132 Ancient Art & Architecture Collection; 142 Novosti; 143 Mary Evans Picture Library; 146 Camera Press; 147 Novosti; 148 Camera Press; 151 Camera Press; 165 Camera Press; 184 Camera Press; 210 Camera Press; 213 Camera Press; 223 Camera Press; 234 Camera Press; 259 Toyota; 268 Ancient Art & Architecture Collection; 270 Mary Evans Picture Library; 273 Popperfoto; 278 + 9 Mansell Collection; 284 Camera Press; 290 Mary Evans Picture Library; 293 Hulton Picture Company; 300 Mansell Collection (top), Visual Arts Library (middle); 301 Visual Arts Library; 302 Camera Press; 304 Michael Holford; 308 Camera Press; 309 Mansell Collection (top), Camera Press (bottom); 311 Mansell Collection; 312 Mansell Collection; 318 Camera Press (top), Mansell Collection (bottom); 321 Camera Press; 322 Kobal Collection; 323 Hulton Picture Company; 324 Mary Evans Picture Library (left), Mansell Collection (right); 326 Kobal Collection; 328 Kobal Collection; 329 Kobal Collection; 330 Kobal Collection; 331 Kobal Collection; 332 Camera Press; 333 Camera Press; 334 Camera Press; 335 Camera Press; 337 Camera Press; 340 Camera Press; 341 Camera Press; 342 Allsport; 343 Camera Press; 344 Allsport; 347 Camera Press; 349 Camera Press; 350 Camera Press; 352 Camera Press; 353 Camera Press; 357 Hulton Picture Company; 358 Camera Press; 361 Camera Press; 362 Camera Press; 363 Camera Press; 364 Camera Press; 366 Mansell Collection.